The Victorian Comic Spirit

New Perspectives

Edited by
Jennifer A. Wagner-Lawlor

Taylor & Francis Group

LONDON AND NEW YORK

First published 2000 by Ashgate Publishing

Reissued 2018 by Routledge
2 Park Square, Milton Park, Abingdon, Oxon OX14 4RN
711 Third Avenue, New York, NY 10017, USA

Routledge is an imprint of the Taylor & Francis Group, an informa business

Publisher's Note
The publisher has gone to great lengths to ensure the quality of this reprint but points out that some imperfections in the original copies may be apparent.

Disclaimer
The publisher has made every effort to trace copyright holders and welcomes correspondence from those they have been unable to contact.

A Library of Congress record exists under LC control number: 99066723

ISBN 13: 978-1-138-70108-3 (hbk)
ISBN 13: 978-1-138-70106-9 (pbk)
ISBN 13: 978-1-315-20427-7 (ebk)

Contents

List of Figures   vii

The Nineteenth Century General Editors' Preface   ix

Acknowledgments   xi

Introduction: New Perspectives on the Victorian Comic Spirit   xiii

1   Parody, Pastiche, and the Play of Genres: The Savoy Operas of
Gilbert and Sullivan   1
Carolyn Williams

2   The Fissure *King*: Parody, Ideology, and the Imperialist
Narrative   23
Patricia Murphy

3   Laughing at the Almighty: Freethinking Lampoon, Satire,
and Parody in Victorian England   43
David Nash

4   Tipping Mr. Punch "the Haffable Wink": E. J. Milliken's
Cockney Verse Letters   67
Patricia Marks

5   American Humor: The Mark of Twain on Jerome K. Jerome   91
John S. Batts

6.   Humor as Daughterly Defense in *Cranford*   115
Eileen Gillooly

7.   Dickens's Dystopian Metacomedy: *Hard Times*, Morals,
and Religion   141
Joseph H. Gardner

8.   Transcendence through Incongruity: The Background of
Humor in Carlyle's *Sartor Resartus*   153
Abigail Burnham Bloom

9.   "Falling into Philistine Hands": Swinburne's Transgressive
     Correspondence   173
     Nicholas Freeman

10. Arnold's Irony and the Deployment of Dandyism   191
     James Najarian

11. *Salomé:* Re/Dressing Wilde on the Rim   205
     Rob K. Baum

12. The Laugh of the New Woman   219
     Margaret D. Stetz

Notes on Contributors   243

Index   247

List of Figures

3.1 A MERRY CHRISTMAS: INSIDE AND OUTSIDE   50
     (*Freethinker*, Christmas Number, December 1882)

3.2 CLERICAL TYPES (*Freethinker*, Summer Special Issue, 1884)   52

3.3 THE SALVATION DODGE (*Freethinker*, 1 October 1882)   53

3.4 GOING TO GLORY (*Freethinker*, 3 September 1882)   54

3.5 AN INQUIRING BISHOP (*Freethinker*, 24 July 1882)   57

3.6 "COMIC BIBLE" SKETCHES.—XLI: THE ORIGINAL   58
     SALVATION ARMY (*Freethinker*, 8 October 1882)

3.7 "COMIC BIBLE" SKETCHES.—VII: SAMSON AND   59
     THE FOXES (*Freethinker*, 1 January 1882)

3.8 "COMIC BIBLE" SKETCHES.—XXIV: THE FIRST   59
     RELIGIOUS MURDER (*Freethinker*, 30 April 1882)

3.9 MOSES GETTING A BACK VIEW (*Freethinker*, Christmas   60
     Number, December 1882)

3.10 "COMIC BIBLE" SKETCHES.—XXXIII: JESUS RESCUES   62
     PETER (*Freethinker*, 2 July 1882)

4.1 'ARRY AT STONEHENGE (*Punch*, 28 August 1886)   69

4.2 EXTREMES MEET ('ARRY AT THE FANCY FAIR)   71
     (*Punch*, 12 July 1879)

4.3 HAPPY THOUGHT FOR MADAME TUSSAUD   77
     (*Punch*, 14 December 1878)

The Nineteenth Century
General Editors' Preface

The aim of this series is to reflect, develop and extend the great burgeoning of interest in the nineteenth century that has been an inevitable feature of recent decades, as that former epoch has come more sharply into focus as a locus for our understanding not only of the past but of the contours of our modernity. Though it is dedicated principally to the publication of original monographs and symposia in literature, history, cultural analysis, and associated fields, there will be a salient role for reprints of significant text from, or about, the period. Our overarching policy is to address the spectrum of nineteenth-century studies without exception, achieving the widest scope in chronology, approach and range of concern. This, we believe, distinguishes our project from comparable ones, and means, for example, that in the relevant areas of scholarship we both recognize and cut innovatively across such parameters as those suggested by the designations "Romantic" and "Victorian." We welcome new ideas, while valuing tradition. It is hoped that the world which predates yet so forcibly predicts and engages our own will emerge in parts, as a whole, and in the lively currents of debate and change that are so manifest an aspect of its intellectual, artistic and social landscape.

Vincent Newey
Joanne Shattock

University of Leicester

Acknowledgments

I would like to express my tremendous gratitude to Linda K. Sadler, Editorial Assistant at *The Southern Journal of Philosophy* at The University of Memphis, who took on the task of helping me edit this text. All the computer formatting was done by her, and she proofread and copy-edited each essay with care and expertise. My offer of dinner at the fancy restaurant of her choice is a poor exchange for the retention of my sanity, which I surely would have lost without her help.

I would also like to thank the following organizations for their generosity: The Johns Hopkins University Press, for permission to reprint Eileen Gillooly's essay, "Humor as Daughterly Defense in *Cranford*," which originally appeared in *ELH* (*English Literary History*) 59: 883–901; G. W. Foote & Co. Ltd., for permission to reproduce the illustrations in chapter 3 (David Nash's "Laughing at the Almighty"), which originally appeared in the *Freethinker*; and Punch Ltd. for permission to reproduce the cartoons included in chapter 4 (Patricia Marks's "Tipping Mr. Punch 'the Haffable Wink'"), which originally appeared in *Punch*.

This book is dedicated to my husband Len, and to our son, Jonathan Lenn Lawlor.

Introduction: New Perspectives on the Victorian Comic Spirit

Jennifer A. Wagner-Lawlor

The attitude of scholars and nonscholars alike to the very notion of Victorian humor is remarkably similar: that it sounds like a contradiction in terms. This can hardly be wondered at. Even Victorian scholars tend to think of the Victorian Sage before they think of a Victorian Harlequin; the stentorian genius of the former went far to define, for their own as well as for later times, the "spirit of the age" with a character more akin to Arnoldian-type meditations on "this strange disease of modern life" than to the satiric observations of Mr. Punch. Harold Orel's 1961 *The World of Victorian Humor*, itself a serious effort to reintroduce to modern audiences some of the many lively manifestations of Victorian humor, would nevertheless take away with one hand what it gave with the other: Orel introduces his collection by stating that

> [t]he miracle of Victorian humor may lie in the fact that it existed ... The problems created by industrialization, the conflict between men of faith and men of science, and political cross-currents were so serious that many Victorians believed humor to be inappropriate in any discussion of them. (3)

Thus does he perpetuate, however unintentionally, the general image of the Victorian period as morbid and dour that has allowed Victorian humor to remain so long unanalyzed and untheorized. But at least some commentators closer to the last century seem to have perceived things a bit differently. Stephen Leacock for example, himself a noted humorist, would write in 1935 that far from being a time of relentless seriousness, the Victorian period "represents an epoch in the history of letters greater than any that preceded it"—not only in the realm of "pure letters," but also "in the domain of humor" (14). Victorian humor, both in England and America, consisted of more than "verbal incongruities," he claims, "the effects of jangling syllables and misused words"; rather, it reached toward "the higher stage of the humor of character, turning on the contrasts of incongruities that make up 'queer' people":

> [Victorian humor] finds its basis in the incongruity of life itself, the contrast between the fretting cares and the petty sorrows of the day and the long mystery of the tomorrow. Here laughter and tears become one, and humor becomes the contemplation and interpretation of our life. In this aspect the thought of the nineteenth century far excelled all that had preceded it. The very wistfulness of its new ignorance—contrasted with the brazen certain[t]y of bygone dogma—lends it something pathetic. (15)

Humor, he concludes, turns on "a contrast between the thing as it is, or ought to be, and the thing smashed out of shape and as it ought not to be.... [T]his broadened into a general notion of contrast, of incongruity, of a disharmony between a thing and its setting" (11). Most importantly, Leacock himself saw the relationship between the ambiguities of Victorian ideology and the outpouring of all kinds of humor, literary and popular, which served "to portray and to satirize not merely the written books of a period but the life and manners of the period itself," particularly "the defects of its noble qualities": its "prudery and overdone morality, and the hypocrisy that apes the moral attitude" (68-69).

. Despite this early and promising assessment of Victorian humor as, in essence, politically and ideologically engaged, the critical atmosphere for analysis of Victorian humor does not seem to have arrived until recently. There were certainly exceptions to this; most notable is Robert Bernard Martin's valuable and unequaled *The Triumph of Wit: A Study of Victorian Comic Theory* (1974). This study, while surveying the large number of essays and treatises—many philosophical in nature—on humor during the Victorian age, focuses its discussion around central distinctions in nineteenth-century humor theory between wit (central to eighteenth-century theories) and humor, and between the claims of the intellect and the imagination. Because of his explicit concern primarily with rhetorical and philosophical notions of humor, Martin necessarily underplays the theoretical connections between humor and what Umberto Eco would call "cultural and intertextual frames" (8), connections which make it more easily possible to look at humor as "a form of social criticism" by means of its challenging of cultural codes (8). This is not to fault Martin's valuable study; it is a matter of emphasis— and indeed Martin glimpses the social implications of his work when he observes that "it was dangerous to laugh because laughter revealed the fundamental dislocation of both the individual and society" (5).

Indeed, it should hardly be surprising that during a period so conscious of social relations at least some commentators on humor—of whom, as Martin shows us, there were many—should recognize it precisely as a social and political phenomenon, what Altick refers to, in his recently published tome on the history of *Punch*, as "social psychology" (introduction, xx). In

1852, for example, Edwin Hood would see contemporary humor precisely in terms of its ability to hunt out "cant," to critique ideological dogma or "formalism":

> Wonderful is *the detective power of ridicule and mirth*. Penetrating through the finest pretences, all the most brilliant but shallow patriotisms, exaggerated opinions, and well drest shams in top boots, are transparent to its eye; the defects of character are instantly weighed and understood; the defects of an argument, or a book, the defects of faith or of formalism ... To the eye of humour he [the hollow orator] stands unmasked ... (67)

This metaphor of unmasking and exposure, of spying out pretense and prejudice, brings us much closer to the kind of political significances that later scholars of humor would come to highlight. Just a few years later, in 1876, Leslie Stephen would remark that "the use of such modes of controversy necessarily jars upon reverent minds ... When a phantom dogma persists in haunting the living world, a laugh will cause it to vanish more rapidly than the keenest logical slashing" (qtd. in Martin, 15).

Certainly other Victorian commentators observed the power of humor to function as a social corrective by foregrounding cultural fissures. H. D. Traill (himself a famous humorist), in an 1888 article in the *National Review* entitled "The Evolution of Humour," would concur with arguments like Hood's and Stephen's, and would make even more explicit the "play" of cultural voices. While he more or less rehearses old arguments about humor as the "perception of incongruity" and contrast, Traill begins pointing toward this new direction by quoting Diogenes: "'The multitude,' ... 'enjoy banter and ridicule most of all when it is the holiest of things that are made mock of'" (813). Traill goes on to make the interesting point that the Athenians themselves, in this as in so many things, had an almost "modern" sense of humor: "The capacity of self-detachment which could enable a people to laugh at a burlesque of their own mythology is already a long stage on the way towards appreciation of the modern introspective variety of the humorous" (828). Traill sees this "capacity for self-detachment" as a possible vehicle for criticism and change. He recognizes, in other words, what twentieth-century humor theorists would begin to study in more rigorous terms: namely, the political in the humorous, and the way in which humor can be employed to break forms and formalisms at every level of social dynamics.

As commentators like Hood, Stephen, and Traill sensed, humor could be, and was, used to create a cultural self-consciousness, to make visible or unmask almost invisible relationships between rule and violation. The most famous of Victorian commentators on humor and comedy, George Meredith, would again employ tropes of "illumination" and visibility to describe the action of the Comic Spirit: "The Spirit overhead will look humanely malign [at the offenders of common sense, manners, reason, justice, and so on] and cast an oblique light on them, followed by volleys of silvery laughter. That is the Comic Spirit" (48). While theoreticians today can continue to debate whether or not comedy and humor are themselves instances of transgression—Eco, for instance, argues that "on the contrary, [comedy and carnival] represent paramount examples of law reinforcement ... [reminding] us of the existence of the rule" (6)—one can still conclude that humor can and often does act as a form of social criticism insofar as "at least it obliges us to acknowledge" the existence of a "system of values" (7–8).

It is the "making visible" of cultural and intertextual frames that has characterized so much of cultural studies (neo-Bakhtinian and, then, neo-Derridean), with its reexploration of so-called high as well as popular culture in the context of a dynamic of opposing voices; this in turn has created a much more fertile critical context for the study of humor and comedy, both verbal and visual. And it is in the light of these new critical approaches that twelve noted scholars offer the following essays on the Victorian comic spirit. The aim of this book is not merely to remind readers of the multifarious faces of Harlequin in the last century; it is also to provide new contexts for considering an area of Victorian culture that has remained more or less unilluminated by the kind of theoretical attention that would serve it best.

What ties each of the essays to the other, no matter what the particular subject of analysis, is a common supposition that there exists a dialogic interchange between the humorous text and its culture. These essays assume, in other words, that humorous and comic representations function politically by revealing contradictions in ideological discourses, by exposing repressed illogicalities and prejudices, by way of irony or ridicule, attendant to nineteenth-century ideologies of gender, class, race, nationalism. The Victorian "Comic Spirit," as Meredith would call it in his famous lectures and essay on comedy, emerges from these essays not as an empty jester, but as the most ruthless of critics. Its object is not merely playful entertainment, but the "interpretation of life," as Leacock put it, and the self-conscious exploration of the interplay of the various complexities of social relations that make up Victorian culture. The essays were chosen to reflect the multiplicity both of Victorian modes and forms of humor—from irony to parody to blasphemy to burlesque—and to reflect the variety of approaches one might take to the recuperation of these texts and to their analysis. Together, they offer a rich and varied view of how humor has operated historically, and what was at stake politically and ideologically for Victorian writers and critics who employed humor as a technique for the unmasking of some aspect of social dynamics.

The first two essays open the volume with a consideration of literary parody and the way in which it animates not only intertextual correspondences and deviations, but also the dynamics between the textual and the cultural. Carolyn Williams's "Parody, Pastiche, and the Play of Genres: The Savoy Operas of Gilbert and Sullivan" looks at the generic play that undergirds so many of the humorous effects in Gilbert and Sullivan's exceptional operas. The role of literary pastiche in particular is more than a merely formalist matter, according to Williams: the operas resonate with the "recombinant mixtures of several generic parodies" jostling against one another to create sophisticated social satires. This essay analyzes issues both of formal intertextuality and of social signification, teasing out the operas' complex interanimation of "social and theatrical registers"—particularly as they critique Victorian gender and class ideologies, and also explore Victorian notions of theatricality itself.

Patricia Murphy's "The Fissure *King*: Parody, Ideology, and the Imperialist Narrative" is an analysis of "Hyder Ragged's" *King Solomon's Wives: or, The Phantom Mines* (1887). Through the humor that emerges from this close and careful parody of H. Rider Haggard's popular *King Solomon's Mines* (1885), argues Murphy, the author foregrounds the ideologically unstable moments in Haggard's own text, thereby interrogating and often demolishing the distinction between the "civilized" British and the "barbaric" natives of the colonies. The essay focuses particularly on "paradigmatic linguistic, behavioral and epistemological strategies" that challenge the original novel's assumption of British cultural superiority; it also explores the parody's demystification of Haggard's employment of the male quest romance as the form best suited to endorsing European imperialism.

David Nash's "Laughing at the Almighty: Freethinking Lampoon, Satire, and Parody in Victorian England" considers the multiple weaponry, from blasphemous lampooning to satire and parody, brought to bear against Victorian religious intolerance. The often derisive humor that found its way into periodical and pamphlet literature—including the satiric cartoons in such publications as *The Freethinker*—becomes the evidence of a powerful resistance to the pressures of a hegemonic religious sensibility in Victorian England. The impact of these comic attacks was palpable: the law against blasphemy, by which many of the cultural texts Nash explores were judged, was effectively liberalized as a result of one humorist's legal challenges.

Patricia Marks turns to that most famous organ of Victorian humor, *Punch, or The London Charivari*, in her "Tipping Mr. Punch 'the Haffable Wink': E. J. Milliken's Cockney Verse Letters." Marks illuminates the ambivalent development of that magazine's ideological stances toward class dynamics, imperialism, aestheticism, and the New Woman by tracing the attitudes of its comic spokesperson for over two decades: the Cockney figure of 'Arry, invented by E. J. Milliken. As Victorians laughed at 'Arry,

Marks argues, they also laughed, perhaps unwittingly, at themselves, for Milliken's social satire was masked by the obvious hypocrisies and comic blunders of his deceptively amiable *Punch* persona.

John S. Batts's essay, "American Humor: The Mark of Twain on Jerome K. Jerome," looks at the transatlantic influences of so-called new—that is, "American"—humor on the work of a Victorian humorist of the 1880s and 1890s, Jerome K. Jerome. The essay first explores the influence of Twain's brand of American humor on British humor writing; it goes on to analyze what the various responses to Jerome's hybrid humor reveal about its function in both literary and cultural contexts. In particular, these responses betray a middle-class deprecation of American-style humor that Batts reads as an index of middle-class interests and traditional British mores.

Eileen Gillooly's "Humor as Daughterly Defense in *Cranford*" turns to the ways in which the seemingly innocent irony of "Mary Smith," the narrator of Elizabeth Gaskell's masterpiece, can be read as a powerful weapon, and as a means of transforming anxiety and conflict. Careful rhetorical analysis of the narrator's many jokes and of other rhetorical plays exposes Mary Smith's aggressive critique of the small town of Cranford—and particularly of her oppressive daughterly role within its society. Beyond the multi-layered humor of the novel's narrator, the essay explores the ways in which Gaskell's use of humor against her editor Charles Dickens barely disguises her resentment of his role in her publication, and undercuts not only his authority as a literary model, but also the authority of a male-oriented world that denigrates any female perspective, much less the work of women writers.

Gaskell's resentments notwithstanding, no book on Victorian humor can exclude Charles Dickens, and Joseph H. Gardner's essay reads *Hard Times* as a metacomedy that fiercely resists the hardening of Victorian hearts and minds by the various mechanistic ideologies of that period. Dickens's humor in this novel is deadly serious in its effort to break down these rigidities, so crushing to the imagination and indeed to life itself in this novel. As in the previous essay, irony becomes the central device, a rhetorical weapon that provides a means of liberation from all the Gradgrindian "Ologies."

Abigail Burnham Bloom's "Transcendence through Incongruity: The Background of Humor in Carlyle's *Sartor Resartus*," explores Carlyle's complex brand of humor in relation to contemporary and earlier theories of humor. While it had long been said that the essence of humor resides in incongruity, Carlyle, according to Burnham Bloom, explores the unique manner in which he employs humor not just as a method of satire and critique, but as a mode of the visionary. Burnham Bloom traces the development of this "transcendent" use of humor in Carlyle's work, particularly through the influence of Jean Paul Friedrich Richter's notion of the "inverse sublime," and then analyzes the text in which it is most effectively employed—the inimitable *Sartor Resartus*—to bridge the gulf between the finite and the infinite, the tragic and the humorous.

Nicholas Freeman looks at the comic devices of one of the period's most subtle—and most subtly humorous—poets, Algernon Charles Swinburne. Freeman mines the under-read body of Swinburne's letters in order to define a kind of "aesthetics of humor" that Swinburne employs to such brilliant effect in his more famous literary works. Central to this consideration is, of course, Swinburne's unrivaled talent for parody; but Freeman also looks at his power of satire, and at the particular strategies of comic diction and linguistic play, all of which come to hand in his always aggressive and often blasphemous attacks on the most rigid Victorian social and religious mores.

Matthew Arnold is a figure that few would approach as a "humorous" writer. But as Najarian points out, his contemporaries did not see him as grave, and in his essay, "Arnold's Irony and the Deployment of Dandyism," Najarian traces the great critic's stance of detachment from his youthful stance of rebellion and aestheticism. Arnold's early dandyism, in particular, is crucial: the dandy typically employs a strategy of display, of self-dramatization that modulates in Arnold's case to a mode of self-irony. This subtle form of humor, and the detachment that it encourages, help to create both the style and the critical stance for the "objective" critic that we think of as "Matthew Arnold." Irony, then, the humorous mode of the dandy, is for Najarian an unacknowledged foundation for Arnoldian literary and social criticism.

If Arnold "engendered the ironic poses that made Wilde possible," as Najarian concludes, it is appropriate that Rob K. Baum's essay on Oscar Wilde's more flamboyant modes of humor should follow. Baum's essay on *Salomé* explores the various ways in which Wilde's least overtly "funny" drama nevertheless employs strategies of critical humor that are as powerfully transgressive as one finds in *The Importance of Being Ernest*. Wilde's elaborately subtle puns as well as his resonant complex of allusions "underwrite" a play that Baum calls a "darker comic vision" of fiercely enforced limitations on gender ideology.

The volume's final essay picks up where Eileen Gillooly's essay on humor in *Cranford* leaves off. Margaret D. Stetz's "The Laugh of the New Woman" explores strategies employed by end-of-the-century writers who still faced intellectual assaults and critical dismissal from male contemporaries. As frequent victims of ridicule themselves, she argues, the New Women chose not only their battles carefully, but also their literary weaponry. Humor was just one such weapon, used uncertainly sometimes, but ultimately to potent effect. Stetz's survey of texts by E. Nesbit, Alice Meynell, Laura Marholm Hansson, and others confirms that "long before Freud published his findings about the links between comedy and aggression, women intellectuals of the late nineteenth century were pressed ... into discerning this connection."

Stetz is only one of several authors to point out that we must be careful not to assume, as critics after Bakhtin tend to do, that humor is "always" transgressive or subversive. These essays show us that during the Victorian period the use of humor is not uniform in either its strategies or its effects. Humor could be employed to conservative ends as well as to radical or transgressive ends. If we cannot claim humor to be always subversive of too-narrow cultural formalisms, however, we can at least say that it is always revealing of them, and always relevant to the study of them. As was argued earlier in this introduction, Victorian humor serves to unmask cultural and intertextual frames, whether or not to a "liberatory" effect. But "to the eye of humour," as Edwin Hood reminds us, all things can be made visible—and for the scholar of Victorian culture it is therefore a remarkable and illuminating area of study.

Works Cited

Altick, Richard D. *Punch: The Lively Youth of a British Institution 1841–1851*. Columbus: Ohio State University Press, 1997.

Apte, Mahadev L. *Humor and Laughter: An Anthropological Approach*. Ithaca: Cornell University Press, 1985.

Boston, Richard. *An Anatomy of Laughter*. London: Collins, 1974.

Eco, Umberto. "The Frames of Comic 'Freedom.'" In *Carnival!* Ed. Thomas A. Sebeok. New York and Amsterdam: Mouton Publishers, 1984. 1–9.

Hood, Edwin. *The Mental and Moral Philosophy of Laughter*. London: Partridge & Oakey, 1852.

Keith-Spiegel, Patricia. "Early Conceptions of Humor: Varieties and Issues." In *The Psychology of Humor: Theoretical Perspectives and Empirical Issues*. Eds. Jeffrey H. Goldstein and Paul E. McGhee. New York: Academic Press, 1972. 3–39.

Leacock, Stephen. *Humor: Its Theory and Technique*. New York: Dodd, Mead & Company, 1935.

Meredith, George. "An Essay on Comedy." In *Comedy* [including Meredith's essay and Henri Bergson's "Laughter"]. 1956. Ed. Wylie Sypher. Baltimore: The Johns Hopkins University Press, 1980.

Martin, Robert Bernard. *The Triumph of Wit: A Study of Victorian Comic Theory*. Oxford: Clarendon Press, 1974.

Morson, Gary Saul and Caryl Emerson. *Mikhail Bakhtin: Creation of a Prosaics*. Stanford: Stanford University Press, 1990.

Mulkay, Michael. *On Humor: Its Nature and Its Place in Modern Society*. Oxford: Basil Blackwell, 1988.

Orel, Harold, ed. *The World of Victorian Humor*. New York: Appleton-Century-Crofts, 1961.

Simon, Richard Keller. *The Labyrinth of the Comic: Theory and Practice from Fielding to Freud*. Tallahassee: Florida State University Press, 1985.

Swabey, Marie Collins. *Comic Laughter: A Philosophical Essay*. New Haven: Yale University Press, 1961.

Sypher, Wylie, ed. *Comedy: "An Essay on Comedy" by George Meredith; "Laughter" by Henri Bergson*. 1956. Baltimore: The Johns Hopkins University Press, 1980.

Traill, H. D. "The Evolution of Humour." *National Review* 10 (February 1888): 813–30.

Parody, Pastiche, and the Play of Genres: The Savoy Operas of Gilbert and Sullivan

Carolyn Williams

The play of genres activates a particular set of humorous effects in the Savoy operas of Gilbert and Sullivan. These comic operas are anthological and formally ironic, a pastiche of nineteenth-century theatrical, literary, and popular genres turned against themselves and mixed up together to form a capacious novelty. Of course, topical ironies and various strands of social satire abound in the operas, pointed against all sorts of political and cultural targets; but beyond their more readily graspable allusiveness, a comprehensive irony resides in their form. This is not merely a formalist issue, however, since the operas' playful pastiche—especially their pastiche of genres and other forms of cultural generalization—has social and cultural significance as well as formal.

It is not unusual, certainly, for the constitution of social significance to be exposed through its theatricalization, but the Savoy operas depend for their sense of humorous absurdity upon a particular hybrid of theatricalized social types (Peers, sailors, policemen, wards of Chancery) and old-fashioned, ironically-recreated literary or theatrical types (fairies, milkmaids, Arcadian shepherds, pirates), thus tipping the balance of signification from the social toward the metatheatrical. This short essay will focus on the humor of the cultural and metatheatrical pastiche (using *Patience* as my example) and the play of genres (both in *Patience* and in *Iolanthe*). This humorously mixed form of the Savoy operas demanded a certain kind of appreciation for its effects to be recognized: an urbane, sophisticated (and perhaps somewhat self-satisfied) sense of knowingness on the part of the audience—or, at least, an upwardly-mobile aspiration toward such a sense of cultural facility—was part of the charm, part of the light but distinctly intellectual pleasure afforded by Gilbert and Sullivan.

Let us begin with pastiche and move toward parody. I should stress that I mean to use "pastiche" as a term of praise. Fredric Jameson's notion of pastiche as "blank" and neutralized is an overly-restricted notion of the practice.[1] One aesthetic sense of the term "pastiche" derives from the Italian, *pasticcio*, a pie or pasty containing a number of various ingredients, and this Italian sense was still active in the nineteenth-century theatrical context as a name for certain forms of mixed parody, burlesque, and musical entertainment. This hodgepodge variety, this rampant eclecticism should be as important to our historical sense of pastiche as is the more dominant sense of the term, which indicates an extensive, pervasive, or diffuse imitation of one stylistic model. The Savoy operas take advantage of pastiche in both these senses, revelling as they do both in general parodies of style and in recombinant mixtures of disparate generic take-offs, juxtaposed and jostling against one another.

As Margaret Rose points out (with reference to the eclecticism of both nineteenth-century and postmodern architecture), "a compilation of different styles [may] deliberately [be] used to constitute a new historicist style" (74). This practice of eclectic citation is not necessarily (or, at least it is not only) nostalgic; for just as much as it may cherish old forms of social and theatrical life, representing them in a bid for fond recognition, it can also show them to be outmoded and ridiculous. As is the case with the related notion of parody, pastiche can equally imply critique and homage, dismantling and reconstruction. Both aesthetic modes, however, have the historicizing effect of seeming to cast the objects of their representation into the past, even while momentarily reviving them. Because parody makes its object a part of its own structure, it preserves, transmits, and makes its object traditional, while at the same time it provides a *frisson* of historicizing modernization, placing its object within a new, present context, and rejuvenating it—while making fun of it—within that novel ambience. Pastiche can, at the least, exaggerate these effects by intensifying the sense of historical accumulation and present fragmentation: how very much must be taken into account! The Savoy operas of Gilbert and Sullivan (1871–96) may be seen in this light, as a formidable late nineteenth-century experiment in the humor of aesthetic historicism.

I

The famous "list" songs mimic in small form the Savoy operas' overarching principles of formation, their recombinant, anthological fusion of disparate popular ingredients. This "list" format can involve a coster's cry in the mobile marketplace like that of Little Buttercup in *HMS Pinafore*, who lists her wares as she introduces herself, or the bilious competitiveness and resentment of Ko-Ko in *The Mikado*, who has "got a little list" of "society offenders ... who never would be missed." These songs, in other words, have both sociological and metatheatrical resonance, the one a bill of fare, and the other a personification of the satirical bite of the operas, impulsively snarling out in all directions. But the best example of the microcosmic representation of this formal principle of popularizing pastiche may be found in Colonel Calverly's song from Act I of *Patience*:

> If you want a receipt for that popular mystery,
> Known to the world as a Heavy Dragoon,
> Take all the remarkable people in history,
> Rattle them off to a popular tune. (161–62)[2]

After this introductory salvo there follows the most incredible "list" of ingredients, a grab-bag of cultural topics of the day and names in current circulation. The "rattle" of this patter song makes fun of the superficial jingle of the "popular tune," enjoying even as it condescends toward a boisterous popular culture composed of superficial chatter and name recognition. Meanwhile the audience is provided with a *tour de force* in rapid-fire musical, linguistic, elocutionary, and social pyrotechnics:

> The science of Jullien, the eminent musico—
> Wit of Macaulay who wrote of Queen Anne—
> The pathos of Paddy as rendered by Boucicault—
> Style of the Bishop of Sodor and Man—
> The dash of a D'Orsay, divested of quackery—
> Narrative powers of Dickens and Thackeray—
> Victor Emmanuel—peak-haunting Peveril—
> Thomas Acquinas, and Doctor Sacheverell—

And so forth.[3] The fact that most audience members today need glosses and identifying annotations only underscores the point of such an intensely contemporaneous topicality. There is a humorous lightness in this chock-full emptiness, this knowingness without depth, which nevertheless has an additive density and boils down into a rich stew:

> Take of these elements all that is fusible,
> Melt them all down in a pipkin or crucible,
> Set them to simmer and take off the scum,
> And a Heavy Dragoon is the residuum!

This alchemical mixture (and reduction) is not only a recipe for that "popular mystery" known to the world as a Heavy Dragoon, but is also a recipe for the mystery of the popular.[4] For this song argues that popular culture operates like the pastiche form, circulating its topics on the surface of social life, boiling them down into a recognizable type (after the "scum" has been skimmed off, of course). Perhaps it is unnecessary to stress the attitude of superior knowingness implied on the part of an amused, rapidly bourgeoisifying theater audience in the 1880s; but a similar attitude obtains today on the part of fans who pride themselves on knowing all the words, or catching all the period allusions. There is a pleasure in "getting" it all, even if in the end the point is that it adds up merely to a fascinating rattle.

The major structural principle of *Patience* places the Dragoon Guards'
representation of popular culture against the pseudo-"high" culture of the
aesthetic poet Bunthorne. This structural division between cultural strata is
also underscored and embodied in the play as gender. In Act I, at the time
of the "list" patter song ("If you want a receipt for that popular mystery"),
the Heavy Dragoons are seen as representations of a discarded, dense and
outmoded masculinity, while the "twenty love-sick maidens" of the female
chorus prefer another sort of man, newly emergent on the cultural scene,
the aesthete and poet, Bunthorne. In this context, the pastiche-list of
popular ingredients, the boiled-down "residuum" represents one sort of
masculinity: a densely packed grab-bag, humorously "rattling" or marching
to a familiar oom-pah, but above all, residual.

Thus, the structured divisions of gender in *Patience* tend to represent
divisions within "culture" more generally. The wittily gendered bifurcation of
the Savoy Chorus almost always speaks to this point. Gilbert's great innovation
was to characterize the chorus and to make it an active participant in the
dramatic action of the play; through both song and dance, it aided the unfolding
of the plot, rather than standing around on stage like the singing "extras" in
much grand opera. Often explained as the influence of classical drama,
especially of Aristophanes, to whom Gilbert's satire is frequently compared, the
social commentary offered by the Savoy Choruses seems to me to serve a
much more modern, sociological and metatheatrical purpose. When in *HMS
Pinafore*, for example, sailors and female relatives of the Admiralty's First Lord
form the two choruses, the gender division emphasizes the opera's
consideration of class divisions at the same time that it recalls nautical
melodrama. Or when, in *Iolanthe*, the choruses are composed of fairies and
British representative Peers, the differences between their two wildly disparate
worlds, hilariously juxtaposed, indicate the differences between Parliament and
the theater, politics and romance, men and women. C. A. Alington discusses the
humorous absurdity of many people doing and saying exactly the same thing,
using as his chief example military discipline and its parody in *Patience*. Since
the gendered choruses in *Patience* are composed of military men and
lovestruck "aesthetic" maidens who no longer like their former Dragoon
Guard lovers, the implicit point is obviously that militarism and literary
aestheticism are antagonistic forces. This opposition is visually conveyed in the
color-blocks formed in the stage-picture by the costumes: "primary colors" for
the Dragoon Guards' uniforms, which are scorned by the maidens, who prefer
"a cobwebby grey velvet, with a tender bloom like cold gravy" and who wear
"aesthetic draperies" themselves, alluding to a supposedly medieval or "early
English" palette. Thus, the "lovesick maidens" are structurally opposed to
"Dragoon Guards" as aestheticism is opposed to an ordinary, everyday
patriotism, militarism, and "uniform" manliness, now, it seems, in danger of
displacement.

But the question of gender in this opera goes deeper than the structural opposition between aesthetic maidens and military men. These large structural groupings of masculinity and femininity are themselves both subdivided: masculinity between rival poets, one manly and one effeminate, who espouse very different styles of verse; and femininity between the lovesick maidens and Patience, the play's eponymous milkmaid heroine, who has never known what it is to love. Her "innocence" and simplicity match the Dragoon Guards' bluff obliviousness, though her characterization is an even more piquant blend of sociological and theatrical elements than theirs. On the one hand, I suppose, the play intends to suggest that the girl of the lower classes is a frequent target of seduction (in melodrama and the novel as well as in social reality); but her role is also a joke on the supposed innocence of pastoral characters such as shepherdesses and milkmaids. Her chaste "innocence" is parodically made to seem dense and "naive." Together, though, Patience and the Dragoon Guards are united in their total inability to understand Bunthorne's "high" poetic language. A sign of the Guards' falling fortunes in love, this linguistic inflexibility is a sign of her simple and "honest" sex appeal, of which she is "modestly" (and absurdly) unaware, and which attracts both of the rival poets. Thus the play of gender underscores the play of poetic genres, and vice versa.

The staging of Bunthorne's poem "Oh, Hollow! Hollow! Hollow!" offers a good case in point (165). Hearing the title, Patience asks "Is it a hunting song?" She cannot recognize the "poetic" notion of emptiness and yearning, but only hears the "hulloa" of the hunting cry. (Later, when Bunthorne asks her if she is "hollow," she answers, "No, thanks, I have dined.") The satire expressed in the lines of Bunthorne's poem turns its distinction between the "high" and the "low" on the poetic obfuscation of bodily necessity. For, coded (and indeed, nearly hidden) in almost impenetrably intertwining sonorities—surely a parody of Swinburne's ultragorgeous difficulty, the way his verse can be so beautiful that it sometimes verges on nonsense—the poem's content is quite bodily indeed. The content is as satirical as the form is parodic, for it describes languishing maidens who misunderstand their inward feelings: their lovesick yearning is revealed to be a need for laxative pills! The poem performs a sublimation of bodily signals as beautiful, "poetic" sentiment, and the scatalogical joke humorously and tacitly equates romantic love, poetry, and excrement. Its impacted difficulty is a large part of its pleasure; not only does the poetic obfuscation get the *risqué* content past the censor, but it also provides a satisfaction to those *cognoscenti* in the audience who find themselves able to decipher the dirty joke.

> What time the poet hath hymned
> The writhing maid, lithe-limbed,
>   Quivering on amaranthine asphodel,

How can he paint her woes,
Knowing, as well he knows,
    That all can be set right with calomel?

This discovery that beautiful forms contain excremental content prompts
Bunthorne's interpretation of the poem as "the wail of the poet's heart on
discovering that everything is commonplace." Can it be, he asks, that
"nothing poetic in the world shall dwell?" High culture seems to disguise
in beautiful sound the "wail" produced when everything inside is revealed
as excrement; yet it is the high-culture poet who says so, who delivers
himself of a poetic utterance with digestive regularity (his "soul [goes]
out into it ... three times a day"). In other words, perhaps it is he who is
full of it, and also hollow, shallow, empty. At the end of his poem, he holds
out the hope that maybe "something poetic lurks" even in the laxative
ingredients and their mysterious workings; and, as we shall see, the play's
conclusion will end up supporting this deeply satiric notion that "everything
is commonplace," and that poetry "lurks" there, or nowhere.

Bunthorne's poetic rival, Archibald Grosvenor, is a good example of
"commonplace" poetry. He recites bone-headed poetic lessons in "morals,"
verses in which feminine docility is rewarded with an upwardly-mobile
marriage, while masculine, bad-boy high jinks are punished with a
downwardly-mobile theatrical one. This poetic parody targets a certain Low-
Church Christian homiletic moralism that was very familiar at the time.
(Think of the Reverend Brocklehurst's initial interaction with Jane Eyre.) In
preparation for Bunthorne's reading of "Oh, Hollow!" the aesthetic maidens
were instructed to "cling passionately to one another and think of faint lilies"
but now, in preparation for Grosvenor's poem, they are told that "to
appreciate it, it is not necessary to think of anything at all" (165, 182). (You,
reading the following verse, should think of it being recited in a loud, blandly
pretentious and heavily portentous "oratorical" style):

Gentle Jane was good as gold,
She always did as she was told;
She never spoke when her mouth was full,
Or caught bluebottles their legs to pull,
Or spilt plum jam on her nice new frock,
Or put white mice in the eight-day clock,
Or vivisected her last new doll,
Or fostered a passion for alcohol.
And when she grew up she was given in marriage
To a first-class earl who keeps his carriage!

Grosvenor proudly claims that "there is not one word in that decalet which
is calculated to bring the blush of shame to the cheek of modesty," and an

aesthetic maiden replies, "Not one—it is purity itself." This sort of "purity," of course, should be as suspect as the aesthetic poet's beautifully dirty "wail." Unlike Bunthorne's sonorous evacuation, these "decalets" are overloaded with childish, utilitarian content:

> Teasing Tom was a very bad boy,
> A great big squirt was his favorite toy;
> He put live shrimps in his father's boots,
> And sewed up the sleeves of his Sunday suits;
> He punched his poor little sisters' heads,
> And cayenne-peppered their four-post beds,
> He plastered their hair with cobbler's wax,
> And dropped hot halfpennies down their backs.
>> The consequence was he was lost to*tal*ly,
>> And married a girl in the *corps de bally!* (182–83)

This penultimate emphasis on the second syllable of to*tal*ly points the joke simultaneously against his lack of technical skill in versification (since he distorts the rhythm to achieve his rhyme); against his accent (for the word must rhyme with the casual—even slightly Cockney—pronunciation of ballet); and also perhaps against the aesthetic affectation of "poetically" and "medievally" twisting pronunciation (as, for example, "li*ly*" is made to rhyme with "die" in the Act II finale of this very opera). The simplicity of the "moral" is mocked by the aesthetic maidens' rapturous response: "Marked you how grandly—how relentlessly—the damning catalogue of crime strode on, till Retribution, like a poiséd hawk, came swooping down upon the Wrong-Doer? Oh, it was terrible!" This mock-heroic delusion inflates the low, mistaking it for the high, but in a very different way than Bunthorne's poem did. Of course, within this pastiche of cultural strata, the high can also suddenly be brought low. And the ultimate humor of this play is, perhaps, that in the battle of the poetic genres, Grosvenor's "every-day" mode is destined to prevail.

For Bunthorne reveals that "the high aesthetic line" is utterly theatrical and insincere, a set of attitudes or poses. His melodramatic "aside" announces this confession in recitative: "Am I alone, / And unobserved? I am! / Then, let me own / I'm an aesthetic sham!" (168). After this confession, the aesthete's gentle patter song trips through the various secrets of how to seem aesthetic. Unlike the Heavy Dragoons' recipe for making the "residuum" that is essentially themselves, the aesthete gives the script and method for a way of acting. What seems so deep and impenetrable is merely another set of performance conventions:

> If you're anxious for to shine in the high aesthetic line as a man
>> of culture rare,

> You must get up all the germs of the transcendental terms and
>   plant them everywhere.
> You must lie upon the daisies and discourse in novel phrases of
>   your complicated state of mind,
> The meaning doesn't matter if it's only idle chatter of a
>   transcendental kind.

These and other confidential lessons are interrupted by a refrain that explains what the effect of this transcendental script will be on a hypothetical audience (what "everyone will say") and, of course, the aesthete imagines that everyone will be gullible, impressed, and taken in. Meanwhile, the actual theater audience at the Savoy is decidedly not being taken in, but quite to the contrary is being shown how to read this performance for the scripted "act" it is.

Performance will be defeated by essence and commonplace identity in this play, as the maidens cast off aestheticism in favor of Grosvenor— whom they nickname "the All-Right"—and all he stands for: "If the All-Right chooses to discard aestheticism, it proves that aestheticism ought to be discarded." Toward the end of Act II, the triumph of ordinary, commonplace, and everyday values are celebrated in yet another "list" song, "When I go out of door," which juxtaposes a pastiche of topically descriptive phrases for the "every-day young man" against the identifying associations of the aesthete (things Japanese, blue-and-white china, etc). The "commonplace young man" is characterized by such things as Somerset House, Chancery Lane, "Monday Pops," Sewell & Cross, Howell & James, a threepenny bus, and a jolly bank-holiday—a list of workaday places, consumer brand-names, and customary practices in the urban present. Against the "high aesthetic" valuation of past over present ("of course you will pooh-pooh whatever's fresh and new / And declare it crude and mean"), Grosvenor's list values present over past—and relegates the aesthete to the outmoded past. This last pastiche song offers the privileged terms of the opera's comic and parodic conclusion, as well as a framed insight on the comic opera's overall form. And what a pastiche of commonplaces that has turned out to be! We should be able to see by now, too, that "high" and "low" are relative and recombinant terms within this aesthetic regime. Bunthorne's "high" aesthetic band can only be highlighted against the displacement of the "Heavy" Dragoon Guards, and Archibald Grosvenor can only be exalted as an "every-day ... commonplace ... matter-of-fact young man" when Bunthorne has been "crushed again." Part of Gilbert's legendary attraction to "topsy-turveydom" involves this double sense of overturning: the high brought low and the low elevated, in both social and theatrical registers at once.

Of course, the rejection of "high" or "transcendental" language as an aesthetic affectation in social life is one thing, but the rejection of theatricality is entirely another. The girls pair off with the Dragoon Guards, who don't do well at "posing," and with Grosvenor, who is too self-satisfied even to think of posing. To be sincere seems to mean to be oblivious, moralistic, antitheatrical, and "every-day" rather than "out-of-the-way." In turning for its conclusion toward the "every-day" and away from the theatrical, this comic opera engineers an elaborately complicated and back-handed compliment to its audience—at the expense of its own principles—for the audience might recognize themselves as part of an everyday, mundanely nontheatrical world. But at the same time, the present tense with Grosvenor's winning, "every-day" values is very far from being idealized in the play, and the implication of ridicule tends to pull the rug out from under any self-satisfaction the audience might feel in identifying with it. Nevertheless, an uncannily strange profundity hovers over the ending, as the play (with a purportedly antitheatrical theatricality) turns against the notion of acting in the social space of "real" life.

II

The first phase of the aesthetic craze was a thing of the past (though not the very distant past) in 1881, when *Patience* produced it as the object of its parody. Moreover, many other theatrical parodies of the craze had already preceded *Patience*; and, of course, parodies such as *Patience* contributed to its outmoding. *Patience* is the only one that has survived into our present. So far, I have used *Patience,* in other words, to provide an extended example of pastiche at work in both form and content, but the discussion of *Patience* has also demonstrated the satiric parody of a few specific genres of "high" and "low" culture ("Pre-Raphaelite" and "aesthetic" fashions of costume and behavior, Swinburnean lyric, melodramatic soliloquy, Low-Church homiletics). In each of these cases, a generalized social resonance goes hand in hand with a generalized literary and theatrical resonance; and in each case, the generic parody works to thrust its object out of present-day modishness and into an outmoded past. Another form of the play of genres involves the thorough-going response to one generic model. In the case of *Iolanthe* (1882), which we will soon consider, genre parody is put to the service of different effects, and the relative constitution of past and present, high and low, works differently as well.

Sometimes Gilbert did base his parodic humor on a certain specific textual or theatrical model. For example, he wrote hilarious parody-reviews of current dramatic productions for *Fun* magazine from 1865 until 1871—each only a page long, and all masterpieces of pointed wit and concise critical judgment. My own favorite is Gilbert's parody-review of *East Lynne* from 17 February 1866,[5] in which the actress playing Lady Isabel was represented thus: "Though I am the wife of a mere country mumble, yet I am the daughter of an Earl. Mumble, mumble, mumble. My husband is wealthy and mumble, and I love him mumbly." Embracing her own child while disguised as his governess, she cries: "Ha! Ha! Mumble! It is my own mumble!" (And it keeps going in this vein quite mercilessly and hilariously.) Or, for example, Gilbert wrote five opera burlesques (in the form of extravaganzas) from 1866 to 1869. Perhaps a title or two will suffice to convey the sort of humor—much broader than that of the Savoy operas—that obtained in this genre: Donizetti's *L'elisir d'amore* was travestied as *Dulcamara, or The Little Duck and the Great Quack*, whereas Balfe and Bunn's remarkably popular *The Bohemian Girl* became, under Gilbert's hand, *The Merry Zingara, or The Tipsy Gipsy and the Pipsy Wipsy* (see Goldberg, ed.).

The greatest and most lasting examples of Gilbert's practice of strict parody are surely his responses to Tennyson's poetic "medley" of lyric, dramatic and narrative forms, *The Princess* (1847–51). Gilbert understood his play *The Princess* (1870) to be "a blank verse burlesque in which a picturesque story [is] told in a strain of mock-heroic seriousness"—that is, as he said, "a respectful perversion" of Tennyson's poem (Stedman, *W. S. Gilbert*, 77). The later Savoy opera, *Princess Ida* (1884), took off on Tennyson yet again, less respectfully perhaps, but much more humorously and much more in keeping with Tennyson's notion of a generic "medley." Often, in fact, Gilbert recycled his own previous works in new forms and once even parodied himself, in *The Happy Land* (1873), which was a direct take-off on his own very successful fairy play of that same year, *The Wicked World.*[6] Gilbert's publication history is replete with various versions of recycling, and it seems that parody and self-parody were fundamental sources of his creativity.

But more often—in the formula that made the Savoy operas so popular—the parody was not of a specific work but of a genre, taken whole (so to speak). The Savoy parodies of melodrama surely provide the best example, though I will only glance briefly at that perennially popular topic[7] here, in the interests of moving soon to consider *Iolanthe*'s parody of another popular genre, the fairy extravaganza. Both *HMS Pinafore* (1878), the first blockbuster hit of the Savoy series, and *The Pirates of Penzance* (1880) derive their entire structure and rationale from the conventions of their precursor form, the nautical melodrama. As Ashley (and many others) have pointed out, the conventions of melodrama were thoroughly "incorporated and burlesqued," not only abused but also used; the parody is so pervasive, in other words, that it shows up in large structural features (the captain's daughter in love with a common sailor, class conflict on board ship, the revelation of switched babies at the end of *Pinafore*) as well as in a panoply of more limited, local effects. Each of these parodied conventions can be far-reaching in its implications. The theatricalized figure of the "Jolly Jack Tar," for example, predates melodrama (as both Clinton-Baddeley and Cottis have shown), but it certainly reaches its most obsessively considered treatment there. That hearty, patriotic, hornpipe-dancing "common sailor," with his identifying salty language compounded of nautical metaphor, manly eloquence, and unrestrained though earnest swearing, is transformed on board the *Pinafore*, whose sailors must be taught the hornpipe by their bureaucratic First Lord, and whose Captain "never [or hardly ever] swears a big, big D."

When Gilbert hypothesizes new figures—polite sailors or sentimental pirates—the joke goes deep, but the total form of the parody reaches even further than these major figural revisions. One could easily argue that the depth and pervasiveness of the parody indicate a thorough critique not only of the conventions, but also of the ideology of nautical melodrama, concerned as it is with class conflict, law and order on land and sea, the relation between domesticity and naval or military service, and the relations of country to city. Gothic melodrama concerns itself with a variant of these clustered thematic issues: the relations between a degenerate aristocracy and the rising common people; the secularization of spirit (as ghosts and other half-psychologized, half-supernatural phenomena). Gilbert parodies these Gothic conventions, too, though somewhat more superficially than he handles the nautical melodrama. *Ruddigore* (1887) parodied both, with its ancestral portrait gallery come to life and its comic sailor, "Dick Dauntless."

The accumulative, recombinant richness of Gilbert's parodic humor must be partly understood in the context of a period without theatrical copyright. Borrowing, adaptation, translation, and "piracy" were standard practice in the English theater until quite late in the nineteenth century. "When they weren't doing Shakespeare,"[8] all the other major genres—pantomime and extravaganza, melodrama and other forms of musical theater—quite regularly depended for their plots on earlier texts, often in German or French. Early melodrama especially relied on adaptation—the supposed first melodrama in English, Thomas Holcroft's *A Tale of Mystery* (1802), for example, was a close adaptation of Pixerécourt's *Coelina*—while pantomime and extravaganza were characterized by a more rambunctious sort of borrowing. A wholesale combination of pastiche and parody, those genres characteristically mixed characters and plots from several classical, folktale, or fairy-tale sources in a gigantic and somewhat unwieldy mass of elements that pointed to the exuberance, if often also to the potential incoherence, of this over-the-top, excessive form of fun. The title of Gilbert's first pantomime will easily illustrate this point: *Harlequin Cock Robin and Jenny Wren, or Fortunatus and the Water of Life, The Three Bears, The Three Gifts, The Three Wishes, and the Little Man Who Woo'd the Little Maid* (1867).

Pantomime and extravaganza were closely allied forms. During the genre's prime, when the form was at the peak of its complex development, a pantomime would open with a verbal combat between mock-representatives of good and evil, usually a demon and a fairy, who were often generic (Demon and Fairy Queen), but were sometimes specified thematically (The Good Fairy of Learning against the Demon of Ignorance, for example, or in Gilbert's pantomime, which was partly based on the theme of sanitation, the Spirit of Fresh Air against the Demon of Miasma). After several phases of skit-like dramatic action, loosely based on one or more folk- or fairy tales, there is a grand "transformation scene," in which the stage set wondrously unfolds to reveal another realm altogether, a spectacular scene of magical bliss, or a version of Fairyland; then, the main characters of the dramatic action are transformed into the familiar figures of the *commedia dell'arte*, and a boisterous harlequinade follows. This is topsy-turvydom indeed, for the main structural premise of pantomime involves this transformation of one world into another.[9]

The extravaganza on the other hand—whether based on classical or fairy-tale models—was more urbane, sedate and elegant. Though it did not end in a harlequinade, it did often end in a spectacular version of the transformation scene. But both generic forms were characterized by dialogue in rhymed couplets; wordplay and egregious punning (italicized in playtexts and playbills to aid audience recognition); parody lyrics, composed of new words set to familiar tunes (airs from current operas, parlor ballads, and other popular music of the day); topical references to issues, personalities, inventions, or anything else in circulation at the time (in London or on the Continent); and literary references (particularly to Shakespeare) scattered humorously throughout. Both the references to Shakespeare and the cosmopolitan references to contemporary cultural life demanded recognition on the part of a knowing, urbane (if middlebrow) theater audience.

Gilbert's most notable "fairy play," *The Wicked World*, was not an extravaganza, but, written in blank verse, aspired to (and was received as) serious drama.[10] *The Wicked World*, like pantomime and extravaganza, assumes the existence of two worlds, one mundane and the other magical, and takes as its double premise that every fairy in Fairyland has his or her mortal counterpart on earth, and that the bliss of the fairies is predicated on their never having experienced "mortal love." In the play, fairy emissaries are dispatched to earth, and the correlative earthly representatives—mortal men—come to Fairyland, with dreadful results. The fairies fall in love with the men, feel all the attendant emotions of yearning, jealousy, anger, and dependence, and are generally made miserable. The play offers a critique of nineteenth-century gender and heterosexual relations, despite the fact that it ends by reestablishing Fairyland and "the wicked world" as separate realms, one chaste and the other still plagued with "mortal love." In fact, the concept of the "fairy" in the period seems to offer a lot of room for the imagination to play with alternatives to the usual gender and sexual relations in the social realm, bridging as it does an unworldly, hyperbolic chastity or domestic bliss on the one hand (as in the frequently-used colloquial phrase for domestic bliss, "fairy cottage") and, on the other hand, a more open and less restrictive sexuality than obtained in "the real world" (as in fairy painting or theater). The utopian, spectacular, supernatural otherworld of "Fairyland" is variously imagined as an escape from or as a perfection of the "real world."

In the theater, fairies provided the vehicle for a light though barely sublimated form of sexual display. Exposure of the female leg was quite a fetishistic pleasure at the time, as numerous illustrations and anecdotes attest, and fairies were a familiar "cover" for this interest—as were, for example, the tableaux vivants and *poses plastiques* in which women wearing fewer, more clinging, or tighter clothes than usual imitated classical statuary or famous paintings. On stage, chorus girls dressed as fairies could show their legs, wear gauzy, short, or otherwise scanty clothing, and display their "fairy forms" rising, falling, turning, and flying on lifts or wires. This interest in the female form was further advanced by particularly nineteenth-century practices of theatrical transvestism. In the fairy extravaganzas of James Robinson Planché, the early master of the genre (as well as one of Gilbert's primary influences), Madame Vestris often took the hero's role (see Fletcher). This feature of the extravaganza would later inform the role of the "principal boy" in the pantomime (see Rowell, Granville Barker). The principal boy was an attractive young woman dressed as a youth, wearing (for example) a doublet and (most definitely) tights. The other side of this coin, the "Dame" figure, was a broad or "low" comic man dressed as an older woman, another staple of the pantomime and later of the music hall as well. Both figures influenced Gilbert's characterizations in *Iolanthe*.

The genre of the fairy extravaganza is almost completely unknown today, and the nineteenth-century pantomime is only barely recognizable in today's "panto," though the current genre retains (and exaggerates) the element of cross-dressing. *Iolanthe*, which draws its inspiration especially from extravaganza, is probably our chief reminder that the earlier genre ever existed at all. Whereas *Iolanthe* can certainly still be enjoyed without any audience awareness of the nineteenth-century fairy extravaganza, a feel for the opera's parodic relation to an earlier genre would surely add to the present-day audience's understanding that Gilbert and Sullivan are engaged in a witty intellectual exercise in literary and theatrical historicism, and that audiences in their own day were likely to have recognized the resonance. Indeed, despite its humor, *Iolanthe* was meant to be a "higher" form of entertainment than the extravaganza. There are no rhymed couplets in the dialogue, and there is very little word play; the music consists not of familiar tunes, but brilliantly original ones; the topically allusive wit remains, but Gilbert and Sullivan made a concerted decision to eschew transvestism in the interest of respectability. *Iolanthe* has its tongue very much in its cheek on this issue, however, drawing on a contextualizing memory of genre conventions, while overturning and even erasing some of them.

Despite the absence of transvestism, in other words, its aura remained. The Fairy Queen, for example, broadly alludes to the stock "Fairy Queen" role in the pantomime as well as to the "Dame" role. As Jane Stedman has argued, Gilbert capitalizes on these precursor figures, while harnessing their authority toward characterizations of powerful women (see her "From Dame to Woman"). A palpable part of the wit would have been felt in the fact that this imposing "Dame"-like figure was played not by a "low" comic man, but by an imposing diva, a large, powerful, charismatic, "operatic" and somewhat threatening woman. When the Lord Chancellor is taught to recognize the Fairy Queen, his response makes this humor clear:

> A plague on this vagary,
> I'm in a nice quandary!
>   Of hasty tone
>   With dames unknown
> I ought to be more chary;
> It seems that she's a fairy
> From Andersen's library,
>   And I took her for
>   The proprietor
> Of a Ladies' Seminary! (224)

He took her for a familiar and forbiddingly repressive social figure, when in fact her type inhabits both page and stage. We might say today that these stage "Dames" expressed the ambivalence (and misogyny) felt toward such figures from social life.[11] Gilbert's humor here seems to me to make this feminist point by capitalizing on the low comedy of a conventional transvestism hovering behind the scenes. Similarly, though "low" theatrical practices of sexual display were toned down and made much less overt in the Savoy operas, it is not unfair to say that they were still present, sublimated to a "higher" form in the Savoy Chorus, whose members were renowned for their beauty and appeal. The band of fairies still showed the charms of their "fairy forms," in other words, though the Savoy Chorus girls were carefully constructed as chaste, good girls, despite their performance of allure (see Davis).

The depth and scope of *Iolanthe*'s indebtedness to the pantomime and extravaganza shows most clearly in a feature whose seeming obviousness belies its subtlety: the fundamental structural division between "Fairyland" and the real world, which is articulated by the gendered, divided chorus of male Peers and female Peris. This juxtaposition is funny on the face of things, especially the comic refunctioning of "high" as supernatural and "low" as sublunary. Thus from the outset the highest representatives of English society are humorously seen to be lower than the fairies in all sorts of ways, including power and intelligence. As Lord Tolloler admits, the Lords are "persons of no capacity whatever" (239); and the Fairy Queen refers to them at one point as "puny mortals" (224). The play engages many times in a hilarious running joke about the uselessness of the House of Lords in particular and the stupidity of party politics in general; and so the gendered significance of this playful redistribution of power is subsumed in its more general political significance. The comic implication that women are to men as "high" is to "low" would, in any case, be overturned in the end (as it was in *Patience*) by the conventional comic ending (marriage and the domestication of female desire). But until that ending, the Fairy Queen is all-powerful; and the humor in the fact that her structural opposite is a Lord Chancellor will be felt more clearly if the "Demon" figure opposing the usual pantomime Fairy Queen is recalled.

Their realms are utterly separate, for they operate according to two distinct "systems" or "laws." As the Fairy Queen must enforce her "fairy laws," so the Lord Chancellor claims that in his realm, "I, my Lords, embody the Law" (208). Of course, this structural division exists in order to be transgressed; the two realms will infiltrate one another, both in matters of parliamentary politics and (as in *The Wicked World*) in matters of "mortal love." In fact the play opens with the premise that the most important fairy law—"every fairy must die who marries a mortal"—has already been broken (244). Iolanthe, who did in former times marry a mortal, has been mercifully banished instead of killed, and in the opening scene of the play her Queen pardons her and welcomes her back. It turns out that from her union with a mortal, Iolanthe has a son Strephon, an Arcadian shepherd who is "half a fairy." This hybrid being is the occasion of much sexual innuendo, since he's a "fairy down to the waist," but below the waist he's "mortal," a word which, as we know, is closely associated in the fairy plays with the idea of "love." For a complicated set of reasons, Strephon is put into Parliament by the Fairy Queen, and this affords Gilbert the opportunity to joke about a "fairy member," while at the same time suggesting the idea that women are messily infiltrating men's territory. Lord Mountararat makes this implication clear when he exclaims in frustration: "This comes of women interfering in politics" (229).

Thus the implications of fairy "law" or a fairy "system" include not only a supernatural sort of feminine influence, but also a more relaxed sexual regime than respectable Victorian gender arrangements made possible. The play's critique of gender arrangements involves the rather heavy-handed point (akin to the lampooning of the Dragoon Guards in *Patience*) that the Lords are dense and incapacitated, but that the fairies find them attractive nonetheless. That the Peers' behavior could be taken for a decidedly masculine style of sexual attractiveness hilariously exposes the absurdity of gendered role assignments in the social world. One fairy, sighing with longing, explains why they seem so attractive: "For self-contained dignity, combined with airy condescension, give me a British representative Peer!" (231).

Likewise, it is funny to find the Fairy Queen holding herself up as a model of sexual restraint by making a grand histrionic display of her own barely-suppressed passion for Private Willis: "Now here is a man whose physical attributes are simply godlike. That man has a most extraordinary effect upon me. If I yielded to a natural impulse, I should fall down and worship that man. But I mortify this inclination; I wrestle with it, and it lies beneath my feet!" (232). Long before Freud or Foucault, Gilbert seems to have grasped something of the range of contradictions implicit in the notion of repression. The Fairy Queen's protestations of restraint, like the Savoy operas' particularly restrained style of sexual display, remind us that there is a decorous middlebrow sexiness in the very displacement of sexuality to the realm of Fairyland. That sexual decorum is both prurient and "innocent," exposing the absurdity of simultaneously gratifying and denying sexual expressiveness. The humor of this restrained form of transgression is emphasized when Strephon turns out to be the son of Iolanthe and the Lord Chancellor, but that *coup* of the plot is not revealed until the conclusion of the play. By that time, all the fairies are in love with the Peers, who explain: "It's not their fault. They couldn't help themselves." To which the Queen replies: "It seems they *have* helped themselves, and pretty freely, too." For now they are "all fairy duchesses, marchionesses, countesses, viscountesses, and baronesses" (244), impossible hybrids of the two realms of representation. Unfortunately, fairy law stipulates that the whole band of them must therefore be slaughtered.

At this point the Lord Chancellor's earthly ways of construing the law come in handy. He intervenes "as an old Equity draftsman" and suggests that "the subtleties of the legal mind are equal to the emergency." The addition of a single word will adjust the fairy law to read "Every fairy must die who *doesn't* marry a mortal" (245). In the end, then, the separate realms are utterly intertwined on a stage full of married and soon-to-be-married pairs. This comic resolution is *Iolanthe*'s equivalent for the "transformation scene" in the pantomime and extravaganza. Like magic—as easy as changing the law into its precise opposite with the addition of single word—everything is transformed! With one last joke about the uselessness of representative Peers—they might as well be transformed into fairies, for, as Lord Mountararat puts it, "I really don't see what use *we* are down here, do you Tolloller?" (245)—the Fairy Queen gives the final command: "Then away we go to Fairyland." Suddenly, electric lights illuminate the fairies' headdresses, and *"Wings sprout from [the] shoulders"* of the Peers (245). The theatrical world overcomes the mundane, social world, with all the liberating promise of that transformation. Singing and dancing exuberantly at the Act II finale, Peers and Peris alike rejoice: "Happy are we / As you can see / Every one is now a fairy!"

III

The deepest humor of this scene resides in its grand transformation of genre, affording a pleasure more subtle and pervasive than that afforded by the comic refunctioning of a single, specific prior work. *Iolanthe*'s general parody of the fairy extravaganza involves the same double motives that any parody involves: imitation and critique; memorialization and trashing or hashing; preservation and dismantling. Parody always implicitly casts its object into the past, making itself modish, popular, and absolutely up to date by partially outmoding its objects of regard. Thus a knowing, historicized connoisseurship is an active part of the appreciation. The courtliness of this sort of turn toward an earlier genre—as if to pay homage at the very moment that the new form also turns away—is braced and balanced by the Savoy operas' social satire. That satirical bite, in turn, is softened or muted by the historical and aesthetic distancing of the parody and pastiche.

By means of this exuberantly mixed form, Gilbert and Sullivan instituted a new genre. The widespread nineteenth-century obsession with the issue of a national music—or rather, with the lack of one—was answered by Gilbert and Sullivan's development of the "comic opera." Soon, however, that general form became almost entirely specified to their own productions, and now "Gilbert-and-Sullivan" names its own recognizable theatrical genre, with its own tradition and history.[12] The Savoy operas are themselves now famously subject to being taken off and parodied, or to being taken up piecemeal into current postmodern pastiches. Among the various theoretical conclusions that could be drawn from this fact is an insight into the close connection between parody and tradition. At the furthest extension of this line of argument, "tradition" itself may be seen as a sequence of parodic intertextual and intergeneric relations, repeated acts of internalization and refunctioning, of absorption and revision.

In the history of establishing Gilbert and Sullivan as a national tradition—a huge topic that we can barely glance at here—Richard D'Oyly Carte played the most important role, for his entrepreneurial genius at capital consolidation allowed the operas to be disseminated in space (by means of touring companies in the provinces and in the United States especially), while his family-controlled corporation allowed them to be stabilized as performance traditions and reproduced over time, long after his death. However, the traditional aesthetic of production was largely Gilbert's legacy, for his strict— even obsessive—control of the stage direction and the acting style was legendary.[13] Gilbert insisted on more rehearsal than was common at the time, and on more precision in all aspects of the production, but also on an absolutely deadpan acting style, in which "the most improbable things [were] done in the most earnest manner by persons of every-day life." E. B. Hindle, writing in the 1880s, calls this Gilbert's "chief discovery" (72). But in fact Gilbert's "chief discovery" was not exactly a discovery at all, for it was another traditional feature of the fairy extravaganza itself. Roy points out (discussing Planché) that a particular form of urbane humor derives from the unexpected juxtaposition of the contemporary urban world with the world of the fairies, and the unremarked expectation that the topical jokes of the city would all be duly understood in Fairyland. Planché himself developed a tacit acting style to accompany his full-fledged antirealistic extravaganzas, which "presuppose the existence of a cultivated and intellectually alert audience" (Roy, 14) to catch the humor.

Restraint in the style of exposure to the parody allows the audience to be the "knowing" ones. As long as the tacit absurdity of the parody never descends into the explicitness of broad (or "low") comedy, the audience can rest within the comfortable ambience of an elegant, urbane, and relatively "high" entertainment (no matter how silly it is). Gilbert theoretically justifies this acting style in *Rosencrantz and Guildenstern* (1891), his parody of Hamlet, just at the moment when Hamlet gives his advice to the company of Players:

> he who doth so mark, label, and underscore his antick speeches as to show that he is alive to their absurdity seemeth to utter them under protest, and to take part with his audience against himself. (*Turning to* Players.) For which reason, I pray you, let there be no huge red noses, nor extravagant monstrous wigs, nor coarse men garbed as women, in this comi-tragedy; for such things are as much as to say, "I am a comick fellow—I pray you laugh at me, and hold what I say to be cleverly ridiculous." Such labelling of humor is an impertinence to your audience, for it seemeth to imply that they are unable to recognize a joke unless it be pointed out to them. I pray you avoid it. (III, 86)

Gilbert's acting style never allows for this impertinence. The Savoy operas— with their pastiche of genre parodies, social and theatrical types, various levels and forms of humor, many of them unmarked, unlabelled, and underplayed—offer an elaborately mixed dish, a tribute to their audience's presumed ability to recognize a wide variety of topical humor in the world around them as well as on the stage.

Notes

[1] Fredric Jameson's notion of pastiche as "blank parody" (neutralized, non-intentional, normless) is developed in "Postmodernism and Consumer Society" and in "Postmodernism, or the Cultural Logic of Late Capitalism." Jameson ties his definition to a historical critique of postmodernism and late capitalism, so perhaps in the present context it is enough to claim that the retrieval of a late nineteenth-century form of pastiche would perforce allow for other valuations. However, a stronger argument can be mounted against Jameson's "wilful redefinition of pastiche as postmodern." See for example Margaret A. Rose, *Parody: Ancient, Modern, and Post-Modern* (220–32 and *passim*). My exemplary conjunction here of the Savoy operas with Rose's claim that "postmodern parody" displays "the rehabilitation of parody as both comic and meta-fictional" suggests that certain practices now usually named "postmodern" are common in late nineteenth-century variants.

[2] In the case of the Savoy operas, I will quote from the Norton paperback edition, as it is perhaps the most accessible edition at this time. All other works of Gilbert's will be cited from the *Original Plays of W. S. Gilbert,* by volume and page number.

[3] The most accessible annotations at this time may be found in Bradley.

[4] The word "residuum" had recently come into current usage to refer to a "dangerous class" of "unregenerate poor." See Stedman Jones, 11. This possible association suggests a distant and more bitter slur than the song's tone and tempo would immediately suggest.

[5] Jane Stedman also mentions this example prominently. See her *W. S. Gilbert: A Classic Victorian and his Theatre,* 23–26.

[6] *The Wicked World* was itself a dramatized version of a previously published story with that same title; and from *The Wicked World,* in turn, *Iolanthe, Utopia Limited,* and *Fallen Fairies* may be seen to derive.

[7] Note, for example, three essays on this topic (Ashley, Bargainnier, and Cottis) in the volume of papers from the 1970 conference (ed. Helyar).

[8] I mean to refer to the distinction between "legitimate" and "illegitimate" theater, which obtained until the Theatre Regulation Act of 1843. Before that time, "legitimate" theater was restricted to the Patent Houses, while all other theater displayed one version of mixed form or another in order to be covered as "burletta."

[9] For a wonderful description of the transformation scene, see Fitzgerald. Gilbert played on this convention elsewhere in his work. One great example may be found in the British Library prompt-book for *Trial By Jury,* which reveals that the closing scene was meant to be seen as a humorous allusion to such a scene. A handwritten notation reads "GRAND TRANSFORMATION SCENE!" (underlined twice in red, and prefigured in the prompt-book directions by a "Gong for Change"). These prompt-book stage directions begin with the Judge's reprise ("Oh yes, I am a Judge") and end, with the play's end, on the choral acknowledgment: "And a good Judge, too!" Whereupon the prompt-book specifies "Picture and Curtain // Red fire R & L," and the left margin specifies again in bold letters, underlined: "Red fire." (Prompt-book for *Trial By Jury,* in Volume XXII of the W. S. Gilbert Papers, British Library [Add. MS 49310]: 14.) Fredric Woodbridge Wilson called my attention to this prompt-book and its importance. See his valuable guide to the collections in the British Library.

[10] Though serious fairy drama dates at least from Shakespeare, the Victorian period experienced a major resurgence. See both Silver, and Maas et al.

[11] Adrienne Munich expands upon this point, seeing a satirical commentary on Queen Victoria's body, person, and role in many of the Savoy operas. See "Queen of a Certain Age" (104–26).

[12] For a good treatment of the formation of the "tradition," see Cannadine.

[13] On Gilbert as a director, see Cox-Ife and also Stedman, "Gilbert's Stagecraft: Little Blocks of Wood."

Works Cited

Alington, C. A. "Aristophanes and Gilbert." *Empire Review* 41 (March 1925): 257–68.

Ashley, Leonard. "Gilbert and Melodrama." In Helyar (ed.) 1–6.

Bargainnier, Earl F. "*Ruddigore*: Gilbert's Burlesque of Melodrama." In Helyar (ed.) 7–16.

Booth, Michael R. *Victorian Spectacular Theatre 1850–1910*. London: Routledge & Kegan Paul, 1981.

Bradley, Ian, ed. *The Complete Annotated Gilbert and Sullivan*. Oxford: Oxford University Press, 1996.

Cannadine, David. "Gilbert and Sullivan: The Making and Unmaking of a British 'Tradition.'" In *Myths of the English*. Ed. Roy Porter. Cambridge: Polity Press in association with Blackwell, 1992. 12–32.

Clinton-Baddeley, V. C. *The Burlesque Tradition in the English Theatre after 1600*. London: Methuen & Co., 1952.

Cottis, Eileen F. "Gilbert and the British Tar." In Helyar (ed.) 33–42.

Cox-Ife, William. *W. S. Gilbert: Stage Director*. London: Dennis Dobson, 1977.

Davis, Tracy C. "The Savoy Chorus." *Theatre Notebook* 44 (1990): 26–38.

Fitzgerald, Percy. *The World Behind the Scenes*. London, 1881.

Fletcher, Kathy. "Planché, Vestris, and the Transvestite Role: Sexuality and Gender in Victorian Popular Theatre." *Nineteenth Century Theatre* 15.1 (Summer 1987): 9–33.

Gilbert, W. S. *Complete Plays of Gilbert and Sullivan*. Illus. W. S. Gilbert. New York: W. W. Norton & Co., 1976.

———. *New and Original Extravaganzas by W. S. Gilbert*. Ed. Isaac Goldberg. Boston: John W. Luce & Co., 1931.

———. *Original Plays of W. S. Gilbert*. 4 vols. London: Chatto & Windus, 1923.

Goldberg, Isaac. *The Story of Gilbert and Sullivan, or The 'Compleat' Savoyard*. New York: Simon & Schuster, 1928.

Granville-Barker, Harley. "Exit Planché—Enter Gilbert." In *The Eighteen-Sixties*. Royal Society of Literature. Ed. John Drinkwater. New York: Macmillan; Cambridge: Cambridge University Press, 1932. 102–48.

Helyar, James, ed. *Gilbert and Sullivan*. (Papers presented at the International Conference held at the University of Kansas in May 1970.) Lawrence, KS: University of Kansas Libraries, 1971.

Hindle, E. B. "W. S. Gilbert, Playwright and Humorist." *Manchester Quarterly* (January 1885): 55–85.

Hughes, Gervase. *The Music of Arthur Sullivan*. Westport, CT: Greenwood Press, 1959.

Jameson, Fredric. "Postmodernism and Consumer Society." In *The Anti-Aesthetic: Essays on Postmodern Culture*. Ed. Hal Foster. Port Townsend, WA: Bay, 1983. 111–25.

———. "Postmodernism, or the Cultural Logic of Late Capitalism." *New Left Review* 146 (1984): 53–92.

Maas, Jeremy, Pamela White Trimpe, Charlotte Gere, et al. (eds.) *Victorian Fairy Painting*. London: Merrell Holberton, 1997.

Munich, Andienne. *Queen Victoria's Secrets*. New York: Columbia University Press, 1996.

Planché, James Robinson. *Plays by James Robinson Planché*. Ed. Donald Roy. Cambridge: Cambridge University Press, 1986.

Rose, Margaret A. *Parody: Ancient, Modern, and Post-Modern*. Cambridge: Cambridge University Press, 1993.

Rowell, George. *The Victorian Theatre 1792–1914*. Cambridge: Cambridge University Press, 1956.

Roy, Donald, ed. *Plays by James Robinson Planché*. Cambridge: Cambridge University Press, 1986.

Silver, Carole G. *Strange and Secret Peoples: Fairies and Victorian Consciousness*. Oxford: Oxford University Press, 1999.

Stedman, Jane W. "From Dame to Woman: W. S. Gilbert and Theatrical Transvestism." In *Suffer and Be Still: Women in the Victorian Age*. Ed. Martha Vicinus. Bloomington: Indiana University Press, 1972. 20–37.

————, ed. and introduction. *Gilbert Before Sullivan: Six Comic Plays By W. S. Gilbert*. Chicago: University of Chicago Press, 1967.

————. "Gilbert's Stagecraft: Little Blocks of Wood." In Helyar (ed.): 195–211.

————. *W. S. Gilbert: A Classic Victorian and His Theatre*. Oxford: Oxford University Press, 1996.

Stedman Jones, Gareth. *Outcast London: A Study in the Relationship Between Classes in Victorian Society*. New York: Pantheon, 1971.

Wilson, Fredric Woodbridge. "The W. S. Gilbert Papers in the British Library." *W. S. Gilbert Society Journal* 1.4 (Autumn 1986): 105–119.

2

The Fissure *King*: Parody, Ideology, and the Imperialist Narrative

Patricia Murphy

With its espousal of imperialist ideology, *King Solomon's Mines* strives to convey the social, political, and ethical values that informed late Victorian conceptions of Africa. Yet the 1885 novel does not provide a seamless, totalizing narrative through which the virtues of imperialism, as envisioned by apologist H. Rider Haggard, emerge as monolithic or incontestable. Instead, the novel is marked by fissures through which the tenets of imperialism—especially the notion that the "civilized" European was destined to exert control over the "primitive" African—are attenuated even as they are being valorized. An 1887 parody, "Hyder Ragged's" *King Solomon's Wives: or, The Phantom Mines*, foregrounds through humor these destabilizing moments in Haggard's text that erase the distinction between the two cultures and allow putative British superiority to be interrogated and undermined.[1]

Victorian writings, both fictional and nonfictional, insistently sought to illuminate the differences between the inhabitants of the "Dark Continent" and the immeasurably enlightened society of their English saviors to provide the familiar rationale for British expansion.[2] In David Livingstone's *Travels and Researches in South Africa*, for instance, the popular missionary–explorer adopts a vocabulary that carefully establishes a binary relationship. Africans are essentialized as "heathens," an uncivilized group so dissimilar to Europeans that "[w]e cannot fairly compare these poor people with ourselves" (61); in fact, "no one can realize the degradation to which their minds have been sunk by centuries of barbarism" (86).[3] Scientific discourses, shaped by Darwin's distinctions between "civilized" and "savage" races in the 1871 *Descent of Man,* reinforced comforting presumptions of European ascendancy on the evolutionary ladder.[4] Typical of Darwin's attitude is his "astonishment" at seeing a group of tribesmen on one of his journeys and his bemused realization that "such were our ancestors" (643). Indeed, as Patrick Brantlinger argues in discussing the rhetoric of explorers, missionaries, and scientists, "humanitarianism did point insistently toward imperialism" on moral, religious, and scientific grounds (174).

As critics have additionally noted, the guiding national ideology of the imperialist mission was not immune to dissent and attack, nor could Victorians ignore apprehensions that the empire was headed toward decline. "Hyder

Ragged's" parody points to disparate elements of *King Solomon's Mines* that reveal such broader cultural inconsistencies.[5] Viewing the 1885 novel within the larger domain of societal discussion makes the text's lack of unity in its representations of Africans and Europeans an oddly logical response to the fractured British discourse on imperialism. As Daniel Bivona observes, this "culture-wide 'debate'" became "a complex discussion of the foundations both of the modern ideology of imperialism and of the critique of that ideology"—a discursive domain that "eschew[ed] the goal of simple 'coherence' in favour of revealing the contradictions in these discourses" (vii–viii). Rather than representing a cohesive univocality, *King Solomon's Mines* functions as a site of conflict through which multiple voices can be discovered and heard in a Bakhtinian dialogic interchange. Haggard's text thus offers not a consistent ideological position and stable meaning but a periodic resistance to the semblance of coherence, made more visible through the microscopic gaze of the parodic vehicle.

My project is to locate moments in the parody that respond to scenes in Haggard's novel wherein the ostensible boundary between African and European collapses, thereby problematizing the distinctions between the two cultures. The indeterminacy of this boundary is a crucial point: if the British cannot establish themselves firmly above Africans on the ladder of civilization, then the justification for imperialism is weakened and the ideological structure is vulnerable to challenge. I focus particularly on paradigmatic linguistic, behavioral, and epistemological strategies that the parody employs to unsettle this questionable binarism. Also confusing the dichotomy, I argue, are abundant analogies established between African and British societies. Finally, I examine the parody's exposure of the male quest romance as a construct, unmasked as an imperialist vehicle that disguises ideology within seemingly innocuous generic conventions.

I

The best-selling *King Solomon's Mines* traces the adventures of three English explorers: Allan Quatermain, the narrator; Sir Henry Curtis, a wealthy nobleman; and Captain John Good, a seaman.[6] Urged by Sir Henry to accompany him to the African interior in search of his long-lost brother, Quatermain agrees, hoping to find the lost treasures of King Solomon along the way. The explorers hire several Africans to accompany them on their trek, including the inscrutable Umbopa, who initially conceals his intent of reclaiming the throne in Kukuanaland that had been usurped by the brutal King Twala. Guided by a map created by a Portuguese trader who died in his quest for King Solomon's riches, the party eventually reaches its destination. After a fierce battle in which the Englishmen successfully join with Umbopa to capture his throne, they are guided to the mines by the wizened witch-hunter, Gagool, who traps them in a rock chamber from which they narrowly escape—but not before collecting sufficient diamonds to ensure their lifelong wealth. The Englishmen leave the grateful Umbopa, who nevertheless vows to ban future imperialists from his kingdom, and begin their journey home. In the novel's tidy closure, the Englishmen encounter Sir Henry's brother, and the party contentedly returns to England.

In *King Solomon's Wives*, penned by British barrister Sir Chartres Biron,[7] the three main characters—the Irish MP Ananias Quarterman, the aristocratic Sir Harry of Danish appearance, and the half-pay Captain Noegood of the Royal Horse Marines—retrace the steps of their Haggardian counterparts to Ipecacuanha Land, along with the displaced African royal, Umbugs. There they encounter the usurper Twosh, who is eventually deposed, and travel to the famous mines. Again they are trapped in a chamber and eventually freed. As in the original novel, they meet Sir Harry's brother on their return journey and book passage back to England, where Quarterman retires to write his story.

Particularly indicative of the difficulty in maintaining a neat dichotomy between African and European, demonstrated in both Haggard's text and the parody, is the complex linguistic interplay between the two cultures through which an ostensibly preeminent British facility with language is repeatedly destabilized. In *King Solomon's Mines*, a characteristic African primitivism is suggested in part through the simplistic speech of occasionally encountered tribesmen. A group of "wretched natives," for example, merely "jabbered" (71–72), and one "wild-bred" man communicates through a preverbal "guttural exclamation" (84). More significantly, the Kukuana culture is marked by its anachronistic speech, an "old-fashioned form of the Zulu tongue" that is as comparatively distant from the contemporary version as Chaucerian English is from its modern Victorian counterpart (112).

In contrast, Quatermain strives to demonstrate linguistic sophistication on multiple levels. Although he disparages his "blunt way of writing" in the novel's preface, Quatermain immediately positions himself as an adept writer in arguing that "I cannot help thinking that simple things are always the most impressive ... when they are written in plain language" (6). Familiar with African dialects, including Zulu, its antiquated Kukuana derivative, and the Dutch-influenced speech of other tribesmen, Quatermain converses deftly with the diverse individuals he encounters in his passage across the continent. Presumably he is even more skilled than native speakers since, at one point, he feels compelled to speak "very slow"— albeit ungrammatically in this description—so that one African "might understand me" (112). Smugly attesting to his linguistic acumen, Quatermain informs the Kukuanas that "I have prepared myself by learning your language," to which a chorus of "astonished aborigines" respectfully replies, "It is so, it is so" (114–15).

The imperialists' supposed verbal superiority is continually questioned in Haggard's text, however, either directly or implicitly. Though Quatermain asserts his mastery of the Kukuana tongue, one dissenter negates the aborigines' choric approval by replying that "thou hast learnt it very badly" (115). Suggestive of verbal dexterity, Quatermain serves as translator for his two companions, but this function ironically foregrounds the pair's own linguistic incompetence. Sir Henry never even attempts direct communication, while Captain Good's "foreign vocabulary" is so "extremely limited" that he brings Quatermain to meetings with his paramour Foulata "to interpret in case he could not make his meaning clear to her" (248). Belying the notion of British linguistic supremacy, Foulata understands the inarticulate Good "marvellously as a rule."

Moreover, Quatermain's ostensible competency with language comes under question with his self-admitted inadequacy in describing "the extraordinary grandeur and beauty" of a panoramic landscape (85). He laments, for instance, that "language seems to fail me" and indeed is "impotent even before its memory"—a curious equation of linguistic mastery and virility through which Quatermain's very masculinity is problematized. Conversely, one Kukuana adeptly narrates "in vigorous and graceful language," consistently displaying the enviable talents of his class of "born orator[s]" (190), which includes Umbopa among its ranks. Unlike the more diminutive and "impotent" Quatermain, Umbopa is characterized by his physical prowess and "powerful speech" (191); linguistic potency matches the appearance of this "magnificent-looking man ... [s]tanding about six foot three high ... broad in proportion and very shapely" (49).

The characterization of Umbopa's speech represents the novel's most compelling querying of British linguistic predominance. In an early encounter with Umbopa, Quatermain comments, for example, on "a certain assumption of dignity in the man's mode of speech" (47), and he later expounds on Umbopa's demonstration of "one of those strange bursts of rhetorical eloquence which Zulus sometimes indulge in" (67). Nevertheless, Quatermain persists in diminishing Umbopa's linguistic ability. The narrator notes the plethora of "vain repetitions" indicative of Zulu speech in general, remarks condescendingly that "the race is by no means devoid of poetic instinct and of intellectual power" (68), and opines that Zulus prefer "the language of hyperbole" (155).

The most significant vacillation between admiring and deprecating Umbopa's rhetorical skills appears when the Englishman describes the Kukuana's triumphant chant at the conclusion of the battle against Twala, "a paean of victory, so beautiful, and yet so utterly savage" (237). Intimating his own inability to capture an event in language, Quatermain admits his "despair of being able to give an adequate idea of it." Quatermain can describe the moment only by relying upon an analogy between Umbopa's language and that of one of Western civilization's most esteemed poets:

> I once heard a scholar with a fine voice read aloud from the Greek poet Homer, and I remember that the sound of the rolling lines seemed to make my blood stand still. Ignosi's [Umbopa's] chant, uttered as it was in a language as beautiful and sonorous as the old Greek, produced exactly the same effect on me. (237)

In striking contrast to the Africans' poetic language in this passage and throughout the text, the Englishmen's speech is punctuated by syntactic simplicity, grammatical improprieties, and idiomatic trivialities. Quatermain's narrative as a whole is presented in conversational English, nowhere evincing the "bursts of rhetorical eloquence" characteristic of Kukuana speech.

Umbopa's linguistic capacity not only undermines the comforting Western belief in its own comparatively advanced civilization; more threateningly, it suggests an underlying measure of subversion and power over the imperialist transgressors. In their first conversation, for example, Quatermain is "struck" by Umbopa's relentless questioning about the adventurers' plans, replying: "You forget yourself a little ... Your words come out unawares. That is not the way to speak" (47–48). Attempting to reassert authority, Quatermain advises Umbopa to reveal his name and village so "that we may know with whom we have to deal" (48). Although Umbopa complies, he counters Quatermain's attempt at control by concluding his response with an emphatic "I have spoken," thus ending the conversation on his own terms and causing Quatermain to disclose, "I was rather puzzled at this man and his way of speech" (48). As Quatermain ponders the troubling conversation, he translates it for his companions, eliciting a response in English from Sir Henry—one that Umbopa "evidently understood," as he places Englishman and African on an equal plane by responding, in Zulu, "[W]e are men, thou and I" (49).

Umbopa's comprehension of English is clear—but his reluctance to use it, hinted in this scene, is confirmed later by Quatermain in observing that Umbopa "understood English, though he rarely spoke it" (66). The text suggests an element of dominance by the African over his British translator. Quatermain's knowledge of the African language initially serves as a means of establishing power; thus, for instance, he can insert himself into the Other's discourse to convince reluctant Africans in their own familiar language to accompany the explorers on their dangerous mission to the mines. The control that Quatermain's linguistic knowledge confers, however, can also be turned back upon him, as evidenced by Umbopa's request that Quatermain translate his remarks to Sir Henry:

"Be my mouth, oh Macumazahn, and say my words to the

> Inkoos Incubu [Sir Henry], my master, for I would speak to him
> and to thee."
>   I was angry with the man, for I am not accustomed to be
> talked to in that way by Kafirs, but somehow he impressed me,
> and besides I was curious to know what he had to say, so I
> translated, expressing my opinion at the same time that he was
> an impudent fellow, and that his swagger was outrageous. (65)

In effect, Quatermain becomes a vessel, to be filled and to transmit Umbopa's words. Umbopa, then, has invaded Quatermain's discourse to achieve the same objective of control that the Englishman periodically seeks in entering African discourse. Although Umbopa presumably positions himself as a servant in referring to Sir Henry as his "master," the African instead has transformed Quatermain, in effect, into his own servant through the Englishman's acceptance of this mediating role. As the exchange between Umbopa and Sir Henry continues, Quatermain accentuates this subaltern function by punctuating the narrative with the revelatory admission, "I translated."[8]

The quoted passage reveals another reversal of linguistic predominance: the power over nomination. Naming functions as a form of control, converting a subject into an object through the imposition of an identity that originates outside of the discursive context of an individual's culture; that new identity derives from the authoritative figure who has imposed the name. The transformation from subject to object therefore becomes a transference of agency and a tool for domination in the imperialist armamentarium. African characters in the novel are occasionally given such monikers as "Jim" and "Tom," which relegate them to a subordinate position—indeed, they are servants—and implicitly deny the authority of the culture in which they were originally named.

The imperialist command of nomination is nonetheless contested in *King Solomon's Mines* via appropriation, principally by Umbopa. In the quoted passage, Umbopa addresses Quatermain and Sir Henry by their African names, a practice that the Kukuana adopts throughout the text and one that Quatermain deems unseemly, as indicated by his response to Umbopa's reference to the nobleman:

> I asked him sharply what he meant by addressing his master in
> that familiar way. It is very well for natives to have a name for
> one among themselves, but it is not decent that they should call
> one by their heathenish appellations to one's face. The man
> laughed a quiet little laugh which angered me. (65)

Interestingly, Quatermain has conceded that Africans will privately use their own names for the Englishmen. Though Quatermain immediately disputes their right to use these names in direct address to the explorers, he significantly proceeds to identify himself and his companions in such terms as "we three, Incubu the Elephant, Bougwan the clear-eyed, and Macumazahn, who watches in the night" (174). Following Umbopa's lead, all of the Kukuanas whom the Englishmen encounter use these names in hailing the adventurers. In contrast, though the imperialists frequently designate Africans by such pejorative terms as "beggars," "savages," and "Kafirs," they customarily address the Kukuanas by their Zulu designations, even switching respectfully to Umbopa's new appellation, "Ignosi," in recognition of his royal status.

II

King Solomon's Wives widens the numerous lacunae in Haggard's text that weaken imperialist attempts to establish authority through language. The parody establishes correspondences with the original text but then twists parallel references into absurd reconfigurations that nullify British pretensions to superiority. Although "Quarterman" patronizingly mentions the prelinguistic and simplistic expressions of "natives"—noting, for example, the "guttural sounds" of "six of the most intelligent" of one group (34–35) and the "uncouth tongue" of Africans as a whole (51)—Quarterman's language itself is the most primitive in the text, displayed in his conversational improprieties and his narrative style.

Throughout the parody, Quarterman lapses into atrocious slang expressions that suggest a linguistic indolence, relying on trite wording rather than imaginative phrasing. He asserts, for instance, that "[w]e will give them a wigging" (51), notes that the adventurers "rack[ed] our brains" (64), and characterizes a woman as a "petticoat" (61). In one signal exchange, Quarterman's linguistic failings are thrown into sharp relief against the far more inventive speech of one African, the son of the despotic Twosh, as they discuss the explorers' various attempts to impress the Ipecacuanhas through trickery:

> "Stay!" said Scraggi. "Have the pale faces—who come from over the sea" (as if we had never got over the crossing), "who roar out thunder and slay from afar—the death-dealing tubes with which the great medicine men spread their lightning and make their enemies as is a sieve?"
>
> This I could not stand.
>
> "Hang it all," I said. "You call our business with the wig and teeth old (I don't believe the leg has ever been done before), and want the old death-dealing tube swindle! Why, it's as old as Robinson Crusoe. No savage with a grain of self-respect could stand it any longer. I had not the face to try it on you; besides

which, Sir Harry, if he does look like a Dane, could not hit a
haystack sitting to save his life." (53)

The other British characters similarly indulge in slang. Noegood complains,
for example, that his dress clothes make him look "like a beastly waiter"
(64) and barks, "Hang it," at an interlocutor (60). Sir Harry, whose linguistic
insufficiencies are insinuated through his habit of "mutter[ing] in his
beard," brusquely comments, "Done with you," when Quarterman agrees to
accompany him to Africa (23).

As in *King Solomon's Mines*, the speech of the African characters—
particularly Umbugs—is more complex than that of the British. Like his
prototype Umbopa, Umbugs "drop[s] into metaphor, as is their [the
Africans'] tiresome custom on the least provocation" (115). Umbugs's
varied soliloquies, though parodying the ornate language that Haggard
attributed to the Kukuanas, are nevertheless replete with colorful phrases
and clever wordplay that the Britons' speech lacks. The linguistic contrast
between the two cultures is heightened as the seaman Noegood attempts,
with comedic results, to adopt the "language of hyperbole, in which all
these good people delight" (111). Refusing to marry his paramour, Noegood
grumbles, "The sun, that's me, cannot mate with the darkness" (111–12).
When Quarterman disagrees, Noegood mixes slang (misspelled by
Quarterman, underscoring Noegood's imprecise speech), execrable French,
clumsy syntax, and strained literary references in replying, "That's all
dooced fine, ... but this is not 'Locksley Hall,' this is 'Sixty Years After.'
Nous avong changee tout cela" (112). Emphasizing Noegood's questionable
language skills, Quarterman responds, "These sailors are such linguists."

King Solomon's Wives further destabilizes British linguistic superiority
through paradigmatic deviations in the speech patterns of the Africans; their
diction strays from the formal phraseology mimicking the Zulu translations
in Haggard's text to clipped British speech and idiomatic fluency. Although
African characters interject slang in much the same fashion as the British
explorers do, it is a repetition with a difference. Uttered by the supposedly
primitive Africans, the phrases mock rather than merely imitate the
Europeans, especially in light of Quarterman's condescending comments
about the "uncouth tongue" of the Africans. In effect, these linguistic forays
into English allow the invaded to become the invaders, again unsettling the
balance of power in the text and attesting to Roland Barthes's claim that
conventionally-read texts are "always haunted by the appropriation of
speech" (41). Moreover, these semantic incursions underscore the
similarities between the two cultures; speech acts of African and Briton
become interchangeable rather than distinctive.

Throughout the parody, African speech is laced with such quintessentially
British expressions as " 'pon my word," "lovely," "my boy," "gentlemen,"
"chap," and "three cheers." In one typical passage, a conversation between

the royal rivals progresses immediately from the archaic phraseology of indigenous speech to idiomatic English, identical in form to the exchanges between the imperialists:

> "Has thy servant leave to speak?"
> "By all means," said Umbugs, with affability.
> "Well, look here," continued Twosh, "as a savage king I can't
>   give the whole thing up without a fight."
> "No, no!" said Umbugs, "certainly not. Who will you take on?"
> "Jumbo [Sir Harry] for choice," said Twosh.
> "Capital," said Umbugs ... "I'll see fair play."
> ... "Queensberry rules?" said Umbugs.
> "Of course," said Twosh. (77–78)

As the passage suggests with such stuffy phrases as "certainly not," African speech in the parody habitually mimics the stilted syntax of middle- and upper-class Englishmen. Umbugs, for example, retorts when advised of a planned marriage, "This must be stopped at all hazards" (111). His uncle sniffs that "I did not think it worth an inquiry" when asked if he questioned whether the explorers were gods but implies that "perhaps as a matter of form" an investigation is necessary (59). Twosh invites the imperialists to an annual witch hunt with an air of ennui as he drones, "It is not bad fun sometimes" (61).

The linguistic binarism disintegrates further through the homonymic equivalence of English and seemingly peculiar African words. An African "drug of great potency," for instance, "only known in these distant regions," is termed "wiskaye" (22), and the travelers learn that certain inscriptions "were called 'Postâhs' in the native vernacular" (47). One "African" word is not only akin but identical to its English equivalent, a fact Quarterman fails to recognize in another subtle attenuation of British linguistic preeminence through the suggestion that he is unfamiliar with his own tongue. Quarterman remarks that the amorous Noegood "declares nothing will induce him to give up his 'tart,'" causing the narrator to muse: "What this means, I do not know. It is an Ipecacuanha expression, which Noegood has picked up. No one will tell me its meaning; they seem afraid to explain" (63–64).

Also helping to erase the linguistic dichotomy is the Africans' frequent punning—a signifier of sensitivity to the workings of language—which is made a habitual practice of Europeans in the parody's early chapters. Quarterman, for instance, recalls an Irish priest presenting him with a prosthetic leg to replace the one he unheroically lost "[d]uring a brief career as an Irish MP of Nationalist leanings" (14). Demonstrating "a humour racy of the soil," the priest intones, "Ye have stood for Cork for some time, me boy, now cork shall stand for you" (15). Later, the narrator counters Sir

Harry's gibe that he is "not half a man" with the "dignified reproof" that "Quarterman is my name" (23). After the Britons enter Ipecacuanha Land, however, the puns are wielded almost exclusively by Africans. Umbugs echoes Quarterman's pun on his own name in urging "[a] good fight, and no quarter man" as the party's motto (78). Twosh castigates a sneezing soldier for dishonoring him, crying, "I'll show you if I am to be sneezed at" (60). He follows that pun with a second as the apologetic soldier addresses him as "O son of cow," to which Twosh retorts, "Oh! I'm a son of cow now, am I? I'll heifer word with you" (60). The sole pun an imperialist makes in Ipecacuanha Land is immediately appropriated by Umbugs, who "would repeat it as his own" (116), effectually denying its originator, Quarterman, of authorship.

As in *King Solomon's Mines*, nomination plays an inconspicuous but vital role in asserting dominance through language. The Ipecacuanhas ignore the explorers' given names and confer their own versions—pejorative terms that underline the subversive effect that nomination carries in Haggard's text. Sir Harry is called "Incubus," a variation on Haggard's "Incubu," along with the insulting "Jumbo," "fat Jumbo," and "White Elephant"; Quarterman is "the bald fox"; and Noegood is "the dusty swallow with one tail" or simply "pale face," corresponding to his own derogatory name of "black dog" for Umbugs. The Africans' power over nomination is as unnerving to the explorers in the parody as in the original text, imparted through Sir Harry's "annoyed" reaction to his new names and Quarterman's disgruntled observation that "[t]his was carrying a joke too far" (32–33). Quarterman likewise protests his own sobriquet, querulously declaring, "[A] nice way to speak of me!" (54). Though the explorers periodically refer to Africans in general by demeaning terms, they tend to use indigenous names in direct address. Even Boss and Joss, two Ipecacuanhas whose rhyming appellations seem the work of condescending Europeans, like the "Jim" and "Tom" of Haggard's novel, apparently have legitimate names: "We called them Boss and Joss," Quarterman explains, "I do not know why, unless from the fact that these happened to be their names" (31). Furthermore, Noegood's abusive agnomens for Umbugs lose their stinging impact when they are read instead as critiques of the Englishman's linguistic acumen. "[T]hese sailors will use such language," Quarterman disgustedly comments (55).

The reference to "pale face" applied not only to Noegood but to all of the adventurers, also suggests a diminution of British supremacy. In Haggard's text, Umbopa disregards his early propensity for the term "inkoosi," or chiefs, with its connotation of a master–servant relationship, and adopts "white men," which equates difference with race rather than eminence. In the parody, the Ipecacuanhas avoid the respectful "chiefs." Indeed, the Britons' custom of referring to Africans as an indistinguishable mass of "natives" or "savages," which denies individuality in favor of an essentialized African identity—"a very familiar, widespread, and stable form of 'othering,'" as Mary Louise Pratt argues (139)[9]—is reversed as Umbugs's uncle, Fairdooes, introduces the British to himself and Twosh's son. "Pale faces, Scraggi," he says. "Scraggi, Pale faces ... I am Fairdooes" (55). Relegated to the position of an amorphous group of inferiors in this exchange, the imperialists merely "bowed our acknowledgments."

III

The shifting boundary between "civilized" and "savage" that the parody's many linguistic maneuvers have signaled also emerges on a behavioral level. As critical commentary has suggested, Haggard's Quatermain attempts to depict his companions—and, by extension, Westerners in their entirety—as the epitome of civilization. Sir Henry is not merely a wealthy and educated aristocrat trained in the classics but seemingly a representation of centuries of tradition, "somehow ... remind[ing] me of an ancient Dane" (11). Captain Good appears to be civilization personified, with his well-groomed appearance and the trappings of a progressive society. Early in the novel, Good looks "just as though he had come in from a comfortable day's shooting in a civilised country, absolutely clean, tidy, and well-dressed," expressing an unwavering determination to "look like a gentleman" (54).

Yet *King Solomon's Mines* also hints at Victorian misgivings about British superiority and at a fear of regression to the Africans' level, a widespread apprehension about "the ease with which civilization can revert to barbarism or savagery," as Brantlinger terms it in theorizing the "imperial Gothic" (229). Haggard's text conveys that anxiety through unsettling likenesses between European and African, both physically and behaviorally. The initial description of Sir Henry as an ancient Dane is quickly followed by a remark that undermines the distinction between Englishman and African, as Quatermain recalls "once seeing a picture of some of those gentry, who, I take it, were a kind of white Zulus" (11). The bifurcation is again complicated when the Englishman repeatedly traces physical correspondences between Sir Henry and Umbopa.[10] The peer "was one of the biggest-chested and longest-armed men I ever saw" (11), Quatermain explains, while Umbopa "was broad in proportion"; like the "fine-looking" Sir Henry (11), Umbopa has a "proud, handsome face" (49).

Cultural differences are further occluded in one of the novel's pivotal episodes: the Britons' participation in the Kukuana civil war.[11] The imperialists' conduct becomes increasingly inseparable from African "savagery" when the explorers act as an integral part of the forces preparing to transform Umbopa into Ignosi, the rightful leader of the Kukuanas. Sir Henry is the nexus of this confusion of identity, taking on the stereotypical traits of barbaric Africanism. At his request, for example, Sir Henry is furnished with a complete Kukuana war uniform, which "was, no doubt, a savage one"; nevertheless, Quatermain is "bound to say I never saw a finer sight" (200). Moreover, the Kukuana military bears unmistakable resemblances to a European army, which again obscures the difference between civilization and barbarism. A "crack corps" of warriors acts like a well-disciplined regiment, standing "like a collection of bronze statues" until given a signal at which "every spear was raised into the air, and from three hundred throats sprang forth" a royal salute (128). Every fit Kukuana is a soldier, "as among the Germans" (133).[12] Even the Kukuanas' uniforms suggest European military dress, for the warriors wear plumed headgear and belt-like circlets.

Once the battle erupts, the British and Africans become virtually conflated. Quatermain identifies Umbopa's forces as "our people" (206), and the Englishman is "brute enough to feel delighted" at killing an opponent (204). He recalls that "there came upon me a savage desire to kill and spare not" and makes the revealing comment that "somehow, all in an instant, [I] began to wonder if my face looked like theirs" (224). Sir Henry throws himself "into the hottest of the fray" (206), brandishing a bloody ax and periodically consulting with Umbopa and his lieutenants. The distinction between Briton and Kukuana becomes even murkier when Sir Henry enters into hand-to-hand combat with Twala. Invariably depicted as ruthless, Twala nonetheless forms "a well-matched pair" with Sir Henry (234). Also complicating the issue is Sir Henry's decapitation of Twala, an act as vicious as any the adventurers have witnessed in Kukuanaland. The two characters merge, in a sense, when "it was on Twala's own couch, and wrapped in Twala's own particular kaross [blanket], that Sir Henry, the man who had slain him, slept that night" (242).

The parody builds on the equivalencies between African and Englishman conveyed in this scene and others in *King Solomon's Mines*, mainly by presenting Ipecacuanha Land as a bizarre but recognizable simulacrum of British society. The battle between the Kukuana forces is replayed as a boxing match between Sir Harry and Twosh, more of a gaming opportunity than a struggle to the death. Indeed, the fight "excite[d] much interest in sporting circles" (80), and "stakes were deposited with the editor of the local sporting paper" (78). To prevent police intervention, the site "is fixed in the private park of a popular nobleman of sporting proclivities," and Scraggi misdirects the authorities by spreading a rumor "that a body of Socialists" planned to disrupt a church service (81–82). Scraggi serves as Twosh's second, Noegood as Sir Harry's, and Quarterman as timekeeper and referee. The prize fight itself begins in proper sporting fashion when the opponents move to the center and shake hands, but the match is quickly broken up by "the famous Blues," donned "in their striking uniform—in highlows and helmets, and white Berlin gloves, their buttons gleaming in the sun" (85). All participants in the illegal fight are fined "five shillings each, with the option of being skinned alive, and costs" (86).

Other seminal events in *King Solomon's Mines* are accorded analogous treatment to blend African and British culture. The brutal witch-hunt in Haggard's text, in which suspects are summarily murdered during a ritualistic ceremony, becomes in *King Solomon's Wives* a performance "[a]t the Hall of Varieties, one of the favourite places of amusement in the —" (61). The setting itself is an amusing variation on Victorian theater: Twosh and his minions "enter the royal box," and the entertainment opens with an "overture, composed of the popular airs of the day" (69). As the witch-hunter Gargle begins searching for victims, one "well-known bill discounter hid himself under his seat," while "Sir Harry could hardly keep his place, so anxious was he to go and see what time the carriages were ordered for" (70). Chaos ensues as "three money-lenders, the court tailor, and a sheriff's officer" are deposited in a cauldron, accompanied by vigorous applause (71).

In numerous other scenes, British and Ipecacuanha culture are likewise merged. As Quarterman and his party prepare to journey to the fabled mines, for example, "church-bells ring and the bands are playing," and "[p]reparations are being made for fireworks in the evening" (35). Noegood arrives at the meeting place in a hansom, and Sir Harry on a tricycle "chartered by the hour." Moreover, the Ipecacuanha landscape is depicted like an English one. When the travelers proceed to the mines, they encounter a signpost with the inscription, "To King Solomon's Road, 1 Mile. Nearest Route to the Treasures," complete with the common typographical figure of a lace-bedecked pointing hand (46). Like their Haggardian complements, the parody's adventurers are stunned by the engineering complexities of the great road, which has been tunneled through rock so expertly that it evokes "[t]he metropolitan subway at South Kensington" (47). Under "quaint designs" are "inscriptions in the native tongue," blazing in capital letters, italics, and emphatic underlinings the proclamations, "Great attraction! Special holiday programme! Bullock waggons run every half hour for the convenience of visitors from the suburbs."

Such descriptions hint that the two cultures are as alike as they are dissimilar. That mutable boundary becomes even more indeterminable through the parody's characterization of savagery as a kind of performance, particularly in the portrayal of Twosh. Multiple references suggest that Twosh is no more barbarous than the British visitors—in fact, Quarterman admits, he "comes out very well on acquaintance" (87). Even though Twosh "looked every inch ... a savage king," Quarterman reveals that he is "made up very carefully for the part" to present a "mask of savagery" (58). In one

indicative passage, Twosh confirms Quarterman's suspicions of the
questionable division between "savage" and "civilized" demeanor:

> "[T]he trouble and anxiety it gave me to keep up my
> character consistently as a savage potentate no one can ever
> fathom. Personally I would not hurt a fly ... It was my *rôle* to
> be bloodthirsty, and bloodthirsty I had to be. I had to go on
> committing atrocities, no one regretting them more than myself,
> as if I revelled in the acts ...
> "Ah!" he continued, "it's a thankless life is a savage king's,
> to say nothing of never being able to talk like a Christian, but
> having to twaddle on about pale faces and Great Spirits, besides
> having to live in a kraal, which is generally draughty and
> always uncomfortable." (88–89)

The barrier between the two cultures is problematized further through
persistent reminders of one Victorian anxiety over imperialism—that the
presumed superior knowledge of the British would be appropriated by
Africans and used against the transgressors. In *King Solomon's Mines* that
double-edged effect of epistemological supremacy emerges early in the
novel when Umbopa tells Quatermain that he "wanted to see the white
man's ways" (48) and learn from those "who are wise, who know the
secrets of the world" (68). Quatermain surmises, however, that the African's
acquisition of knowledge poses a threat, uncomfortably noting at one point
that "[t]he man knew too much" (69). In part, Umbopa's accumulation of
knowledge is perceived as disturbing because he refuses to share it, leaving
the Britons at the mercy of one whom they have inadvertently educated. "I
don't like his little ways," Sir Henry says of Umbopa as they journey
toward Kukuanaland. "He knows something, and won't speak out" (69).

The appropriation of knowledge is perhaps most unnervingly presented
in the characterization of the centuries-old Gagool, who functions as a link
between the current and the ancient imperial presences in Kukuanaland, as
Laura Chrisman argues. Gagool is the repository of imperial knowledge,
Chrisman observes, and consequently both vital and menacing to the
adventurers; because Gagool alone knows the imperialists' full history, only
she can help the explorers recuperate their past (53).[13] "I have seen the
white man, and know his desires," she says; "[y]e know not, but I know"
(Haggard, 148–49). Gagool's grotesque appearance, mirroring her sinister
behavior, provides a corporeal locus for imperialists' qualms that their
knowledge can be turned against them. Gagool, for instance, is the only
person who can gain entry to and negotiate the secret passages of the mines
built by the ancient imperialists, and as a result she can imprison their
Victorian descendants. Indeed, the novel obliquely suggests that the imperialists'
learning may be the source of their own destruction once it has been

disseminated to the Other; after all, the original imperialists did not survive but the Kukuanas did, taking over control of the road and mines imposed upon their land and maintaining the structures for their own purposes.

Veiled apprehensions about the transfer of knowledge underlying *King Solomon's Mines* are transformed into humorous but still threatening incidents in the parody. Sir Harry, for example, introduces Umbugs to a card game, winning their early matches with dubious skill, but Umbugs rapidly becomes "quite a proficient" who "wants to scalp his dummy for not seeing his call for trumps" (38–39). When the explorers nervously await the start of the witch hunt, Umbugs "keeps us posted in all the news, and seems to know his way about here wonderfully"; the implications of that knowledge, however, lead Quarterman to muse that "I fear we must get rid of him soon" (62), a concern he uneasily reiterates. Frequently demonstrating a penchant for magic acts to confound the Africans, Quarterman worries at one point that Twosh "is getting too sharp, and finds out all my tricks" (104), later fearing that "with us out of the way, he might start on his own account" (108). In the parody's final pages, Quarterman encounters Dr. Carlyon, a European acquaintance also exploring Ipecacuanha Land, who laments that "those savages know such a lot now-a-days," an "awful" result that "comes of educating the lower orders" (115).

It is in the parody's description of the visit to the mines, though, where the African appropriation of knowledge and of the resulting control over imperialist interlopers is most forcefully conveyed in incident after incident. When the adventurers arrive at the structure's door, for example, they must each pay to pass through a turnstile regulating access to the interior. When they subsequently approach one exhibit, Umbugs advises that entrance "will be six-pence extra including catalogue" (94). As the party confronts a mass of solid rock, Umbugs demands more money to lift the barrier. Led into a chamber from which Umbugs quietly escapes as a door descends and traps them, the Britons beg Umbugs for their release. As they consider prying open the door, the explorers are warned, "Any one seen tampering with the machinery is liable to a fine of £10 on conviction" (101). The British are spared only when they agree to Umbugs's demands, including the surrender of their watches, prime signifiers of civilizational advancement that will now be in African hands. Claiming that he now has "the talisman which opens the solid rock," Umbugs inserts a penny—"*our* penny," Quarterman snorts—and frees the men (103).

Part of the anxiety stemming from the Other's knowledge of Western ways can be attributed to a belief that Africans will cease being complicit in their own domination and reject dubious imperialist claims of superiority. The parody builds on this fear in its rewriting of a scene from *King Solomon's Mines* in which the explorers awe the Kukuanas by pretending they will cause the sky to darken, fully aware that an eclipse will occur, thereby allowing the

Englishmen to pose as invulnerable celestial gods.[14] In the parody, however, the maneuver is exposed as a tiresome ploy that produces boredom rather than respect. As Quarterman asserts that "we will put out the sun"—the Britons' "great *coup*" (73)—the reaction is far from the expected response:

> A groan arose from the onlookers. Twosh the king gave a wild yell of anguish and fell off his throne and lay moaning piteously in the dust.
> "Oh, spare me that! spare me that! be merciful! Anything—anything but that ancient fraud!" he just found strength to gasp.
> ... "Sooner, ay sooner than submit to another eclipse at the hands of the strangers who come from the stars, will I leave this throne ..." (73–75)

Though the explorers have apparently achieved their goal of defeating Twosh, since he has decided to abdicate, the outcome instead reflects another Victorian fear stemming from imperialist ventures: invasion by the Other. As Stephen D. Arata explains, such "reverse colonization" represents "a terrifying reversal" because "the colonizer finds himself in the position of the colonized, the exploiter becomes exploited, the victimizer victimized" (623). In the parody, that anxiety emerges when Twosh ominously announces his intention to "take a cheap ticket to England" (75). The incident presages Haggard's own revelation of this apprehension in his 1887 *She*, in which the eponymous character schemes to invade England and capture Victoria's throne.

Elsewhere, the parody hints that the imperialists, not the Africans, are successfully duped. When the Britons attend the witch-hunt performance, for example, Quarterman blithely observes that, despite a large crowd, "[c]uriously enough, in the front rows there seemed plenty of room" (68). Oblivious to the fact that the adventurers are being set up as easy victims, Quarterman naively surmises, "I suppose they do not wish to intrude on our privacy," for "[t]hose savages, simple children of the desert though they be, have sometimes wonderful tact." Displaying similar credulity, Quarterman assumes that the tarring and feathering he undergoes shortly before the explorers leave Ipecacuanha Land is a mark of honor, reporting that "[i]t is a ceremony of the country reserved exclusively for distinguished strangers on their departure" (123).

IV

The subtextual nervousness in *King Solomon's Mines* about the Eurocentric presumption of superiority is emphasized in the parody through its demystification of the literary genre that most aims to perpetuate that notion: the male quest romance. As Wendy R. Katz argues, this popular genre was particularly well-suited to ideological ends. The form, she notes, "can be controlled and manipulated so easily that it can be made to do the romancer's ideological bidding" (44). *King Solomon's Wives* is positioned as a typical exemplar of these romances, recognizable in part by their stereotypic characters and incidents. In the parody's closing chapters, Quarterman's friend Carlyon suddenly enters the narrative when his balloon descends into Ipecacuanha Land. "Hallo!" says Quarterman, "there's some mistake here ... You've gotten into the wrong book," to which Carlyon petulantly responds: "The covers"—like the narratives themselves—"are so alike" (113). Before emerging in Quarterman's story, Carlyon had enacted a typical generic scenario. "I've had great fun," he informs Quarterman, recalling in true imperialist fashion that he had "discovered a new city" in South America and inscribed his name "on all the principal monuments" (114).

Other conventions ally *King Solomon's Wives* with the romance genre. Mimicking Haggard's text, the parody includes the occasional footnote, which in *King Solomon's Mines* is inserted to convey a sense of authenticity. In the parody, however, often the footnotes are amusing interchanges between the narrator and the editor. "Is not this sentence rather ambiguous?" asks the editor at one point. "Not a bit," replies the narrator; it is "one of my pet passages" (14). Aside from mocking the authoritative pretensions of *King Solomon's Mines*, the parody's footnotes emphasize the separation between narrative construction and the "reality" it presumably represents. In addition, the parody features numerous illustrations, as found in the original Cassell edition of *King Solomon's Mines* and frequently in its generic cousins, but the parody alters the register from a serious to a humorous one, confusing the delineation between British and African culture in the process. A cartoon of the signpost to the mines, for instance, carries a notice that "bill stickers will be prosecuted if caught," and one African politely requests, "Get off my toe, please" (46). A depiction of an eclipse includes a telescope, an African shouting, "Walk up," and signs indicating "one penny per view" and "royalty [at] half price" (66). The fight scene between Twosh and Sir Harry is portrayed with the two men prostrate in the boxing ring, adorned with an advertisement urging spectators, "Try Twosh's Bitters. No Credit," while an official announces, "Time, Gentlemen!" (84).

The artificiality of the quest romance genre is conveyed more overtly in the parody's penultimate chapter. Quarterman complains to Sir Harry that the latter has inappropriately raised the issue of his lost brother, whom Quarterman "had forgotten all about" in narrating "the excitement of our adventures" (105).

> I was very annoyed, and did not conceal it.
> "Look here," I said, "this is too bad. Here have I got to my last chapter but one, and you suddenly spring your long-lost brother on me. He cannot be worked in now, I cannot spare the

space.

    ... "Hang it," I exclaimed, "do you expect me to write another volume to find your beastly brother? It is too much to expect; it is not reasonable."

    "You can do it shortly," said Sir Harry, in a conciliatory manner.... "[B]ut find him, there's a good chap, if it's only in a foot-note, it will make the thing so complete." (105–6)

Despite his misgivings, Quarterman proceeds to describe the party's encounter with Sir Harry's brother, "which shows how wonderfully things can be brought about by a writer of Romance who knows his work" (106).

Among those wonders, the parody suggests in its entirety, is the myopic ability of Victorian society to position itself as the world's most enlightened, advanced, and altruistic nation. As intimated in *King Solomon's Mines* but made blatantly manifest in *King Solomon's Wives*, the comforting belief in British supremacy is vulnerable to disconcerting evidence that the dividing line between civilization and primitivism is not only permeable but indiscernible. Through its hyperbolic interpretations of the linguistic, behavioral, and epistemological nuances of *King Solomon's Mines*, the parody transforms Haggard's uneasy hints into unmistakable barbs. The gaps in imperialist ideology, which become troubling but traversable interstices in *King Solomon's Mines*, instead become yawning fissures that cannot be sidestepped in the parodic *King*.

Notes

¹   I use the terms "British" and "Britons" broadly in this essay to encompass both the English and Irish (the parody's main character is an Irish MP) as a way of distinguishing between the imperialists and the Africans. The relationship between Ireland and England was, of course, a vexed one in the nineteenth century, even though the countries were unified. I also use the term "European" broadly to include the United Kingdom and distinguish between Westerners and Africans.

²   See Patrick Brantlinger's *Rule of Darkness* for a fascinating explanation of the factors shaping the Victorian perception of imperialism, particularly chapter 6.

³   Daniel Bivona makes an important point in noting the Victorian tendency of "the equation of the childlike and the primitive" (78). He adds, however, that Haggard's texts "go well beyond a simple-minded recapitulation of the Victorian cultural hierarchy of the civilized over the primitive." Brantlinger remarks that even though Haggard "contrasts primitive customs favorably with civilized ones," the novelist "nevertheless maintains a sharp division between civilized and savage" (192).

⁴   As Brantlinger points out, "Darwinism lent scientific status to the view that there were higher and lower races, progressive and nonprogressive ones" (187). Also see Alan Sandison (chapter 2) and Norman Etherington (107–10) for discussions of Haggard's responses to Darwinism and anthropological discourse.

⁵   Critical commentary also reflects Haggard's own ambivalent views of the imperialist mission and African "inferiority." Etherington notes, for instance, that "Haggard was no political maverick" but a reasonably typical specimen of the

Conservative "New Imperialist"; nevertheless, "a paradox arises" with his political pronouncements and novels (98). Wendy R. Katz claims that Haggard's texts mirror "the anxieties of the imperial age" and its "disordered psyche" (45). Sandison asserts that Haggard "repudiates without fuss the whole arrogant notion of the white man's burden" (31), while Brian V. Street comments that Haggard "believes firmly in ... the superiority of European and particularly English culture" (123). Jeff D. Bass argues that Haggard's novel "is a rhetorical attempt to purify an image of imperialism that many Britons found disturbing," and suggests that *King Solomon's Mines* "emphasize[s] the ability and duty of a superior culture to impose its beliefs, attitudes, and values upon less advanced cultures" (260). I take the position that *King Solomon's Mines* both endorses and questions the imperialist project. Like Laura Chrisman, I view Haggard as "an apologist of Empire" who "serves as an example of how imperialism even at its most basic is capable of constructing itself as a contradictory process, of commenting upon its own self-mythologising" (41).

⁶ *King Solomon's Mines* was one of the most popular novels of its time, with 31,000 sales in its first year of publication in England. The figure comes from Morton N. Cohen, who adds that thirteen American editions were published the same year (95). Although Victorian reviewers noted some flaws with *King Solomon's Mines,* they overwhelmingly gave it high marks. The *Spectator,* for instance, opined in November 1885 that "we were in the hands of a story-teller of no common powers" (1473), and in an earlier review commented that the novel was "one of the most exciting of its kind ever published in a modern language" (1365). The *Saturday Review* similarly applauded "the very remarkable and uncommon powers of invention and gift of 'vision' which Mr. Haggard displays" (485), while the *Athenaeum* described the novel as "one of the best books for boys— young and old—which we remember to have read" (568).

⁷ Authorship of the parody has been variously attributed to Andrew Lang and John De Morgan, as Lloyd Siemens reports (104). In Biron's 1936 autobiography, *Without Prejudice,* the barrister acknowledges his authorship and characterizes the parody as "my best success" as a writer (96). Unfortunately, Biron does not discuss his rationale for writing the parody, nor does he reveal his own views on imperialism in this text. The autobiography primarily recalls, as its subtitle portends, his "impressions of life and law" as a specialist in criminal trials.

⁸ This incident offers an interesting twist to Brantlinger's discussion of the "invasion of ... largely preliterate societies by men with industrialized communications" and the "deluge of ruling discourse on one side and, on the other, what appeared to be total acquiescence and silence" (198). He adds, "Victorian imperialism both created and was in part created by a growing monopoly on discourse," and Africans were either mimics or "stripped of articulation."

⁹ Katz likewise remarks, "Individual African lives are either dispensable or invisible," and she notes the "lack of individuality in the character of the African" (142).

¹⁰ Etherington reads the likenesses between Sir Henry and Umbopa as displaying "[t]wo hidden aspects of the self," commenting on "strong suggestions that the real aim of the search [for Sir Henry's brother] is to rediscover or uncover lost aspects of oneself" (43).

¹¹ See Etherington for a similar reading of the significance of English participation in the battle (42–43), which demonstrates "the savagery of the whites and the civilization of the blacks" (42).

¹² As Katz explains, African militarism "sparked Haggard's enthusiasm and admiration," and "he brings home the relevance of their militarism by introducing Germany into the African context" (45). Quatermain, she adds, "is clearly impressed by the effectiveness of the Kukuana army."

¹³ Chrisman expands on the point in observing, "Imperialism's mythical pretensions (primeval and absolute rightfulness of occupation of Africa) are belied by the very fact that it needs a Gagool to testify to, and bring into representation (and therefore into

question) its 'mythical' origin" (53). Indeed, "Gagool may ... be seen as a product of imperial discourse's own bad faith"—"its bad mirror, engendered by the conflicting desires, fears and self-knowledges that imperialism cannot acknowledge to itself."
[14] In commenting on this scene, Street observes that "[g]ullibility is a feature which enables British sovereignty to be maintained by the use of western knowledge and technology to frighten the simple native into submission" (61). Despite the incredulity of some Kukuanas, whose "scepticism is devalued by selfishness and ambition," Street argues that "the final impression is not of a considerable degree of scepticism among the natives but of their gullibility, superstition and stupidity" (61–62). In the parody, however, the skepticism is refigured from ineffective dissent to outright disbelief.

Works Cited

Arata, Stephen D. "The Occidental Tourist: *Dracula* and the Anxiety of Reverse Colonization." *Victorian Studies* 33 (1990): 621–45.

Barthes, Roland. *S/Z*. Trans. Richard Miller. New York: Hill & Wang, 1974.

Bass, Jeff D. "The Romance as Rhetorical Dissociation: The Purification of Imperialism in *King Solomon's Mines*." *Quarterly Journal of Speech* 67 (1981): 259–69.

Bivona, Daniel. *Desire and Contradiction: Imperial Visions and Domestic Debates in Victorian Literature*. Manchester: Manchester University Press, 1990.

Biron, Sir Chartres. *King Solomon's Wives; or, The Phantom Mines*. London: Vizetelly, 1887.

———. *Without Prejudice: Impressions of Life and Law*. London: Faber, 1936.

Brantlinger, Patrick. *Rule of Darkness: British Literature and Imperialism, 1830–1914*. Ithaca: Cornell University Press, 1988.

Chrisman, Laura. "The Imperial Unconscious? Representations of Imperial Discourse." *Critical Quarterly* 32.3 (1990): 38–58.

Cohen, Morton N. *Rider Haggard: His Life and Works*. New York: Walker, 1960.

Darwin, Charles. *The Descent of Man, and Selection in Relation to Sex*. New York: Hurst, n.d.

Etherington, Norman. *Rider Haggard*. Boston: Twayne, 1984.

Haggard, H. Rider. *King Solomon's Mines*. 1885. Oxford: Oxford University Press, 1989. Rev. of *King Solomon's Mines*.

———. *Athenaeum*. 31 October 1885: 568.

———. *Saturday Review*. 10 October 1885: 485–86.

———. *Spectator*. 17 October 1885: 1365.

———. *Spectator*. 7 November 1885: 1473.

Katz, Wendy R. *Rider Haggard and the Fiction of Empire: A Critical Study of British Imperial Fiction*. Cambridge: Cambridge University Press, 1987.

Livingstone, David. *Livingstone's Travels and Researches in South Africa*. Philadelphia: J. W. Bradley, 1859.

Pratt, Mary Louise. "Scratches on the Face of the Country; or, What Mr. Barrow Saw in the Land of the Bushmen." *"Race," Writing, and Difference*. Ed. Henry Louis Gates, Jr. Chicago: University of Chicago Press, 1985. 138–62.

Sandison, Alan. *The Wheel of Empire: A Study of the Imperial Idea in Some Late Nineteenth and Early Twentieth-Century Fiction*. London: Macmillan, 1967.

Siemens, Lloyd. "The Critical Reception of Sir Henry Rider Haggard: An Annotated Bibliography, 1881–1991." *ELT* (*English Literature in Transition, 1880–1920*) Special Series 5 (1991).

Street, Brian V. *The Savage in Literature: Representations of 'Primitive' Society in English Fiction 1857–1920*. London: Routledge & Kegan Paul, 1975.

3

Laughing at the Almighty: Freethinking Lampoon, Satire, and Parody in Victorian England

David Nash

The renowned historian of prerevolutionary France, Robert Darnton, once famously suggested that jokes and humor presented cultural historians simultaneously with their greatest opportunity and their greatest challenge. Humor, for Darnton, was a window onto mental worlds we had lost, and it could also illuminate the differences between historically remote societies with an engaging immediacy that other cultural contexts seemed to lack. Following the lead and inspiration of anthropologists, such as Clifford Geertz, Darnton's investigation of a historically remote society concentrated deliberately upon the "gap" of understanding between such societies and our own. As he put it, quite succinctly, it was the task of the cultural historian to enable his or her readership to "get" the joke of the Great Cat Massacre— essentially the hilarity which the eighteenth-century chronicler of this episode was able to derive from the ritual slaughter of his employer's cats. What makes this example of interest is the suggestion that such cruelty, conspicuously absent from contemporary life, has become in contemporary eyes a source of revulsion and not mirth. Thus it is Darnton's conclusion that the job of the cultural historian is to explain the gulf between the responses that are distanced by over two and a half centuries (11, 79–104).

In a sense the value and success of this episode in cultural history emphasizes the remote, the distant, and the curious, an element in the interpretation further fostered by the use of quasi-anthropological approaches. It should be remembered that there are numerous episodes in more recent cultural history where the "joke" is not so much not understood but that the full depth of its humor and the relevance of its attacks upon powerful institutions and individuals are lost upon a contemporary audience. Thus there are occasions where the cultural gulf is not nearly so great, enabling the joke to be "got," but its significance may be misunderstood or more often, and importantly, may be dismissed as juvenile or simply offensive. To follow Darnton's advice, in these many instances, it is the job of the cultural historian to peel away these layers of misunderstanding and anachronistic judgment. In doing so, the subjects and targets of the humor involved can frequently be appreciated and even take on a renewed significance.

Thus there is a legion of lesser studies to be done, where a glance at the slightly less odd and errant provides evidence of the precise level of seriousness a particular phenomenon excited in the past that, to an extent, can be unappreciated by the present. In other words, such studies are not engaged in the rescue work of recovering lost contexts, but rather in rejuvenating ones that have become a faint and dusty memory to contemporaries. Such a phenomenon worthy of study is the popular and official place of religious belief in nineteenth-century contexts. Whilst important work has been done on elements of folk custom and of popular quasi-religious belief which differed from that prescribed by established and dissenting religion, there are other areas of investigation that remain relatively unexplored (Smith *passim*). One of these is the panoply of world views of those who entertained antipathies of various kinds to the phenomenon of religious belief and practice. Whilst it may be possible to understand in part the considered rejection of religion that some studies have illuminated, a more popular antipathy is sometimes hard to illuminate (see Berman *passim*; Budd [1967] *passim*; Budd [1971] *passim*; Murphy; Neusch). A particular aspect of this is demonstrated by the problem that a contemporary historian has in convincing a modern audience (especially in Britain) that some of their Victorian ancestors not only found religion to be a pernicious evil but also found it, perhaps most historically remote from modern experience, a monolithic and all-pervasive influence on the culture of the society in which they lived.

The small but incredibly vocal and well-organized minority of secularists in Victorian England were throughout the early Victorian period denied a number of significant civil rights—a fact which was a keenly-felt grievance. As late as the late 1890s, secularists who tried to take a solemn affirmation in preference to a religious oath could still encounter animosity and prejudicial procedures used against them by an unsympathetic bench. Perhaps most keenly felt of all was the sheer pervasiveness of Christian culture which itself was constantly taking on new and apparently aggressive forms. The perceived intrusiveness of such a phenomenon is probably very difficult to grasp for those used to a modernized culture where popular forms have readily downgraded the importance of religion. Religion was, in a very real sense, everywhere in Victorian England, and it was confident enough to engage with society wholly on its own terms at least until the last years of the period. It dominated in education, was a dynamic force in the politics of the Victorian era, and still played a central role in cultural life. Perhaps only in the area of popular culture was religion's role genuinely under threat, and it was this opening that secularists were to exploit.

As the nineteenth century progressed, the popular appeal of homespun evangelism, as offered by Hannah More and her compatriots, had lost ground to the unnumbered publications offering a wide and ever expanding range of both benign and malignant secular alternatives. Although there was a substantial literature in existence that outlined the repugnance many secularists felt towards organized religion, there was also a significant tradition which considered that religion deserved a less exalted status as an object of ridicule. Ian McCalman has done much to illuminate the dark literary underground of post-Napoleonic London, and some of his figures traded in literature that was at least irreverent, and at its strongest reflective of more Continental forms of anticlericalism (McCalman [1984; 1987; 1993] *passim*). Evidence from the thought and writings of Thomas Paine recognized the inherent potential for ridicule that religion contained. Many of his monarchical and clerical targets were regularly made figures of fun and worse. His often-repeated axiom that lampoon and ridicule were the best weapons to be used against spurious forms of authority was a message that was taken graphically to heart by the infidel Richard Carlile and his shopmen. Paine had likened debunking the mystery surrounding the exalted nature of the monarchy to pulling aside a curtain in order to gaze upon a frail and ridiculous farce of an institution. As such, the shedding of light, the exposition to the public gaze, and the application of reason and discernment were crucial weapons with which to forge a better existence freed from such deceitful forms of authority. Whilst Paine himself was a deist, this ideological position was strengthened and informed by a strong antipathy towards forms of established religion which actively sought to wield both secular and spiritual authority. In essence, Paine's creation and propagation of the philosophical arguments surrounding the natural rights of the individual acted as a further supplement to his anticlericalism. This removed the justification for wielding authority in the secular sphere that religion claimed, yet it also went further, to make the lingering claims of that authority appear tyrannical.

What was also to become another important dimension to the atheist and secularist use of laughter was that individuals involved in this movement, ideology, and cultural outlook were most likely to want to frame their beliefs around forms of individualism. In doing so, other holistic and all-embracing systems needed to be discredited in the mind of the individual concerned. In other words, these were made to be unacceptable, even ridiculous, and a psychologically comfortable and successful way of achieving this was to make such systems the raw material of laughter and humor.[1] However it should also be remembered that humor carried a special devastating quality in the hands of critics of Christianity. Levity and the lampooning of sacred matters were of course considered serious offenses in English law; in effect, to draw comic inspiration from or to portray Christianity as in any way deserving of humorous depictions was considered to be blasphemy. Indeed, the law itself had a number of specific words to refer to this phenomenon. Phrases like "contumely," "contumelious," "scoffingly," and "injurious" regularly appeared in legal treatises, account of trials, Judge's summings-up, and newspaper reports during this period. Thus the expression of these opinions as humor had a genuinely subversive side that was actually punishable by imprisonment for blasphemy enshrined in English law—a constitution and society that some historians are increasingly persuading us to regard as the epitome of tolerance.[2]

There is also a clear gulf between two cultures evident in these clashes of expression—one at least outwardly Christian and linked to forms of secular governance and authority, and the other a culture of doubt, deism, and atheism which saw itself as the vanguard of modernity. A governmental concern to control and regulate opinions expressed about morality came increasingly to the fore as the nineteenth century dawned. Perhaps the most important example of all this was the work of Hannah More, who clearly did more than most to assist the government in its increasingly arduous task of policing public morals and popular culture. In particular, she indicted atheist and blasphemous works as depriving the poor of the hope of salvation. However, very frequently this cultural outlook was juxtaposed with a popular and accessible atheist culture in which humor and levity were constantly near the surface. Perhaps the best example of how this clash could work in practice is demonstrated by the incident that resulted in the imprisonment of George Jacob Holyoake for blasphemy. Holyoake had been lecturing in Cheltenham on the subject of Owenite land reform, when a local teetotal clergyman named Maitland questioned him from the floor about what he conceived mankind's duty to God to be. Holyoake reached instinctively for a humorous riposte. Drawing a disparaging comparison with army officers, he declared that he considered that God was discharging his responsibilities so ineptly that He should be placed on half pay for his incompetence. Holyoake was applauded by many present (Holyoake [1871] 14). The lecturer's sober denial of belief in God as well as his ability to humbug the question simultaneously uplifted the friends he had in the audience, and introduced a denigration of the Almighty.

The humor that found its way into the periodical and pamphlet literature of the early nineteenth century, as has been noted by McCalman, had its roots firmly in Regency cultural sensibilities. Its appearance in this literature was considerably more episodic, and generally was aimed at specific individuals or was a response to specific events. In some respects the Holyoake episode is a classic demonstration of how this sensibility lay close to the surface, only appearing occasionally and even then only in response to forms of provocation. What turned humor from an instinctive response to a concerted strategy was the advent of a new style of secularist publishing. Newspapers that spoke for and wrote for freethinkers up until the early 1880s, such as the *National Reformer*, the *Secular Review*, and the *Secular Chronicle*, were sober, bookish, and overtly serious. This stereotype was challenged by the arrival of the *Freethinker* in 1882. The paper, the brainchild of its editor George William Foote, adopted an approach and style that antedated the full-blown tabloid style of *Titbits* and W. T. Stead's *Pall Mall Gazette*.[3] From the first, the paper pulled no punches. It chose to largely leave behind the freethinking tradition of informed debate and erudite writing on practical, philosophical, and scientific issues. Instead, alongside articles which nonetheless catered for amateur scholars of these areas, there were parts of the paper which were intended to pour invective upon organized religion in all its forms. Three particular columns were important in furthering this strategy: the first of these was entitled "Acid Drops" and was closely followed by sections entitled "Rib Ticklers" and "Profane Jokes." Another significant part of the paper, the "To Correspondents" column, found an ingenious number of ways in which it could put down and remove the seriousness of critical and sometimes irate letters which it received from orthodox and dissenting Christians. Just as the three previously mentioned columns contain too much material to analyze systematically, the same is true of the "To Correspondents" column. However, any sample of the replies to these letters from one edition conveys the range of humorous techniques and voices at work in the paper's attempts to belittle Christianity. The summer number for 1884 serves well as a miscellany and distillation of the paper's style and content and is thus a particularly apposite example to use. As can be seen, the paper has a whole host of targets ranging from biblical characters to contemporary religious figures and phenomena:

> HOLY JOE—We prefer washing in cold water to the blood of the Lamb.
> PARCHED—It is very improbable that it will rain for forty days and forty nights next week.
> A. BELL—There are no Cook's excursions to the Garden of Eden. But you can go to the Dead Sea and look for Lot's wife.
> MATTHEW—Your verses are not up to the Mark. You want more practice—not at lying.
> SALVATION JENNY—Balaam did not ass-ass-innate his donkey; but he tried to.
> MERCIFUL FATHER—Glad to hear you only killed off a dozen human beings and a few hundred sheep with your lightning the other day. Is that the way you indulge in summer sports?
> LAZARUS—Have you taken out a license yet for that dog, you beggar?
> E. NOCK—Please drop us a postcard when you arrive at your destination.

> ONE OF THE WISE MEN—Have you found Jesus? By the
> way, are you the cardinal wise man?
> UN-SAVED—The *War Cry* is of ancient date. It was heard of
> when the walls of Jericho fell at the shout of the *Little
> Soldiers*—i.e. The Children of Israel.

Present in this list are many of the joke genres Foote used. The juxtaposition of the mundane and the sacred in the cold water/Lamb reference, the puns in the Matthew reference and the reinvocation of Balaam's ass (a perennial Freethought favorite) as well as the pun on Cardinal Wiseman were all intended to please somebody in the Freethought movement. The diversity of these jokes perhaps in this way mirrored the diversity of requests and statements that inundated the "To Correspondents" column, which themselves indicated the multifarious interests and obsessions of individuals in the movement. Much of the material which appeared in these columns was repeated and reworked many times— certainly far too often for the historian to trace and analyze. The columns maintained a presence in the paper until well into the twentieth century, and their remarkable consistency of tone suggests that examples can be chosen almost at random to demonstrate the range of cadences the humor conveyed. Joss Marsh has done much to demonstrate how this was a conscious attempt to desacrilize the text of the Bible and make it capable of carrying alternative readings. Similarly, through Bakhtin the cultural historians Stallybrass and White have emphasized that the use of puns can be a means of initiating counter meanings and thus destabilizing dominant cultures which might seem to have applicability in this case (Stallybrass and White, 10). However, we should nonetheless be wary of seeing this destabilizing and playfulness as a prototype for postmodern-style textual intervention. Whilst Foote, the *Freethinker*, and many secularists might appear to be engaged in the task of relativizing and de-authorizing the texts of a powerful meta-narrative, they nonetheless worked with a series of moral absolutes, and with convictions that the system they were undermining was flawed and iniquitous. This is demonstrated in part by observing that the essential themes on which the paper concentrated were also remarkably consistent.

The clergy were frequently attacked for their incompetence and in particular for the failures of tact and understanding which secularists saw in missionary work. A particularly poignant example of how the criticism of missionaries could contain hard-hitting and barbed humor is evident from the following example, which comes from the 2 April 1899 issue of the *Freethinker*:

> A West African, on a visit to England in connection with a
> missionary society, was shown a collection of photographs.
> "What is this?" he asked, gazing wonderingly at one of them.
> "That is a snapshot taken during a scrimmage at a Rugby

football game." "But has your Church no missionaries to send
among these people?" he demanded.

This joke, which at first sight relies upon the misunderstanding of an
innocent placed in a challenging cultural encounter, also contains many more
targets for its humor. On one level, the West African is making assumptions
about the culture he is viewing in exactly the same manner adopted by
Christian missionaries in Africa. The strange is misunderstood as the
barbaric, and the civilizing mission proceeds apace in the mind of the
individual encountering this scene, apparently content and satisfied that his
own culture is devoid of such barbaric tendencies. Yet again the direct
parallel with the alleged complacency of Christian missions to Africa is here
emphasized. There are also some apparent sources of amusement in the
indication that a rugby scrum could be mistaken for a religious rite. This
invites the mind to indulge in amateur forms of anthropological analysis of
contemporary Christian religious services and forms, with predictably
humorous results for the paper's readership. However, there is also clearly
humor involved in the context used to interest the West African in the
photograph since the involvement of the pious in such sporting activity
would be in some sense pleasing to the clergyman turning the pages.

The clear target here is muscular Christianity in its various forms, which
informed some evangelicals from the 1880s onwards, particularly those
interested in missionary work. The collision, in this context, between sport
and religion is made to be anthropologically humorous. In a sense this was,
like many other forms of secularist humor, the popular end, conveyed with
sharp immediacy, of deep and sustained moral and philosophical arguments
against trends within contemporary society, where religion's intrusion could
be demonstrated to be malevolent. In this case, the more sophisticated
critique of missionary work was employed by the radical journalist John
Robertson, who saw in it the benign end of an ultimately savage imperialism.
His contemporary reports on the Second Boer War, which emerged in the
Morning Leader newspaper, were some of the first to question the conduct of
the war and its aims.

While the *Freethinker* regularly contained lampoons, skits, and
satirizations of biblical and imaginary religious episodes, it was the cartoons,
which Foote inaugurated, which inspired the public's imagination and
indignation in equal measure. These cartoons were of varying artistic quality
and effectiveness, but they nonetheless were a consistent feature of the paper
until the turn of the nineteenth century and even beyond. It was these, far
more than any of the text-based stories and satirizations, that carried Foote's
message swiftly and penetratingly to all corners of Britain.[4] His targets were
numerous but remarkably consistent with older forms of critique. An earlier
staple of anticlericalism was the sustained attack upon the apparent gulf

between the Christian doctrine of charity and the failure to practice this doctrine. This was in response to Christian arguments that only Christianity stimulated the charitable impulse and that without it there would be no moral reason to care for the less fortunate. In the provinces, secular societies often held "hospital Sundays" or other charitable occasions to raise money for worthy causes. It is thus really no surprise to discover that the inconsistency and apparent hypocrisy of Christian charity in practice was a theme that ran

Figure 3.1: A MERRY CHRISTMAS: Inside and Outside

through the *Freethinker*. Likewise, the Christian clergy were frequently indicted for their failure to seek out and explain the underlying causes of poverty. The cartoon, "A Merry Christmas: Inside and Outside" (fig. 3.1), which appeared on the cover of the infamous Christmas number for 1882, uses irony to expose what it sees as the true message of Christian charity.

The diverse denominational make-up of Christianity and its supposed idiosyncrasies was itself a source of considerable humor which the *Freethinker* exploited mercilessly. Once again, the summer number for 1884 provides a particularly useful example of an attempt to invoke a series of well-established images of clergymen. The full-page collection of cartoons entitled "Clerical Types" (fig. 3.2) presents a physiognomy of clergymen which would have been partly familiar to the paper's readers from a range of traditional jokes and stereotypes which found their way into popular culture. However, this particular cartoon also includes a Salvation Army captain, the representative of a religious innovation less than ten years old. Throughout Foote's writings, the Salvation Army was an unceasing target for the *Freethinker*'s comments and wit. His argument was that its approach, style, and content were as potentially offensive and vulgar as his critics claimed his own was. In this, Foote was less interested in defending the bona fides of his publishing venture than in securing equal cultural treatment for what were, nonetheless, two very different religious responses. The single-minded vulgarity of the Salvation Army and its attempts to wrestle street-corner conversions from unwitting and unwilling passers-by is the main subject of perhaps the *Freethinker*'s best known depiction of them, "The Salvation Dodge" (fig. 3.3). Whilst there is undoubted humor in the bombastic seated figure of Booth elevated by a large pile of collecting boxes, and the overcrowded and cluttered surroundings filled with tambourines and copies of the *War Cry*, there is a serious side to this cartoon. The sternness of the two figures at the front of the cartoon plays upon rapidly established stereotypes of the Salvation Army, but also suggests that encountering an opportunity to see "King Jesus in Blood and Fire" on the street corner is obviously intolerable. This was one of many depictions in which the Salvation Army was the serious target of considerable scorn and repugnance. These were a part of a whole range of serious cartoons that Foote produced that ran alongside the more obviously comic ones. With legal, and often subsequent scholarly, focus upon the offensive and scoffing, it is easy to forget those with a more serious target. The cartoon "Going to Glory" (fig. 3.4) is a case in point, and shows secularist distaste for the logic of the doctrine of forgiveness. In this case a murderer is welcomed into heaven whilst his victim is consigned to the depths of hell. The only humorous touch in this particular cartoon is the depiction of angels wearing Salvation Army caps, which has a serious sting in the tale since they are shown welcoming the murderer into heaven.

1. The Tea-Meeting Curate.

2. The Calvinist.

3. Salvation Captain.

4. The Infallible One.

5. The Revivalist.

6. Broad Church.

7. Low church.

Figure 3.2: CLERICAL TYPES

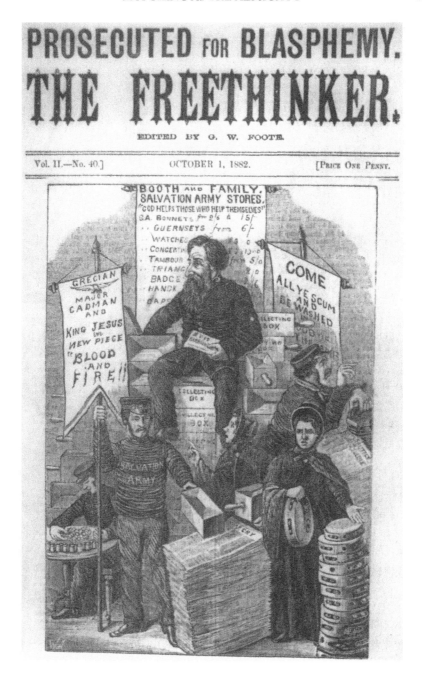

Figure 3.3: THE SALVATION DODGE

Figure 3.4: GOING TO GLORY

Whilst the shortcomings of all denominations were ruthlessly exposed by the *Freethinker*, Foote and most secularists aimed most of their attacks upon the Established Church. It was this which upheld a religious morality with the active support of the state in most areas of society. Anticlericalism had always been a component of atheistic and infidel humor and the tithe-hungry squarson had long been a figure of satirical attack and derision in equal measure (Evans *passim*). However, the *Freethinker* took the basic genre of anticlericalism into new dimensions of criticism and subtlety. One of Foote's favorite depictions of the clergy was to show them actively consuming and enjoying his own publications. This had an important purpose, which turned around Foote's attempts to make his material appear scurrilous and to court a prosecution of blasphemy. Most of the complaints about the *Freethinker* newspaper which found their way to the Home Office noted explicitly that the unsuspecting could encounter this material in the street when and where they least expected it. This "casual encounter," which resonated throughout the court cases and the briefing documents circulating around the Home Office, was ruthlessly reworked by Foote to show his own power both to shock and also to defuse the seriousness of the offense he was accused of. Foote's depiction of clergymen laughing at his literary products showed that the *Freethinker* was not afraid to put itself in the way of trouble, but also demonstrated that the paper and its opinions could crop up anywhere in contemporary Victorian Society. This was a cultural phenomenon over which Christianity and established religion had previously exercised a monopoly.

Thus the "casual encounter" was an encouraged literal collision between two cultures—one which the *Freethinker*, Foote, and his compatriots all hoped was a collision between old and new with, of course, the new triumphant. As a part of this clash, the *Freethinker* demonstrated that the older religious culture it sought to attack received what was effectively legal protection and special consideration from the state and government. What the paper frequently argued for was a free market in philosophical discussion—a market where truth would apparently succeed backed by the buying power of public opinion. The crucial role played by this last interest group is demonstrated by Foote's regular campaigns to show that the blasphemy laws were operated with considerable partisanship by local legal authorities and the central administration of the Home Office. This frequently-aired argument suggested that upper-class and academic doubt were permitted whilst lower-class profanity and blasphemy were the subject of police harassment, arrest, and ultimately prosecution. In this manner, so the argument went, critically aware and scientifically enlightening material was kept from the scrutiny of the public at large. This argument was particularly adept at demonstrating that the cultural attitudes that held sway in the minds of those who wrote letters of complaint to Sir William Harcourt (and arguably those of Harcourt himself) had scarcely changed since Hannah More and her times.

However, it is important that we should not forget the sheer comic appeal of secularist literature displaying itself and surprising clergy in unexpected circumstances, which must have pleased secularists forced into outward conformity or overwhelmed by the clerical presence in their society. The paper was similarly adept at stating the obvious; just as the purchase of copies of the paper to provide evidence for prosecution seemed to provide it with a readership to address in mockingly pompous tones, so the depiction of the clergy as avid readers served this similar purpose. The regular purchase and consumption of the *Freethinker* by members of the clergy in search of material to denounce was clearly an irony which Foote played upon. This could also be used to suggest that one of the greatest criticisms of the *Freethinker*, namely that it was capable of corrupting its readers, could simultaneously be shown to be exaggerated and flawed.

An example of this wider attack upon the clergy is provided by the cartoon "An Inquiring Bishop" (fig. 3.5). This depicts the Bishop of Manchester, an early violent critic of the *Freethinker*, attending his local newsagent in search of reading materials "suitable for a converted ballet girl." Immediately this takes us into the realm of traditional stock images of anticlericalism, and in particular the twin evils of licentiousness and abuse of power that was considered to be endemic within the clergy. The bishop is confronted by what the cartoon describes as a "smart shop girl" who proceeds to offer him a selection of the works sold from the newspaper's address. Whilst obvious humor is derived from the incongruity of the bishop buying these materials in person, there is also an appeal to a conception of morality in which the *Freethinker* and its publications were seen by its audience as genuinely instructive and morally uplifting. In other words, the irony is that such supposedly immoral material is, so the *Freethinker* suggests, actually quite suitable for the ballet girl.

However, the depiction of the casual encounter also had other important cultural resonances for Foote and his audiences. In some respects, it was a prepared defense against those who accused the *Freethinker*'s attacks upon literalism of constituting an anachronistic strategy. At times, the focus upon the absurdity, barbarism, or banality of certain biblical texts could seem to be attacking a religious straw man. Christianity, and forms of Anglicanism in particular, had been supervising a skilled and orderly retreat from biblical literalism. The depiction of the clergy consuming Foote's publications followed Christianity into its own territory with hope of an ideological rout. If a significant number of Christians no longer believed in the literal interpretation of the Bible, then there was clearly no reason why they should not laugh at biblical absurdities, as secularists were actively doing. The inherent suggestion was that no sane individual could continue to believe the truth of certain absurd episodes, nor actively condone certain barbaric acts portrayed in the Old Testament. Yet the rest of Foote's paper and indeed many of his anticlerical cartoons still maintained that certain other consistent beliefs, various practices, and forms of hypocrisy were still staples of Christian attitudes and behavior. Here Foote was proffering an underhanded compliment only to snatch it away in an instant.

Building upon this, a central part of the *Freethinker*'s appeal and its mission was to make the religiously revered look stupid by association. On

Figure 3.5: AN INQUIRING BISHOP: S[ce]ne—SHOP IN MANCHESTER. BISHOP F——R: I want something suitable for a converted ballet girl, something entertaining as well as instructive. SMART SHOPWOMAN: Here, Sir, is just the thing—Foote's "Bible Romances"; or perhaps you would prefer Ingersoll's "Mistakes of Moses." There's a great demand for both amongst the clergy just now. The Freethinker, Sir, you know already.

occasions this could pile target upon target, such as in the "Comic Bible" sketch XLI "The Original Salvation Army" (fig. 3.6). This took the use of comic physiognomy still further and depicted the twelve disciples with a variety of comic expressions which might have been drawn from any Salvation Army band. A more regular feature of the *Freethinker* was the comic depiction of incidents drawn from the Bible which illuminated the

Figure 3.6: "COMIC BIBLE" SKETCHES.—XLI: THE ORIGINAL SALVATION ARMY. These twelve Jesus sent forth, and commanded them, saying, Go not into the way of the Gentiles, and into any city of the Samaritans enter ye not.— Matthew x, 5.

bizarre and absurd from the scriptures. An example of how this worked in practice is provided by cartoon sketch VII entitled "Samson and the Foxes" (fig. 3.7). This was an illustration of the text from the Book of Judges (15: 4–5) in which Samson uses foxes to spread fire amongst the crops of the Philistines. The cartoon depicts Samson dipping a fox's tail in petrol before preparing it to be set alight and sent after two others who are about to disappear into the crops. Whilst this is clearly an obscure biblical text, elements of contemporary culture lend further humor to the scene. A bucket of petrol and a box of Bryant and May matches attempt to demonstrate how this feat might be achieved in contemporary Britain, and this theme is continued by the inclusion of a Home Counties cottage and a church steeple in the middle distance.[5]

Occasionally the uses of humor could sit uneasily close to the repugnance or even horror felt by some secularists towards Christian scripture. A "Comic

Figure 3.7: "COMIC BIBLE" SKETCHES.—VII. SAMSON AND THE FOXES. And Samson went and caught three hundred foxes, and took fire-brands, and turned tail to tail, and put a firebrand in the midst ... — Judges xv, 4–5.

Figure 3.8: "COMIC BIBLE" SKETCHES.—XXIV. THE FIRST RELIGIOUS MURDER. And the Lord said unto Cain, where is Abel thy brother? And he said, I know not: Am I my brother's keeper?—Genesis iv, 9.

Bible" sketch entitled "The First Religious Murder" (fig. 3.8) gives us a clear flavor of this. In portraying the story of Cain and Abel, the cartoon uses humor juxtaposed with horror as a device to highlight what was seen as the barbaric nature of the whole episode, and to illuminate some inconsistencies with the other sections of the Bible. The cartoon is pointedly called "The First Religious Murder"—a direct implication that numerous subsequent murders followed Cain and Abel's example. The illustration itself has Abel's feet protruding from a sea chest on which Cain (portrayed as a seafarer) sits smoking a pipe. That Cain is sitting on the chest which supposedly hides (or rather comically fails to hide) his brother, allows a direct joke to be made from the text underneath—"am I my brother's keeper?"—and to invest this vernacular phrase with resonant and not easily forgotten comic potential. Moreover, God as depicted in this cartoon fails to see Abel's feet, patently obvious to the reader, which further serves to question the Almighty's apparent claims of omnipotence.

The cartoons sometimes made a point of emphasizing that some Bible incidents actually need no satirization and could appear absurd on their own. An example is provided by probably the most notorious of Foote's "Comic Bible" sketches. Foote had noted the comic possibilities inherent in the text from Exodus (33: 23)[6] which effectively appeared to be the Almighty exposing his rear and genital area to a surprised and apparently shocked Moses (fig. 3.9). Foote had come across an illustration of this episode, which must have jumped out at him

Figure 3.9: MOSES GETTING A BACK VIEW. And it shall come to pass that I will put thee in a clift of the rock, and I shall take away my hand, and thou shalt see my back parts.—Exodus xxxiii, 23.

for its sheer incongruity, from a seventeenth-century Dutch Bible. It seemed absurd in its original context yet Foote decided to elevate this still further and produced his own version. This appeared in the Christmas number of the *Freethinker* for December 1882 and was greeted with scandalous amazement by the authorities. Whilst this whole issue of the paper was indicted for blasphemy (including a two-page cartoon comic history of Christ), the Moses cartoon was singled out specifically for mention in court (Nash [1995] 16).

The cartoon itself contains classic elements of carnivalesque inversion that Bakhtin would obviously recognize. The emphasis upon the rear of the Almighty is a clear subversion of the natural order as Christians perceived it to be. The cartoon gives us not the face and word of God but a representation of the Almighty's rear from which emanates what could either be a rogue shirt tail or, if the reader wished to see it as such, what appears to be flatulence. Whilst this representation was obviously itself calculated to offend, Foote was nonetheless drawing attention to the fact that a supposedly sacred divinely inspired text could produce such patently ridiculous illustrations—even from reverent believers. Foote made this revelation public by printing the seventeenth-century version in a subsequent edition of the *Freethinker*. Whilst obviously not ribald, this illustration served to perplex the orthodox public still further since the meaning of the text remained obscure with the loss of its textual context. In a sense, this highlighting of specific incidents and their removal from conventional discourses was a weapon which Foote used in a variety of ways (see Marsh [1991]).

Throughout the cartoons, depictions of biblical characters were invariably pejorative, and obviously Semitic racial characteristics were especially dwelt upon. Inevitably, we have to consider the precise nature of the anti-Semitism present in these depictions of the Jewish race and of individuals associated with the core of the Jewish religion. The danger of the cartoons being looked at beyond their historical context should persuade us into sounding important notes of caution. This is not to say that there was not a strong vein of anti-Semitism which could permeate secularism, as indeed it could many other forms of radicalism from Urquhartism in the 1850s through to pacifist and anticapitalist critiques of the Boer War. Nonetheless, there was some cause for Freethinkers to view Jews uncharitably if they wished to. Two of Bradlaugh's opponents in his quest to enter Parliament (Sir Henry Drummond Wolfe and Baron de Worms) were of Jewish origin, and the *National Reformer* commented specifically on this. However, Bradlaugh himself carefully separated religion from political action and pointed out that enough liberal Jews supported his push for wider religious toleration (Royle, 412).

But depictions of the Jewish race in cartoons and some secularist writings could be relentlessly unforgiving. Whilst Charles Southwell's conviction for blasphemy in 1841 for a publication which denounced the Bible as "The

Jew Book" could be attributed to a species of rage these were nonetheless
the sort of sentiments that survived long enough for Foote to reiterate. If
we, for example, consider the "Comic Bible" sketch "Jesus rescues Peter"
(fig. 3.10) there is quite obviously a specific joke being broadcast about
Jewish physiognomy—Christ plucks Peter from the waters literally by his
nose. In this context it should be remembered that Foote's Bible sketches

*Figure 3.10: "COMIC BIBLE" SKETCHES.—XXXIII. JESUS RESCUES PETER.
And ... Jesus went unto them walking on the sea ... And Peter walked on the
water to go to Jesus. But when he saw the wind boisterous, he was afraid; and
beginning to sink, he cried, saying, Lord, save me. And immediately Jesus
stretched forth his hand and caught him, and said unto him, O, thou of little faith,
wherefore didst thou doubt?—Matthew xiv, 25–31.*

were clearly doing the Jewish race no favors since they were finding their way into homes, taverns, and workshops just as the refugees from the Eastern European pogroms of the early 1880s were arriving in London. This could be construed as a cheap attempt to cash in upon a comic stereotype with popular and immediate resonance. However, Leonard Levy points out that the important distinction was between attitudes towards the Jewish race and its history, and attitudes towards individual Jews in everyday public and private life (449). In this way, it is also easy to mistake an attack upon a persecuted race for an attack upon their religion—or far more importantly, an attack upon a universally observed religious sensibility. In popular culture and understanding, orthodox Jews were considered to be the most outwardly pious and religious group in the community at large. If religion itself were seen purely as the enemy, then Jews came in for criticism for being the most religious, although even here some freethinking commentators such as Mazzini Wheeler noted that many Western Jews had virtually become secularized (Royle, 416). When secularists did convey blame upon the Jews in their writings, it was for a perhaps unexpected reason. In a characteristic inversion of the traditional guilt for the death of Christ which Christians blamed upon the Jews, secularists blamed them for being (whether wittingly or not) the originators of Western civilization's obsession with Christianity. Nevertheless, this criticism was aimed solely at the extreme religious sensibilities that orthodox Judaism represented. Moreover, this attack was genuinely even-handed. The secularist papers, and the *Freethinker* in particular, were ready and eager to attack the intolerant attitude of both individual Christians and Christian government in their attitude toward Jews in contemporary society.[7] Foote criticized the persecution meted out to the Jews of Eastern Europe and saw in it a further manifestation of the persecuting tendency that clung to Christianity, even in a supposedly modern world.

Whilst many examples could be chosen a particularly striking instance of this even-handedness is provided by the "Acid Drops" column in—once again—the summer number of 1884. One article notes that the traditional representation of the Deity in Jewish culture was tantamount to proof that the Jewish race had once been savages. Whilst on the surface this might appear to be a particularly shallow and ill-conceived piece of amateur anthropology, the fact remained that the findings of the new social science could easily be put to the construction of such aphorisms that invariably brought a smile to the face of many Freethinkers. But clearly in this instance the reader is invited to press home the attack upon the Christian religion that has been the consequence of Judaism. Less than two inches lower is an article applauding a letter in the *Jewish World* written by Oswald J. Simon. This attacks the Dean of Lichfield's attempt to solicit money intended for the conversion of the Jews. Simon suggests that such money would be far better spent in rescuing fallen Christian women or in converting Christian drunks to the ways of temperance. Just a little further below this second item is a favorable report of local Freethinkers protesting against the growth of an anti-Semitic movement in Antwerp. This group objected "to religious prejudice being displayed against any class or nation" (*Freethinker*, 16 January 1887).

The *Freethinker* represents the high-water mark of secularist humor, and its explosively successful formula was never to be surpassed. This was emphasized when one of Foote's fellow defendants in the *Freethinker* trial, William James Ramsay, launched a paper in 1895 entitled the *Jerusalem Star* devoted entirely to biblical spoofs. Each edition was dated BC and the legend under the title claimed to insure its readers against fire in this world and the next. All serious content was eschewed in favor of satires on biblical stories and reports of others as though they were contemporary events. Advertisements sought contractors for the Tower of Babel and speculated upon the unsanitary conditions that Noah and his family must have endured upon the Ark. The paper, however, was short-lived since it very quickly lost its novelty value and, unlike the *Freethinker*, ran out of entertaining copy long before recycling earlier material was a viable possibility.[8]

So what was the intention behind these attacks, and what was their wider cultural significance? Some species of postmodern theory in some senses stop short of analyzing the historical context of such phenomena. As such, blasphemy becomes an area where texts and their destabilization are the primary area of study, and transgression the ultimate end in view. The cultural analysis of forms of transgression offered by Stallybrass and White would appear at first sight to offer some useful tools of analysis. The jokes, satires, and cartoons of Freethinkers were at an obvious level transgressions, and Foote's cultural attacks upon another transgressing phenomenon, the Salvation Army, served to heap transgression upon transgression (Stallybrass and White *passim*; Walkowitz *passim*). However, there is a tendency in this to make blasphemy a tool and blueprint for investigation, rather than a subject in and of itself.[9] Thus, to see blasphemy and the humor associated with it as transgression can easily slide into accepting that all forms of transgression are themselves forms of blasphemy. This analysis is in danger of seeing carnivalesque inversion and transgression as almost an end in itself, and of portraying this as what transgressors in all chronological periods and contexts clearly have uppermost in their minds through the use of destabilization. This rather neglects the agendas of Freethinkers (and other groups in the Victorian period and beyond) who had their own stringent and absolute moral orders to defend. They were ultimately more interested in promoting these than in relativizing existing ones, since they were clearly unable to anticipate the confident tolerance that is supposedly a facet of postmodern culture. It is also perhaps difficult in this context to accept one of Stallybrass and White's most important suggestions about how cultural "others" are created. Foote was not solely demonized by a worried governing and moral order—he carefully and skillfully created himself and his paper with wider goals than mere transgression. Moreover, his approach could be seen as an attempt to reverse the Stallybrass and White dictum about the peripheral in reality being central. Foote and other Freethinkers wished to make peripheral that which persistently claimed symbolic and concrete centrality. What is particularly important is that in this instance secularists had possession of the process.

Ultimately it should also be remembered that these comic attacks were more than simply playful episodes, and that they did have an impact on how the law viewed meditated attack upon Christianity. Indeed, as a result of the Foote case, the Common Law of blasphemy was effectively liberalized for roughly a century. As such, these comic depictions of Christianity are a vital method of reclaiming the importance of non- and antireligious outlooks, and of actually grasping their depth, their conviction, and on occasions their sophistication. They deserve to have their context fully appreciated before they are too readily dismissed as juvenilia, or their content and idiom misappropriated for the toolbox of cultural studies. These were real sentiments with real effects, and those converted or inadvertently shocked by encountering them would never have viewed the Christian religion in quite the same way again.

Notes

[1]   Marsh suggests that the power of humor was that it made secularists part of a community of criticism. This "community" conception was by no means incompatible with such expressions of individualism (see *Word Crimes*).

[2]   The theme of tolerance allowing British society to become more cohesive and counter external threats as well as develop material prosperity is intrinsic in Linda Colley's *Britons: Forging the Nation*.

[3]   Marsh suggests that the early 1880s witnessed a systematic "dumbing down" of popular journalism which produced *Titbits* and, so she suggests, probably inspired the *Freethinker* (*Word Crimes*, 139).

[4]   See Marsh, 143.

[5]   Marsh describes this as a tendency to "incongruous modernization" which Foote inherited from Taxil, although Foote clearly anglicized and elaborated upon this (140).

[6]   The text is "And it shall come to pass, that I will put thee in a cleft of the rock, and I shall take away my hands, and thou shalt see my back parts."

[7]   Marsh has described this as a "functional" anti-Semitism, and the use of the clearly non-European stereotype as "an alienation tactic" which attempted to make Christianity appear foreign and dangerous. This view should be considered alongside the attacks that secularist writers made upon anti-Semitism in other contexts, including the Dreyfus affair (*Word Crimes*, 113).

[8]   See Nash, "'Unfettered investigation'—the Secularist Press and the Creation of Audience in Victorian England," 130. See also *Jerusalem Star* 1, June 1895 BC (*sic*).

⁹　The primary analysis of blasphemy in a postmodern vein is David Lawton's 1993 *Blasphemy*.

Works Cited

Berman, David. *A History of Atheism in Britain: From Hobbes to Russell*. New York: Croom Helm, 1988.

Budd, Susan. "The Loss of Faith in England, 1850–1950." *Past and Present* 36 (1967): 106–25.

———. *Varieties of Unbelief*. London: Heineman, 1971.

Calder-Marshall, Arthur. *Lewd, Blasphemous and Obscene*. London: Hutchinson, 1972.

Colley, Linda. *Britons: Forging the Nation, 1707–1837*. New Haven: Yale University Press, 1992.

Darnton, Robert. *The Great Cat Massacre and Other Episodes in French Cultural History*. London: Allen Lane, 1984.

Evans, E. J. "Some Reasons for the Growth of English Rural Anti-Clericalism c. 1750–1839." *Past and Present* 66 (1975): 84–109.

Holyoake, George Jacob. *The Last Trial for Alleged Atheism in England. A Fragment of an Autobiography*. London, 1871.

Lawton, David. *Blasphemy*. London: Harvester Wheatsheaf, 1993.

Levy, Leonard. *Blasphemy: Verbal Offense against the Sacred, from Moses to Salman Rushdie*. New York: Knopf, 1993.

Marsh, Joss Lutz. "'Bibliolatry' and 'Bible Smashing': G. W. Foote, George Meredith, and the Heretic Trope of the Book." *Victorian Studies* 34 (1991): 315–36.

———. *Word Crimes: Blasphemy, Culture and Literature in Nineteenth Century England*. Chicago: University of Chicago Press, 1998.

McCalman, I. D. *Radical Underworld: Prophets, Revolutionaries, and Pornographers in London, 1795–1840*. Cambridge: Cambridge University Press, 1993.

———. "Ultra-radicalism and Convivial Debating Clubs in London, 1795–1838." *English Historical Review* 102 (1987): 309–33.

———. "Unrespectable Radicalism: Infidels and Pornography in Early Nineteenth Century London Movement." *Past and Present* 104 (1984): 74–110.

Murphy, H. R. "The Ethical Revolt Against Christian Orthodoxy in Early Victorian England." *American Historical Review* 60 (1955): 800–17.

Nash, David S. "Blasphemy in Victorian Britain? Foote and the *Freethinker*." *History Today* 45 (1995): 13–19.

———. "'Unfettered Investigation'—the Secularist Press and the Creation of Audience in Victorian England." *Victorian Periodicals Review* 28 (1995): 123–35.

Neusch, Marcel. *The Sources of Modern Atheism: One Hundred Years of Debate over God*. Trans. Matthew J. O'Connell. New York: Paulist, 1982.

Royle, Edward. "The Faces of Janus: Free-thinkers, Jews, and Christianity in Nineteenth Century Britain." *Studies in Church History* 29 (1993): 409–18.

———. *Radicals, Secularists and Republicans: Popular Freethought in Britain, 1866–1915*. Manchester: Manchester University Press, 1980.

Smith, A. "Popular Religion." *Past and Present* 40 (1968): 181–86.

Stallybrass, Peter, and Allon White. *The Politics and Poetics of Transgression*. Ithaca and London: Cornell University Press, 1986.

Walkowitz, Judith. *City of Dreadful Delight: Narratives of Sexual Danger in Nineteenth Century London*. London: Virago, 1992.

4

Tipping Mr. Punch "the Haffable Wink": E. J. Milliken's Cockney Verse Letters

Patricia Marks

A rub of class on class, of Cockney impertinence upon upper-class reticence, is generated by the intrusion of 'Arry into the clubby world of nineteenth-century *Punch*. This Cockney figure, whose name became the epithet for low breeding and irrepressible vulgarity, was the creation of E. J. Milliken, who joined the magazine in 1877 under Tom Taylor's editorship. As Mr. Punch's *bête noire*, 'Arry commented on the events of the day in a series of comic dialect letters, the last of which appeared on 27 March 1897, almost five months before Milliken's death. Over the years of his life at *Punch*, 'Arry broadens his intellectual and aesthetic horizons, adopting establishment attitudes and expressing them with his own brand of brashness and self-seeking. With this shift, the function of Milliken's satire also shifts, now to include an indictment of the upper classes. In the end, the figure of 'Arry embodies a contradiction: that in their penchant for good food and drink, fashion, seasonal vacations, and the racecourse, and in their dislike of hard work, their snobbery, and their political conservatism, the Cad and the Toff[1] were almost identical. The contradiction reflects the ambivalent development of *Punch* itself, which struggled in the latter years of the century as its youthful radicalism mellowed into a comfortable Old Boyishness ill-suited to the changing social scene.

'Arry debuted on 29 August 1874[2] in a verse letter that gives little hint of his later verve and wit. As "a Cook's tourist about the Continong," 'Arry 'Higgins is an unsympathetic graffiti artist thoughtlessly destroying national monuments:

> On Ston'henge's rummy pillar you've but to cast a squint
> For to find my neat A-R-R-Y carved in conspicuous print.
> 'Arry's name will live for ever, 'Arry's mark by 'Arry's 'and
> Stands out on all the monuments of 'Arry's native land!

The rough meter is matched by an unattractive sketch of an auger metamorphosed into a face and of a blade mutilating a druidical pillar. When Milliken's "'Arry On His 'Oliday" appears three years later, however, the figure is younger and more cocky, and some of the long-term thematic emphases are established. On 13 October 1877, he is on a "golumshusly fine" seaside visit, enjoying "good grub and prime larks," a "tuppeny smoke" and bitter ale. A ladykiller, his "bags" are a "gridiron pattern in treacle and mustard," his "merstarsh" has started to grow, and he has his eye on a "tidy young parcel in pink." Like his 1874 predecessor, he chisels his name "on the cheek of a rummy stone Saint"; for the same caper ten years later, he is menaced by a ghostly druid at Stonehenge for defacing the monument (28 August 1886: 98; fig. 4.1). Aside from his diction and tastes, his activities differ little from those of a better class; in fact, he has "[b]een took for a Nob." As Milliken writes,

> ['Arry] is not a creature to be laughed at or with. My main purpose was satirical—an analysis of and an attack on the spirit of Caddishness, rampant in our days in many grades of life, coarse, corrupting, revolting in all.... So it was a compromise: not a consistent study of an individual Cad, but of the various aspects of Caddishness. (Qtd. in Spielmann, 380)

Milliken's persona has well-known literary and historical roots. Writers like Charles Kingsley and Charles Dickens, for instance, and illustrators like John Leech and Charles Keene, prodded private conscience and promoted public legislation in works about working-class neighborhoods and their inhabitants (Keating, 21–23). Spielmann, however, in his history of *Punch*, dismisses both Keene and F. Anstey, whose experiments in dialect verse and drama seem natural antecedents to 'Arry.[3] He argues that Milliken means "a great deal more. 'Arry with him is not so much a personage as a type— ... an impersonal symbol" that is "amusing ... his forms of speech, the quaint turns of his vulgar thought, being in themselves irresistibly laughable, their grossness merged in their genuine humour" (378–80). Similar contemporary assessments were important to a publication hypersensitive about its reputation as a family magazine; the review in the *Somerset County Gazette* remarks that *Punch* "is the first comic we ever saw which was not vulgar. It will provoke many a hearty laugh, but never call a blush to the most delicate cheek" (qtd. in Price, 30).

Milliken, well-suited to furthering that desired reputation, had written anonymously for a variety of publications, including Dickens's *All the Year Round* and *The Gentleman's Magazine*. His first published *Punch* contribution, "A Voice from Venus" (2 January 1875), is unexpectedly mannered, but he quickly became indispensable as a satirist, cutting his initials near the foot of the venerable *Punch* table, to the left of Phil May and across from George Du Maurier. Milliken, modest and well-respected, became "Suggestor-in-Chief" to Tom Taylor, a literary position akin to that of Chief Cartoonist (Spielmann, 377). According to Arthur á Beckett's chatty memoir, "When everybody was lazy, the custom was to fall back upon Milliken," who would read from his notebook during "a pause in the rather

Figure 4.1: 'ARRY AT STONEHENGE

frivolous conversation" (211). The *Times* obituary agrees: Milliken is "one of the first to be consulted on the subject of the weekly cartoon, his judgments being regarded by his colleagues on the staff with the highest respect" (1 September 1897: 4). Spielmann also credits him with writing the memorials for such important dignitaries as Disraeli, John Bright, and Tennyson (377).

Contextualized by the development of *Punch*, 'Arry holds an ambiguous position. In its more rambunctious youth, with a stable of inquisitive, energetic, and socially-conscious staff members like Henry Mayhew, the magazine wielded its editorial cudgels vigorously, publishing such works as Thomas Hood's "Song of the Shirt," a lament about the seamstress's plight. Yet Mr. Punch's stance on foreign despotism was conservative—Britannia's job was to rule the waves abroad and be suspicious of the German Prince Albert at home. In the mouth of 'Arry the Cad, however, these ideas become questionable. Like Mr. Punch, 'Arry preferred womanly women; and like members of Parliament, he enjoyed "bird season" and Ascot. Like them, too, he believed in moving in "correct" society, dressing in the height of fashion, and affirming pronounced, often conservative, political views. Carried to an extreme by 'Arry, however, these views and behavior become caddish: the women are "pooty parcels," the holidays are spent "chi-iking" and gulping shrimps and ale, his sartorial splendor is in poor taste, and his political stance entails rioting in the streets. Unlike Hood's seamstress, however, Milliken's Cockney creation rarely evokes sympathy, except in those late pieces like "'Arry at Harrowgate" or "'Arry on Diamond Jubilee Charity in General," when the narrative voice takes on a gentler tone, consistent with the actual state of Milliken's own declining health. Rather, the effect of Milliken's satire is to problematize the editorial stance of the magazine. While Milliken seems to be commenting on the social disabilities of the lower class, he is not calling for tolerance; instead, he is presenting a case against the "Toffs" themselves by reminding *Punch* editors and readers that a very thin line divides pride in British nationalism and culture from intolerant boorishness (fig. 4.2).

"We Don't Want to Fight, but by Jingo If We Do ...": 'Arry, Class and Politics

In 1878 *Punch* "respected" Gladstone and distrusted Disraeli, but became more cautious in its approach to contemporary problems as Tom Taylor solidified the periodical's intellectual reputation and furthered its dissemination (Price, 110–13). Leery of growing American power but intrigued by that new phenomenon, the American girl; uncomfortable with the idea of Irish independence but unhappy about Irish starvation; concerned about imperialism but fervent about nationalism: these views created a political polyphony reflected in the 'Arry poems.

Figure 4.2: EXTREMES MEET. ('ARRY AT THE FANCY FAIR.) Fashionable Beauties. "Pocket-Comb, sir! Only Half-a-Crown!"— "Box of Toothpicks, Half-a-Crown!"— "Flower for your Button-hole, Half-a-Crown!"— "My Carte de Visite, Half-a-Crown!"—"cigars a shilling-a-Piece. Half-a-Crown, if I bite off the end!" (In the 'ighth of his 'appiness, our 'Arry drops his 'Arf-Crowns as 'andsome as a bloomin' Lord.)

On 9 March 1878, 'Arry announced his support for Disraeli, who was "a drorin' the clarses together" by contending that the working class was naturally Conservative because of its pride in "a great country" and its belief that "the greatness and the empire of England are to be attributed to the ancient institutions of the land" (Morley, 523). "Old Beakey's a brick," ready to give a "larrup" to Russia, 'Arry says; but "... there's a Party, a nasty, mean, snivelling gang, / Led on by that gassy old GLADSTONE—a traitor they'll yet have to 'ang—." As the 1874–80 Conservative Prime Minister, Disraeli confronted Russia, the "Bear" that threatened to invade Turkey, but while offering Britain as a neutral mediator, he signed a secret pact to protect Constantinople (Blake, 629–49). On the other hand, when Gladstone, the leader of the Liberal Party, became Prime Minister again in 1880, he spoke against the threat of war and was called one of "Russia's principal agents" by the Duke of Sutherland (Blake, 607). 'Arry and his pals, who would agree with that assessment, engage in riotous "patriot capers," shouting "the Great BOUNCE'S row-de-row chants." It was G. H. Macdermott, the "Lion Comique," who gained lasting fame by singing "the famous music-hall song, and night after night the numbers swelled of those who did not want to fight, but by jingo if they did ..." (Blake, 637). The song, written by G. W. Hunt, had one memorable chorus:

> We don't want to fight, but by Jingo if we do,
> We've got the men, we've got the ships, we've got the money too;
> We've fought the Bear before, and while we're Britons true,
> The Russians shall not have Constantinople! (Bratton, 54)

As George Scotson-Clark comments at the turn of the century, "'Jingoism' once meant a nondesire to fight, coupled with a fitness ... to do so. 'Jingoism' now means war at any price ..." (15). The song, which was wildly popular, was rumored to have been financially backed by the Conservative Party (Pearsall, 48).

Along with singing, 'Arry throws bricks at Gladstone's supporters (one of the speakers—a "spouter"—has been hit in the mouth, or "tater-trap"). As Gladstone records the mob attack on his own house on 24 February:

> Between four and six, three parties of the populace arrived here, the first with cheers, the two others hostile. Windows were broken and much hooting. The last detachment was only kept away by mounted police in line across the street both ways. This is not very sabbatical. There is strange work behind the curtain, if one could only get at it. The instigators are those really guilty; no one can wonder at the tools. (Qtd. in Morley 2: 574)

'Arry feels justified, however; as a member of "the new *'Arry-stockracy*," he and the upper class have similar ideas: "A Toff *is* a man and a brother:

it's mainly a matter of dress; / Their rule's 'Number One and no Snivel'..."
(11 May 1878: 113). He invokes and misapplies the phrase "Am I not a
man and a brother" popularized by Josiah Wedgwood on a medallion used
by the Anti-Slavery Society of London. Here, 'Arry puts the toffs in the
position of the chained Negro on the medallion, and, connecting himself
with the upper classes, unwittingly calls himself a slave.

Since Milliken challenged political assumptions by means of satire, even
his title "'Arry on Niggers" (15 March 1879) is misleadingly racist;
although published before F. C. Burnand's editorship banned jokes against
minorities, the letter militates against bigotry by its overt insensitivity.
Milliken is writing upon the occasion when the "festive Zulu," an army
20,000 strong, had decimated Lord Chelmsford's forces. The sneak attack
was precipitated by an unauthorized ultimatum given to Chief Cetewayo by
Sir Bartle Frere, the Governor of the colony and the High Commissioner
for South Africa, who wanted to govern a federated South Africa. Cetewayo
was defeated on 4 July (Blake, 666–71). For 'Arry the Zulus are "Warmint—
that's putting it plain, and no kid; / And to talk of their rights and their
wrongs is all bosh;—let 'em do as they're bid"; his solution to any question
is "Wy smash 'em, like fun...." In her *Victorian Attitudes to Race*, Christine
Bolt gives a comprehensive summary of the intolerant attitudes that 'Arry
represents: even though "observers with some pretensions to knowledge
deplored the confusing of Arab, Moorish, Abyssinian, Egyptian, Nubian,
and Berber peoples," she writes, the influence of such disparate groups as
phrenologists and *Encyclopedia Britannica* writers fostered and validated a
pervasively racist attitude by putting the African on the lowest evolutionary
rung (121–38). Some influence was exercised by the Aborigines' Protection
Society, one of whose poems about the captured Zulu chief Cetewayo
revealed its schizophrenic position: "Savage, brutal, if you will; /He fought
for home, a hero still" (qtd. in Bolt, 145). In Milliken's 1879 poem, 'Arry's
comprehensive xenophobia and national chauvinism are answered by the
corrective voice of the "Methody," who appeals to civilized behavior and
Christian principles. The irony invoked by a rational, civilized speech
coming from the lips of an outsider to the established church suggests that
Milliken may be as disturbed by prejudice as his persona is attached to it.

Seventeen years later in "'Arry on African Affairs" (22 February 1896: 90,
93), Milliken has dropped invective altogether. 'Arry is a staunch patriot,
complaining about Kaiser Wilhelm: "It's clear 'e's no class, that young
Sossige, as ought to know better, yes, much, / Than to chip at 'is Good
Gracious Grandma, along of a hugly Old Dutch." He sees the Transvaal
situation "like good old times of 'eads up, and 'We don't want to fight.'" He
supports "Doctor Jim," the Administrator of Rhodesia and leader of a raid
into the Transvaal to foment an uprising against President Kruger's control
over rail and river transport and against his exacting of high freight

charges; Jameson's claim that Kruger had endangered English women and children in Johannesburg energized his forces, who surrounded and captured Krugersdorp on 4 January 1896. Although "Brummagem Joe"—Joseph Chamberlain, Secretary of State and Colonial Minister—denounced the raid and ordered Cecil Rhodes of the British South Africa Company to do the same, the government was implicated in the scheme, as the epithet "brummagem," meaning "false" or "showy," suggests. Liberals demanded an inquiry, and Rhodes resigned; after the trial, Jameson and others received fines and short sentences in England, while the Uitlanders, including Cecil Rhodes's brother, received two-year sentences in the Transvaal (Gretton, 384–91; Longford, 544–45).

In the 1880s, 'Arry still fancies himself a "Tory right down to [his] bluchers." His coupling of his political position with boots named after the Prussian Field-Marshall von Blucher and his own militancy pose an irony in light of *Punch*'s distrust of Germany:

> Sech larks, my dear CHARLIE, sech shindies, sech row-de-dow
> meetings all round!
> Sech turns at the chucker-out bizness, wich suits me right down to
> the ground!
> 'Most as funny as 'unting a Welsher. Chap 'isses, that puts up yer
> blood,
> So you go for him, six on yer, thump him, and leave him to cool in
> the mud. ("'Arry on the Elections," 12 December 1885: 270)

He joins the Primrose League, a Conservative organization fostered by a *Morning Post* editorial that had hailed the wearing of primroses on 19 April 1883 as "a perpetual reminder" of Disraeli, dead two years previously. Whether the primrose was really Disraeli's favorite flower (Longford, 437–38) or whether the inscription on the funeral wreath from Queen Victoria—"His favourite flower"—really referred to Prince Albert (Robb, 36–37, 42–43) is debatable. The league, promoting Disraeli's conviction in *Sybil* that the Two Nations should be unified, tried "to realize the 'true union of the classes' as a practical program" (Robb, 140). 'Arry, vociferously opposed to the "Rads," benefits from one of the avowed goals of the league—"To instruct working men and women how to answer the arguments of the Radicals and the Socialists and the Atheists ..." (qtd. in Robb, 49). 'Arry is therefore present at the riot that took place in Trafalgar Square on "Bloody Sunday," 14 November, one of the more serious occasioned by the unemployment situation. On 13 November, the Socialist Democratic Federation leaders and the unemployed tried to break through a police cordon, the most bitter fighting occurring on the Strand, where Foot Guards with bayonets and balls were stationed (Gretton, 221). 'Arry takes umbrage at being collared: "Wen that cop got his hand on my collar he ought to 'ave knowed like a shot, / By the Astrykan only, that I wasn't one o' the Socherlist lot."[4]

In the next decade *Punch* focused its attention on the Boer War, imperialism, and labor agitation; as Price says, *Punch*'s interests reflected right-wing liberalism, not radicalism bent on resolving social problems. In this milieu, 'Arry's forthright commentary becomes an internal voice operating at a number of levels. His brash, opinionated diatribes serve to articulate particular issues—Jameson's Raid, the disappearance of serious drama, the economic situation—but his lower-class diction and behavior make him into a satirical whip, provoking reactions against the causes he espouses. His insistence that he and the "Toffs" held similar ideas must have been discomfiting and unsettling. At the turn of the decade, in "'Arry on the Battle of Life" (21 September 1889), Milliken connects 'Arry's political stance and social pretensions with Darwinianism, in answer to a series of letters on "Are men really born free and equal?" that appeared in the *Daily Telegraph* in January and February 1890:

> Orful nice to see Science confirming wot *I* always held. Blow me
>   tight,
> If I don't rayther cotton to HUXLEY; he's racy, old pal, and he's
>   right.
> The skim-milk of life's for the many, the lardy few lap up the
>   cream,
> And all talk about trimming the balance is rubbish, a mere
>   ROOSO'S Dream.

In his letter, reprinted in *The Coming Terror*, Robert Buchanan discusses Rousseau's "sane and sublime" thesis about the equality of man and the artificiality of class distinctions, and quotes Huxley's defense of legal recourse to defend "might makes right": "Force, effectually and thoroughly used so as to render further opposition hopeless, establishes an ownership which should be recognised as soon as possible" (45–52). 'Arry misquotes Huxley to say that "*High priori* hideas about Justice ... is all rot": Huxley, who is arguing that experience, not theory, determines the "'necessary limitations' of freedom," concludes that neither "the celestial courts of Poesy nor ... the tribunals of speculative cloudland" are adequate to the question (qtd. in Buchanan, 72–73). For 'Arry, what "Science" confirms is that his egotism is natural and that cynicism gathers more money than sentiment:

> I'm a Darwinite all up to my back. If my hancestor perched on
>   a tree,
> He made shift to get top and nail nuts; the result, arter ages, is
>   Me! ...

> Sloppy sentiment mucks the best mill, and our spouters keep all
>   on the slop;
> From GLADSTONE to Cardinal MANNING, they snivel all
>   over the shop,
> About "own flesh and blood," and Wealth's duties, the
>   Sweaters, and Housing the Poor.
> Bah! The oof bird flies out o' the winder when sentiment dabs
>   at the door.

"A Reglar Philistian": 'Arry and the Arts

'Arry's predisposition for "lap[ping] up the cream" allies him with the Philistines, those for whom Matthew Arnold's call for culture, for "learning the best that has been thought and said," is absurd. In his 21 September 1878 letter, his insensitivity to "High" art is magnified in comparison to "Loo," a third cousin and foil to his artistic ignorance; yet *Punch*'s own cartoons of Maudle, the Oscar Wilde burlesque, and of languishing Pre-Raphaelite women indicate a tenderness for some of 'Arry's more "Philistian" opinions. On the whole, 'Arry prefers racy photographs to high art: "That gal in Turk togs[5] is a screamer. Wot eyes! and her figger!—well, there!" he says: "That's Art, my dear boy." 'Arry is enjoying a collection of inexpensive cartes-de-visite photographs, developed by Louis Dodero in 1851 and popularized by André Disdéri some years later. Like the music hall, these "photygraff fakements" of royalty, the middle class, and actresses in "*dishabille*" were a great leveler (Howarth-Loomes, 81–83). Photographs of the famous and the infamous, the fashionable and the flash (or, as 'Arry would have it, "the pink of the swell and the fast") appeared side by side:

> There's the QUEEN—*she* ain't much to be sure—and there's
>   BESSIE BOLAIR of the "Cri."
> By Jingo, 'er bust is a buster, and hasn't she jest got an eye? ...
>
> "Mixed pickles," my boy, and no kid. Oh, I've got a whole pile at
>   my den;
> They'd be flattered to hear the remarks when I'm trottin' 'em
>   hout to our men....

His other artistic enjoyment is visiting "Madame TWO-SWORDS" (1 February 1879: 42; fig. 4.3). Madame Tussaud's Waxworks, originally a traveling show with thirty-five wax figures, opened in 1835 in Baker Street; by the time Milliken mentions it, the exhibition had increased in size at least tenfold and included such special effects as moving figures and lifelike wax impressions, some taken from actual death masks; Napoleonic curios; and a curious and horrific display of effigies of executed criminals

Figure 4.3: HAPPY THOUGHT FOR MADAME TUSSAUD. A Chamber of Beauties! (The Scale, say 13 inches to the Foot.) 'ARRY. "Oh! S'y!! Nyam—Nyam!!! Just ain't she my form to a T, Bill! None o' yer bloomin' Photergraphs for me, *after* that!"

(Altick, 335–38). Popular figures in wax would have been more to 'Arry's liking than classical sculpture and Pre-Raphaelite paintings:

> I like limbs as *is* limbs, my dear CHARLIE, and faces as ain't got the chalks;
> A fig for your Classical attitoods, wobbles, and slommocking walks!
> Slantindicular saints on the goggle, and mooney young women in grey,
> With their muslins all twisted tight round 'em don't elevate *me*, I must say.

Rather, he would take "them old fogies in marble" and "paint 'em sky-blue, or dab on a moustarch, on the strictest Q. T." 'Arry's cousin, Loo, who has read her Matthew Arnold, calls him a "Philistian."

Six years later, 'Arry has learned more about art. He has witnessed Ruskin's mental deterioration and is aware of the aging critic's glorification of Nature—"It's Town makes a man of one, CHARLIE, as me and the Nobs 'as found out, ... / Old RUSKIN, I know, sez quite t'other, but then *he* is clean off his chump" (16 May 1885: 229). Ruskin indeed had a breakdown after Rose LaTouche's death and resigned the Slade Professorship in 1879 (and again in 1885), in the meantime publishing *The Storm Cloud of the Nineteenth Century*. His detailed and painterly description of clouds, rain, and sunlight, the verbal equivalent of Turner's luminescent landscapes, carried a somber social and religious message, one that 'Arry would be quick to reject: that because of a combination of wars, moral backsliding, and industrial pollution, "the empire of England, on which formerly the sun never set, has become one on which he never rises" (Ruskin, 13). 'Arry, part of the problem Ruskin cites, is an urban character; "Where's the *Life* in long lanes with no gas-lamps?" he asks. For him, the good life is beer, "good goods in pink musling," and song:

> *I*'d make Mister RUSKIN sit up, and the rest of the 'owlers see snakes,
> With their rot about old Mother Nature, as *never* don't make no mistakes …
>
> Lor bless yer, dear boy, Picter Galleries, Balls, Sandwich Sworries and all;—
> It's fun and the fizz makes 'em go, not the picter, the speech, or the squall.

While the objection to Ruskin seems tongue-in-cheek, 'Arry recognizes in James Abbott MacNeill Whistler and in Wilde his own consummate showmanship. As he comments, "I've seen HOSCAR WILDE, yus, and WISTLER, and tipped 'em the haffable wink"—"we snide 'uns are birds of a feather," he maintains. As a reviewer, 'Arry ignores their paintings, concentrating, perhaps like Milliken and Anstey before him, on the crowd as spectacle:

> As to WISTLER, I went to his Show. Sech a spree!
> Not the Picters—they didn't count much, but the pick o' the fun was to see
> The Swells gawping round at his scratches, like lunatics puzzled and flustered,
> In a room like a big padded cell as they'd used for the stowage of mustard.
>
> I carn't say I like HOSCAR'S hair, and a kink in the waist ain't my style,
> I'm more *ah lar militare*, CHARLIE, close cropping and plenty of ile;
> But if fluffing and flopping was fetching in suckles in which I might spin,
> Wy I'd flop with the best of 'em, CHARLIE, so long as it pulled in the tin. (14 April 1883: 180)

Much later, in the Christmas number for 1890, 'Arry dreams that he plays "Enjimmyun" to the goddess "Dianner." Among the inhabitants of "lunar Limbo" he sees two familiar faces: Whistler, who was awarded a farthing in damages in his lawsuit against Ruskin, whom he charged with libel for saying that his *Nocturne in Black and Gold* was like "flinging a pot of paint in the public's face"; and the writer, wit, and aesthete Oscar Wilde, who in the spring had published *Dorian Gray* in *Lippincott's* (Ellmann, 305–14). 'Arry's observations take on a more somber tone, reflecting the public opinion that led to Wilde's 1895 trial:

> Then I twigged Penny WHISTLER'S white plume, and the
>   haddypose HOSCAR upreared,
> His big hairy horryflame, CHARLIE, whilst Phillistines looked on
>   and jeered.
> I see Nature, as Narstiness, ramping at wot Nambypamby dubbed
>   Nice,
> And Twoddle parading as Virtue, and Silliness playing at Vice.

While 'Arry has little use for the aesthetes, he reacts very differently to the January 1885 exhibition at Sir Coutts Lindsay's Grosvenor Gallery. Intended, in part, to provide a venue for Pre-Raphaelites like Burne-Jones and others largely excluded from the Royal Academy, the Grosvenor, which featured a West Gallery frieze designed by Whistler, had opened with a private showing on 30 April 1877 for selected guests like Wilde (Ellmann, 78). The 1885 exhibit comprised works by Thomas Gainsborough and *Punch*'s own Richard Doyle, who at seventeen drew his first border for the 1843 *Almanac* and who began his popular series *Manners and Customs of Ye Englyshe* six years later. Responsible for designing the covers, he left *Punch* in 1850 over its antipapist stance (Prager, 110; Price, 66) and went on to a long, varied career until his death in 1883—creating a wealth of fairyland drawings, illustrating Thackeray's *Newcomes*, and exhibiting landscapes at the Royal Academy and Grosvenor (Hambourg, 10–29). 'Arry's review (10 January 1885: 24) is uncharacteristically gentle, his comments naïve, rather than sharp, the difference in tone suggesting a closeness between author and persona, and loyalty to the old *Punch* gang.

Less the cad than the innocent, 'Arry sees Gainsborough as a "a top-sawyer at painting the toffs of his time"; he likes the "sweet things in tailoring," like the "pink breeches and plum-colored coats," but thinks the landscapes somewhat shadowy: "they must 'ave 'ad jolly rum hoptics, they seemed to see everythink brown." It is Dicky Doyle, however, who draws the most praise: "Don't know as I'm filberts on fairies, and dragons, and toadstools and things, / But you find yourself looking at *his* till you wish you wos small and 'ad wings," says 'Arry: "But his dwarfs and his goblins and sech are the rummest most rollicking chaps; ... / Seems to paint 'em with moonshine and jewel dust, dashed if he don't, my dear boy." 'Arry's aesthetic voice has changed as he moves from being a "Philistian" to an art "crickit" who rejects art as spectacle (a "snide" cad can recognize others like himself) and praises both an old master like Gainsborough and a *Punch* legend like Doyle.

As art and drama critic, 'Arry points up inconsistencies between theory and practice. Theatrical fare, for instance, allows for music and "spice"—"Sly sarce, don't yer know, 'ot and sweet, with a dash of the blue, but mixed weak" (2 November 1878)—to the dismay of the "*soap-board crawlers*," who are more interested in decorum than in entertainment. In 1878, despite "my Lord Chamberling" E. F. Pigott, imported French comedies were plentiful. To 'Arry's delight, music-hall morality has affected the legitimate stage, driving out plays about "Connoobial yum-yum"; for that kind of tame offering, audiences needed to go to the New Victoria Theatre, which, opening in 1816–18 as the Royal Coburg Theatre, had become a temperance music hall for the working class managed by Emma Cons. 'Arry, like the "Swells," avoids seeing "Virtue wop Vice at the Vic"; as he boasts, "... our taste and theirs in sech things is as like as two peas,—no mistake!"

> We men o' the world, mate, knows better. *Pink Dominos*, hay?—
>   that's yer style.
> Lor', 'ow I did larf! and P[olly]. J[ane]. had a struggle to smooth
>   out a smile.
> Then *The Idol* that widder's warm-waterworks—quickly turned
>   off at the main—
> And the no-never-mention-'em larks as they play in that sweet
>   *Marjerlaine!*[6]

Milliken addresses the public argument over theatrical morality in several ways. As a connoisseur of continental drama, 'Arry goes to see Sarah Bernhardt at the Gaiety, where the Comedie Française opened on 4 June 1879 in Racine's *Phaedre* (Skinner, 36). While for 'Arry being seen at the "Comerdee Frongsay" is quite "le fromage" (quite "the cheese" or "correct thing"), he nonetheless prefers the melodramatic *Pink Dominoes* to French understatement; he complains that he cannot quite understand the "naughty-nice business" and would much rather have strong-flavored speech than French "sooflays" or "fine ess" (2 November 1878; 5 July 1879). By 31 January 1885, 'Arry is more outspoken on "'Onesty." He espouses "Free Trade—In Beauty," a version of *laissez-faire* in which the consumer wants his "tin's" worth, while the showgirl (who is scornful of preachy "tracts") and her showman earn whatever her beauty can fetch. "Beauty must prance it for pelf," he says; "And as to the *risk*, that's 'er bizness—she's got to look out for 'erself." He opts for plain speaking, for "plain fack without painting or pad," since the principle of theatrical Free Trade is very much like the interaction of prostitutes and pimps, and complains that he has been called a "hapostle of snideness" for his honesty, a possible reference to Matthew Arnold, who called Macaulay "the great apostle of the Philistines" (3: 210). In extending political theory to the theater, 'Arry is consistent in his Conservative ideology, while Milliken is, through irony, criticizing a system that markets beauty for money.

Away from the dramatic scene, 'Arry remains true to his class by frequenting "smoking-concerts"; other venues like Monday Pops and Ballad Concerts are "rare tommy-rot to a man / Who cannot be 'appy ten minutes aways from his pipe and his can" (13 November 1886: 229). He joins the "Old Peckham Puffers," who dislike Gladstone, support Churchill, and take full advantage of the Lord Chamberlain's lax censorship on music-hall songs to gather for a "bellows and blow." The audience participates so vociferously that, in some songs, the chorus completely replaces the narrative (Bratton, 201):

> Rap! rap! Tingle-ting! "Gents, pray silence for Mr. BOKANKY'S
>   new song.
> No ladies are here, so he'll tip us '*I Mustn't Sing Anything
>   Wrong.*'"
>
> *Larf*, CHARLIE? I jolly nigh busted. BOKANKY'S own version
>   it wos,
> But for touch-and-go slyness and winking, he beats ARTHUR
>   ROBERTS,[7] that's poz.
> Anyone looking on might have fancied the roomfull of pals was a
>   lot
> Of purple-faced 'ogs in convulsions, he *was* that cerulean and 'ot!

Like his real-life cohorts, 'Arry likes "spice," the pervasive sexual innuendoes that characterize music-hall songs (Bratton, 155–202). "These 'ere Nineties," then, with their problem plays, present a realignment of human relationships difficult to incorporate into 'Arry's perspective.

"Probblems in Petticoats": 'Arry and the New Woman

'Arry's brashness is an expression of his sexual prowess, while his distaste for the problem or New Woman play is part of the conservative spectrum. In 1895 he grumbles about New Women and *fin de siècle* changes, his arguments typically dismissive of those variously called the "screaming sisterhood," "redundant women," or "varmity women."[8] The "Problem play" he takes his girlfriend Lil to see is "dashed rot [which] gave poor LIL 'ARRIS the 'orrors"; as she complains, "I feel just as creepy and 'oller, along o' these 'ere warmed-up ghosts, / As if I'd bin dining on spiders" (18 May 1895: 230). Lil's mother is considerably more direct:

> "There ain't nothink new in *their* Newness; it's only old garbige
>   warmed up.
> Mere bubble-and-squeak. The stale taters and greens on which
>   poor people sup

> Is 'olesome compared with sich offal. Yah! Weddings'll outlast
>   *that* lot;
> And while gals is gals the old Eve'll jest make the new evil seem
>   rot."

The very coarseness of the speech clarifies the choice: to reject the New Woman is to become allied with Old Dutch, whose sentiments, class, and behavior offer little. The same effect is achieved by 'Arry's analysis:

> All splutter-sludge, CHARLIE! On styge or on cinder-path,
>   sillypop things
> As want to play Man and *be* Woman are trying to fly without
>   wings,
> Or fight without fistes. Are Men, the world's masters—like you,
>   mate, and Me—
> To be knocked out by probblems in petticoats? Wot bloomin'
>   fiddle-de-dee!

On the whole, *Punch* was less misogynistic than some of its contemporaries, but its perspective was that of the "bachelor clubman"—"The dear creatures must be fled when nagging and petted when feather-headed" (Price, 109). Milliken's sly suggestion that Charlie and 'Arry consider themselves the "world's masters" is subtly critical of the *Punch* stance, since it allies 'Arryism with Old Boyishness.

In 1888 a number of periodicals ran readers' polls that asked "Is Marriage a Failure?", a discussion impelled by the legal activity that followed the 1883 Married Woman's Property Act. As a declared man-about-town, 'Arry identifies himself with the toffs:[9]

> "Is Marriage a failure?" old mivvies are asking. Of course that
>   depends;
> But a dashing young feller like me, with good looks, and good
>   'ealth, and good friends,
> Knows a trick that's worth two on it, CHARLIE. While life goes
>   on nutty and nice,
> And the ochre slings in pooty slick, it is blooming bad bizness to
>   splice....
>
> When [the "swells"] do get stone-broke prematoor like, as 'appen
>   it may to the best,
> Then they looks for a Missus with money, and rucks in along o'
>   the rest.

'Arry's mercenary comments are slangy versions of the mid-century dictum that most marriages took place "from some interested motive, such as wealth, social position, or other advantages"; by 1888, however, love and early marriage had been argued as a solution to prostitution, the "great social evil" (Houghton, 381–85). Milliken turns the argument around, juxtaposing the antifeminist Eliza Lynn Linton with 'Arryism to mischievous effect:

> If the country took care of the kids, and diworce was made easy all
>   round,
> Wy, *I'd* marry mate, early and often, and so would lots more, I'll
>   be bound....
>
> In one thing, old pal, I go pairs, with this Mrs. LYNN LINTON
>   exact.
> She sez it's a—let'see, wot is it?—a "physiological fact"
> That some chaps who're fair flamers as lovers, are failures as
>   'usbands. That's me!
> So I mean spooning round like permiskus, and Mrs. L. L.
>   would agree.

Eliza Lynn Linton, well known for her *Saturday Review* article "Girl of the Period" (14 March 1886), in which she castigates the modern young woman, commented in the *Universal Review* for September 1888 that irrespective of polygamy or polyandry, what is important is that society acknowledge both marriage and children (Van Thal, 175–77). 'Arry twists Mrs. Linton's comment about licit and illicit relationships to suggest that she condones adultery: she actually says:

> It is a psychological fact that many men are charming as
> proprietary lovers who are impossible as husbands, and many
> women make the most complacent and delightful mistresses
> who, as wives, would give points to Xanthippe. (Qtd. in Van
> Thal, 176)

In April 1889, 'Arry again allies himself with Linton in Robert Buchanan's *Daily Telegraph* debate, reprinted in his *Coming Terror and Other Essays and Letters*. Buchanan railed against the "Modern Young Man," the "half-educated, semi-cultivated, small pessimist" who has lost faith in the "purity of womanhood" (Buchanan, 186) and wants, in 'Arry's words, to make "the Woman a speeches of gingerbread Saint" and himself into a Gladstone, a "gushing Grand Old Man in metre." For 'Arry:

> ... Woman's all right enough, not arf a bad sort of thing
> When a fellow is young and permiskus. And when he has 'ad his
>   fair fling,
> And wants quiet diggings or nussing, she do come in 'andy no
>   doubt;
> In fack, taking Woman all round, she's good goods the world
>   carn't do without.

> But washup 'er, CHARLIE? Wot bunkum!—as Mrs. LYNN
> LINTON remarks.
> To watch *her* wire into 'er sex like Jemimer, old man, is rare
> larks ...

Mrs. Linton's "Wot bunkum!" is actually expressed somewhat differently. In one of his letters, Buchanan complains that the "fallen" woman has become a "Magdalene," the victim of the "barbarity and savagery of the pseudoscientist" (187); Linton answers that Buchanan "talks sentimental bunkum with splendid literary power." She complains that women's "deadliest wrong" is being too sentimental about their fallen sisters, writes of the "absolute authority" of the mother to shape her sons' attitudes, and objects that the "smaller" and "weaker" woman does not deserve worship (qtd. in Buchanan, 191–94). 'Arry's enthusiastic support of Mrs. Linton's arguments and his identification with upper-class pretensions about money and social standing erode the plausibility of both; again, Milliken's satire is a quiet debunking of the conservative position.

Similarly, "'Arry on the 'Igher Education of Women" (5 April 1879) presents an unpalatable choice: those who object to women's education are consigning women to being household drudges.

> I see it a comin', my pippin, yer Girtons, and Art Schools, and
> such,
> Teach the women to take the men's measure, and that's just a trifle
> too much.
> Education has spiled all our servants, and now if our sisters and
> wives
> Gets too fine for the fireside and faggin' *we* shan't have no peace
> of our lives.
>
> *I* don't want a wife as can paint, or pick 'oles in my grammar; no
> fear!
> But one as can bile a pertater and keep in her own proper
> spheer ...

While this poem appeared at the beginning of his career, "'Arry on Blues and Bluestockings" appeared at the end, on 21 March 1896, when 'Arry simultaneously upholds the *Punch* position against higher degrees for women and brings it into question, even though the women's rights defender himself lacks credibility: "... old SNIPE of our club. Was a schoolmaster once, so 'tis said; / But 'is duds are as seedy as *Guy Fox*, 'is nose end's remarkable red" (135). As a foil to 'Arry, Snips is not entirely successful and perhaps represents the indecisiveness of Mr. Punch on the women's issue. Even Linley Sambourne's cartoon on 21 March 1896 seems to question the conviction that barring women admission to Oxford is appropriate: the unpleasant mien of the Don who, blinded by spectacles, prevents a woman from entering academe contrasts unfavorably with the shape of the woman who, garbed as Minerva in a helmet and carrying an owl, is prepared to lay siege. 'Arry, weighing in on the side of the establishment and thus undercutting its arguments, exclaims, "No, no, sling your hook, Miss Bluestocking, and cart your old poultry away!"

Women were not awarded degrees at Oxford until 1925, although they had, for over thirty years, been allowed to take selected Honors examinations. It was not the women's inability to compete that was at stake, but rather their perceived potential for distracting young men from study. Serious opposition came from the clergy, who feared that women in academia would be outside Church jurisdiction since they were barred from the priesthood (Burstyn, 100–101). 'Arry suggests an economic reason—"we must 'ave first cut at the screw"—and conveys a very real fear that women will eventually succeed in "sneaking our rights":

> A man as is really a man, mate, and not a mere molly in bags,
> Knows that women was *made* to knock under, in spite of them
> Radical rags.
> While us men set the pace, my dear CHARLIE, no doubt we can
> romp in in front;
> But if *she* males git sprinting away, on their own, *we* mayn't be in
> the 'unt.

If *Punch* did not fully realize that men were not "setting the pace," Milliken did, in his comical way. In "'Arry and the Battersea Park Lady Cyclists" (15 June 1895: 285), 'Arry the "Scorcher" takes his friend Lil cycling and comments that even the "lydies … borrow their barnies from *hus*, arterall":

> World shifts it, old man, that's a moral! We'll 'ave some duchess,
> on wheels,
> A-cuttin' all records, and showing young ZIMMY a clean pair of
> 'eels.
> Hadvanced Women? Jimminy-Whizz! With the spars and the sails
> they now carry
> They'll race us all round, pooty soon, and romp in heasy winners.
> Yours, 'Arry.

A Final Wink from 'Arry

From a vacation at the seaside to serious issues of women's rights, racism, and class, Milliken's Cockney verse letters mirror the life-cycle of the last third of the Victorian Age. Like the time itself, 'Arry is contentious and changeable, reflecting contemporary arguments about class, art, politics, gender, and economics. Despite their cautious, white-gloved attempts at egalitarianism—opening estate lawns to political gatherings, welcoming all comers at bazaars—the upper class preserved a measurable distance from their less well-bred brothers and sisters, taking seriously Alexander Pope's "insuperable line" in the Great Social Chain of Being. Milliken effectively subverted that view by identifying and giving voice to a class-neutral trait, "the spirit of Caddishness." "'Arryism," he suggested, could exist at any level. In that sense Milliken condemned the overt class system, based on birth and wealth, and harked back to an older understanding of honor and gentlemanliness that cuts across social pretension.

With that understanding as a measure, Milliken compels an in-depth examination of the social scene and especially of establishment attitudes. His method—the use of a persona to hide the author and the use of satire to deflect criticism—is appropriate to his subject; what he succeeds in doing is to reveal through humor the hypocrisies of the age, especially those involving the classes. In a periodical in which Cabinet ministers, the members of the House of Lords, and the religious establishment read about themselves regularly, a long-running social commentary from a brash, lower-class figure seems to be an anomaly. 'Arry the Cad and Sir Harry the Toff, however, have a good deal in common. Both spend far too much money on clothes, although one favors loud checkered suits and the other dark, costly materials; both engage in holiday parties and in political dogfights with equal fervor, although one uses fists and the other words. Both gamble and bet on dogs and horses; both love the "piffle" of vaudeville; and both have their "pooty parcels in pink," although the "Toff's" *demi-mondaine* is disguised by a French name. Both are contemptuous of women's rights, but have a sneaking suspicion that women are more devious, more intelligent, and more powerful than men.

There is, Milliken seems to suggest, little to choose between them; what is problematical is the "Toff's" assumption that he represents Britannia's best. The effect of Milliken's satire was to introduce 'Arry into the breakfast rooms and parlors of his betters and to trick them through laughter into seeing themselves. Milliken's campaign against "caddishness" was less a campaign against vulgar tailoring, defacing public monuments, knee-jerk political affiliations, thriftlessness, and the like; rather, it was a crusade against an attitude that fostered intolerance and racism and narrow-mindedness. Such blind egotism reinterpreted the Darwinian dictum to suggest that the "Toff" and his imitators are at the top of the tree. As is the way with satire, the ideal of honorable behavior was revealed at the moment that 'Arry's brashness became most pronounced. In the history of *Punch*, a reminder of that ideal was perhaps most needed in the two decades that Milliken wrote his verse letters, when it had moved from its earlier stance as "the champion of justice, the crusader against poverty, the defender of the weak and oppressed" to a "stuffy and imperialistic establishment paper, dull and highly respectable, with only an occasional flash of its old magic" (Price, 107). 'Arry, who comes down on the side of "Love, Lotion, and Larks," provides some of that flash:

> You see larks are larks. They're the "relish" as life ain't worth living without,
> To any young fellow of sperrit who knows his meander about.
> Wot hodds if it's chivvying swells with red ties, doing spoons at the "gai,"
> Or leading a rush along Fleet street, as *we* did that last Lord Mare's Day?
>
> It's only the jugginses grumbles at me and the Mashers, dear boy,
> Young pidgins too funky to flutter, old roosters too stale to enjoy.
> We smart 'uns must put on the pace, that's a moral, and if in the run,
> We bump or bowl over the stodgies, wy, that's more than arf of the fun. (14 April 1883: 180)

Notes

[1] "Toffs" have all the physical, moral, and attitudinal characteristics typical of the upper class. C. Stoeffel, *Studies in English Written and Spoken for the Use of Continental Students*, is helpful in deciphering 'Arry's Cockneyisms.

[2] The *Oxford English Dictionary* cites 23 December 1873 as the first occurrence of the nomenclature, when a cartoon of 'Arry posing in "checked ditters" on "'Orseback" appeared in the 1874 *Punch Almanack*. For details, see Spielmann (381) and my article "'Love, Larks, and Lotion': A Descriptive Bibliography of E. J. Milliken's 'Arry Poems."

[3] Thomas Anstey Guthrie, who acquired his *nom de plume* from a printer's error, which he appropriated (Price, 152–53), contributed a wealth of material to *Punch*, including *Voces Populi*, first-hand accounts of ordinary people in which he tried "to present commonplace characters and conversations and incidents as humorously as I could ..." (qtd. in Price, 153). Milliken seems to adopt the "music-hall" versification and meter popularized by Anstey's *Mr. Punch's Model Music Hall Songs*. Other *Punch* predecessors to Milliken mentioned by Spielmann include, at opposite ends of the social scale, Albert Smith, drummed out of the *Punch* circle for both plagiarism and "low" connections (Price, 41), and Thackeray, whose *The Snobs of England, by one of themselves* appeared in 1846–47.

[4] As crown territory, Trafalgar Square had been closed to meetings, which were thereupon moved to Hyde Park, Westminster Abbey, and St. Paul's. Once the square was reopened, Social Democratic Federation leader M. H. Hyndeman, who was instrumental in the 8 February 1886 Fair Trade/Free Trade riot in Trafalgar Square, demanded that the government curtail its workshop workday, cultivate its waste lands, and set up relief. Hyndeman, along with the anarchist Kropotkin, was tried and acquitted at the Old Bailey after conducting his own defense (Gretton, 178–79). In the hubbub that preceded the riot, as *The Times* for 9 November 1887 reports, two *Daily Telegraph* journalists, Bennett Burleigh and Albert Winkes, along with a printer, Joseph Knight, were arrested and charged with being "loose, idle, and disorderly persons, disturbing the peace with intent to commit a felony" and with "obstructing and resisting the police" (3). The next day's report of Winkes's speech, likening the gathering to the French Revolution (13), shows that the fear of social breakdown was very near the surface.

[5]   An example of the kind of picture 'Arry might have enjoyed appears in Sansom's *Victorian Life in Photographs.*

[6]   The plays he mentions were popular ones in 1878. *Pink Dominoes* opened at the Criterion Theatre on 31 March 1877; the play, "which seemed so risqué to society of its day, and in which the sentimental comedy is laid aside in favor of a rather mawkish cynicism," is by James Albery (Nicoll, 1: 156), adapted from *Les Dominos Roses* by Maurice Henniquin and A. C. Delacoeur. It starred Charles Wyndham, Mary Eastlake, and Fanny Josephs. *The Idol* opened at the Folly Theatre in September 1878; adapted by Charles Wyndham from the French play *La Veuve* by Henri Meilhac and Ludovic Halévy, *The Idol* starred Mary Eastlake and Lionel Brough. "Sweet *Marjerlaine*" may be Daniel Bandmann's *Madelaine Morel,* which opened at Queen's Theatre in April 1878, or the Paris favorite *La Marjolaine,* produced by Kate Santley, which opened in 1877 at the Royalty and closed in 1879 (Gänzl, 115, 151).

[7]   Roberts is a well-known figure: in 1886 he was a star in the role of "the gormless miller, Matt o' the Mill" in Farnie's *Indiana,* itself not a success (Gänzl, 297–98).

[8]   Ellen Jordan discusses the genesis of the term in "The Christening of the New Woman." See also my *Bicycles, Bangs, and Bloomers* (7–11).

[9]   "'Arriet on Labour" (26 August 1893) provides arguments that are parallel to 'Arry's but undercut them. Appearing in the conservative *Punch,* the poem is a radical indictment of marriage from the working-class woman's perspective:

> I'm only just a work-girl, Poll, one of the larky drudges
> As swarm acrost the bridge at night and 'omeward gaily trudges, ...
>
> As vulgar as they make 'em, Poll. Leastways the chaps whose trade is
> To write and dror in Comics, call hus "anythink but ladies."
> Ladies? O lor! On thirteen bob a week, less sundry tanners
> For fines, it's none so easy, Poll, to keep up style and manners.

As 'Arriet points out, working "Mothers can't strike, or unionise, or make demonsterations":

> But 'twixt the cradle and the tub, the old man and 'er needle,
> A married woman's tied up tight. Yus, Mick might spoon and wheedle,
> But when a woman's got four kids, bad 'ealth, and toke for tiffin,
> Then marriage *is* a failure, Poll, I give yer the straight griffin.

Works Cited

á Beckett, Arthur William. *The á Becketts of Punch; Memories of Father and Sons.* 1903. Detroit: Singing Tree Press, 1969.

Altick, Richard. *Victorian People and Ideas.* New York and London: Norton, 1973.

Arnold, Matthew. *Culture and Anarchy. The Complete Prose Works of Matthew Arnold.* Ed. R. H. Super. 10 vols. Ann Arbor: University of Michigan Press, 1965.

Blake, Robert. *Disraeli.* New York: St. Martin's Press, 1966.

Bolt, Christine. *Victorian Attitudes to Race.* London: Routledge, 1971.

Bratton, J[acquelin] S. *The Victorian Popular Ballad.* London: Macmillan, 1975.

Buchanan, Robert. *The Coming Terror and Other Essays and Letters.* London: Heinemann, 1891.

Burstyn, Joan N. *Victorian Education and the Ideal of Womanhood.* London: Croom Helm; Totowa: Barnes & Noble, 1980.

Ellmann, Richard. *Oscar Wilde.* New York: Knopf, 1988.

Gänzl, Kurt. *The British Musical Theatre*. Vol. 1. New York: Oxford University Press, 1986.

Gretton, R. H. *A Modern History of the English People 1880–1922*. New York: Dial, 1930.

Hambourg, Daria. *Richard Doyle: His Life and Work*. London: Art and Technics, 1948.

Helsinger, Elizabeth K., Robin Lauterback Sheets, and William Veeder. *The Woman Question: Social Issues, 1837–1883*. Vol. 2. New York and London: Garland, 1983.

Hotten, John Camden. *The Slang Dictionary*. London: Chatto & Windus, 1874.

Houghton, Walter. *The Victorian Frame of Mind 1830–1870*. New Haven and London: Yale University Press, 1957.

Howarth-Loomes, B. *Victorian Photography: An Introduction for Collectors and Connoisseurs*. New York: St. Martin's Press, 1974.

Jordan, Ellen. "The Christening of the New Woman: May 1894." *Victorian Newsletter* 63 (1983): 19–21.

Judd, Dennis. *Radical Joe: A Life of Joseph Chamberlain*. London: Hamish Hamilton, 1977.

Keating, P. J. *The Working Classes in Victorian Fiction*. London: Routledge, 1971.

Longford, Elizabeth. *Queen Victoria: Born to Succeed*. New York: Harper & Row, 1964.

Marks, Patricia. *Bicycles, Bangs, and Bloomers: The New Woman in the Popular Press*. Lexington: University of Kentucky Press, 1990.

———. "'Love, Larks, and Lotion': A Descriptive Bibliography of E. J. Milliken's 'Arry Poems in *Punch*." *Victorian Periodicals Review* 26 (1993): 67–78.

Morley, John. *The Life of William Ewart Gladstone*. 1903. 3 vols. New York: Greenwood, 1968.

Nicoll, Allardyce. *A History of Late Nineteenth-Century Drama 1850–1900*. 2 vols. Cambridge: Cambridge University Press, 1949.

Pearsall, Ronald. *Victorian Popular Music*. London: Newton & Abbot, 1973.

Prager, Arthur. *The Mahogany Tree: An Informal History of Punch*. New York: Hawthorn, 1979.

Price, R. G. G. *A History of Punch*. London: Collins, 1957.

Robb, Janet Henderson. *The Primrose League, 1883–1906*. New York: AMS, 1968.

Ruskin, John. *The Storm Cloud of the Nineteenth Century. Two Lectures Delivered at the London Institution, February 4th and 11th, 1884*. New York: Wylie, 1884.

Sansom, William. *Victorian Life in Photographs*. London: Thames & Hudson, 1974.

Scotson-Clark, George Frederick. *The "Halls."* London: Unwin, 1879.

Skinner, Cornelia Otis. *Madame Sarah*. Boston: Houghton, 1967.

Spielmann, M. H. *The History of Punch*. London: Cassell, 1895.

Stoeffel, C. *Studies in English Written and Spoken for the Use of Continental Students*. Series 1. Zutphen: Thieme, 1894.

Van Thal, Herbert Maurice. *Eliza Lynn Linton: The Girl of the Period*. London and Boston: Allen & Unwin, 1979.

Weinreb, Ben, and Christopher Hibbert, eds. *The London Encyclopedia*. London: Macmillan, 1983. Bethesda: Adler & Adler, 1986.

5

American Humor: The Mark of Twain on Jerome K. Jerome

John S. Batts

One area in the world of literary humor has been surprisingly undervalued when not neglected. A look at the early career of Jerome K. Jerome reveals not only the emergence of a successful English writer of humor but also the response to literary humor among different classes in England at the end of the nineteenth century.[1] In late 1897, responding from Italy to a suggested list of members for a proposed English Academy of Letters—a list which included heavyweights like Gladstone, Gilbert, Gosse, Hardy, Kipling, Lang, Meredith, Ruskin, Spencer, Swinburne, and Yeats—a snobbish Oscar Wilde strikes a not uncommon note among the educated class of readership. Writing to Leonard Smithers about the composition of this putative academy, Wilde snidely remarks: "I have seen the Academy with its lists of Immortals. It is very funny what sort of people are proposed. But it is difficult no doubt to make out a list. Personally I cannot make up my mind as to whether the Duke of Argyll or Jerome K. Jerome has the better claim—I think the former. The unread is always better than the unreadable" (6 December 1897; Hart-Davis, 692). Despite a flood of suggestions to the *Academy* after its 20 November issue printed a list of forty names, including that of the Duke of Argyll, no one mentioned Jerome. Yet Wilde alludes to his contemporary, Jerome, only to be dismissive and to opt cheekily for the unread duke.[2] Supposed "unreadable" by Wilde, Jerome was certainly not unread during the 1890s. Yet Wilde's flippancy indicates a fissure in literary culture of that decade, a sharp crack along class lines where humor was concerned. After all, Jerome K. Jerome was an exponent of American-style humor, a so-called new humor that middle-class England did not appreciate.

At that point in the 1890s, Jerome's standing as a creator of literary humor was based on a couple of works, principally on what J. B. Priestley calls the "smash-hit" of the Victorian period, *Three Men in a Boat: (To Say Nothing of the Dog)* (1889; see Priestley, 96). Enthusiasm for that book has continued to the present day.[3] Jerry Palmer for example, in a recent survey of humor in Great Britain, acknowledges Jerome's contribution, citing briefly the two *Three Men* novels (92). There are at least two earlier Jerome writings which show his leaning toward humor, but his reputation was made by the first of the *Three Men* books and secured by his three collections of

Idler essays published between 1889 and 1905.[4] However, Wilde's dislike of "unreadable" Jerome was not uncommon; acknowledging Jerome's success was rare among English critics if not among a broader spectrum of readers.[5] The reason for this disparity is that Jerome wrote in the manner of American humorists, notably Mark Twain, about whom middle-class England, loyal to traditional English humor, felt at best ambivalent during the 1870s and 1880s.[6] Pivotally, Jerome was popularly linked with the "new humor"—a phrase used during the last two decades of the century according to Priestley (94)—also referred to as "American humor."[7] Two contemporaries in the Jerome circle, Arthur Adcock and Israel Zangwill, testify to this division.[8]

There are links between Twain and Jerome in addition to their stylistic traits, though there is little to suggest that the two met in person. Jerome admired Twain, whose books had sold well in England for twenty years prior to the younger man's success.[9] Not surprisingly, Jerome, co-editor of *The Idler* with Robert Barr at its inaugural issue in 1892, chose a full-page frontispiece of Mark Twain and published serially the latter's "The American Claimant."[10] But initially, and well before Oxford awarded Twain an honorary degree and *Punch* magazine feted Twain, American humor was a controversial commodity in late Victorian England.[11] During the 1880s, for example, Andrew Lang not unappreciatively puzzled over the humor of the Americans as represented by Twain, Bret Harte, and Artemus Ward, noting its differences from English humor and probing the reasons for it.[12] Nor was Jerome favorably viewed by *Punch, or the London Charivari*, a distinctively middle-class magazine with a formidable reputation.[13] A partial explanation can be found in Jerome's delight in lower-class diction, but his American humor also counts. In the 1860s, as Michael Barsley reminded wartime readers, *Punch* could look down on the writing of Artemus Ward and his backwoods philosophizing complete with dialect "illiterature" because a largely middle-class public enjoyed the fact that dialect humor came from the United States (x–xii). From its early days, this very English magazine could be quite rude to its ex-colonial cousins, though, as one of its historians has noticed, this attitude modified to a "warier hostility" (Price, 115).[14] *Punch* had originally disliked Twain and his compatriots, and Jerome suffered as part of this cultural clash, even after Twain's reputation in middle-class England had risen by the mid-1890s.[15]

Beyond Jerome K. Jerome's enthusiastic reading of Mark Twain, I have briefly argued elsewhere that Jerome was an unofficial disciple of Twain.[16] Don Nilsen, in *Humor in American Literature*, has kindly noticed these views outlining Jerome's indebtedness to Twain (504). Nilsen distills salient ingredients of American humor as used by Twain: an exaggerated narrative told by a self-deprecating speaker in a colorful, slangy idiom, with an emphasis on whimsical ways of looking at otherwise serious experiences (504).[17] The following sections detect components of "new humor" among Jerome's books, a writer finding his voice as a humorist and developing his skills in the American style. Responses by readers of Jerome on either side of the Atlantic are also glanced at alongside *Punch*'s broadsides. These suggest that in Britain there is a culture clash underpinned by class, for overall where English critics (unlike readers) are unappreciative, American responses are enthusiastic.

I

A look at two early works of humor by Jerome K. Jerome is instructive. Dealing with Victorian theater and acting, both *On the Stage—and Off: The Brief Career of a Would-Be Actor* (1885) and *Stage-land: Curious Habits and Customs of Its Inhabitants* (1890) precede his best-known writing. Each book is structured as a series of descriptive chapters or sketches, and shows a humorist developing that characteristic fare which *Punch* and contemporaries like Max Beerbohm perceived as an affront to traditional English humor.

On the Stage was Jerome's first humorous publication. It drew on a personal knowledge of the theater by recounting his experiences as a would-be professional actor. There can be no mistaking the intention to amuse. The opening paragraph establishes the tone: "There comes a time in every one's life when he feels he was born to be an actor ... Then he burns with a desire to shew them how the thing's done, and to draw a salary of three hundred a week. This sort of thing generally takes a man when he is about nineteen, and lasts till he is nearly twenty" (1). Exaggeration is soon established as a strong suit with a narrator's remarks like this: "I was at the theater one evening seeing *Romeo and Juliet* played, when it suddenly flashed across me that that was my vocation. I thought all acting was making love in tights to pretty women, and I determined to devote my life to it" (2). Cumulative remarks such as these also build up a sense of a talkative silly-billy narrator determined to appear engagingly dim-witted, a well-known trait of American frontier humor.[18] Other chapters, largely relying on the guise of quoting from supposed letters, deal with the author's experience of sundry aspects of the theater, such as rehearsals, dressing, debuts, lodgings and landladies, the stock company, and so forth. Like Twain, Jerome likes to reproduce the language of foreigners or provincials; a French landlady, for example, married to an English dullard, is well-caught in speech-patterns for humorous effect (114). Such a passage is reminiscent of Twain's encounter with guides in Paris in chapter 13 of *The Innocents Abroad* (102 ff). Narrator self-deprecation is commonplace in Jerome: "I have tasted fame and don't like it. I have been recognised in the

street, and followed by a small crowd of children. They evidently expected
me to stop at some corner and sing" (99). Exposing his own naïvety is also
common, as when he learns from the company manager that he will have a
"ben." or benefit performance; but the pleasure is short-lived when the
"walking gent." discloses that "he never lost more than thirty shillings at
his benefit" (98). Other humorous tropes remind one of the culminating
one-liners of the music halls: "He [the stage manager] has been carrying on
down here, and swelling around to that extent you'd have thought him a
station-master at the very least. Now he's like a bladder with the air let out.
His wife's come" (102). Part of the appreciation of the humor here hinges
on the all-too-English class concern with appearance, the "smartness" of
petty officials, and the battle of the sexes. Finally, this early work suggests
Jerome also strives for humor via slang-phrases such as "shut up" (99)—in
strange contexts.[19]

With Wilde's quip about "unreadable" Jerome in mind, one might recall
Leonard Russell's distinction between wit and humor. For Russell, wit "is
reason on its judgement seat ...[w]hereas humor always has in it some idea
of the humorist himself being entangled with the difficulties and
contradictions of human life" (ix).[20] Jerome is generally the humorist rather
than the wit, because in his recounting he is, in Russell's phrase, "very
much of this imperfect world" (ix). And this distinction often applies to
Twain's humor. Jerome's career as an actor as reflected in this book had
been notably unsuccessful; small acting companies knew the imperfect
world well enough. Jerome writes, for example, of a struggle with elocution
lessons: "I have the misfortune to possess a keen sense of the ludicrous,
and to have a morbid dread of appearing ridiculous" (*On the Stage*, 4).
Happily, a sense of the ludicrous served the humorist better than the actor.

Initial public response to *On the Stage* suggests that there was a market
for Jerome's style—especially his strategies of a narrator's habitual
exaggeration and self-deprecation, to say nothing of a prose embedded with
humorous ploys. Not that success was immediate.[21] The book "sold fairly
well" as Jerome recalled in his autobiography (*My Life* [1992 ed.], 57),
though as his friend Adcock recalled, "the critics were not particularly kind
to it" (Adcock, 162). The key to this puzzle is that critics were generally
middle class, like Beerbohm or Wilde or *Punch* itself, whereas readers were
a newly literate class, less sophisticated, and more open to Jerome's humor.

II

The series of essays which constitutes Jerome's next book, *Stage-land*, a
look at the English theater from an actor's viewpoint, had appeared as
unsigned articles in the magazine *The Playgoer* over the four previous

years. This writing also displays the emerging Jeromian style and familiar strategies for engendering humor. *Stage-land* indicates that Twain continued to be a model for Jerome. The traits of humor are much the same. My contention in either case is that in these works Jerome is still a few sandwiches short of a good humorous picnic, even though the hamper that is *Three Men in a Boat* was soon to follow. In *Stage-land*, Jerome sketches fourteen characteristic roles of Victorian melodrama and comedy; brief accounts include the Hero and Heroine, the Villain, the Child, the Comic Man, the Servant Girl, the Adventuress, and so forth.

Most pervasive as a technique for generating the "new humor" is an assumed mask of the narrator as a slow-witted, if knowledgeable, observer notable for a strained sense of logic. Twain in *The Innocents Abroad* and *Roughing It* had made some use of this strategy. Jerome's commentator induces humor in this way by providing a workable context for often wild and zany generalizations. Occasionally this comes attached to a three-part formula, as in this example: Statement A makes parallel proposals: "It is marvelous how short-sighted people on the stage are," and "Then again, their hearing is so terribly weak" (22). Statement B follows up with the sane reflection: "It really ought to be seen to" (22). But Statement C takes one into the realm of the daffy uncomprehending dim-wit: "People talk and chatter at the very top of their voices, close behind them, and they never hear a word—don't know anybody's there even" (22). A more appealing example of the silly narrator is his description of the stage snowstorm that brings Stage Heroines into jeopardy. This is effected by much exaggeration, supported by broad generalizations, such as: "The Stage Heroine's only pleasure in life is to go out in a snowstorm without an umbrella, and with no bonnet on" (16). Humor is sustained tolerably well throughout this sketch. The Heroine, we are told, even goes out in the snow with her child who finds it cold. But this is no Lucy Gray. Here the Jeromian narrator tells us that the Heroine must be irritated by the way in which the snow "seems to lie in wait for her, and follow her about ... It is quite a fine night, before she comes on the scene: the moment she appears, it begins to snow. It snows heavily all the while she remains about, and, the instant she goes, it clears up again, and keeps dry for the rest of the evening" (17). Here Jerome sustains the mood with some success, and not without a slang verb: "The way the snow 'goes' for that woman is most unfair. It always snows much heavier in the particular spot where she is sitting, than it does anywhere else in the whole street" (17). Then follows the amusing observation on the phenomena by the narrator: "Why, we have sometimes seen a Heroine, sitting in the midst of a blinding snowstorm, while the other side of the road was as dry as a bone. And it never seemed to occur to her to cross over." To maintain the delicate balance requisite for sustaining humor in this context, the narrator tops that recollection of the Heroine's perversity with: "We have even known a more than usually malignant snowstorm to follow a Heroine three times round the stage, and then go off R. [stage right] with her" (17). The account then abandons any pretence to rational explanation in favor of a whimsical, Victorian-risqué climax: "Of course, you can't get away from a snowstorm like that! A Stage Snowstorm is the kind of snowstorm that would follow you up stairs, and want to come into bed with you" (17).

In each chapter supposedly typical stage qualities of these stock characters are adumbrated, the Jeromian narrator blending straightforward comments with the exaggerated. The Stage Heroine, we are told, is exquisitely good, has a hard life, is always in trouble, and weeps a good deal; her father (white-haired, of course) becomes bankrupt, her childhood home is sold up, her husband is found guilty of murder, and her infant contracts a lingering fever (16). But any maudlin elements in Jerome's analysis of the Stage Heroine's litany of woes are offset by the humor, as in this manner: "It is over the child that she does most of her weeping. The child has a damp time of it altogether. We sometimes wonder that it never catches rheumatism" (16). In this kind of whimsical formula, Statement A makes a reasonably faithful description of the Heroine. Then Statement B moves into a different key, with a probable half-truth heightened dramatically by exaggeration in sentiment, yet kept in equilibrium by the euphemistic phrase, "damp time." Finally, Statement C climaxes the description by returning to exaggeration, this time tinged with irreverence; it takes the notion of the bawling infant— in the text cleverly neutralized to "it"—as far as possible with a speculative generalization that yokes two unlikely ideas, namely, a baby linked to rheumatism (an affliction usually associated with adulthood, especially old age). This is not to suggest that in Statement C we have a candidate for metaphysical wit with heterogeneous ideas suddenly brought into propinquity, but rather that humor is spawned by an awareness of the incongruity of the notions of a crying babe being linked to typically adult suffering. Notice there is also an undertow of sentimentality, which Jerome generally liked to exploit.

Aiding this sparking of humor is the *gravitas* of tone in the commentator who slyly makes the reader his accomplice with the adoption of the first person plural, "we." Thereby Jerome has provided a context for his silly-billy narrator to essay such serious observations delivered in a dead-pan voice. Little wonder that in continuing he can lean towards an obtuse reflection involving a reversal of norms about Stage Heroines: "Our only consolation ... is that there are not many good women off the stage. Life is bad enough as it is; if there were many women, in real life, as good as the Stage Heroine, it would be unbearable" (16).

In the chapter on the Adventuress, Jerome uses a similar three-statement formula, playing with reader expectations: "Some folks like to die in bed, but stage people don't. They like to die on the floor. We all have our different tastes" (36). Statement A points to a generally understood distinction between stage and real life; Statement B of the second clause elaborates on the sentiment in a related key, making the point that popular theater loves dramatic deaths on stage. Then Statement C concludes tangentially, implying that the narrator is a simpleton, because the reflection stemming from A and B is inadequate, a rather weak explanation of the phenomenon. Yet there's a pleasing hint of euphemism too (via the word "taste") as one reaches his weak conclusion, for, after all, nobody dies to taste. A reader can be distracted, perhaps amused, by this bringing together of two words ("die" and "taste") with such remote connotations.

At another weak-headed moment the trick is observable again when Jerome's narrator asserts in Statement A: "It is repentance that kills off the bad people in plays." Statement B provides the evidence: "They always repent, and the moment they repent they die." Thence, Statement C's whimsical conclusion: "Repentance, on the stage, seems to be one of the most dangerous things a man can be taken with. Our advice to stage wicked people would undoubtedly be, 'Never repent'" (37). When Twain's narrator of *The Innocents Abroad* is approaching Gibraltar, for example, there is a similar playful tone in the prose: "The ancients considered the Pillars of Hercules the head of navigation and the end of the world. The information the ancients didn't have was very voluminous. Even the prophets wrote book after book and epistle after epistle, yet never once hinted at the existence of a great continent on our side of the water; yet they must have known it was there, I should think" (49).

Perhaps a final example of quirky logic at the service of Jerome's humor will suffice: a series of statements that also involve inversion and exaggeration. This one deals with the way in which death on stage for the Adventuress seems not to be final. Statement A observes "Most people like to die once and have done with it." Then comes the Statement B clause, "but the Adventuress, after once or twice trying it, seems to get quite to like it" and he concludes whimsically, "and then it grows upon her until she can't help herself, and it becomes a sort of craving with her" (34). Little wonder the Jeromian guide to *Stage-land* can perversely conclude "It must be most disheartening to the murderers" (35), or in similar droll tone and making the best of stage practice of reviving its "dead": "and, bless you, it does them good—it is like a tonic to them" (35).

Underlying most observations in *Stage-land*, one presumes an element of truth. One concedes that second-rate Victorian theater in performance had less than exacting standards for acting often ephemeral texts. The Jeromian narrator relies on a degree of inside knowledge of lax standards, but consistently and unfailingly manages to blend his description of the stage character with a Twain staple, exaggeration. Generally the reader is in no doubt as to when precisely the tall-tale element takes over. There's a similar feel here to Mark Twain's fiction reportage of his frontier experiences in *Roughing It*, where its writer has knowledge of riding in a coach for days, has encountered curious people such as Mr. Arkansas or Captain Ned Blakely and their habits in a lawless part of the world, and generally has undergone privations of frontier life.

An account of a traditional stage character by Jerome is also aided humorously by the infusion of preposterous witty asides and even some extended digressions—their only justification being a potential for exploring humorous angles. Twain, too, liked digressions at the service of humor. Jerome, moreover, incorporates whimsical comparisons into the prose, such as noting the hero is "as full of noble sentiments as a bladder of wind" (*Stage-land*, 5), or more locally commenting on the extreme purity of a typical audience at a theater by suggesting that the "early Christian martyrs were sinful and worldly compared with an Adelphi [London theater] gallery" (5). This way-out analogy equates with Twain's extravagant descriptions of the qualities of George Bemis's "pepperbox" Allen revolver in *Roughing It* (32).

Sometimes Jerome's comparison is outrageous and it bridles any laughter. His narrator can describe a flirtation between real (as opposed to stage) peasantry as "a singularly solid and substantial affair" that makes him think of "a steam-roller flirting with a cow" (61). Twain can be equally unfeeling, pointed but outrageous. Recall his description of the "inexcusable ugliness" of Moorish women in *The Innocents Abroad* (70), or of the "absolute lord of the Ottoman Empire." Both, too, are snobbish and in poor taste. Abdul Aziz is "clad in dark green European clothes, almost without ornament or insignia of rank: a red Turkish fez on his head—a short, stout, dark man, black-bearded, black-eyed, stupid, unprepossessing—a man whose whole appearance somehow suggested that if he only had a cleaver in his hand and a white apron on, one would not be at all surprised to hear him say: "A mutton-roast to-day, or will you have a nice porterhouse steak?" (109–10). The social snobbery here is something most readers would associate more readily with English Victorian writers—not least with Wilde, perhaps even with the Duke of Argyll! Underpinning the humor of Jerome and Twain is a class consciousness, though Jerome above seems to be sneering at the peasantry and Twain at not only foreign potentates but also the bourgeoise of little shopkeepers and tradesmen.

Additional ploys for humor in *Stage-land* involve Jerome's reliance on nonliterary low words or phrases.[22] Andrew Lang, an English contemporary writing about American humor in 1889, singled out the slang of Twain and Artemus Ward as one of two remarkable features of the new humor (*Lost Leaders*, 73). Jerome certainly loves to introduce slang terms like these into *Stage-land*: "ducky" (7), "a goner" (65), "drivels on" (7), "a bob's worth" (70), or "nabbed" (14). Then there's the Stage Child who is taken out in the snow to "freshen it up" (17); the Villain who is "fairly mashed on" the Heroine (10); and the Adventuress who has "grit and go in her" (38). Similarly, romantic Peasants are described as "spooning" (62) and the Comic Lover's girl is not only a "regular" (54) but also a "bit of a spanker" (54). Finally there is the House Guest who is expected "to chuck the housemaid under the chin" (30). The Comic Man, says Jerome, refers on stage to his wife as my "old Dutch Clock" and "my old Geyser" (25). If these are identifiably English, there are also words with a recognizable transatlantic quality, such as describing a fellow, Twain-like, as "so cussed mean" (24), or even that notably North American "stoopid" (54).

III

Of *Stage-land*'s public reception, Jerome recalled that "journals that had been denouncing me and all my works as an insult to English literature hastened to crib them" (*My Life* [1983 ed.], 64). Yet with attractive illustrations by Bernard Partridge, *Stage-land* "was quite a success" (64). It sold well too. Chatto and Windus, also a publisher of Mark Twain in England, printed 12,000 copies within a year of publication. Responses to early Jerome differed significantly in England and the United States.[23] In England, *The Athenaeum*, for example, had given at least a polite nod to *On the Stage*; in a column titled "Dramatic Gossip" an unsigned reviewer had noticed "a brightly written work, and an agreeable addition to stage literature" (3004 [23 May 1885]: 674). But four years later a brief notice of *Stage-land* seems to hedge rather: "[it] gives comic sketches of the various characters in melodrama, and has a certain amount of humour" (3229 [14 September 1889]: 362). This is surely grudging and ultimately dismissive. The same journal's review of Jerome's *Tales Told After Supper* (1891) gives a clearer idea of the hostility:

> As one of Mr. Jerome K. Jerome's books is said to be in its 119th edition, he must be the most popular of living British authors. If there is anybody who has never opened a single copy of any of the 119 editions, he should read Mr. Jerome's new book, *Tales Told After Supper* (Leadenhall Press). He may well be astounded at the popular taste. The book is very poor stuff: but it is printed in very large type, on thick paper (but of an unpleasant blue colour), with many blank pages, so that half an hour will suffice for reading every word. The exquisite fun of it appears to consist in the supposed fact that the ghost stories which it contains are told by people who are drunk or in one of those states which witnesses in criminal courts are apt to distinguish with so much nicety. (*Athenaeum* 3298 [10 January 1891]: 51)

For all that book's weakness, snootiness is offensive. Little wonder Jerome's autobiography characteristically lamented:

> I think I may claim to have been, for the first twenty years of
> my career, the best abused author in England. *Punch* invariably
> referred to me as "'Arry K. 'Arry," and would then proceed to
> solemnly lecture me on the sin of mistaking vulgarity for
> humour and impertinence for wit. As for *The National
> Observer*, the Jackdaw of Rheims himself was not more cursed
> than I was, week in, week out, by W. E. Henley and his
> superior young men. I ought, of course, to have felt
> complimented; but at the time I took it all quite seriously, and it
> hurt. Max Beerbohm was always very angry with me. *The
> Standard* spoke of me as a menace to English letters; and *The
> Morning Post* as an example of the sad results to be expected
> from the over-education of the lower orders. (*My Life*, 58)

By contrast, *Stage-land* was subject of an appreciation in *The New York Times* for Henry Holt's American edition. There, one reviewer suggested that American newspapers had already made numerous quotations from Jerome; the book was compared favorably with both Dickens and Thackeray. Finally, the reviewer enthused: "*Stage-land* is exceedingly bright and worth reading, and it explains more clearly than his other books, the growing vogue of this young writer in London and his success there as a comic playwright" (27 April 1890: 12).[24] Equally intriguing is the same newspaper's notice of *On the Stage*, an American edition of which appeared in 1891. While generally approving ("This book is an exception to a very good rule—it is easy writing that is not hard reading") the reviewer noted that Jerome K. Jerome was in fashion, but qualified his remarks in suggesting that the humor is "of the most obvious sort. The sophisticated reader knows just what to expect and is never disappointed" (*The New York Times* [21 June 1891]: 19). These phrases, incidentally, may offer some explanation for Oscar Wilde's hostility. Nonetheless, this American reviewer thought that the would-be actor's career as presented may well have been a true statement of facts: "it is probably not exaggerated." And this brought him to observe one national difference of humor: "he has not the real comedy instinct of the American writer. There is never a hint of irony in his pages." Maybe what is at stake here—irony apart—is the degree of exaggeration present. Persistent use of hyperbole is a feature of Jerome's humor, though maybe not as outrageous as in the staple of the American tall tale as used by Twain. That same reviewer's take on the book's factual reportage is puzzling. However, differences of opinion between reviewers English (negative) and American (positive) as to Jerome's talent are notable.

IV

Jerome's slangy idiom seems to be especially the "low" kind of humor that enraged late nineteenth-century *Punch*. In the late 1860s, the American humorist Artemus Ward, renowned for his countrified misspellings, had been invited to contribute to *Punch*.[25] A kindly historian of *Punch*, Marion Spielmann, has explained that Ward was then in failing health and writing under difficulty so that "little of his rollicking humour is to be found" (370). In any case, a generation later, taste had shifted.[26] When that same magazine mocked Jerome in its satirical spoof of modern novelists (see below), his slang was a clear target. *Punch*, after all, mirrored respectable "society" life. Both its jokes and cartoons reflected attitudes of the middle classes, and typically it took satirical aim at those who failed to conform to its own norms of acceptable behavior, language, even looks. Writing in the early 1890s, Spielmann discerned a shift: "The social and political attitude of *Punch* today is a very different thing from what it was when the paper first claimed public attention and support" (99). Spielmann also noted the metropolitan rather than international nature of this repository of English humor: "In considering *Punch*'s attitude during his long career, it must be borne in mind that he has always aimed at representing the sentiments of the better part of the country—seeing with London's eyes, and judging by London's standards. 'Punch' is an Englishman of intense patriotism, but primarily a Citizen of London" (111).

Jerome, however, was an East End Londoner; he did not represent what Spielmann termed "sentiments of the better part of the country." Those sentiments, according to Spielmann, were broad-minded; he saw the journal as less confrontational than in its early days: "it may be said that there is today no effort on *Punch*'s part to be 'smart,' anti-popular, anti-bourgeois, or anti-anything, save anti-virulent and anti-vulgar" (101). It was this last category in which *Punch* was especially watchful, and where it found Jerome offensive. Americans could laugh at vulgarity, because the old rebel colony was relatively classless. By 1890, though, vigilant Mr. Punch could not or would not join in; nor seemingly would he allow others to enjoy indigenous writing in imitation of American humor. One alternative explanation might be available: that Jerome was an ineffective humorist and strove to imitate the styles of American humor to hack out a living as a writer.[27] One hundred years on, it seems safer to say that *Punch* got it wrong. Little wonder, as Spielmann ruefully remarked, "nowadays many Americans prefer to regard *Punch* with a scornful amusement" and acknowledged that "the same line is taken in England by New Journalists and Newer Critics" (370).

There is an important footnote to this late Victorian reading of American humor. Though *Punch* had formerly sneered at an English "Speling Reform moovement" (317), Spielmann makes a case that humor generated through the deplorably inaccurate writing of an illiterate, as exemplified by Artemus Ward and others, is following a humorous device introduced in 1841 by Thackeray[28]: "All the American humourists who have adopted the same idea, are but followers where the great Titmarsh led" (317).[29] If that is contentious, Spielmann believed that another element of American humor had roots in *Punch*: "even what is known in England as 'modern American humour' has been claimed as a leaf out of *Punch*'s book, quaint exaggeration forming its staple feature, as in the case [where] we are told that 'a young artist in Picayune takes such perfect likenesses that a lady married the portrait of her lover instead of the original'"(163).[30] Perhaps this is only to be explained by a self-professed enthusiast for *Punch*; the "Preface" to the *History* does warn readers of Spielmann's loyal affiliation. His judgment, however, does seem without knowledge *inter alia* of either Sam Slick or Major Jack Downing.[31]

There were sniping reviews of Jerome in *Punch* by "The Baron de Book-Worms,"[32] probably the work of the editor himself, Francis Burnand, though he had an occasional deputy for that nom de plume.[33] Perhaps Burnand's educational background (Eton and Trinity College, Cambridge) immediately disclosed why he lacked sympathy with the writings of a poorly-educated Jerome who struggled in the East End of London and was never able to consider a university education.[34] Two of three reviews link Jerome with American humor, suggesting that the Englishman is a weak imitator. The first is more guarded but makes *Three Men in a Boat*'s connection with American humor explicit: "The Baron may well be wrong, and the humour of this book, which seems to consist in weak imitations of American fun ... a style the Baron believes to have been introduced from Yankee-land, and patented here by the *Sporting Times* and its imitators, ... is not to his particular taste" (1 February 1890: 57). Next, *Punch* wrote: "Jerumky Jerum still somewhat affects Yankee humour, not, however, in so forced a manner as in his over-praised *Three Men in a Boat*" (3 January 1891: 4); this review also goes on to contrast Jerome unfavorably with Dickens.[35]

The most revealing attack by *Punch* on Jerome, however, is an extended mockery in a series of parodies of contemporary novelists under the heading "Mr. Punch's Prize Novels" that opened in the fall of 1890. Price attributes this series to R. C. Lehmann (151). Almost two dozen writers were eventually targeted. Significantly, the very first attack was on Jerome under the thinly veiled disguise of reviewing "One Man in a Coat," supposedly by "'Arry O.K. 'Arry, Author of Cheap Words of a Chippie Chappie, etsetterer" (*Punch* 99 [4 October 1890]: 157).[36] Keats had endured the sneer of "Cockney poet" earlier in that century, and a century later again *Punch*'s 1890s' snigger at the expense of Jerome seems equally inept.[37] The attack seems indicative of a *Punch* still in awe of the humor of Dickens and Thackeray, of a magazine peculiarly unaware that a vigorous Victorian counter-culture was alive, and dismissive of a new class of reader which responded enthusiastically to the "new humor" of Jerome. The purported "Prefatory Note" pointedly reminded readers of

Jerome's associations with Mark Twain: "This novel was carefully wrapped up in some odd leaves of Mark Twain's *The Innocents Abroad*, and was accompanied by a letter in which the author declared that book was worth £3000, but that 'to save any more blooming trouble,' he would be willing to take the prize of £1000 by return of post, and say no more about it.—Ed."[38] Here the mockery suggests a deliberate ploy by Jerome to gain readership on the reputation of the American humorist. Further, the use of the low word "blooming" is calculated to link Jerome with slovenly expression and working-class speech. The ruse of accepting less than the supposed worth of the manuscript alleges an author desperate to publish.

A deliberately nonsensical *Punch* spoof presents a narrator who reflects on difficulties with both his "slavey" [maid][39] and his landlady in contrast with his friend, Pottle. The lack of shaping does accurately reflect the way in which *Three Men in a Boat* mixes slabs of factual history with a whimsical adventure yarn that makes frequent use of dialogue and digressions. The mock is also replete with slang and mini-climaxes such as the arrival of a new coat:

> Well, when the coat came home the Slavey brought it up, and put it on my best three-legged chair, and then flung out of the room with a toss of her head, as much as to say, "'Ere's extravagance!" First I looked at the coat, and then the coat seemed to look at me. Then I lifted it up and put it down again, and sent out for three-ha'porth of gin. Then I tackled the blooming thing again. One arm went in with a ten-horse-power shove. Next I tried the other. After no end of fumbling I found the sleeve. "In you go!" I said to my arm, and in he went, only it happened to be the breast pocket. I jammed, the pocket creaked, but I jammed hardest, and in went my fist and out went the pocket. (*Punch* 99 [4 October 1890]: 157)

Apart from the silliness of the three-legged chair (whether best or not), there is a parody of working-class speech underlined by the use of "slavey" for occasional help and her "three-ha'porth."[40] The allusion to the gin shops of Victorian England, for the working poor "the quickest way out of Manchester" as one contemporary adage put it, must have been equally applicable to darkest London too, firmly placing the mocked author in lowest Cockneydom.

The final paragraph quickly moves from the ridiculous to the incredible; it deals with the arrival of the lodging-house cat which drinks the narrator's milk for tea, with the local butcher's dog which runs off with his trouser leg, and with a small boy who seeing a red-faced narrator causes the local fire brigade to be called. With a dollop of frontier-like exaggeration this narrator then assures his reader that the firemen gave up after ten minutes and found him "Inextinguishable." The adversity out of which Jerome generally weaves his comic material is an acceptable target for fun, as is the mockery of lower-class speech and the excited dramatization of personal matter, but the ridiculous climax is well over the top. The *Punch* spoof has one more jab: "Three words more and the Editor has intervened with 'No, thank you. No more.'"

The hostility of *Punch* to Jerome is unmistakable. The discernment of Jeromian qualities is not unreasonable, especially a dim-witted narrator who forever seems to be on the receiving end of life's mishaps; likewise, the American-style seasoning of quaint exaggeration and slangy speech for humorous effect. The *reductio ad absurdum*, of course, is not supposed to be funny, but the overall satire has its edge. A century later one can see that *Punch* is overreacting and overplaying the class card.

V

As a modern addendum to this matter of broad, even silly humor, it may be significant to note that in his important study, Roger Henkle pays no attention to Jerome. His thesis shows how as the nineteenth century developed, comic modes and techniques moved towards either lower-middle class humor, notably among *Punch* writers, or the more reflexive, elaborate comedy of paradox and intellect present in Wilde, Beerbohm, and George Meredith. In effect, Henkle's interest is in comedy as a middle-class concern. Similarly, Robert Martin, after surveying numerous Victorian periodical debates on the issue of humor versus wit, links the change to the revival of wit after the 1860s (38). Jerome, more understandably, does not fit in.

On the particular matter of slang as a constituent of humor, one might reflect that Martin had gauged nineteenth-century humor as Henkle was later to do. Detecting a marked change in Victorian comic theory (as reflected in George Meredith's essay), Martin surmises that as the age matured, wit became increasingly accepted as the essence of comedy. Noticeably, Martin also ignores Jerome. But given the concerns of both with wit and middle-class humor, these scholars' omissions do suggest, inadvertently, possible explanations. First, one assumes that Jerome's humorous writing had a broad appeal principally among the English lower classes—not the typical *Punch* readership. Secondly, one may judge that Jerome is not notably a witty writer like Beerbohm and Wilde. Perhaps, finally, Jerome may have been more in touch with the new and American in humor, and possessed affinities with contemporary music-hall comedians, especially the raconteurs of his own day (I think here of George Robey); he thus anticipates British radio comedy shows around mid-century. Revealingly, one recent critic has compared the best of Jerome with Benchley and Thurber (Bishop, 16). But the slang-for-humor link in Jerome's time is probably with the music halls, places which, like most such institutions of popular culture in Victorian England, according to Jerry Palmer, lacked respectability (93–94). Little wonder, then, that the middle-class *Punch* was hostile to Jerome's success.

VI

Before glancing at Jerome's major book of humor, *Three Men in a Boat*, one should mention his *Idle Thoughts of an Idle Fellow* (1886), a humorous collection of fourteen essays which first appeared serially in the magazine *Home Chimes*. Its editor had also solicited contributions from Mark Twain (Connolly, 38). Jerome's pieces were collected for publication in 1886, and he eventually added two further books of miscellaneous "idle" essays. Therein the humor quotient varies. It need not concern one here beyond remarking that some American humor and specific traits of early Twain are once more discernible: exaggeration, the slow-witted narrator-cum-essayist, wilful digression, slang to trigger amusement, and a persistent whimsical inventiveness.[41]

Three Men in a Boat: (To Say Nothing of the Dog), to give its eventual full title of 1889, is notably pervaded by Twain's brand of American humor.[42] Structurally it relies on a loose narrative describing the exploits of the storyteller "J" and two friends, George and Harris. Jerome's trio, who attempt a holiday afloat, are innocents abroad, English city tenderfoots inadvertently forced to rough it while in pursuit of "rest and a complete change" (9). The leisurely storytelling, as in *The Innocents Abroad*, digresses frequently, conveys a few historical facts along the way, but basically deals with real experiences of Jerome and two friends who had often spent weekends boating on the Thames. Twain, too, had been exercised by the search for ways of converting personal experience into literature (Covici, 537). Jerome did not need to look beyond Twain to find a means of converting a personal past into an entertaining book.[43]

Not a little overcome by the historical richness of Europe and being aware that tourists are ever exploited in cities such as Marseilles or Paris, Rome or Naples, Twain had injected humor frequently, perhaps as a personal means of coping with what he saw and what his American party had to put up with as visitors. To dub all his Parisian guides as "Ferguson" while especially disliking one suitably named Billfinger is a small example of the viewpoint; so too is Twain's response to the overdose of Michael Angelo in Italy (264). The visit to Père la Chaise cemetery in Paris, and being overwhelmed by the memorials of celebrities interred there, trigger similar irreverence; at the grave of Abelard and Heloise, Twain's narrator can cap his own rhapsody with humor thus: "Go when you will, you find it furnished with those bouquets and immortelles. Go when you will, you find a gravel-train from Marseilles arriving to supply the deficiencies caused by memento-confiscating vandals whose affections have miscarried" (121). Similarly, when he recounts the story of the famous lovers, we learn of the role of "her uncle the howitzer" (122). Likewise, when in Rome Twain delights in his discovery of "the only playbill of that establishment [the Coliseum] now extant" (254) for all the fact that it smells of mint-drops.

Analogously, Jerome's city-boy stance is the English writer's strategy when confronted with the pastoral delights of the Thames Valley. Humor is his way of coping with boating which involves "heathenish tow-lines" (130), "impertinent" rowing boats (267), a floating dead dog (219), the appearance of a water rat (cf. Twain's sail to Hawaii in *The Innocents Abroad*) etc.; and rowing brings recollections of the perils of punting (257) and rafting (245), hair-raising escapades while sailing on the Norfolk Broads (262), even the danger of swimming (261). Similarly, Twain-like irreverence also marks some of Jerome's recounting of history, like the George and Dragon at Wargrave where the pub sign has two sides painted by distinguished artists: "Leslie has depicted the fight; Hodgson has imagined the scene 'After the Fight'—George, the work done, enjoying his pint of beer" (224). Jerome's encounter with an all too enthusiastic church sexton who perceives a stranger at Hampton (chapter 7) and sounds inadvertently, if tellingly, American— "Yuise a stranger in these parts?" (105)—is reminiscent of Twain's reportage of an Italian guide who blathers to Americans about Columbus in *The Innocents Abroad* (266–69).

Exaggeration, that stalwart ploy of American humor, is prominent from the opening pages as the narrator discloses how he suffered from symptoms for most diseases but housemaid's knee.[44] Further, one notices the use of Twain's poker-faced narrator in "J," who engages his reader in active collusion, seemingly nudging the reader and saying "You know that I'm spinning a tall tale, but let's pretend that I'm not so that you can enjoy this yarn with its far-fetched incidents." In following three English mock-musketeers battling unsuccessfully with the vicissitudes of river travel, the plot of *Three Men in a Boat* also bears an American stamp.[45] The motive had been to bring relief to maladies ascribed to city employment by "a change of scene, and the absence of the necessity of thought" (9). Overruling the dog's objections, they had opted for two weeks on the river (18). Their plans go awry at every turn and the narrative piles digressions upon asides in addition to recording holiday failures. Yet the appeal of the book lies in Jerome's unflagging ability to make these incidents the focus of shared amusement. This excursion up the Thames from west London is crammed with the difficulties of rowing upstream, key embarrassments in the locks, tangles with others' tow-lines, even run-ins with riparian owners. Worse, there is evidence of citified ineptitude in every facet of their organization. They have brought with them unnecessary garments, and have left behind indispensable utensils. Simple tasks like putting up a canvas awning over the boat for the first night prove epical struggles (149–52). But frustration is rendered humorous. Exaggeration is present in generous portions, along with frequent endowment of inanimate objects with human traits, a device also used by Twain. Descriptions of action also make clear Jerome's predilection for broad slapstick. Dialogue, too, as in an encounter with an old sexton who is determined to show them church treasures (104–107), is given a local flavor, and if not as pronounced as frontier humor, it is still akin to Twain's interest in local speech in *The Innocents Abroad*.

Notably American are occasional one-liners reminiscent of vaudeville embedded in *Three Men in a Boat*: "Everything has its drawbacks, as the man said when his mother-in-law died, and they came down on him for the funeral expenses" (39). Another is a borrowing from Twain when the narrator "J" remarks: "I like work: it fascinates me. I can sit and look at it for hours. I love to keep it by me: the idea of getting rid of it nearly breaks my heart" (244). Action in the novel is in the key of lightness. The three boaters find adversity at all points of the compass and Jerome digresses at every opportunity for humor. The famed digression about carrying two cheeses by train for a friend is long but less sustained (46–53)—but there are sprightly shorter ones, such as the recollection of some dangerous posing for a photo while in the lock (286–91).

Perhaps the most notable of the extended asides is the one recalling the ability of Uncle Podger "so ready to take the burden of everything himself, and put it on the backs of other people" (30). Twain liked to introduce character-portraits into his early fiction, like Jim Blaine (*Roughing It*) or the "Oracle" (*The Innocents Abroad*). Jerome's most memorable sketch must be of his Uncle Podger, a man associated with slapstick actions as well as being a compendium of less admirable traits of the Victorian *Pater*; he is absent-minded, boastful, bumbling, clumsy, cantankerous, disorganized, exasperating, self-centered and small-minded. To a simple task of hanging a picture he brings all the hallmarks of a do-it-yourself bungler. He insists on doing the job while commanding the whole household to his aid. Beginning without tools or materials, he contrives to cut himself, fall off the chair, lose his temper, wreck the appearance of the wall and break the glass frame before the picture, "very crooked and insecure" (36), is hung at midnight. Podger has had his mounting problems but he concludes triumphantly: "Why, some people would have had a man in to do a little thing like that!" (36). The irony of the situation is granted a delicious twist as "J," having remonstrated with Harris for being like Podger, unblinkingly takes on the role himself (36). Podger's tale has become a universal domestic myth (see Pritchett, 783–84). Like Twain, Jerome knew a natural target for the comic vision.

Eventually the holiday is abandoned prematurely in damp chill and rain. Wearying of the prospect of a fortnight afloat, the intrepid adventurers, unrested and exhausted, eventually reach rare unanimity. Unable to face another night in the boat, or as George terms it "this bally old coffin" (311)— a joke used in Twain's *Roughing It* (chapter 69)—they catch a return train for their urban bolt-hole with visions of an evening at the Alhambra and a good restaurant. The so-called holiday has been one extended failure for the characters and one extended laugh for readers.

From this survey of a late Victorian English humorist writing in the vicinity of Twain, several conclusions may be drawn about Jerome. Conceding that his work is unevenly successful, one notices a mixed reception among contemporaries, a polarization between hostility from the English middle classes, and encouragement by the general readership. This is a reaction underpinned by both class and national sentiments in England and highlighted by approval from America. Crucially, one observes that staple devices for Jerome's humor show American influence; the so-called new or American humor allowed him to write a humor less in touch with older-established Victorian mores, and more in touch with the coming age (see Hall, 578). With Cockney irreverence and native whimsy, Jerome K. Jerome is neither simply an English Twain nor an unalloyed American humorist. Despite Wilde's opinion, Jerome is not unreadable, though the Duke of Argyll probably remains unread. Happily for the world of laughter, Jerome was surprisingly able and his humor does bear the mark of Twain.

Notes

[1]   A version of this chapter was originally given as part of a paper to a meeting of the International Society for Humor Studies. Extensive revision and expansion has been possible thanks to two summer study leaves granted by the University of Ottawa, Canada. I also wish to acknowledge the hospitality of the School of English, University of New South Wales, Sydney, Australia, my host during those leaves.

[2]   Here I assume that Wilde is amusingly punning, not so much to suggest that whatever the duke had written was unread or unknown to the public but rather to point at the usual philistinism of the aristocracy, namely that the duke lacked any background in reading.

[3]   D. C. Browning, the compiler, reckons that *Three Men in a Boat* sold one million pirated copies in America (364).

[4]   Jerome K. Jerome, *Idle Thoughts of an Idle Fellow: A Book for an Idle Holiday* (1886). Jerome's *Three Men on the Bummel* (1900) appeared in its American editions with a different title, *Three Men on Wheels*, as in the current Penguin edition.

[5]   Wilde, too, had been the subject of an anonymous but offensive and vulgar (Wilde's terms) *Punch* review (19 July 1890) of *The Picture of Dorian Gray* (see Hart-Davis, 267).

[6]   I am aware of the note of caution raised by scholars like Jesse Bier about speaking blithely about American humor without specifying region or time. The term is used in this chapter to refer to American humor in the second part of the nineteenth century, principally the writings of Twain.

[7]   The first recorded use of the phrase "American humor" in the *Oxford English Dictionary* is supposedly in 1879, though John Robertson had certainly used it prior to

that in an interesting essay dealing with the humor of Sam Slick, David Crockett, et al., while noting that a distinctive national humor has emerged in the United States. See his article "Yankeeana" in the *London and Westminster Review* 32:1; this attribution to Robertson is made in *The Wellesley Index* 3: 876.

⁸ Adcock wrote: "He [Jerome] and most of the group gathered round him had been dubbed 'the new humorists,' what they wrote was indiscriminately called 'new humor,' and the terms were not always meant to be complimentary, though why humorists or humor should be any the worse for being new it is not easy to understand, except that our critics are a conservative race, wedded to precedent and averse from change" (8). He added: "It bewildered others of us who were living in those times, for the term [new humorist] was applied impartially to Jerome and Barry Pain, to Pett Ridge and Zangwill, as if they were all exactly alike and each had not a brand of humor that was distinctively his own" (166–67).

⁹ Recognition of literary links between Twain and Jerome is not new. I have not seen a copy of a German article that claims that Jerome repeatedly reminds the reader of Twain, but it is cited by Carl Markgraf's bibliography of Jerome, namely, Heinrich Schmitz's "Kurt Schladenbach, Jerome K. Jerome, Fact and Fiction" (see *Works Cited*). Jerome's *Diary of a Pilgrimage* (1891) was seen by at least one contemporary critic to be based on the style of Twain's *The Innocents Abroad* (see "Books of Travel and Description," *Dial* 12 [August 1891]: 103–104).

¹⁰ The *Idler*, a sixpenny monthly, first appeared in February 1892, edited by Jerome and Robert Barr. The latter provided the capital; Jerome provided the title, having been chosen for the editorship over Rudyard Kipling.

¹¹ For details of Mark Twain's reputation in England from 1870 onwards, see Welland.

¹² See Lang's comments in *Lost Leaders* (1889), 70–77. These are reprints of articles that had formerly appeared in the *Daily News*.

¹³ For surveys of *Punch*'s political leanings in the nineteenth century, see Spielmann, Price, Prager, and Altick.

¹⁴ For a glimpse of the early formation of the magazine's suspiciousness of foreigners, see especially chapter 3 of Jerrold.

¹⁵ Having seen an article about himself in a May 1897 issue of *Harper* in South Africa, Twain was able to write to its author, his American friend the Revd. Joseph Twichell, of *Punch*'s new esteem: "Thank you a thousand times, Joe, you have praised me away above my deserts, but I am not the man to quarrel with you for that ... Between you and *Punch* and Brander Matthews, I am like to have my opinion of myself raised sufficiently high" (*Letters*, 329). Ten years later, Twain was a man of considerable stature in England; Oxford conferred an honorary doctorate on him and *Punch* granted him the accolade of one of its celebrated office dinners. "Mark Twain's extraordinary reception and triumph in England was, in fact, the crowning glory of his career. Perhaps one of the most satisfactory incidents of his sojourn was a dinner given to him by the staff of *Punch* in the historic offices at 10 Bouverie Street, where no other foreign visitor had been thus honoured—a notable distinction. When the dinner ended, little Joy Agnew, daughter of the chief editor, entered and presented to the chief guest the original drawing of a cartoon by Bernard Partridge, which had appeared on the front page of *Punch*. In this picture the presiding genius of the paper is offering Mark Twain health, long life, and happiness from 'The Punch Bowl'" (*Letters*, 414–15n).

¹⁶ John S. Batts, "American Humor: A Late Victorian View" (1987).

¹⁷ Also see Donelson.

¹⁸ Andrew Lang noted this trait in his 1880s essay on "American Humour," focusing on Artemus Ward and Twain: "a good deal of the amusement is derived from the extreme dryness, the countryfied slowness of the narrative" (*Lost Leaders*, 74).

¹⁹ Yet some of the attempts at humor are too obvious. Twain seems to have better judgment than to write thus: "Bad language is another thing that the profession might spare a lot of, and still have enough remaining for all ordinary purposes. I remember one

night at —— we all agreed to fine ourselves a penny each time we swore. We gave it up after two hours' trial: none of us had any money left" (155–56).

²⁰ Similarly, Arthur Adcock's view: "Like every humorist, he takes life seriously; no man lacking a sense of humor can do that; unless he can also see the fun of things he cannot rightly see the sadness of them" (167).

²¹ The manuscript of this book, having been rejected by two or three magazines, was "purchased outright for five pounds, for serial purposes by the [journal] *Play*.... Publishers fought shy of it when it was offered as a book, and at last it was accepted as a gift by the Leadenhall Press [Field and Tuer] and duly made its appearance in 1885" (Adcock, 162).

²² Jerome must have noted how Twain and his American contemporaries relied on unusual coinages and eccentric spellings; the trait was widespread. See Pinkser, 186.

²³ For contemporary reviews of Jerome, see Carl Markgraf's "Jerome K. Jerome: An Annotated Bibliography of Writings About Him," *ELT* (*English Literature in Transition, 1880–1920*) 26 (1983): 83–132. There is also an update by Markgraf in vol. 30 (1987), 180–211.

²⁴ Similar enthusiasm for Jerome can be found in the same American journal's review of *The Observations of Henry*: "Mr. Jerome K. Jerome is a master merrymaker, with the exceptional quality of inoculating his joyousness. He has the true 'gaieté de coeur,' and is never anything else than decorous" (*The New York Times* [20 April 1901]: 272).

²⁵ For the texts of the eight papers, "Artemus Ward in London," see his *Complete Works* (Sydney, NSW: E. W. Cole, [n.d.]) 409–45.

²⁶ The "Robert" contributions in *Punch* are contemporary with Jerome's first success; these continue to ridicule funny spelling and speech among other classes. See, for example, "Robert on English and Foreign Waiters" which opens: "Well, things is cumming to a pretty pass, things is, when I'm acshally told that, as it used to be said formerly, 'No Hirish need apply for nothing,' so now, we are told, that no English Waiters need apply at the Royal Nawal Xhibishun unless he bes a German!" (*Punch* 100 [3 January 1891]: 239).

²⁷ One Baron de Book-Worms review claims that, but the publication history of Jerome suggests otherwise. In any case, there was a serious side to some of his other books and plays, though these have never attained the popularity of his lighter writings.

²⁸ Thomas Inge, however, reminds one of the admiration expressed by Thackeray for the humor of the old southwest, especially Hooper's *Some Adventures of Captain Simon Suggs* and Baldwin's *Flush Times* (8).

²⁹ Thackeray seized on the comic side of this movement [Sir Isaac Pitman's Spelling Reform] for whimsical spelling always delighted him" (Spielmann, 318). Thackeray's papers signed by "Fitz-Jeames de la Pluche" were first created in *The Britannia* (1841) as "Mr. Yellowplush, my lord's body-servant." The style was continued as a "Diary" series by the same Jeames's hand in *Punch* (1845).

³⁰ I have not been able to identify the source to which Spielmann refers.

³¹ Two obvious sources for American humor using strange spellings and speech, both of which antedate Thackeray, are: Thomas C. Haliburton, *The Clockmaker: or, the Sayings and Doings of Samuel Slick, of Slickville* (1837); and Seba Smith, *The Life and Writings of Major Jack Downing, of Downingville. Written by Himself* (1833).

³² Baron de Book-Worms & Co. in "Our Booking Office" deals with *Three Men in a Boat* and three other books (*Punch* 98 [1 February 1890]: 57). Further reviews of Jerome appeared in *Punch* (100 [3 January 1891]: 4) and, under the same "Our Booking Office" column, the Baron later takes a dismissive swipe at another Jerome book, *Diary of a Pilgrimage* (*Punch* 100 [16 May 1891]: 239).

³³ This was H. W. Lucy, then on the staff of *Punch*.

³⁴ For details of Jerome's difficult family circumstances and upbringing, see (in addition to his own autobiography, *My Life*) Faurot and Connolly.

³⁵ Interestingly enough, Burnand had also written a light piece describing a yachting

holiday in the Hebrides with four friends, "Another Little Holiday Cruise" in *Punch* (1 September 1887); he, too, describes people and places with humor, as Price reminds one (149–50). This may suggest a personal sense of jealousy over Jerome's public success with similar material.

[36] Some of these attempts at spoof will strike a modern reader as English schoolboy humor, as may be gleaned from the inventive titles. Rider Haggard was mocked via an invented "The Book of Kokarie" written by "Reader Faghard" (11); Jules Verne was ridiculed with supposed extracts from "Through Space on a Formula" by "Rules Spurn" (13). Other indicators of humor are with George Meredith being transformed to "George Verimyth" (3), R. D. Blackmore to "R. D. Exmore" (18), Kipling to "Kippierd Herring" (2) and Zola (perhaps inevitably so, granted the low caliber of punning) to "Gorgon-Zola" (14). Can it also be that the slang "OK" was already identifiably American?

[37] Non-British readers may need reminding that the dropped "H" (from Harry to 'Arry) is especially associated with working-class speech. Incidentally, Max Miller was a twentieth-century comedian of the music halls and of BBC radio, a Cockney who cheerfully used the popular sobriquet "the Cheeky Chappie."

[38] *Punch* 99 (4 October 1890): 157.

[39] 'Arry's parodic "contribution" capitalizes on this favored Jeromian slang word, "slavey," and is replete with slangy phrases such as "Well, I nevers ..." and even one enduring Cockney mispronunciation, an Alf Garnett-like "You don't know everythink!"

[40] "Three ha'porth" is a corruption of "three half-pennies' worth," that is, a very small amount in monetary worth, a common working-class expression and sometimes metaphorically applied.

[41] Among the slangy phrases in the first *Idler* collection, words like "shindy" (11) and "spiffin" (92), is a revealingly American colloquialism, "a one-horse town" (57) such as is found in Twain's "This poor little one-horse town" in *The Undertaker's Chat* (1875). While reviewing this book in the *Pall Mall Gazette*, one contemporary English critic made the link between Jerome's technique in *Idle Thoughts* and Twain's humorous exaggeration. See Markgraf, 107.

[42] One Victorian reviewer for a middle-class readership alerted his audience to unmistakable American humor but found the book a failure ("*Three Men in a Boat* and *Idle Thoughts of an Idle Fellow*," *Nation* 50 [17 April 1890]: 321). Alice Turner, among modern reviewers, finds Jerome's imitation of Twain shameless but nonetheless funny ("Have Sitcoms Killed Litcoms?" *Nation* 232 [28 March 1981]: 377–78).

[43] A curious sidelight on my comparison is that Jerome's *Three Men in a Boat* does traverse some of the specific concepts of a holiday, as mentioned by Twain in the opening page of *The Innocents Abroad*, as to what his grand picnic would avoid: "The participants ... instead of freighting ... a ferry boat with youth and beauty and pies and donuts, and paddling up some obscure creek to disembark upon a grassy lawn and wear themselves out with a long summer day's laborious frolicking under the impression that it was fun" (5).

[44] Clarence Gohdes concludes that by the middle of the nineteenth century, the fixed critical view was that the essence of American humor was exaggeration (qtd. in Blair and Hill, 40). Max Eastman had thought that exaggeration distinguished American humor from British, but he may have been thinking of middle-class humor in the manner of *Punch* (see Blair and Hill, 40).

[45] Jerome uses a character called Harris; Twain had used the name "Harris" for the agent in *The Innocents Abroad*.

Works Cited

[Anon.] "Books of Travel and Description." *Dial* 12 (August 1891): 103–104.
[Anon.] "One Man in a Coat." *Punch, or The London Charivari* 99 (4 October 1890): 157.
Adcock, Arthur St. John. *The Glory That Was Grub Street: Impressions of Contemporary*

Authors. 1928. New York: Books for Libraries Press, 1969.

Altick, R. D. *Punch: The Lively Youth of a British Institution*. Columbus, OH: Ohio State University Press, 1997.

Barsley, Michael, ed. *Modern American Humour*. London: The Pilot Press, 1942.

Batts, John. "American Humor: A Late Victorian View." *Whimsy* 5 (1987): 26–28.

Bier, Jesse. *The Rise and Fall of American Humor*. New York: Holt, Rinehart, & Winston, 1968.

Bishop, Charles. "Jerome K. Jerome's *Three Men in a Boat*." *Reprint Bulletin Book Reviews* 26.2 (1981): 16.

Blair, Walter, and Hamlin Hill. *America's Humor: From Poor Richard to Doonesbury*. New York: Oxford University Press, 1978.

Browning, D. C. *Everyman's Dictionary of Literary Biography—English and American*. London: Dent, 1960.

Covici, Pascal. "Mark Twain." Vol. 11. *Dictionary of Literary Biography*. Ed. Stanley Trachtenberg. Detroit: Gale, 1982. 526–55.

Clark, W. Bedford, and W. Craig Turner. *Critical Essays on American Humor*. Boston: G. K. Hall, 1984.

Connolly, Joseph. *Jerome K. Jerome: A Critical Biography*. London: Orbis, 1982.

Donelson, Ken. "Traits of Humor in the United States." *National Styles of Humor*. (The Study of Popular Culture series, no. 18). Ed. Avner Ziv. Westport, CT: Greenwood Press, 1988. 157–88.

Faurot, Ruth. *Jerome K. Jerome*. New York: Twayne, 1974.

Haliburton, Thomas C. *The Clockmaker; or, the Sayings and Doings of Samuel Slick, of Slickville*. 1837. Toronto: McClelland & Stewart, 1958.

Hall, Peter C. "Jerome Klapka Jerome." *Encyclopedia of English Humorists*. Ed. Steven Gale. New York: Garland, 1997.

Hart-Davis, Rupert, ed. *The Letters of Oscar Wilde*. London: Hart-Davis, 1963.

Henkle, Roger B. *Comedy and Culture: England, 1820–1900*. Princeton: Princeton University Press, 1980.

Inge, M. Thomas, ed. *The Frontier Humorists: Critical Views*. Hamden, CT: The Shoe String Press, 1975.

Jerome, Jerome K. *Diary of a Pilgrimage*. 1891. Gloucester, England: Alan Sutten, 1982.

———. *Idle Thoughts of an Idle Fellow: A Book for an Idle Holiday*. 1886. London: Tuer and Tuer, 1886; Arrowsmith, 1889 and 1928.

———. *My Life and Times*. 1926. London: The Folio Society, 1992; London: John Murray, 1983.

———. *On the Stage—and Off: The Brief Career of a Would-Be Actor*. London: Field and Tuer, The Leadenhall P; Simpkin, Marshall; Hamilton, Adams, 1885.

———. *Stage-land: Curious Habits and Customs of Its Inhabitants* with drawings by J. Bernard Partridge. London: Chatto & Windus, 1890.

———. *Three Men in a Boat: (To Say Nothing of the Dog)*. 1889. Bristol: J. W. Arrowsmith, 1899.

———. *Three Men on the Bummel*. Bristol: J. W. Arrowsmith, 1900.

———. *Tales Told After Supper*. London: Leadenhall Press, 1891.

Jerrold, Walter. *Douglas Jerrold and* Punch. London: Macmillan, 1910.

Lang, Andrew. *Lost Leaders*. Selected by Pett Ridge. London: Kegan Paul & Trench, 1889.

Markgraf, Carl. "Jerome K. Kerome: An Annotated Bibliography of Writings About Him." *ELT (English Literature in Transition, 1880–1920)* 26 (1983): 83–132.

Martin, Robert B. *The Triumph of Wit: A Study of Victorian Comic Theory*. Oxford: Clarendon Press, 1974.

Nilsen, Don, comp. *Humor in American Literature: A Selected Bibliography*. New York: Garland, 1992.

Palmer, Jerry. "Humor in Great Britain." *National Styles of Humor*. (The Study of Popular Culture series, no. 18). Ed. Avner Ziv. Westport, CT: Greenwood Press, 1988.

Pinkser, Sanford. "On or About December 1910: When Human Character—and American Humor—Changed." *Critical Essays on American Humor.* Ed. W. Bedford Clark and Craig Turner. Boston: G. K. Hall, 1984.

Prager, Arthur. *The Mahogany Tree: An Informal History of* Punch. New York: Hawthorne Books, 1979.

Price, R. G. G. *A History of* Punch. London: Collins, 1957.

Priestley, J. B. *English Humor.* 1929. New York: Stein and Day, 1976.

Pritchett, V. S. "The Tin-Openers." Rev. of *Three Men in a Boat. New Statesman and Nation* (15 June 1957): 783–84.

Robertson, John. "Yankeeana." *London and Westminster Review* 32 (1838): 137–45.

Russell, Leonard, ed. *English Wits.* 1940. Port Washington, NY: Kennikat Press, 1970.

Schmitz, Heinrich. "Kurt Schladenbach, Jerome K. Jerome, Fact and Fiction." *Neue Philologische Rundschau* 26 (1904): 620–21.

Smith, Seba. *The Life and Writings of Major Jack Downing* [pseud.], *of Downingville, Written by Himself away Down East in the State of Maine.* Boston: Lilly, Wait, Colman & Holden, 1933.

Spielmann, Marion H. *The History of* Punch. London: Cassell & Co., 1895.

Twain, Mark. *Letters of Mark Twain with a Biographical Sketch and Commentary.* Ed. Albert B. Paine. London: Chatto & Windus, 1920.

———. *The Innocents Abroad.* London: Robert Hayes, n.d.

———. *Roughing It.* New York: The New American Library, 1962.

Ward, Artemus. *The Complete Works of Artemus Ward (Charles Farrar Browne).* Sydney, NSW: E. W. Cole, n.d.

Welland, Dennis. *Twain in England.* London: Chatto & Windus, 1978.

The Wellesley Index to Victorian Periodicals: 1824–1900.

6

Humor as Daughterly Defense in *Cranford*

Eileen Gillooly

> "She has married for an establishment, that's it. I suppose she takes the surgery with it," said Miss Pole, with a little dry laugh at her own joke. But, like many people who think they have made a severe and sarcastic speech, which yet is clever of its kind, she began to relax in her grimness from the moment when she made this allusion to the surgery.
>
> (Elizabeth Gaskell, *Cranford*)[1]

When, in 1865—nearly fourteen years after the first installment of *Cranford* had appeared in *Household Words* (1851–53)—John Ruskin wrote to Elizabeth Gaskell expressing his fondness for her novel, Gaskell responded with warm thanks and with a curiously amusing insistence upon the veracity of the book: "And it is true too, for I have seen the cow that wore the grey flannel jacket—and I know the cat that swallowed the lace, that belonged to the lady that sent for the doctor, that gave the emetic &c!!!" (*Letters*, 747). What is amusing about her response is not just its nursery rhyme cadence—its House-That-Jack-Built construction—but its evocation of a childish mode of perception and utterance. Although long since displaced in importance by adult thought processes (such as the logic of causation), the repetitive, associational mode of perception and formulation recalled here by Gaskell remains familiar and appealing, both in the psychological distance it offers to the reader and writer who have mastered and surpassed it and in the humor that results when that distance is momentarily abridged. Indeed, the humor of Gaskell's comment to Ruskin depends upon the reader's recognition of its inherently childish perspective.

Such a childish perspective similarly informs both the narrative and the humor of *Cranford*. The familiar yet peculiar world of the novel—its nostalgic, utopian community—is fashioned upon childhood memories viewed from a psychological distance. When that distance is both confidently achieved and temporarily suspended, humor occurs. The eccentricities of the Cranford inhabitants, for example, recalled from the safety of an adult perspective but recorded with the immediacy of a child's, become a laughing matter. So too, in a subtler way, does the episodic narrative structure of *Cranford*, which, built upon association and repetition, harks back to nursery-rhyme convention.

Although steeped in a child's perspective, the humor of *Cranford* is far from innocent. *Cranford* is neither a simple celebration of a pastoral childhood nor an elegy to a bygone way of life, but an ironically amused and amusing tale of an eccentric community told from the viewpoint of a younger, marginal participant. Marginality, no matter how eccentric the cultural community may be, entails isolation and estrangement, provoking frustration and often bitterness in those relegated to its territory. However, as Miss Pole illustrates in the epigraph to this essay, one may sidestep frustration by making a "joke" of its provocation. In this way, the humor of *Cranford* permits the narrative "to relax," to avoid "grimness," while at the same time expressing the pain of its narrator's marginal perspective—marginal not merely in relation to the narrative community but to nineteenth-century culture at large. It is this narrative perspective and the humor to which it gives rise that I wish to disclose in my discussion of *Cranford*.

Locating the Narrator

"In the first place, Cranford is in possession of the Amazons; all the holders of houses, above a certain rent, are women" (39). Although many readers have taken this opening statement of the novel to mean that the Amazons, the upper-middle class female householders of Cranford, form an oligarchy of sorts, the sentence, at least initially, states something quite different.[2] The Amazons may indeed be "in possession of" Cranford, but the sentence reads: "Cranford is in possession of the Amazons"—as though they were a captive population or a historical artifact. To be sure, the subsequent comment that "all the holders of houses, above a certain rent, are women" goes far to reinforce a reading of Amazonian possession; yet the fact remains that the authority of the Amazons, even as it is asserted, is likewise undercut.

Furthermore, despite their appellation, these Amazons' arena of action is domestic, not martial. Cranford is women's sphere become hegemonic; its inhabitants are described in the first pages of the novel in terms less befitting a troop of warriors than a bevy of hens. Their fighting consists of only "an occasional little quarrel, spirited out in a few peppery words and angry jerks of the head" (40), and their conversation constitutes a "clacking noise" (95). Their sole weapon appears to be "verbal retaliation," and their primary source of power to lie in frightening males of all ages: they frighten little boys away from their gardens and frighten gentlemen "to death" (39). Like the phallic Mother (psychologically endowed by the infant with omnipotence despite her relative lack of power in the Real), these latter-day Amazons are perceived as frightening, though their power is largely limited to that perception; they are in fact—or at least are rendered in humor—quite harmless.

Considering that *Cranford* is generally acknowledged to be a "charming" novel, chronicling the domestic adventures of a handful of loyal, kind-hearted women, we might well ask what purpose all this aggressive humor serves. Beyond the convention of the "mock heroic," what accounts for the textual impulse to make fun of the very women whom the novel celebrates? Any investigation of this issue must necessarily consider the generative source of the humor (that is, the narrator); but in most discussions of the novel, Mary Smith the narrator is curiously overlooked. Her neglect by literary critics, indeed, rivals the neglect Mary Smith the character habitually experiences at the hands of the Amazons.[3]

Part of this critical neglect is due to the difficulty of locating the narrator as a distinctive character in *Cranford*. She is not only linguistically evasive (she characteristically and ambiguously narrates with "we," and her infrequent use of "I" is remarkably impersonal), but disembodied: since the narrator remains unnamed until the last pages of the book, there is literally no identifiable body in which to place her. This being the case, the occasion of her naming is itself significant. Shortly following word of Miss Matty's bank failure, the narrator is singled out for the first time to attend a colloquy of the Cranford ladies. After she confirms for them Matty's financial ruin, Miss Pole speaks to her about their collective intention of providing Matty with an income:

> "Miss Smith," she continued, addressing me (familiarly known as "Mary" to all the company assembled, but this was a state occasion),... "our object in requesting you to meet us this morning, is, that believing you are the daughter—that your father is, in fact, her confidential adviser in all pecuniary matters, we imagined that, by consulting with him, you might devise some mode in which our contribution could be made to appear the legal due which Miss Matilda Jenkyns ought to receive from ——. Probably, your father, knowing her investments, can fill up the blank." (191–92)

Although "familiarly known as 'Mary,'" the narrator is first named by her patronym—an appropriate address not only because the occasion is a formal one, but because she owes her presence in the colloquy to her father. By including her in their meeting, the Cranford ladies acknowledge for the first time Mary's maturity; in calling her by name, they both confer upon her a legible identity and affirm her existence as a quasi-participant in Cranford society. However, both of these marks of recognition are dependent upon her status as her father's daughter: Mary Smith by any other name would not be in attendance. The Amazons want neither her

monetary contribution (though Mary's father is financially better able than
they to provide one) nor her personal advice (she is requested simply "to
devise a mode" for anonymous payment to Matty, and only after "consulting
with" her father). Rather, Mary is solicited solely for her daughterly access to
the authority of Mr. Smith, Miss Matty's "confidential adviser in all pecuniary
matters."

Well before she is called upon to make herself useful in this affair of
Matty's, the essentially functional nature of Mary's relationship to the
Amazons has manifested itself in a number of textual details. For example,
although the guest of honor at the card party that produces the famous
Johnson versus Dickens dispute (Deborah and Captain Brown championing
the merits of "the Great Doctor" and "Boz" respectively), Mary is rather
unceremoniously ordered by her hostess to "fetch ... *Rasselas*" (47). She is
frequently imposed upon to assist in household tasks and to execute shopping
errands in Drumble on behalf of the Amazons. Apart from her regular annual
visits, Mary inevitably makes her trips to Cranford in response to an
Amazonian summons or need, whether to deliver a purchase, to conduct a
business task (settling Matty's tea accounts and correspondence on a
quarterly basis), or to perform a delicate personal service (preparing Matty
for the birth of her servant Martha's baby). Once in Cranford, Mary functions
as a generally helpful, and silent, companion to the older women she visits.

Indeed, Mary Smith exists for the Amazons less as an individual, less as
a mature young woman with a self of her own, than as simply a type.
Deprived by fate, and by Gaskell, of daughters of their own, the Amazons
cast Mary in the role of surrogate: a dutiful nineteenth-century daughter,
always "prepared to comfort and cosset" (79), and, being single, useful in
caring for and assisting elder family members, particularly Miss Matty (in
whose house the narrator maintains a room for her "use in case of Miss
Matty's illness" [200]), but also Miss Pole and, before them, Miss Deborah
Jenkyns.

As contemporary accounts of the period make clear, limited extra-
familial activity and the Victorian ethos of self-sacrificing duty combined to
exert great pressure on young middle-class women to devote themselves to
the care and needs of other (especially male) family members.[4] In the case
of a spinster, such devotion was expected to continue as long as the needy
party survived. This cultural insistence on the selflessness of the unmarried
daughter surfaces in *Cranford* in the treatment of Mary Smith both as
subordinated character and elusive narrator and is reinforced by
interpolated stories of other textual daughters, such as the Brown sisters
and Deborah Jenkyns. Although neither Mary Smith nor her history is ever
explicitly under discussion, her narrative voice permeates the text.
Consequently, any struggle between self-denial and desire she experiences
will be most legible in her language: her language, that is, rather than her

story comprises the site of conflict. This being the case, not only her humor but other linguistic acts, such as the complex trope of the "eyes" in the following confession of her secret fear, provide ground for disclosing the aggression and frustration aroused by such conflict:

> Having braved the dangers of Darkness-lane, and thus having a little stock of reputation for courage to fall back upon; and also, I dare say, desirous of proving ourselves superior to men (*videlicet* Mr. Hoggins) in the article of candour, we began to relate our individual fears, and the private precautions we each of us took. I owned that my pet apprehension was eyes—eyes looking at me, and watching me, glittering out from some dull flat wooden surface; and that if I dared to go up to my looking-glass when I was panic stricken, I should certainly turn it round, with its back towards me, for fear of seeing eyes behind me looking out of the darkness. (147)

"Seeing eyes behind me looking out of the darkness" is a manifestation of the double (doppelgänger)—an uncanny experience founded on an unconscious recognition of oneself in the form of an Other: a self-recognition that is textually reinforced here by the implication, strong until the very last line of the passage, that the eyes that Mary fears are actually her own in reflection, "glittering out from some dull flat wooden surface" or observed in "my looking-glass." Psychoanalytic theory suggests that the double gives form to an early phase of narcissistic rage that, having become unacceptable to the maturing self, has long since been mastered (that is, repressed).[5] Accordingly, the appearance of the double in Mary's mirror represents a return of that primary anger, split off and rejected by the self as something alien to it and projected outward, onto the Other. At least part of what Mary fears, then, in the other's eyes (the Other's "I") is her own aggression.[6]

Through synecdoche and homonym (an I for an eye) and inversion (one I for an Other), Mary's fear of eyes also becomes a fear of herself. Her terror at being observed by eyes whose very presence, if not explicit intention, is felt to be aggressive calls into question the aggressive nature of her own observing: indiscretion, she tells us, is her "bugbear fault" (163). In terms of character, her cognizance of her aggression gives rise to anxiety (she becomes "panic stricken"); in terms of narrative, it results in humor, which contains and neutralizes that self-terrorizing aggression. Although the mechanics by which aggression becomes humor are far from explicit in this passage, recourse to another quite different Gaskell story of a double may shed glancing light on this transformative process.

"The Poor Clare" (1856) tells a story of sin, retribution, and redemption.[7] Bridget, a "wild and passionate" woman, rumored by her neighbors to be a witch, curses a stranger named Gisborne who has wantonly killed her beloved late daughter's dog. In doing so, she also unwittingly curses her only grandchild, Lucy (of whose existence she is unaware), causing an evil "Double" (361) of the young woman to spring into existence. This double, who roams the vicinity "always about some mischievous or detestable [that is, lascivious] work," impersonates the "pure" Lucy so successfully that even Gisborne, her father (though his cruelty is responsible for the double), comes quickly to shun his own daughter's presence as repugnant by association.

Banished from her father's house with her faithful nurse, Lucy is spotted by the unnamed male narrator of the story, who falls in love with her "pale, quiet, resigned look of intense suffering" (352). Soon, however, he encounters her double: first as "a peal of ringing laughter ... verging on boisterousness" (358); later, as an image lurking behind her, "a ghastly resemblance, complete in likeness, so far as form and feature and minutest touch of dress could go, but with a loathsome demon soul looking out of the grey eyes, that were in turns mocking and voluptuous" (362). Like the narrator of *Cranford,* this narrator is frightened by "eyes"; like Mary Smith, Lucy can only see those eyes in reflection:

> "I looked up in terror. In the great mirror opposite I saw
> myself, and right behind, another wicked, fearful self, so like
> me that my soul seemed to quiver within me, as though not
> knowing to which similitude of body it belonged." (361)

The intensity of conflict between these selves—the "pure," "resigned" self that goes by the name of Lucy and the "wicked, fearful self" called simply "IT" (363)—begets profound psychic confusion. Caught between internalized cultural demands for female chastity and passivity and the inexorable force of desire (the primal IT/Id) seeking an outlet for expression, Lucy's "soul," like the ego to which it corresponds, is unsure to which "self" it belongs.[8]

Lucy's father's murder of the dog and, more importantly, his sin against Lucy's mother (his "terrible deceit upon her" [366] led to her suicide) are responsible for Lucy's affliction; but because her grandmother has inadvertently called the double into existence, only she can remove it. Reversing the curse, which has resulted from a murderous wish ("my wishes are terrible—their power goes beyond my thought" [348]), requires more than Bridget's wishful thinking, however. Lucy can only be delivered from her double through her grandmother's forgiveness of her father's sins, forgiveness that is partially enacted by Bridget's penitential service in the cloistered religious order of the Poor Clares (hence, the title of the story).

If, as Lucy's nurse declares, this story shows how "'The sins of the fathers shall be visited upon the children'" (363), then it is evident that in this case the only children who suffer are daughters. Lucy not only acts as scapegoat for her father's crimes, but is exiled from society altogether because the mark of the punishment she endures—a splitting of the (female) self into angel and demon—violates, even while it enforces, the Law of the Father.[9] If patriarchal law demands control of female sexuality and speech, then Lucy, in splitting in two, both capitulates to that demand and thwarts it. Like her mother, Mary, another daughter who suffers death for transgressing the law in birthing her (presumably) illegitimate child, Lucy forfeits patriarchal recognition for exposing, in the form of IT/Id, how female sexuality and speech (in the form of IT's boisterous laugh) exceed and outwit phallocratic control, despite heavy psychic and cultural prohibitions against their expression.

Even Bridget ultimately suffers a daughter's fate. Because her uncontrolled speech has released her granddaughter's "demon," she too is implicated in "the sins of the fathers." However, unlike Gisborne, she alone bears the burden of atonement, which requires both that she enter a silent sisterhood and that she forgive the father's sins against her, her daughter, and her granddaughter. The Law of the Father, then, requires not only the (grand)mother's complicity for its enforcement, but her acceptance of wrongs perpetrated by that law upon her and her gender. In order to rid Lucy of her "demon," Bridget must sacrifice her own "passionate anger," "masterful spirit, and vehement force of will" (338). In submitting to the "laws" of the Poor Clares, she relinquishes not only her sexuality and speech, but indeed her selfhood: Bridget becomes Sister Magdalen. Thus, by the example of her own self-abnegation, the mother shows her daughters the way to compliance, duty, and selflessness, to becoming the saintly sister or the domestic angel who both forgives and enforces the law against her.

Although differing in strength, the doubles in "The Poor Clare" and *Cranford* are similar in kind. Lucy's IT may be explicitly more sexual than Mary Smith's, but aggression is common to both. Moreover, at least one mode by which that aggression is expressed is the same: laughter—whether in the mocking eyes and gestures of Lucy's double or in the narrative humor of *Cranford*—is the speech of the double, both an expression of repressed aggression and a response to cultural oppression.[10] Thus, unlike Lucy's double, Mary Smith's is actually twofold: represented not only by the eyes in the mirror but secondarily by her narrative humor. Maintaining the angelic Lucy and the compliant, dutiful Mary Smith requires a repression of primary aggression, which in turn engenders the demonic double and the frightening mirrored eyes. Arguably, the double is less powerful for Mary Smith simply because the aggression it represents finds partial relief and release in the narrative humor.

In other words, humor in *Cranford* arises in part from the narrative sublimation of Mary Smith's aggression—aggression provoked by the conflict between self-denial and desire, between the internalized cultural demand to submit oneself to the role of daughter and a psychological resistance to that demand. The role of daughter is in itself oppressive, particularly so in the nineteenth century, but in *Cranford*, where parent figures are at best inadequate (like Miss Matty) and at worst neglectful and disabling (like Mr. Smith or Deborah Jenkyns), that oppressiveness is aggravated by a sense of loss—the daughter's loss of nurturing—entailed in her becoming a parent to the parent, an affectionate caretaker of her needy surrogate mothers. Humor operates in *Cranford,* then, not only to give derivative expression to the anger at parent figures who prevent rather than assist the narrator to authority and selfhood, but also to defend against the pain invoked by the loss of adequate parenting. Abounding with images of disfigurement and sexual ambiguity, which I will discuss later, the humor discloses itself as a strategy of protection and retaliation against parental authority—authority that the humor reveals as arbitrary, tyrannical, and ultimately destructive of female selfhood.

The Amazons

Even though parents in *Cranford* are the targets of humorous aggression, they are also clearly figures of narrative affection. The Amazons, no matter how snobbish or silly they may be at times, remain fundamentally endearing old women. Moreover, some of these parents are, to use D. W. Winnicott's term, "good enough,"[11] if not exemplary—the deceased Mrs. Jenkyns and Captain Brown, for instance (although it should be noted that in their capacity as "good" parents, such characters are treated with poignancy and pathos, never with humor). Yet because humor has its very origins in ambivalence, constituting itself in the contained irresolution of contrary feelings and impulses, it represents its objects as both "good" and "bad," gratifying and frustrating. It maintains ambivalence, even while it masks and relieves the anxiety that ambivalence provokes. In this way, the Amazons are narratively experienced as a source of both (humorous) satisfaction and (unconscious) resentment.

In relation to the young Mary Smith, the Amazons are figures of apparent maternal authority. Their maternity, however, is not nurturing—they are, as the etymology of their name indicates, "without a breast"—and as we saw even in the opening pages of the novel, their authority is so restricted as to be a source of laughter. Furthermore, authority is theirs strictly by default: gentlemen who enter Cranford society, namely Captain Brown and Peter Jenkyns, assume, however briefly, its leadership. Largely derived as it is from their adherence to a "strict code of gentility" (109), Amazonian authority amounts to little more than the enforcement of class snobbery, a slavish devotion to rules, empty rituals, and archaic forms (Dr. Johnson, for example, is their stylistic model). And, although their "strict code of gentility" is traceable to Rector Jenkyns (noted for "laying down the law" [101]), and thus bears the mark of patriarchal approval, its application is limited to the body (bodies) of upper-middle class Cranford women, restrictively governing their (female) behavior. In this way, the "good-will" (40) that "reigns" in Cranford also reins in its female population.

> Then there were rules and regulations for visiting and calls; and they were announced to any young people, who might be staying in the town, with all the solemnity with which the old Manx laws were read once a year on the Tinwald Mount.
> ... "I dare say your mama has told you, my dear, never to let more than three days elapse between receiving a call and returning it; and also, that you are never to stay longer than a quarter of an hour."
> "But am I to look at my watch? How am I to find out when a quarter of an hour has passed?"
> "You must keep thinking about the time, my dear, and not allow yourself to forget it in conversation." (40–41)

The most authentic (though ultimately self-destructive) authority these women possess lies in silence. Their discourse is restricted by their "gentility" in its content and duration, but they transform this disability into a meager sort of power. They refuse not only to speak on certain subjects, but to acknowledge their existence altogether:

> We none of us spoke of money, because that subject savoured of commerce and trade, and though some might be poor, we were all aristocratic.... When Mrs. Forrester, for instance, gave a party in her baby-house of a dwelling, and the little maiden disturbed the ladies on the sofa by a request that she might get the tea-tray out from underneath, every one took this novel proceeding as the most natural thing in the world;... as if we all believed that our hostess had a regular servants' hall,... instead of the one little charity-school maiden, whose short ruddy arms could never have been strong enough to carry the tray up-stairs, if she had not been assisted in private by her mistress, who now sat in state, pretending not to know what cakes were sent up, though she knew, and we knew, and she knew that we knew, and we knew that she knew we knew, she had been busy all the morning making tea-bread and sponge cakes. (41)

Where silent disavowal fails to ward off the stark character of reality, euphemism generally succeeds. "Elegant economy" is the Cranfordians' description of the penury they suffer in having to eke out an existence from diminutive incomes, which they are prevented by gender and class from increasing through professional employment. Even while this description of their finances cheats the socioeconomic truth of the situation—that these women are hounded by worries of insolvency—it also disarms the pain of poverty, by making money seem ungenteel. Thus, Captain Brown, whose incursion into Cranford society occupies the greater part of the first two chapters of the novel, is rightly perceived by the Amazons as dangerous not merely because he is Other, but because he boldly flouts, however unwittingly, the silence and euphemism upon which their "strict code of gentility" and "elegant economy" are based:

> I never shall forget the dismay felt when a certain Captain Brown came to live at Cranford, and openly spoke about his being poor—not in a whisper to an intimate friend the doors and windows being previously closed; but, in the public street! in a loud military voice! alleging his poverty as a reason for not taking a particular house. The ladies of Cranford were already rather moaning over the invasion of their territories by a man ... [I]f, in addition to his masculine gender, and his connexion with the obnoxious railroad, he was so brazen as to talk of being poor—why! then, indeed, he must be sent to Coventry ... (42)

Eventually, however, the Amazons not only succumb to the masculine appeal of the invader, but elevate him to "an extraordinary place as authority among" them (43):

> It was on this subject; an old lady had an Alderney cow, which she looked upon as a daughter ... The whole town knew and kindly regarded Miss Betty Barker's Alderney; therefore great was the sympathy and regret when, in an unguarded moment, the poor cow tumbled into a lime-pit. She moaned so loudly that she was soon heard, and rescued; but meanwhile the poor beast had lost most of her hair and came out looking naked, cold, and miserable, in bare skin ... Miss Betty Barker absolutely cried with sorrow and dismay; and it was said she thought of trying a bath of oil. This ... proposal, if ever it was made, was knocked on the head by Captain Brown's decided "Get her a flannel waistcoat and flannel drawers, ma'am, if you wish to keep her alive. But my advice is, kill the poor creature at once."
> Miss Betty Barker dried her eyes and thanked the captain heartily; she set to work, and by-and-by all the town turned out to see the Alderney meekly going to her pasture, clad in dark grey flannel. (43–44)

Here jesting, which is trivial, whimsical, disruptive of sober discourse and, as such, an affront to the Law, attains a position of absolute authority. Analogically, such a heightened position raises the status of the jest throughout, lending authority to the humor of the narrative voice (as well as to Peter Jenkyns's pranks) and underscoring the serious implications of humor. Part of the joke about Betty Barker's cow is that she is a natural nurturer turned into an object of superfluous care by an unnurturing (breastless) mother. Similarly, the surrogate mothers of Cranford, as breastless Amazons, have reversed the natural order: they demand care and nurturing from children who themselves are deprived of sufficient care and nurturing. With the possible exception of the late Mrs. Jenkyns, whose mothering Matty recalls in an affecting anecdote, the women "above a certain rent" in Cranford are anything but adequately maternal: Matty Jenkyns is a perpetual child; Deborah Jenkyns is a version of her tyrannical father (a phallic mother); and Betty Barker and the widow Mrs. Jamieson are hysterically, hyperbolically maternal only to their pets. The only one among them who does become a mother (and, following her father's example, an apparently successful one) is Captain Brown's daughter, Jessie; she, however, must escape Cranford before doing so.[12]

Despite their very real charity toward each other and others (nursing Signor Brunoni through his illness, for example), not even their solicitude is exempt from humor. Intent upon showing her gratitude to the Cranford ladies for condescending to be entertained by a former shopkeeper, Betty Barker heaps her serving board high with delicacies ordinarily prohibited—because prohibitively expensive—at Cranford tea parties. "However, Mrs. Jamieson was kindly indulgent to Miss Barker's want of knowledge of the customs of high life; and, to spare her feelings, ate three large pieces of seed-cake, with a placid, ruminating expression of countenance, not unlike a cow's" (111). Besides mocking Mrs. Jamieson, this descriptive linking of Betty's imperiously lethargic guest with her own fashionably-clad Alderney calls into question the value of Betty's solicitude. Her anxious attention to Mrs. Jamieson not only mimics her maternal concern for her bovine "daughter," but, by association, is itself exposed as laughable and, like her mothering of the cow, misplaced.

A more appropriate candidate for maternal concern is Mary Smith. However, though Mary is considered by the Amazons to be a child, not just in her youth but years into her adulthood, she enjoys few of the benefits of such consideration while enduring its disadvantages. Excluded from active participation in Amazonian exploits primarily on account of her exaggerated child-status (she is past nineteen years of age when she is still obliged to look at picture books of sorts as the others play cards at Betty's tea party [112]), Mary also is excluded from the considerate attentions that the Amazons, under normal circumstances, show only to each other. In a community where affection is reserved for pets and petted petty aristocrats, Mary's lifelong designation as a child secures her chronic neglect.

The Amazons are narratively subjected to humor not only for their general lack of authority and maternity, but for their failure to guide and nurture their surrogate daughter to adulthood—a failure that, if Matty is any indication, is endemic to their community if not to middle-class Victorian culture. Often considered to be the most representative of the Cranford ladies, Matty is in some ways the least Amazonian of her cohorts.[13] She is not merely more timid and more easily befuddled than the others (excepting perhaps Mrs. Forrester), but in fact more childish—in her knowledge of the world, in her relations to others, in her latent sexuality. Matty "never could believe that the earth was moving constantly, and ... would not believe it if she could, it made her feel so tired and dizzy whenever she thought about it" (127). Servants and tradesmen spot her gullibility at a glance; some take advantage of her innocence, while others (like Martha, whose "tone to Miss Matty was ... that ... usually kept sacred for little children" [186]) work to protect her from the demands of reality. In general, "People would have felt as much ashamed of presuming on her good faith as they would have done on that of a child" (201).

Once the narrator has identified Matty as a child, she can then identify with her as such. Mary, from her earliest days in Cranford, has been "a favourite" of Matty's (66), and "dear Miss Matty" (218) is clearly a favorite of the narrator's. Their mutual regard is encouraged by their shared status as children, which places them together in submission to Deborah's authority and its legacy. From this position of subordination, they also share a humorous perspective, even though Matty's humor is sporadic and altogether unwitting. Matty, for instance, in leaving a copy of *A Christmas Carol* on the dying Deborah's nightstand, which Flora Gordon then looks at on the sly while reading aloud to Deborah from the *Rambler,* subversively, though not deliberately, undercuts her sister's authority as Mary's narrative commentary intentionally does throughout. Similarly, Matty's remark on her father's Napoleonic War sermons ("'I remember my father rather thought he should be asked to print this last set; but the parish had, perhaps, had enough of them with hearing'" [91]) innocently conveys the public's opinion of the Reverend's pomposity—an opinion heartily endorsed by the narrator ("he could hardly write a letter to his wife without cropping out into Latin" [88]).

The jokes that result from Matty's ingenuous responses to her situation as well as those that are narratively made about her naïvety, link her to the novel's two other children and jokesters, Mary Smith and Peter Jenkyns. Yet, because Mary and Peter are conscious wits as Matty is not, their humor elevates them *vis-à-vis* Matty, granting them an interpretive authority inaccessible to her. As in Freud's "Humour" (1928) where the subject acquires "superiority by assuming the role of the grown-up" and reducing "the other" to the role of child, the stance and strain of their attitude toward Matty is kindly parental, preserving her innocence and protecting her from frustration "as an adult [does] towards a child" (*Collected Papers*, 5: 218). Matty, by the end of the novel, bears much the same relationship to Mary as to Peter: his "little girl" is her "dear Miss Matty," placidly accepting her position as dependent child to both her younger brother and to her fondly anxious surrogate daughter.

The Dutiful Daughter in Drag—Mary Smith and Peter Jenkyns

While some readers consider that Peter—in returning from his self-imposed exile in India to care for Matty and to mediate Amazonian disputes whenever necessary—functions merely as Matty's representative (and thus that Matty is the real authority in Cranford), few if any have considered the ways in which Peter functions as a figure for the narrator.[14] Peter, for example, owes his *deus ex machina* reappearance in the novel to Mary; her letter, her authorship, calls him back into the world of Cranford. Furthermore, even though Peter is male and older than Mary and, upon his return to Cranford, more worldly and exotic than she, they share a childhood spent under patriarchal and Amazonian rule as well as a humorous perspective shaped by that circumstance. Though the textual representation of female selflessness demands the erasure of Mary Smith as both narrator and character, Peter Jenkyns, whose history complements hers, is able by virtue of the visibility of his gender to represent them both.

   As the youngest of the Jenkyns children and the only boy, Peter bears the weight of paternal expectations. Sent "to win honours at Shrewsbury school, and carry them thick to Cambridge, and after that" to settle into a clerical living provided by his aristocratic godfather, "Poor Peter" distinguishes himself only in "the art of practical joking" and is consequently forced to return to Cranford, where he studies under his disappointed father's tutelage (93). Although "like dear Captain Brown in always being ready to help any old person or child" (94), Peter nevertheless "seemed to think that the Cranford people might be joked about, and made fun of" (93), that "the old ladies in the town wanted something to talk about" (94). His joking becomes ever more bold, extending even to his own father, whom he fools "by dressing himself up as a lady that was passing through the town and wished to see the Rector of Cranford, 'who had published that admirable Assize Sermon'" (94). Although Peter is "awfully frightened" by his success at mocking his father with impunity ("more terrified than he ever was before" [94]), having done so once only increases his audacity, and he attempts an even more blatant attack on paternal authority. One day Peter dresses himself in Deborah's clothes and parades around the rectory gardens in view of a group of avid watchers, cuddling a pillow and cooing at it as though it were an infant. Discovered by his father, who flogs him in front of the gathered crowd, Peter flees home and joins the Navy, subsequently rising to the level of lieutenant. Although he once visits Cranford on leave, Peter remains abroad, making his fortune in India. Only some forty years later, upon receiving Mary Smith's letter informing him of Matty's lonely situation, does he return to Cranford permanently.

Peter's fate bears little resemblance to Mary Smith's. Although both are reared according to "the strict code of gentility" that obtains in Cranford, Peter is able (like Austen's Captain Wentworth) to escape its purview by going to sea and earning fame and fortune; Mary, however, like Anne Elliot, must submit to the domestic regime. While Peter establishes independence and authority outside of Cranford—first as a naval lieutenant, later as the Aga Jenkyns—and then transports it back into the community intact, Mary remains forever a child in the eyes of the Amazons, subject to a code of conduct that circumscribes, when it does not simply ignore, her existence.

Yet in spite of their dissimilar destinies, the child Peter—in his character and responses—anticipates Mary. Both children challenge the authority of their fathers and "the old ladies in Cranford" by mocking them: Peter through gross physical parody, Mary through cautious verbal humor. Late in the novel, the fastidiously circumspect Mary curiously remarks that "indiscretion" is her "bugbear fault" (163), suggesting that the lack of restraint—"the animal nature" (92)—characteristic of the young Peter is not foreign to her own character but simply better checked, contained by and in the rebellious counter-meanings of her humor. However compliant Mary appears, her spirit of "indiscretion" links her to Peter and to his active insurrection, his wildest pranks. Conversely, putting on drag transforms Peter into a female jokester. Both figures gain force in their association. Mary as narrator appropriates Peter's jokes and profits by them in the retelling; and Peter enacts more than Oedipal resentment in dressing as a woman to deride his father. In literalizing his identification with the feminine and devalued, he defies not just his father and family structure, but a cultural ideology that forbids such identification. Furthermore, as Peter appears unexpectedly before the townspeople of Cranford with a "baby" in his arms, so Mary appears unexpectedly before the leading lady of Cranford with a baby (Martha's) in hers. That Mary, although under very different circumstances, performs the identical scene of mock mothering for which Peter is flogged implicates her in his act of rebellion even while her own act remains feminine, normative, unexceptional. In this way, through their reflexive association, Mary the narrator's quiet little jokes about her father's temper or the Amazons' code of gentility participate on the sly in Peter's glaring affronts to his father and to the law (note: Peter's baby, being Deborah's, is perforce illegitimate) while Mary the character slips the responsibility—and the flogging—for such trespass.[15]

Humor serves Mary and Peter not only as a means of assault against patriarchal authority, but as a defense against the conscious knowledge of that assault. Since the mechanics of humor allow one to vent hostility while remaining blissfully unconscious of its motivation and significance—and therefore not fully responsible for its consequences (that is, the reception of one's jokes)—Peter can understand his cross-dressing as simply a public service, as providing "the old ladies in town" with "something to talk about" (94), rather than as an act of subversion. Although even Matty interprets his transvestism as intended "to plague Deborah" because she "vexed him," Peter himself "never thought" of his prank "as affecting her" (95). Moreover, because humor appropriates aggressive energy, constituting itself in the conversion of that energy, it defends against the pain that frustrated aggression usually provokes: it allows both Mary and the young Peter to give voice to their alienation from parental authority and affection while avoiding the evocation of loss usually associated with such an admission. Following the cue of their environment, Peter and Mary cast themselves in their jokes as children (ergo innocent) *vis-à-vis* withholding (ergo guilty) parental figures; in doing so, they effectively protect themselves from the wrath of the authority—external and internalized—that they subvert. It is only when Peter's "boy's trick" (96) fails, when it exceeds the indulgence allowed both to children and to dissension couched in humor, that he is punished for insubordination. Furthermore, it is only when his humor does fail to protect him, only when his behavior is perceived as a threat to authority (as Mary's never is), that he is accorded adult status. For unlike Mary, who remains a child throughout, Peter achieves manhood with his flogging: "'Peter came in, looking as haughty as any man—indeed, looking like a man, not like a boy'" (96).

Peter's jokes, however, do not cease with the onset of adulthood. His wildly exaggerated accounts of his adventures in India (he "told more wonderful stories than Sinbad the Sailor") are, like his youthful pranks, extravagant, ostentatious, phallic: "if we swallowed an anecdote of tolerable magnitude one week, we had the dose considerably increased the next" (211). Indeed, Peter so imposes upon the credulity of the Amazons that he convinces Mrs. Jamieson of his having once "shot a cherubim" (217). Mary's jokes, on the other hand, are generally so suppressed as to be barely noticeable. Even those that tend most toward ridicule are muted in effect, at least partially because the audience for them (unlike the audience for Peter's jokes) is limited to the reader. This is true of the jokes perpetrated by both Mary the narrator and Mary the character. When Betty Barker violates the Amazonian rule of elegant economy by serving her guests adequate portions of more than meager fare, the character makes the joke, but silently; the reading audience hears it only by secondary narrative report: "Another tray! 'Oh gentility!' *thought* I, 'can you endure this last shock?' For Miss Barker had ordered (nay, I doubt not, prepared ...) all sorts of good things for supper" (113; emphasis added).

Regardless of their differences in form, audience, and intention, the jokes fashioned by Peter and Mary (as character) share the fate of being habitually misunderstood by the Amazons. Like Captain Brown's advice regarding Betty Barker's cow, Peter's tall tales are taken as truth, while Mary's jokes are taken simply as lapses in feminine decorum:

> I had once said, on receiving a present of an elaborate pair [of garters], that I should feel quite tempted to drop one of them in the street, in order to have it admired; but I found this little joke (and it was a very little one) was such a distress to her [Matty's] sense of propriety, and was taken with such anxious, earnest alarm, lest the temptation might some day prove too strong for me, that I quite regretted having ventured upon it. (185)

Although Mary's sense of humor separates her from the Amazons, it enables her to read Peter correctly. When the town suspects Peter of amorous designs on Mrs. Jamieson, Mary is assured upon overhearing his cherubim-shooting tale that the town's suspicions are as false as his story. Not only does she decipher Peter's meaning (in killing the cupid-like cherubim he intends to kill the rumor of romance between himself and Mrs. Jamieson), but by virtue of the "twinkle" that Peter extends to her, she participates in the enjoyment of his joke as well. Like the relationship between the narrator and reader of humor, the alliance between Mary and Peter hinges upon their shared intellectual and affective understanding of humorous intention.

Narrative and Linguistic Humor—Tropes and Structure, Sub- and Surtext

Even more crucial to the pervasive humor of *Cranford* than the memorable contributions of its joking characters are the narrator's jokes—as distinct from those attributed to the thought or speech of the character Mary. While there is no significant discontinuity between the identity of Mary the narrator and that of Mary the character (that is, Mary when she plays a role in the narrative action), there is a distinction between the narrator's jokes, whose reception is restricted to the reading audience, and Mary Smith's jokes, whose audience potentially includes the other characters. Although some of the narrative jokes are aggressive—targeting the pretension of Deborah's Johnsonian letter-writing, for instance (when "Miss Jenkyns was evidently very much alarmed ... the first part of her letters was often written in pretty intelligible English" [90–91])—most are defensive, transforming potential hurt or pathos into more tolerable affect. Deborah's at first funny indignation at Captain Brown's preference for Dickens threatens to turn sour, when the narrative humor (at the semicolon) intervenes:

> He [Captain Brown] endeavoured to make peace with Miss
> Jenkyns soon after the memorable dispute I have named, by a
> present of a wooden fire-shovel (his own making), having heard
> her say how much the grating of an iron one annoyed her. She
> received the present with cool gratitude, and thanked him
> formally. When he was gone, she bade me put it away in the
> lumber-room; feeling, probably, that no present from a man who
> preferred Mr. Boz to Dr. Johnson could be less jarring than an
> iron fire-shovel. (50)

Distracting attention away from Deborah's mean-spiritedness by alluding to
the primal comedy of the Boz–Johnson feud, the humor cuts short our
growing irritation with Deborah's dismissive treatment of Brown and offers
laughter as a substitute response. Similarly, the narrator's joke about the
inconvenience of Matty's "candle economy" stands as an attempt at defense.
Her complaint of having missed the opportunity to "scorch" herself strives in
its hyperbole to reduce her actual annoyance:

> I had been very much tired of my compulsory "blind man's
> holiday," especially as Miss Matty had fallen asleep, and I did
> not like to stir the fire, and run the risk of awakening her; so I
> could not even sit on the rug, and scorch myself with sewing by
> fire-light, according to my usual custom. (84)

By curtailing the rise of anger and annoyance, which threaten to betray
bitterness, humor enables the narrator to attain a position of detachment
"seriousness," while peripherally gesturing to the source of resentment that
provokes its own existence. Deborah's coldness and Matty's indifference to
her visitors' needs are irritating in a general sense, but particularly so to the
narrator as character who suffers them on a daily and intimate basis.

The persona-protective quality of the narrator's humor extends even to the
linguistic fabric of the novel, to the tropes, signs, grammar, and other
discursive elements that comprise its means of circulation. However, being
widely dispersed throughout the text and, thus, conspicuous and accessible
only in an accumulative act of reading, this linguistic humor is both subtler
and more subversive than the jokes generated or related by the narrator.
Whereas the narrative humor is more or less "conscious" in its conception
and reception (the narrator and reader share an acute sense of its presence
and some immediate, if general, understanding of its significance), the
linguistic humor is "unconscious." Like dreams, it constitutes itself in
repetition and association, giving rise to clusters of words that together create
a pattern of subtextual significance, a pattern that exists independently of plot
and apparent thematics.

Foremost among these linguistic clusters is that of disfigurement or
castration. The Amazons are missing a breast, and Captain Brown is run over

by a (phallic) train. Both the postman and the tailor are lame, and Peter, sitting cross-legged, is compared to the tailor—as (indirectly) are the other Indian exotics who occasionally surface in Cranford. Matty notes in a letter that "a little child's arm" was once eaten by one of "Wombwell's lions" in Cranford (128); and the narrator reports that Matty and Mary "fell to upon the pudding" called a "lion *couchant*" (187). It is Matty also who is prevented from "disfigur[ing] herself with a turban" (129), while her father, the Rector Jenkyns (remotely recalling Oedipus), "disfigured his shirt-frill" with a "strange uncouth brooch" (195). This disfiguring brooch, moreover, links the "castrating" fathers of *Cranford*: it is passed from Matty's father to Mary's father (via their daughters) and includes, by its association with his lack of refinement, Matty's suitor, the "uncouth" Holbrook, in its passage (75). The Amazons, too, who brandish an "array of brooches" on state occasions— one evening the narrator counts "seven brooches ... on Miss Pole's dress" alone—are implicated as castrators or phallic mothers as well (120).

Cross-dressing and, consequently, sexual ambiguity likewise form a knot of association. Deborah wears a helmet; the Rector Jenkyns wears a frill; the umbrella "stick" wears a petticoat. Peter dresses up as a girl, and Betty Barker's daughter/cow—in grey flannel waistcoat and drawers—dresses androgynously. The Alderney cow, furthermore, in receiving nurturance rather than giving it, suggests some fellow beasts: the "ruminating" Mrs. Jamieson and her dog, Carlo, who guzzles cream ("which should have been ours") while her guests get only milk (124); the milk-greedy cat who swallowed in its haste Mrs. Forrester's soaking lace; and the lions— Wombwell's and *couchant*—devouring and devoured.

These knots of association, formed by the accretion of discrete humorous moments, participate both aggressively and defensively in the subtextual significance of the novel. The persistent trope of disfigurement, for example, suggests a narrative desire to destroy the object of its humorous aggression as well as a fear of the object's retaliation for its destructive wish (a fear interjected as guilt). Thus, the fathers and Amazons are aggressively maimed, while the "little child's arm" (metonymically, the narrator's instrument of inscription) is wounded in defensive, guilty self-punishment for its aggression—as is the audaciously derisive Peter, who carries the mark of his castration in his exoticism, his "difference." Although the fear of castration may signal an Oedipal component to the trope of disfigurement, the pervasive images of sexual ambiguity and devouring together suggest that the objects of humorous aggression—the withholding parents of *Cranford*—are in fact primarily pre-Oedipal, sexually undifferentiated, figures. Their withholding inspires both rage—evinced in a desire to bite, to devour (as in Matty's and Mary's devouring of the lion *couchant* and the animal pseudo-children's voracious guzzling)—and a sense of loss and frustration: that "which should have been ours" (nurturance) is withheld (the surrogate mothers of Cranford are breastless). And yet, the pre-Oedipal alternative to withholding, the overwhelming presence of the Mother figure, inspires its own fears: the fear of engulfment, of non-individuation (of the mirrored eyes/I's), of being devoured—of Womb/well's lion.

Not only these knots of signifying tropes, which contribute substantively to the shape and texture of the narrative, but the narrative structure itself—its ordering of event and commentary—contains within its form the ambivalent responses provoked by the objects of humor.[16] Like the "charm" of *The Pickwick Papers,* an episodic narrative saturated with comic humor and interpolated with stories of patricide (in which the children are always abused and the fathers always wicked), the "charm" of Cranford depends in part on the repression of aggression in the text at large and on its limited expression both in humor and in tales of violence, such as "the horrid stories of robbery and murder," "rummaged up, out of the recesses of their memory" (141) by Matty and Miss Pole.[17] These tales, like the instances of humor, serve not only as outlets of aggression at the "bad" parents who withhold nurturance and guidance but as defenses against the frustration and guilt aroused by such aggression. Confined to a joke or a ghost story, aggression cannot harm the "good" parents cherished by the narrative proper.

Conveniently, the narrator herself confirms the ambivalence embedded in the narrative structure and tropes. A third of the way into the novel, at the beginning of the chapter entitled "Old Letters," the narrator comments on the idiosyncratic nature of hoarding: "Almost every one has his own individual small economies—careful habits of saving fractions of pennies in some one peculiar direction—any disturbance of which annoys him more than spending shillings or pounds on some real extravagance" (83). Such small economies function psychologically as a way to cope with anxiety, by delimiting an area of often compulsive control, distinct from, though linked associatively with, the actual source of overwhelming anxiety:

> I am not above owning that I have this human weakness myself. String is my foible. My pockets get full of little hanks of it, picked up and twisted together, ready for uses that never come. I am seriously annoyed if any one cuts the string of a parcel, instead of patiently and faithfully undoing it fold by fold. How people can bring themselves to use India-rubber rings, which are a sort of deification of string, as lightly as they do, I cannot imagine. To me an India-rubber ring is a precious treasure. I have one which is not new; one that I picked up off the floor, nearly six years ago. I have really tried to use it; but my heart failed me, and I could not commit the extravagance. (83)

String, according to Winnicott, symbolically functions "as an extension of all other techniques of communication." On the one hand, string communicates (connects) by joining or securing one thing to another, by holding together "unintegrated material" (22, note 12). Thus, an obsession with string clinically suggests "a fear of separation": an attempt to tie or secure the self to its source of nurturance (to recreate the umbilical cord) and to deny separation by re-enacting oneness (20). On the other hand, string communicates (expresses, informs) by symbolizing in its visible presence the desire for connection. Thus, an obsession with string textually suggests other manifestations or "techniques of communication"—such as letters (in the sense both of correspondence ["Old Letters"] and of marks of inscription)— that forge connection by their visible, (doubly) literal presence. Like string, these other techniques of communication defend against the frustration of separation and against the pain associated with the loss of nurturance by offering themselves as substitute satisfactions for oneness.

In this sense, the narrative of *Cranford*, strung and knotted together by the association and repetition of trope and event, loosely tied by episodic moments rather than driven by inexorable plot, stands as an attempt to connect with the lost source of nurturance, the pre-Oedipal mother (who, despite a number of Amazonian surrogates, is clearly absent in this text). Put another way, in being pre-Oedipal, nonlinear, nonphallocentric, the narrative denies the authority of the Law that has superseded the Mother's presence: it enacts this denial in its encoded discourse of loss, anger, and ambivalence, in its narrative structure, and—in its emphasis on mother/daughter (Amazon/narrator) activities and its lack of nuptial closure—even to some degree in its thematic content.

Although a fetish for string may be understood as a means to communicate, to compensate for loss, and to negotiate frustration, understanding why the narrator's heart should fail her when she tries to use an "India-rubber ring" requires a shift of focus from subtext to surtext. According to Winnicott, when string represents a denial of separation, aggression is its hallmark. String serves then not only as a means to express the lost connection with the mother, but also to retaliate against the person held responsible for the loss. In Winnicott's case, a boy obsessed with string, ties a string "round his sister's neck (the sister whose birth provided the first separation of this boy from his mother)" (20). In Gaskell's case, a narrator, obsessed with string, strings together a text that in its form and substance defies the Law: the paternal principle that has replaced the mother's presence and that dictates (among other things) how texts should be written.[18] Hence, the aggressive use of string in *Cranford* constitutes a narrative attack on authority—authority that is surtextually located in the person of Dickens.

If string is metonymy for Gaskell's narrative technique, and is, as J. Hillis Miller has suggested, in contrast to what one might call the rubber-band, full-circle narrative of Dickens, then the female narrator's preference for string represents not only a defense against loss and anxiety, but also an aggressive undermining of the authority of the prime male practitioner of "rubber-band narrative" and of the culture that privileges it.[19] Having picked up a rubber band "nearly six years ago" (and *Mary Barton*, begun nearly six years earlier, is a rubber-band narrative), the narrator tells us that she "could not commit the extravagance," could not be so imprudent, so unrestrained, as to use it. Although her excuses for not using a rubber band are overvaluation ("a precious treasure") and lack of courage (her "heart failed" her), "extravagance" suggests that there is something improvident, even morally wrong, about availing herself of "India-rubber rings, which are a sort of a *deification* of string" (emphasis added): which represent, in other words, that which surpasses string, an embodiment of the Father, an exaltation of his Law. Prudence and self-interest lie, rather, in string itself: in the tie to the pre-Oedipal Mother.

Gaskell's undercutting of Dickens and male authority is not limited to her narrator's rejection of his "rubber-band" model of narrative; Dickens himself is specifically lampooned at a number of points in the text. Captain Brown is not only killed for reading *The Pickwick Papers*—which as Nina Auerbach points out are the memoirs of a misogynist club, in contrast to the Amazonian community of Cranford—but he is killed in the same manner as Dickens's Carker, who met his demise three years earlier in *Dombey and Son*.[20] Moreover, in the famous contest between Dr. Johnson and Boz, the stylistic and moral authority of the eighteenth century, in Cranford at least, triumphs over his nineteenth-century literary successor. Although Johnson's victory is certainly a hollow one (jokes about Johnsonian style are a staple of the novel's humor), Dickens's defeat is no less of one for that. Johnson may not be an appropriate model for writing daughters, but neither, the text implies, is Dickens.

Gaskell's digs at Dickens—impugning his authority as a literary model, parodying his plot device for getting rid of Carker, murdering him by association when she has Captain Brown killed for reading *The Pickwick Papers*—are astonishing in themselves, but particularly so when we remember that *Cranford* was originally published in Charles Dickens's *Household Words*. Furthermore, while the contributions to *Household Words* were published without bylines, the name "Charles Dickens" literally appeared on every page. Besides being flattered by Gaskell's lionizing him as a literary authority, Dickens, it seems, was also sensitive to the subversive aspect of such treatment: to the possibility that the lion *couchant* was being secretly attacked. In his capacity as editor, he removed all references to himself in *Cranford*, substituting them with those to his contemporary Thomas Hood. Gaskell furiously objected to the substitution and attempted (unsuccessfully) to withdraw *Cranford* from *Household Words* altogether.[21]

Dickens's substitution thwarted Gaskell on two fronts. It weakened the aesthetic integrity of the installment (Hood, unlike Dickens, was no match for

Dr. Johnson), and it constituted a blatant affront to Gaskell's authorship. Although, as editor and publisher, Dickens was clearly entitled to make changes where he saw fit, his rather too comfortably assuming the role of mentor to Gaskell, of Father to daughter, or to use his own analogy of Sultan to "Scheherazade" roused her resentment—resentment, however, which Gaskell, like Mary Smith in relation to Amazonian authority, allowed expression only in humor.[22] In the first book edition of *Cranford*, Gaskell was able to reinstate Boz, but there, without the contextual frame of her anonymous article appearing underneath the rubric "Charles Dickens"—of her voice subsumed by and thereby undermining that of the Father—some of the complexity of her humorously subversive treatment of Dickens and of the cultural authority he represented was inevitably lost.

No matter how personal the provocation for Gaskell's attack on Dickens, the conflict represented by that attack—the daughter's urge for selfhood struggling with internalized cultural demands for female selflessness—was common to legions of other nineteenth-century middle-class daughters. Although denied overt expression in a culture that disallowed female perspectives generally, such daughterly conflict yet finds voice in the humor of *Cranford*: not only in Gaskell's battle of authorship with Dickens, but in the challenge her young female narrator's viewpoint presents to Amazonian authority and in the pre-Oedipal ambivalence embedded in the tropological and narrative structures of the text. Circumventing prohibitions against (female) anger—whether at the prohibiting culture or at the withholding parental figures who represent it—humor gives the daughter's anger derivative utterance even as it defends against both the guilt provoked by her anger and the pain engendered by cultural and familial neglect. In so doing, humor may be said to function less as a reaction to anxiety and conflict than as their means of transformation: rather than simply warding off the pain of daughterly frustration, the humor of *Cranford* miraculously converts it—for reader as well as writer—into a positive source of both psychological enjoyment and aesthetic satisfaction.

Notes

[1]   Elizabeth Gaskell, *Cranford/Cousin Phillis*, 167. Subsequent page references to *Cranford* appear parenthetically in the text.

[2]   See, for example, Auerbach, 79.

[3]   Peter Keating is an exception. The narrator "is by no means anonymous. Her individuality is fixed from the beginning and plays an important part in establishing *Cranford*'s distinctive tone. By making her a woman Mrs. Gaskell allowed her access to the inner lives of the Amazons ... and by emphasizing her youth and connections with industrial Drumble it was possible to heighten the strangeness of Cranford's way of life by a subtle mixture of ironic distancing and affectionate concern" (14). Although he locates the narrator as the source of humor in *Cranford*, Keating refrains from exploring the various implications that arise from such a location.

⁴ See, for example, Florence Nightingale's autobiographical *Cassandra: An Essay*, as well as Josef Breuer and Sigmund Freud, *Studies on Hysteria*. Sarah Stickney Ellis's series of conduct books—*The Women of England, Their Social Duties and Domestic Habits*; *The Wives of England, Their Relative Duties, Domestic Influence, and Social Obligations*; *The Daughters of England, Their Position in Society, Character and Responsibilities*; and *The Mothers of England, Their Influence and Responsibility*—and others like them gave specific, detailed directions on how to serve most selflessly in the domestic roles available to women. Patsy Stoneman reports that *"The New Female Instructor, or Young Woman's Guide to Domestic Happiness, Being an Epitome of all the Acquirements Necessary to Form the Female Character* ... went through six editions between 1811 and 1836, the period of Elizabeth Gaskell's girlhood" (53); furthermore, like Deborah Jenkyns, *"The New Female Instructor* quotes Johnson's letters *verbatim* as models" (89).

⁵ See Freud, "The 'Uncanny'" in *The Standard Edition of the Complete Works of Sigmund Freud*, hereafter abbreviated *SE*); Jacques Lacan, "The Mirror Stage as Formative of the Function of the I" and "Aggressivity in Psychoanalysis" in *Ecrits*, 1–7 and 8–29, on the issue of primary aggression and *imagos*; and Melanie Klein, "Infantile Anxiety Situations Reflected in a Work of Art and in the Creative Impulse (1929)" and "A Study of Envy and Gratitude (1956)" in *The Selected Melanie Klein*, 84–94 and 211–29, on object splitting and its relation to infantile rage.

⁶ For Lacan, the mirrored self is the first Other (in both time and importance). He argues in "The Mirror Stage" that identification with the image in the mirror—the "specular I"—precedes identification with the other—the "social I." Such being the case, the "specular I," which totalizes pre-ego fragments, contradicts the later (false) sense of an incipient, emergent self (associated with the "social I") and stands as evidence that identity is by definition self-alienating, that the ego agency from the beginning is located in "a fictional direction," in its symbolization as the image in the mirror. For an interesting discussion of Gaskell's use of the Mother as mirror and of the mirror/Mother as the daughter's initiation into difference, see Homans, 251–76.

⁷ Elizabeth Gaskell, "The Poor Clare" in *The Works of Mrs. Gaskell* 5: 334. Subsequent page references to "The Poor Clare" appear parenthetically in the text.

⁸ Not only is the presence of Lucy's double signified in the same way as is the presence of Bertha Rochester in Charlotte Brontë's *Jane Eyre*—first as a laugh, then as a mirror image—but Bertha functions much in the same capacity for Jane as the IT does for Lucy. Moreover, the description of Lucy's first glimpse of her double in the mirror inverts that of Jane's first glimpse of her mirrored self in her bridal attire: "I saw a robed and veiled figure, so unlike my usual self that it seemed almost the image of a stranger" (252). For a discussion of Bertha as Jane's double, see Sandra Gilbert and Susan Gubar, 336–71.

⁹ Maureen T. Reddy's "Female Sexuality in 'The Poor Clare': The Demon in the House" discusses the angelic/demonic splitting of the female self as a comment on Victorian culture. Homans, too, points out the splitting of the female self in "The Poor Clare," though her emphasis is on how the mirrored Lucy literalizes the psychic split between female goodness and badness.

¹⁰ See Hélène Cixous's "The Laugh of the Medusa," 245–64.

·¹¹ See Winnicott, 11. The term, however, has such circulation as to have inspired the title of Bruno Bettelheim's *A Good Enough Parent: A Book on Child-Rearing*.

¹² According to some, the Amazons, although admittedly lacking children, demonstrate their maternal instincts in their compassion and sisterly affection for one another. See, for example: Auerbach, 77–97; Lansbury, 83–94; Wolfe, 162–76; and Nestor, 43–56. For a more general discussion of the importance of sororal empathy to narratives of female community, see Zagarell.

¹³ Some readers (Auerbach and Wolfe among them) go so far as to see Matty not only as Queen of the Amazons, but as the heroine of the novel. Auerbach, even while admitting

that the novel is about community (hence the title of her book), elevates Matty to the status of heroine because, as she sees it, Matty's values become the adopted platform of Cranford society, replacing those of Deborah's administration. Edgar Wright in *Mrs. Gaskell: The Basis for Reassessment* ignores the communal subject entirely.

[14]   On the issue of Peter as Matty's adjutant, see Auerbach and Wolfe.

[15]   The association between Peter and Mary extends beyond their characterological similarities to their semiotic significance. Both are marked by gender as Other: Mary in her native femaleness and Peter in "putting on" the accoutrements of such. Peter's transvestism, however, signals only one aspect of his representation of otherness. As the Aga Jenkyns, he is (like Signor Brunoni and the Bluebeardian Hindu servant before him), "'so very Oriental,'" a "cross-legged" Indian who mesmerizes the Amazons with his fantastically tall tales (he "was quite as good as an Arabian Night any evening") and conjures up the unbelievable: the appearance of Mrs. Jamieson and Mrs. Fitz-Adam at the same social event (211). Like Brunoni, Peter must be foreign in order to be considered Other in Cranford; that is, in order for the females of Cranford to be normative, the males must be marked *other*wise. Since middle-class white men are the standard by which difference is judged, they necessarily dominate and define deviance in the context in which they appear (as Captain Brown, before he is killed off, is in danger of doing in Cranford). Thus, Cranford signifies a community of women only because its visible male inhabitants are racially or socially "deviant."

[16]   On the importance of "incremental repetition" of event to the narrative structure of *Cranford*, see Boone, 286.

[17]   Miss Pole's story of the bleeding sack is particularly memorable among these tales of violence in having as its aggressor a daughter who murders without guilt or punishment: "One of the stories ... was of a girl, who was left in charge of a great house when the other servants all went off to the gaieties. The family was away in London, and a peddler came by, and asked to leave his large and heavy pack in the kitchen, saying he would call for it again at night; and the girl (a gamekeeper's daughter), roaming about in search of amusement, chanced to hit upon a gun hanging up in the hall, and took it down to look at the chasing; and it went off through the open kitchen door, hit the pack, and a slow dark thread of blood came oozing out. (How Miss Pole enjoyed this part of the story, dwelling on each word as if she loved it!) She rather hurried over the further account of the girl's bravery, and I have but a confused idea that, somehow she baffled the robbers with Italian irons, heated red hot, and then restored to blackness by being dipped in grease" (141–42). The daughter's phallic weapons and Miss Pole's relish in telling the story are memorable as well.

[18]   Gaskell asserts that "the dear and tender *tie* of Mother and Daughter passeth every earthly love" (*"My Diary,"* 5; emphasis added): mother's love, in other words, is supreme next to that of the Father. A remarkably progressive childrearer, Gaskell is nevertheless obsessed throughout *"My Diary"* with curbing her infant daughter Marianne's obstinacy, presumably because obstinacy, being prohibited by Law (especially in females), will result in her loss. The Father, that is, will punish Gaskell by reclaiming custody of Marianne's soul if either Marianne or she, in her too strong attachment to Marianne, is obstinate; in such a case the Father (Law) will intervene in the love between mother and daughter by replacing the Mother (and her presence) and by appropriating the child to Himself. Gaskell thus prays that she not make "an idol" of her daughter for fear of losing too severely when the Father calls her (punitively or not) to Him.

[19]   J. Hillis Miller, "Tropes and the Narrative Line in Elizabeth Gaskell's *Cranford*," a paper presented at the Modern Language Association Convention, 1986. The exception within Dickens is, of course, *The Pickwick Papers*, which, although a strung-together narrative, is uncharacteristic of Dickens generally and in contradistinction to his "rubber-band" style. If Gaskell, having once written a rubber-band narrative, has temporarily sworn them off, Dickens, having once written a string-tied narrative, has conversely followed suit. Prefiguring Miller's rubber band, Judith Little distinguishes between

women's humor (which "mocks the deepest possible norms") and men's "rounded-off comic fiction" (1).

[20] Auerbach, 81–82.

[21] In a letter dated 4 December 1851, Dickens apologizes:

> I am truly concerned for this [substitution], but hope you will not blame me for what I have done in perfect good faith. Any recollection of me from your pen cannot (as I think you know) be otherwise than truly gratifying for me; but with my name on every page of *Household Words*, there would be—or at least I should feel—an impropriety in so mentioning myself ... I would do anything rather than cause you a minute's vexation arising out of what has given me so much pleasure, and I sincerely beseech you to think better of it, and not to fancy that any shade has been thrown on your charming writing, by—The unfortunate but innocent. (Qtd. in Hopkins, 107)

Dickens himself was aware that his demonstration of power over Gaskell did not go unnoticed for what it was. In a letter to Gaskell, he comments that she was always unkindly suspecting "soft sawder in the purest metal of [his] praise" (21 December 1851; qtd. in Gerin, 120). Adopting the role of (unwanted) mentor, Dickens often made unsolicited suggestions about the plotting of her stories—well-intentioned suggestions that were increasingly looked upon by Gaskell with annoyance. By the last installment of *North and South* (the last major work she would publish with him), their relations were severely strained. Exasperated by her tardiness in submitting installments, Dickens remarked to his sub-editor, "If I were Mr. G. Oh Heaven how I would beat her!" (qtd. in Hopkins, 152). Gaskell, in turn, not only refused to write any faster, but became less circumspect about her poor opinion of Dickens's critical judgment. According to Angus Easson, "'good enough for Mr. Dickens' came to be a pejorative self-criticism" (41).

[22] Dickens, letter to Gaskell of 25 October 1851 (qtd. in Gerin, 123). Like Scheherazade (the author of the Sinbad and Amine stories referred to in *Cranford*), Gaskell spun installments of *Cranford* at Dickens's request, the first installment having been originally intended by Gaskell as a discrete story.

Works Cited

Auerbach, Nina. *Communities of Women: An Idea in Fiction.* Cambridge: Harvard University Press, 1978.

Bettelheim, Bruno. *A Good Enough Parent: A Book on Child-Rearing.* New York: Vintage, 1988.

Boone, Joseph Allen. *Tradition Counter Tradition.* Chicago: University of Chicago Press, 1987.

Breuer, Josef, and Sigmund Freud. *Studies on Hysteria.* New York: Basic Books, n.d.

Brontë, Charlotte. *Jane Eyre.* New York: Norton, 1971.

Cixous, Hélène. "The Laugh of the Medusa." In *New French Feminisms: An Anthology.* Eds. Elaine Marks and Isabelle de Courtivron. Amherst: University of Massachusetts Press, 1980. 245–64.

Easson, Angus. *Elizabeth Gaskell.* London: Routledge, 1979.

Ellis, Sarah Stickney. *The Women of England, Their Social Duties and Domestic Habits.* London: Fisher, Son & Co., 1839.

———. *The Wives of England, Their Relative Duties, Domestic Influence, and Social Obligations.* New York: Appleton, 1843.

———. *The Daughters of England, Their Position in Society, Character and Responsibilities.* New York: Appleton, 1844.

Ellis, Sarah Stickney. *The Mothers of England, Their Influence and Responsibility.* New York: Appleton, 1844.

Freud, Sigmund. "The Uncanny." In *The Standard Edition of the Complete Works of Sigmund Freud.* Vol. 18. Trans. and ed. James Strachey. London: Hogarth, 1961. 219–52.

———. "Humour." In *Collected Papers.* 5 vols. New York: Basic Books, 1959. 5: 215–21.

Gaskell, Elizabeth. *Cranford/Cousin Phillis.* Harmondsworth: Penguin, 1969.

———. *"My Diary": The Early Years of My Daughter Marianne.* London: privately printed by Clement Shorter, 1923.

———. *North and South.* Harmondsworth: Penguin, 1996.

———. *The Letters of Mrs. Gaskell.* Ed. J. A. V. Chapple and Arthur Pollard. Manchester: Manchester University Press, 1966.

———. *The Works of Mrs. Gaskell.* 8 vols. London: Smith, Elder, & Co., 1906.

Gerin, Winifred. *Elizabeth Gaskell: A Biography.* Oxford: Oxford University Press, 1980.

Gilbert, Sandra, and Susan Gubar. *The Madwoman in the Attic: The Woman Writer and the Nineteenth-Century Literary Imagination.* New Haven: Yale University Press, 1979.

Homans, Margaret. *Bearing the Word: Language and Female Experience in Nineteenth-Century Women's Writing.* Chicago: University of Chicago Press, 1987.

Hopkins, A. B. *Elizabeth Gaskell: Her Life and Work.* London: John Lehmann, 1952.

Keating, Peter. Introduction. *Cranford.* Harmondsworth: Penguin, 1976.

Klein, Melanie. *The Selected Melanie Klein.* Ed. Juliet Mitchell. New York: Free Press, 1986.

Lacan, Jacques. *Ecrits: A Selection.* New York: Norton, 1977.

Lansbury, Coral. *Elizabeth Gaskell: The Novel of Social Crisis.* New York: Barnes & Noble, 1975.

Little, Judith. *Comedy and the Woman Writer: Woolf, Spark and Feminism.* Lincoln: University of Nebraska Press, 1983.

Miller, J. Hillis. "Tropes and the Narrative Line in Elizabeth Gaskell's *Cranford.* Paper presented at the Modern Language Association Convention, New York, 1986.

Nestor, Pauline. *Female Friendships and Communities: Charlotte Brontë, George Eliot, Elizabeth Gaskell.* Oxford: Oxford University Press, 1985.

Nightingale, Florence. *Cassandra: An Essay.* Old Westbury, NY: Feminist Press, 1979.

Reddy, Maureen T. "Female Sexuality in 'The Poor Clare': The Demon in the House." *Studies in Short Fiction* 21 (1984): 259–65.

Stoneman, Patsy. *Elizabeth Gaskell.* Brighton, Sussex: Harvester Press, 1987.

Winnicott, D. W. *Playing and Reality.* Harmondsworth: Penguin, 1980.

Wolfe, Patricia. "Structure and Movement in *Cranford.*" *Nineteenth-Century Fiction* 23 (1968): 162–76.

Wright, Edgar. *Mrs. Gaskell: The Basis for Reassessment.* Oxford: Oxford University Press, 1965.

Zagarell, Sandra A. "Narrative of Community: The Identification of a Genre." *Signs* 13 (1988): 498–527.

7

Dickens's Dystopian Metacomedy:
Hard Times, Morals, and Religion

Joseph H. Gardner

I make no apology for the title, especially as it once was "The Modicum is the Massage: *Hard Times* and the Homeric Doodle in Dystopia." But Dickens and dystopias, metacomedy and God as well? In a book on Victorian humor?[1] Surely that is a grotesque enough project, and punishment enough in itself for any disrespect not meant either in the title or in the direction this inquiry will take. Utopias, anti-utopias: both are escapism. Mr. Thomas Gradgrind, secular puritan potentate of Coketown and perfect embodiment of Carlyle's chief bogy, the ruthless logic-grinder, has peremptorily said as much. The Utilitariat had condemned all fantasies as the enemies of the one and only one thing needful, capitalism. Fiction can never be approved by either the Benthamite or the Baptist: it smacks of lying. Hence Utilitarianism, like the fundamentalism it is, always makes trouble for religion because it questions theology.

In *Hard Times*'s first phase, Dickens might have admitted that ancient dogma and the latest fancy, moral rules, and imaginary extravagances, had nothing to do with each other. *Hard Times* explores the Industrial Revolution's most daring speculation and wildest hope. The boom of Manchester's mills, considered by Carlyle to be as sublime as Niagara, spoke of an all-absorbing fascination with the machine. It was the man in the machine, the machine in the man, and not the *deus ex machina*, who was to be the master of things. The Gradgrindian answer to the Pascaline query, "May not the heart have reasons of which the mind is ignorant?" was the reply of another French mathematician a century later, "I have no need of such hypotheses." The Utilitarian universe was, as Teufelsdröckh knew, a vast machine, and the men of Fancy, inventors of social and moral myths, who would explore it, would get furthest by and in machines.

Dickens, founding father of dystopian fantasy, was no mere romantic socialist, despite his influence over G. B. Shaw's Emergent Evolution. And he certainly was not aware of another of Shaw's strange literary godfathers, the Samuel Butler of *Erewhon*, the inverted Utopia wherein man turned against the machines. It was Shaw who descended in 1912 to a preface and a judgment of *Hard Times* he would have ridiculed had it been written by anyone else—an introduction rather metaphysical and moral precisely in the stridency of its special pleading:

> [H]ere he begins at last to exercise quite recklessly his power of presenting a character to you in the most fantastic and outrageous terms, putting into its mouth from one end of the book to the other hardly a word which could conceivably be uttered by any sane human being, and yet leaving you with an unmistakable and exactly truthful portrait of a character that you recognize at once as not only real but typical. (Shaw, 130)

Thus G. B. Shaw. And all over a dystopia that brings into the metallic purity of a world to be made manageable by machines the huge cloudy symbols of high romance.

Romance, it appears, in the inhibited nineteenth century, could only find a place in *Hard Times* as an effeminate desire for private petting which, when thwarted in the interest of social stability, spurs Dickens's hero of the great social effect only to a little rebellion and less profundity. "I ha' fell into th' pit" are the dying words that come from Stephen Blackpool's crushed body, just up from Old Hell Shaft, into which abyss Dickens plunges him literally to drown his sorrows. It is as if a crushed people were speaking from the black pool into which the world of Bentham had stumbled:

> I ha' fell into th' pit ... as have cost wi'in the knowledge o' old fok now livin, hundreds and hundreds o' men's lives—fathers, sons, brothers, dear to thousands an' thousands, an' keepin' 'em fro' want and hunger. I ha' fell into a pit that ha' been wi' th' Fire-damp crueler than battle. I ha' read on't in the public petition, as onny one may read, fro' the men that works in pits, in which they ha' pray'n and pray'n the lawmakers for Christ's sake not to let their work be murder to 'em, but to spare 'em for th' wives and children that they loves as well as gentlefok loves theirs. When it were in work, it killed wi'out need; when 'tis let alone, it kills wi'out need. See how we die an' no need, one way an'another—in a muddle—every day! (272)

Is it the speculations of Utilitarian economists, skeletons of schoolmasters, Commissioners of Fact, genteel and used-up infidels, gabblers of many little dog-eared creeds that have caused this muddle? It is their research results, their actual findings and answers to the prime question: "What is human nature and how is it natural for man to behave?" The great hypothesis of evolution which won out, in hard times, against the elder hypothesis of special creation, disturbed the fundamentalists. We see now it had little effect on the ordinary man. Whether he had climbed up from an ape or fallen out of a Garden, here he was, far and away the wisest of all beasts, able to change his environment to suit his needs and wishes. Darwin and Huxley had far more in common with the bishops with whom they disputed than either party knew. Evolutionary biology, it turns out, made little difference to social mores.

What was human nature? Moralists (as least as Bounderby would define them) had always claimed that the rules they imposed were to prevent deviations from the natural. During Blackpool's first talk with the mysterious Mrs. Pegler, she asks whether the troubles she suspects he has (a drunken wife he cannot divorce—more evidence of Coketown's insistence on social stability and its scrupulous interests) followed him to Bounderby's factory: "No, no; they didn't follow him there, said Stephen. All correct there. (He did not go so far as to say, for her pleasure, that there was a sort of Divine Right there; but, I have heard claims almost as magnificent of late years)" (79).

Perhaps the mechanistic view of *Hard Times* I posited earlier is incomplete. In the past we have supposed or accepted that mere mechanism was the bone of contention between Bounderby (master, mill owner, monster; spokesman for *laissez-faire*, for room at the top, for the humble-virtue school of bullying eloquence; cad and captain of industry) and Blackpool (saint and martyr, dialect spokesman for religious morality). But as a matter of hard-working fact, religious moralism in *Hard Times* finds it far easier to get on with Coketown mechanicalism than perhaps even Dickens first suspected. In the real world of Bentham and Mill, a kind of concordat was devised whereby the realm of values and ends was left to religion while the realm of the tangible was handed over to science and industry. Both sides assumed (although both were mistaken) they were agreed about morality. Whether you were at a machine or a shrine, in a factory or a church, a few general rules were supposed to run and be able to control all issues of ends and means, private behavior and public business. Post the Ten Commandments in M'Choakumchild's schoolroom, and all will be well. But let the author strike his keynote, Coketown, before we pursue this tune:

> First, the perplexing mystery of the place was, Who belonged to the eighteen denominations? Because whoever did, the labouring people did not. It was very strange to walk through the streets on a Sunday morning, and note how few of *them* the barbarous jangling of bells that was driving the sick and nervous mad, called away from their own quarter, from their own close rooms, from the corners of their own streets, where they lounged listlessly, gazing at all the church and chapel going, as at a thing in which they had no manner of concern. Nor was it merely the stranger who noticed this, because there was a native organization in Coketown itself, whose members were to be heard of in the House of Commons every session,

indignantly petitioning for acts of parliament that should make
these people religious by main force. (23)

Religion and morality and questions of human nature are live issues in
Hard Times; still the liveliest of issues for us, as they cut to the heart of
what Utilitarianism and science and industrial management have found out
about life itself. As long as Dickens and his reader—Victorian and
modern—thought Bounderbyism was simply making money off power-
giving gadgetry, *Hard Times* was not mature and was not really anti-
utopian. To sound a new keynote, Dickens faced a hard choice: was *Hard
Times* to be a boy-Bounderby's fairy tale with a machinist-suited Prince
Charming as the arrested idea, or a dystopian counter-myth operating within
and subverting the licensed utopian precincts of Benthamite myth? If ever a
choice was a moral one, this was. If *Hard Times* was to do its job, it could
not merely commandeer inventions, not even those essentially Utilitarian
ones of rhetoric, documentary, or "realistic" fiction. If it was to be worthy
of the name of the true novel and of a truly dystopian vision, it would have
to create real persons and make them develop psychological and moral
maturity under the pressure of unsuspected portentous events.

Would *Hard Times* have the nerve to tell the contemporary truth to the
growing-up? Recent history had come to be dominated by primitive
passions, ultimately irrational, which benevolent rationalists and even
natural supernaturalists like Carlyle seemed incapable of understanding.
The energies that really shaped and drove the world sprang from
emotions—racial pride, nationalism, evangelical intensities and obsessions,
love of even muddled wars—which liberal intellectuals had written off as
anachronisms, and which they had so nearly destroyed in themselves as to
have nearly lost all power of action. The Victorian sage who glorified
industrial captains in good will was too sane to understand the deep, dead-
end center of Coketown's spirit-quenching hideousness: that man could be
subsumed into machine by scientific management. Would Dickens dare say
what the cards, now in the hand and on the table, actually were, what was
in the black pool ready for pick-up, and what the game really was?

The answer, of course, is yes, but to do so put character problems before
him, the master character-draftsman, beside which the old plots and play of
temperament were rudimentary. E. M. Forster held that Tolstoy was both a
psychological genius and the first great novelist because he could show his
characters developing and changing. They are not static puppets or mere
stylized humors as Forster thought so many of Dickens's dramatis personae
to be. Yet in *Hard Times* Dickens is profoundly (and bleakly) aware that
changes of character and even total modification of psyches and physiques
are possible. He is not just satirizing teacher-training schools when he tells us
Mr. M'Choakumchild "and some one hundred and forty other schoolmasters

had been lately turned at the same time, in the same factory, on the same principles, like so many pianoforte legs" (8). Or we can read this description, quasi-mechanical in its very technique, of a prime product of Coketown's "manufacture of the human fabric"; behold Bitzer:

> ... the boy was so light-eyed and light-haired that the [sun's] rays appeared to draw out of him what little colour he ever possessed. His cold eyes would hardly have been eyes, but for the short ends of lashes which, by bringing them into immediate contrast with something paler than themselves, expressed their form. His short-cropped hair might have been a mere continuation of the sandy freckles on his forehead and face. His skin was so unwholesomely deficient in the natural tinge, that he looked as though, if he were cut, he would bleed white. (4–5)

Simply a number of sandy freckles to be filled in or continued and connected a little later on. Even the lines and dots of Bitzer's eyes have not yet been manufactured and must be, by the voyeuristic reader, brought into contrast with the short ends of their paler lashes. Thus the thin-blooded Bitzer. But Dickens further knows that the power to make psychic changes will increase in a way and to a degree Tolstoy would have thought utterly fantastic, utterly beyond any realism and only to be relegated to the absurdities of Sissy Jupe's Arabian Nights entertainments. (Are we to find an irony that the transforming of a man into a woman or vice versa is a favorite bit of magic in these non-Utilitarian tales?)

Perhaps it is about here where all dystopian fiction can be tested as to whether it is fully adult and responsible. Can it, for instance, take a theme which, starting with the basic boy-meets-girl situation, faces up to the fact that each may, like Bitzer, be drafted and so coerced as to be finally transmuted? Dickens sensed that here is the material for a completely new drama, a fresh development of tragedy and an original extension of what Greek poets called irony. We have had in the moral-making forms of drama only two situations, comedy and tragedy. In the first, things turn out well and after some surprises and contretemps all ends in laughter and fun. Nature turns out to be friendly after all to our main design and desire. The master force in us, the desire to make love, is backed by the life force, and a little applause is bribe enough to bring the fairies in to bless the marriage bed. Journeys end in lovers' meetings and only old spoilsport, crabbed age gets fooled and beaten up. In the second, nature does not cooperate; she does not care about man or his happiness, even when he is a breeding animal seeking a mate. The universe is not friendly, but although it can— and will—smash man's body in whatever Old Hell Shaft available, it cannot bend his will or coerce his character. While there is no happy ending, the audience gets its catharsis nonetheless, its sense that you can let the cosmos do its damnedest because beneath the bludgeonings of fate the protagonist has a head that is bloody, of course, but unbowed.

In the moral drama of *Hard Times*, Dickens has worked through tragedy to something beyond. The characters are altered by their crises in Coketown. The irony—the onlooking God's-eye view of the reader seeing through the control of Dickens's language—consists no longer in so simple a formula as being purged of pity and fear. We now really face Facts: if the universe is evolving, so too is human nature. The idea that the one unchangeable thing in the cosmic flux is man's unconquerable soul, with its muddle of prejudices which it calls morality and its lack of humor which it calls dignity, goes, finally, down Old Hell Shaft.

As Professor Leavis proclaimed decades ago, the formal and church-goingly solemn moral of Dickens's fable is placed with the rightness of genius into the asthmatic mouth of brandy-soaked, game-eyed Sleary of the Horse Riding:

> "It theemth to prethent two thingth to a perthon, don't it, Thquire?" said Mr. Sleary, musing as he looked down into the depths of his brandy and water: "one, that there ith a love in the world, not all Thelf-intereth after all, but thomething very different; t'other, that it hath a way of ith own of calculating or not calculating, whith thomehow or another ith at leath ath hard to give a name to, ath the wayth of the dogth ith."
>
> Mr. Gradgrind looked out the window, and made no reply.
> (292–93)

Beyond this formal moralizing lies metacomedy. Comedy thought the universe was fun; tragedy thought man was at least dignified or had something going for him in the end, even if it were only "ath the wayth of the dogth ith" or Stephen's determination to call a spade a spade, a muddle a muddle. *Hard Times* as metacomedy sees man and the cosmos in play. If you can laugh at your expense, suddenly you will get the gigantic point of the joke. For the complete catharsis lies not in brandied tears or stoic expression, but in laughter.

Example: Louisa Gradgrind when her heart has been melted is a far less convincing character than Louisa as the enchanted princess with a heart of ice. Compare her interview with her father to discuss Bounderby's proposal of marriage with the parallel scene where she returns to her father to reproach him for her upbringing and is made to speak what are easily the most embarrassing lines in the novel.

Example: The uneasy alliance between wealth and birth occasions the most sublimely absurd dialogue in the book:

> "At the time when to have been a tumbler in the mud of the streets, would have been a godsend to me, a prize in the lottery to me, you were at the Italian Opera, ma'am, in white satin and

jewels, a blaze of splendour, when I hadn't a penny to buy a link to light you."

"I certainly, Sir" returned Mrs. Sparsit, with a dignity serenely mournful, "was familiar with the Italian Opera at a very early age."

"Egad, ma'am, so was I," said Bounderby, "—with the wrong side of it. A hard bed the pavement of its Arcade used to make, I assure you. People like you, ma'am, accustomed from infancy to lie down on feathers, have no idea *how* hard a paving stone is without trying it." (45)

Example: The stoic dandy, James Harthouse, tries to make himself, as well as Louisa, invulnerable through apathy, and his apologia for genteel cynicism contains a shrewd thrust at the Utilitariat:

> "The only difference between us and the professors of virtue or benevolence, or philanthropy—never mind the name—is, that we know it is all meaningless, and say so; while they know it equally, and never say so."
> Why should she be shocked or warned by this reiteration? It was not so unlike her father's principles, and her early training, that it need startle her. (166)

Example: Mind and body can only be taken apart purposely by suicide, so we are allowed our guess as to a shared ending for Harthouse and young Tom Gradgrind, the novel's "whelp" whose ways are hardly "ath the dogth ith":

> James Harthouse continued to lounge in the same place and attitude, smoking his cigar in his own easy way, and looking pleasant at the whelp, as if he knew himself to be a kind of agreeable demon who had to hover over him, and he must give up his whole soul if required. (133)

Final example (and it's a long one): The only real freedom is achieved by taking a standpoint from which not only the body is seen as ridiculous but the personality as well. Mind and body are regarded with detachment and that detachment is not gravity (which is always full of self-focus and concern, always very Bounderby) but laughter that is full of bemused insight. The dying Mrs. Thomas Gradgrind, a total cipher in her husband's system, writes the unwritten language of her life:

> Her feeble voice sounded so far away in her bundle of shawls, and the sound of another voice addressing her seemed to take such a long time in getting down to her ears, that she might have been at the bottom of a well. The poor lady was nearer Truth than she had ever been: which had much to do with it.
> On being told that Mrs. Bounderby was there, she replied, at

cross-purposes, that she had never called him by that name since he married Louisa; that pending her choice of an objectionable name, she had called him J; and that she could not at present depart from that regulation, not being yet provided with a permanent substitute. Louisa had sat by her for some minutes, and had spoken to her often, before she arrived at a clear understanding who it was. She then seemed to come to it all at once.

"Well, my dear," said Mrs. Gradgrind, "and I hope you are going on satisfactorily to yourself. It was all your father's doing. He set his heart upon it. And he ought to know."

"I want to hear of you, mother; not myself."

"You want to hear of me, my dear? That's something new, I am sure, when anybody wants to hear of me. Not at all well, Louisa. Very faint and giddy."

"Are you in pain, dear mother?"

"I think there's a pain somewhere in the room," said Mrs. Gradgrind, "but I couldn't positively say that I have got it ... You must remember, my dear, that whenever I have said anything, on any subject, I have never heard the last of it; and, consequently, that I have long left off saying anything ... But there is something—not an Ology at all—that your father has missed or forgotten, Louisa. I don't know what it is. I have often sat with Sissy near me, and thought about it. I shall never get its name now. But your father may. It makes me restless. I want to write him, to find out for God's sake, what it is. Give me a pen, give me a pen."

Even the power of restlessness was gone, except for the poor head, which could just turn from side to side.

She fancied, however, that her request had been complied with, and that the pen she could not have held was in her hand. It matters little what figures of wonderful no-meaning she began to trace upon her wrappers. The hand soon stopped in the midst of them; the light that had always been feeble and dim behind the weak transparency, went out; and even Mrs. Gradgrind, emerged from the shadow in which man walketh and disquieteth himself in vain, took upon her the dread solemnity of the sages and patriarchs. (197–99)

Comedy so seen goes far deeper than tragedy and so must be considered as the "real realism" of *Hard Times*.

But where in the extended of the novel's genuinely human plots does dystopian fiction come in? Right in the middle. For what is the blend of men and the universe—the theme of *Hard Times*'s metacomedy—but the emergence into a complete work of art of, if you will, the Bounderby Blessed Dawn Concept: that man and machine must develop together as an integrated symbiot. *Hard Times*, in its attitude to morality, had in its day a double appositeness, in its aim and in its method. In its aim it is bound by its extrapolation of the Industrial Revolution and its use of dramatic event and plot, to view the Coketown mills, their perpetually clanking machinery, and the men the mills turn into "hands" as a threefold whole, the machine being the hyphen linking the other two. *Hard Times* is a prophetic fiction of a particular yet still evolving epoch of crisis. So it explores morality in the traditional sense, that is, man's power to adjust to the demands of natural law. The aim of life, as far as Dickens can see in the novel, is the increase of consciousness. A Utilitarian theology or morality (or a moralized Industrial Revolution) is, of course, something more than the rather jejune formulas of Gradgrindery and its pursuit of truth by sticking to the Facts. That aim itself starts to look fuzzy, even fantastic, when we consider the final summation of Coketown is that the end of Fancy equals the end of real objectivity. The utopian aim of Dickens's dystopian fable in all hard times is to discover that supra-Utilitarian self-control whereby man learns to master, shift, and expand the focal length of consciousness in order to apprehend alternative universes to Coketown, as in Dickens's own times the rise of alternative geometrics really did open the way to new cosmogonies.

Dickens's method, too, is apposite. The old comedy laughed things off. And when things became as grim as Coketown and men grimly dwindled into "hands," such fun was shawled and bundled off the scene. The old broad, undignified (read "Dickensian") pantomime became obscene—what must not be shown on stage. To laugh at Stephen Blackpool's death is precisely as outrageous as Oscar Wilde's reaction to the death of Little Nell. Tragedy, with a J. Bounderby's pretentious solemnity (again the solemnity of Sleary's formal moral) and with a Gradgrindian puritanism (its repressions and censorship) took over. But Utilitarianism itself had shown that truth cannot be regarded as obscene and what actually takes place cannot be called (and banned as) unnatural. The method of *Hard Times* is so to narrate the very facts Thomas Gradgrind has discovered that we may be presented with a new play of character.

So we can view this novel, the immensely enlarged picture of what nature and human nature are in an Industrial Revolutionary utopia, with a new insight, a new humor, a new fun. Solemnity is the sign of psychosis oncoming to utopians; laughter is the boom made by an exploding taboo, not that booming of Manchester mills. For the solemn you must not laugh off pain: you must be stoically tragic toward it. (Scientific progress, with its advances in analgesics, may make this attitude anachronistic.) You must not laugh for pleasure. You must be secretive, whispering, ashamed. But laughter is not merely frankness; it is a necessary force for insight.

A main characteristic of any vigorous dystopian fiction when it keeps in touch, as it should, with Fancy is extravagance. And who could be more extravagant than the folk of the Horse Riding capering so delightedly, so self-forgetfully, in un-Utilitarian findings:

There were two or three handsome young women among them,

with their two or three husbands, and their two or three mothers, and their eight or nine little children, who did the fairy business when required. The father of one of the families was in the habit of balancing the father of another of the families on the top of a great pole; the father of a third family often made a pyramid of both those fathers, with Master Kidderminster for the apex, and himself for the base; all the fathers could dance upon rolling casks, stand upon bottles, catch knives and balls, twirl hand-basins, ride upon anything, jump over everything, and stick at nothing. All the mothers could (and did) dance, upon the slack wire and the tight rope, and perform rapid acts on bare-backed steeds; none of them were at all particular in respect of showing their legs; and one of them, alone in a Greek chariot, drove, six in hand into every town they came to. (35)

In Hobbes's famous definition, laughter is a sudden glory. The profoundest human insights arise from all kinds of mental locomotion, from a making of athletic associations and correlations which seem at first absurd and can only be sustained by regarding them as humorous extravaganza—the intellectual equivalent of dancing on a rolling cask or charging six-in-hand, alone in a Greek chariot, down the High Street of Coketown. Of the circus folk we are told:

They all assumed to be mighty rakish and knowing, they were not very tidy in their private dresses, they were not at all orderly in their domestic arrangements, and the combined literature of the whole company would have produced but a poor letter on any subject. Yet there was a remarkable gentleness and childishness about these people, a special inaptitude for any kind of sharp practice, and an untiring readiness to help and pity one another, deserving often of as much respect, and always of as much generous construction, as the every-day virtues of any class of people in the world. (35)

Alternative consciousnesses do, indeed, create alternate moral universes.

Though the dramatic form and the psychological atmosphere in which *Hard Times* must work is metacomedy, that has nothing to do with the farcical or the burlesque. It and it alone can produce a situation beyond tragedy. Try to think of every actor in the novel as being noble, every one of them as a person who surrenders ordinary domestic happiness because he or she is intellectually convinced (or compelled, or conditioned) that civilization is best served in that way. Most will remain very human nonetheless, that is, melodramatically ridiculous in self-admiration of the sacrifice they are making. So Dickens the realistic, that is, fanciful, novelist can, and does, debunk them—Sleary, Blackpool and Ruth, Sissy too—all of them. But in the process he produces a kind of super irony that leaves us unable to escape the keynote by mockery. There is in the novel that irony the Greek dramatists attempted as the acme of their art. Their irony was the God's-eye view of the hero blinded by his own heroic hubris, the self-sufficient courage will do everything save see itself as ridiculous. The sublimely magic irony of *Hard Times* can watch all its characters, central ones or mere ciphers, undergoing psychological and physical change even though they may not bear off the pageant of a bleeding human heart with a fine exit line. They themselves watch their own metamorphoses with something akin to Dickens's own expanding, always-shifting consciousness and increasing humor. Undergoing the ultimate, final change, even Mrs. Gradgrind sees herself not merely altering in physique, not merely bundled in an Ology shawl of self-imposed suffering. She sees her psyche changing too. She sees her attachment to home and family and to the values of Gradgrindery which she had considered to be eternal, fading away—perhaps as the author himself saw his own taste for social cause and documentary fiction yielding to the social and moral activity of creative myth-making.

Faced with the prospect of being required to box in their limb-ripping, soul-crushing machines, the mill-owners of Coketown assert they'd just as soon "pitch [their] property into the Atlantic" (111). Now that, Dickens says, would be really funny.

Notes

[1] Northrop Frye was the first to identify *Hard Times* as a dystopia, see his "Dickens and the Comedy of Humors," in *Experience in the Novel* (ed. Roy Harvey Pearce). Frye's oft reprinted essay also considers *Hard Times* as a comedy, but as one that follows the structures of classical "New Comedy," not, as I will argue, a metacomedy that transcends those structures and the religious and ethical assumptions they embody.

Jerome Meckier's "Dickens and the Dystopian Novel: From *Hard Times* to *Lady Chatterley*" is still an important discussion of *Hard Times* as dystopia, placing it as a "seminal" work whose seeds took root in Orwell and Huxley as well as Lawrence. See also Gold and Toker.

Apart from Frye, generic discussions of *Hard Times* as comedy (of whatever sort) are rare, most commentators approaching the novel with a high seriousness that depresses me but would make the Arnolds, father and son (as well as the late Professor Leavis) proud. For these critics—fortunately too numerous to mention—"*Hard Times* as comedy" is thinkable only as "comic touches in *Hard Times*." An interesting exception is Grahame Smith's "Comic Subversion in *Hard Times*."

Discussion of religion in *Hard Times* tends to focus either on those eighteen unused churches or on Dickens's use of biblical allusions. Only Edwin Eigner's *The Metaphysical Novel in England and America* addresses the novel in terms relevant to my argument.

Works Cited

Dickens, Charles. *Hard Times*. In *Oxford Illustrated Dickens*. Oxford: Oxford University Press, 1955.

Eigner, Edwin. *The Metaphysical Novel in England and America*. Berkeley and Los

Angeles: University of California Press, 1978.

Frye, Northrop. "Dickens and the Comedy of Humors." In *Experience in the Novel: Selected Papers from the English Institute*. Ed. Roy Harvey Pearce. New York: Columbia University Press, 1968. 49–81.

Gold, Joseph. *Charles Dickens: Radical Moralist*. Minneapolis: University of Minnesota Press, 1972.

Meckier, Jerome. "Dickens and the Dystopian Novel: From *Hard Times* to *Lady Chatterley*." In *The Novel and its Changing Form*. Ed. R. G. Collins. Winnipeg: University of Manitoba Press, 1972. 51–58.

Shaw, G. B. "*Hard Times*." Rpt. in *The Dickens Critics*. Ed. George Ford and Lauriat Lane, Jr. Ithaca: Cornell University Press, 1961.

Smith, Grahame. "Comic Subversion in *Hard Times*." *Dickens Studies Annual* 18 (1989): 145–60.

Toker, Leona. "*Hard Times* and a Critique of Utopia: A Typological Study." *Narrative* 4 (1996): 218–34.

8

Transcendence through Incongruity: The Background of Humor in Carlyle's *Sartor Resartus*

Abigail Burnham Bloom

In 1830 and 1831 when Thomas Carlyle wrote *Sartor Resartus,* he slowly, layer by layer, created a book that departed radically from any that he or anyone else had written before. This unique work was suffused with humor, but of a variety that the world had never experienced. It resulted from Carlyle's own temperament and background, from the influence of German literature, and from "the Edinburgh style of mockery" he eschewed. It went beyond any of the theories of humor current in England. Indeed Carlyle's humor went beyond the theoretical framework he himself had erected. Carlyle used humor to attempt to change the world. He wanted to force his readers to reexamine themselves and their assumptions, and for this purpose developed a unique form of humor. Humor undercuts the accumulated, unquestioned beliefs held by his readers and consequently contributes to his didactic purpose. Humor at its best works in the same manner as literature at its best, as a means of discovering the world anew. In order to write about his own age, Carlyle's humor blends with his didacticism. Carlyle was not writing comedy; he was incorporating humor into his writing of fiction, philosophy, and history.

In *Sartor Resartus*, Carlyle developed a process of transcending seemingly incongruous statements through a technique he called the "inverse sublime." Carlyle, like his character Teufelsdröckh, recognized the incongruity residing in all men:

> "[T]here is something great in the moment when a man first strips himself of adventitious wrappages; and sees indeed that he is naked, and, as Swift has it, 'a forked straddling animal with bandy legs'; yet also a Spirit, an unutterable Mystery of Mysteries." (*SR*, 57)

This quotation consists of a three-part sentence. The first part envisions man without clothes conscious of being without clothes, the second presents a quotation from Swift focusing on man's baser nature as an awkward animal, seeming to undercut the "something great" in the moment of man looking at himself. But Carlyle does not solely have disgust for mankind. The third part of the sentence presents man's sublimity. The spirit transcends the previously represented view of man, but does not erase it. Man partakes of these two extremes simultaneously; he does not exist between them. Man must first learn to look candidly at himself and he will then apprehend the duality of his being and he will transcend his incongruities. It is this view of mankind, partaking of both the humorous and the sublime, that Carlyle perfects in *Sartor Resartus*. The transcendence of incongruities through the three-part structure of the sentence above is reflected in the climactic chapters of the work, "The Everlasting No," "Centre of Indifference," and "The Everlasting Yea," as well as in the three-part structure of the whole. Carlyle's humor becomes a method of vision, through transcendence to a higher plane, that he hopes to impart to his readers.

I

> "[N]o Life-Philosophy ... which originates equally in the Character (Gemüth), and equally speaks thereto, can attain its significance till the Character itself is known and seen; 'till the Author's View of the World (Weltansicht), and how he actively and passively came by such view, are clear: in short till a Biography of him has been philosophico-poetically written, and philosophico-poetically read.'" (*SR*, 75)

Carlyle credited his predilection for humor to his parents: "[T]he most important by far was that of Nature, you would perhaps say, if you ever heard my Father speak, or very often heard my Mother & her inborn melodies of heart and voice!" (Clubbe, 59). He admired his father's speech, especially his tendency towards exaggeration. The sayings of Carlyle's father added to the picturesque, coterie speech used by both Thomas and Jane Welsh Carlyle in their conversations and letters. Certainly, exaggeration was ever an element of his humor. Like his father, Carlyle had a natural gravity of demeanor that lent emphasis to his humor. Yet from an early age, Carlyle's humor must have gone beyond the limited subject matter, use, and audience of his father's stories. Carlyle admired his mother's "sportive vein" of humor, but felt that it was not prominent in him because of the difficult nature of his life (*Reminiscences* 4: 103). Carlyle mentioned the effect that his ill-health had on his character several times, and used it to blame those aspects of his style of which he did not completely approve. Carlyle claimed that the problems of ill-health, physical suffering, and psychological difficulties caused the negative tone in his own humor. He responded to John Stuart Mill's criticism of his writing style in *Sartor Resartus* and "Cagliostro" by stressing these factors:

> Irony is a sharp instrument ... I cannot justify, yet can too well explain what sets me so often on it of late: it is my singularly anomalous position to the world,—and, if you will, my own singularly unreasonable temper. I never know or can even guess what or who my audience is, or whether I have any audience: thus too naturally I adjust myself on the Devil-may-care principle. Besides I have under all my gloom a genuine feeling of the ludicrous; and could have been the merriest of men, *had I not* been the sickest & saddest. (*Collected Letters* 6: 449)

Carlyle sets up an opposition between gloom, sickness, and sadness, which express themselves in irony, and merriment, which expresses itself in the ludicrous. He credits the ludicrous with arising from happiness. Carlyle here, as in several areas in his writing, suggests the inferiority of irony as a type of humor and longs for the ability to create a humor based on health and positive fellow-feeling. At this time in his life, Carlyle's "singularly anomalous position" included having no clear audience, searching to build his own reputation, as well as his struggling to find a voice. This voice came to include a rich supply of humor and irony, but Carlyle was yet unsure of its timbre. However, Carlyle never appreciated the ludicrous for itself; for him, all humor must lead towards a moral end.

J. Anthony Froude, Carlyle's friend and biographer, recognized Carlyle's ability for exaggeration, but like Carlyle himself, criticized what he saw as the darker or negative aspects of his humor:

> He had a natural tendency to exaggeration, and although at such times his extraordinary metaphors and slashes of Titanesque humour made him always worth listening to, he was at his best when talking of history or poetry or biography, or of some contemporary person or incident which had either touched his sympathy or amused his delicate sense of absurdity. His laugh was from his whole nature, voice, eyes, and even his whole body. And there was never any malice in it. His own definition of humour, "a genial sympathy with the under side," was the definition also of his own feeling about all things and all persons, when it was himself that was speaking, and not what he called the devil that was occasionally in possession. (Froude 1: 313–14)

Froude accepts, like Carlyle, that humor, through sympathy, can raise the lowly, "the under side." Humor is, therefore, a powerful force for portraying the world in a positive light. Froude postulates a Carlyle in control of himself, excelling in sympathy and humor—and a second Carlyle who is at times possessed by an ironical devil. The kind of humor that Froude admired was based on feelings of sympathy and absurdity. Describing Carlyle as "Titanesque" (a word that Carlyle used to describe Richter),

Froude indicates Carlyle's ability to raise his subject to a higher level through humor, the process of what Carlyle came to call the "inverse sublime."

Another long-standing friend, David S. Masson, criticized Froude's biography for not emphasizing Carlyle's humor sufficiently:

> Those about him that knew him best always felt that the most proper relation to much that he said and did was to take it humorously or suffuse it with humour; and that he himself had the same feeling and authorised it in others appeared in the frequency, almost the habitual constancy, with which he would check his conscious exaggerations at the last point with some ludicrous touch of self-irony, and would dissolve his fiercest objurgations and tumults of wrath in some sudden phantasy of the sheerly absurd and a burst of uproarious laughter. (*Carlyle Personally*, 18–19)

The Carlyle that Masson describes seems to chase away wrath and the devil with his humor. The humor is felt as a change in direction; Carlyle gives a new spin of a less solemn nature to what he has previously stated. This forces the reader to reconsider what has already been said. Yet another close friend and editor, Charles Eliot Norton, advised that "even in his most serious moods his mind retains a certain playfulness, which finds vent in grim jokes and extravagant exaggerations. He is rarely to be taken *au pied de la lettre*" (Wilson and MacArthur, 191). An American visitor described the general manner in which Carlyle cloaked his ideas by showing how Carlyle used humor to change the nature of what had gone before:

> But that which saved these and all his sharpest words from being actually offensive was this, that, after the most vehement tirade, he would suddenly pause, throw his head back, and give as genuine and kindly a laugh as I ever heard from a human being ... The laugh, in short, revealed the humorist; if I said the genial humorist, wearing a mask of grimness, I should hardly go too far for the impression it left. At any rate, it shifted the ground, and transferred the whole matter to that realm of thought where men play with things. (Higginson, 5–6)

Without the clue of Carlyle's laughter, one might take offense at what he says—but there is a sense on the part of his audience that Carlyle elevates his subject through humor. Here it is not the devil causing Carlyle to use irony, but the humorist wearing a disguise of gravity. Although Carlyle's aspect may have become fiercer and more settled over the years, the substance remains the same.

Carlyle's early letters and works show evidence that he was slowly moving towards the development of his own comic voice. In 1814 Froude commented on Carlyle's letter-writing style:

> I have had the pleasure of receiving, my dear Carlyle, your very
> humorous and friendly letter, a letter remarkable for vivacity, a
> Shandean turn of expression, and affectionate pathos, which
> indicate a peculiar turn of mind, make sincerity doubly striking
> and wit doubly poignant ... A happy flow of language either for
> pathos, description, or humour, and an easy, graceful current of
> ideas appropriate to every subject, characterise your style.
> (Froude 1: 29)

Carlyle's friend was prescient, for this describes Carlyle's adult style more
accurately than his youthful one, when he was still working to achieve a mature
voice and style. His early stories "Cruthers and Jonson" (written 1822), "Illudo
Chartis" (1825–26), and "Wotton Reinfred" (1826–27) lack this characteristic
style. The search for a subject and a style in which to express it continued
throughout Carlyle's apprenticeship. While "Illudo Chartis" has an aspect of free-
wheeling humor, it lacks an encompassing vision; while "Wotton Reinfred" has a
philosophical basis, it lacks any successful attempt at integrating humor with his
ideas.

As a young man, Carlyle expressed interest in many humorous writers,
including Rabelais, Swift, Butler, and Sterne.[1] He wrote in his *Reminiscences*,
that "My *first* favourite Books had been *Hudibras* & *Tristram Shandy*;
everybody was proclaiming it such a feat for a man, 'To have wit, to have
humour' above all! There was always a small secret something of *affectation*,
which is now not secret to me, in that part of my affairs" (Clubbe, 58). As an
adult, he comments on his younger self with a mature understanding. He
implies that he thought it important to have wit and humor "above all." The
"small secret something of *affectation*" may be the realization that he wanted to
win the acclaim of other people by emulating the style of *Hudibras* or *Tristram
Shandy*, that his humor was a deliberate affectation. Indeed, Carlyle's earliest
works lack the sophisticated use of humor present in *Sartor Resartus*. He had
yet to develop the ability to use humor as a means of transcending the real.

II

> "[N]o man who has once heartily and wholly laughed can be
> altogether irreclaimably bad. How much lies in Laughter: the
> cipher-key, wherewith we decipher the whole man!" (*SR*, 33)

Many writers have striven to define the comic. Victorians, for the most part,
based their theories of humor on the works of Thomas Hobbes and
Immanuel Kant, who espoused the superiority theory and the incongruity
theory respectively. Almost all theories of humor focus on an implicit
comparison between two different propositions put forth simultaneously.

"Laughter is a sudden glory," proclaims Hobbes, "arising from the sudden conception of some eminency in ourselves by comparison with the infirmity of others, or with our own formerly" (Hobbes, 3: 46). For Hobbes the two mutually exclusive propositions of humor involve an examination of the self which leads to the pleasure of self-satisfaction. Many theorists who hold with the incongruity explanation for humor cite Aristotle as the first proponent of this theory. Comedy, he states, "consists in some defect or ugliness which is not painful or destructive" (Aristotle, 33). Implicit in this idea is a normal world order against which difference can be measured. Kant first gave voice to the incongruity theory: "Laughter is an affection arising from the sudden transformation of a strained expectation into nothing" (Kant, 33). During the Victorian era, the incongruity theory was frequently cited, perhaps due to the hope of the Victorians that the centuries were making mankind more civilized.

Nineteenth-century discussions of the comic often went over the same issues. Essayists would attempt to distinguish between wit and humor, instances of humor would be given, humor would be classified by type or style, and examples would be enumerated. There was little attempt at definition. Typically, the author would praise comic figures such as Don Quixote, Falstaff, and Uncle Toby. These characters represented positive values which would be scorned or overlooked by the majority of men because the characters reside outside the established norm of society. The number of works written in the nineteenth century on humor indicates the success that comedy had achieved in becoming a legitimate and serious means of expression. Humor was recognized not as something that would cause an audience to forget itself in frivolity, but as a means to attaining reflection and insight into the human situation. Stuart Tave describes the typical discussion of the comic: "By the middle of the nineteenth century, it was a commonplace that the best comic works present amiable originals, often models of good nature, whose little peculiarities are not satirically instructive, but objects of delight and love" (viii).[2] These characters would act to increase the moral sympathy of the audience.

During the Victorian age, there was a shift towards accepting incongruity as the basis of humor, as this theory implies an intellectual attitude on the part of the audience rather than a moral judgment of superiority. Hazlitt, writing his "Lectures on The Comic Writers, Etc. of Great Britain" in 1819, based his theory on ideas of incongruity: "Man is the only animal that laughs and weeps; for he is the only animal that is struck with the difference between what things are, and what they ought to be" (Hazlitt 6: 5). Hazlitt does not connect humor with sympathy; rather, he believes that man laughs to show his self-love. Consequently Hazlitt finds that humor appeals to man's baser nature. He finds that wit detracts from sympathy, and anything that reduces an individual into an abstraction is less than the highest order of the comic. He formulates three kinds of comedy and three degrees of the laughable. First, there is the comedy of nature found in Shakespeare, and such characters as Falstaff, Don Quixote, and Uncle Toby; then there is the comedy of manner or artificial comedy found in Restoration plays. Hazlitt names this the highest comedy. The third kind of comedy he catalogs is sentimental comedy, comedy in form but lacking in essence. Sentimental comedy, Hazlitt states, was prevalent in the eighteenth century and in his own time. Each kind of comedy can have any of three degrees of laughter. The three degrees of laughter are: first, the merely laughable which may originate from an incongruity or an accident resulting in surprise and contrasts; second, the ludicrous, which finds further incongruity in either character or situation, and which is not unpleasant; and third, the ridiculous, which is an artificial comedy composed of satiric wit.[3]

It is beginning with the thought of Hazlitt, according to Tave, that the majority of commentators no longer saw comedy as satiric ridicule, but as amiable humor (241). Many other Victorians proffered theories of the comic or humor. Among those major writers who published theories of humor after the publication of Carlyle's *Sartor Resartus* were William Makepeace Thackeray, George Eliot, and George Meredith. While these were not in any way an influence on Carlyle, they convey the prevailing idea of humor during the Victorian era. The essays written by these authors and the comedy they wrote would have been influenced by many of the same forces as Carlyle's theory and practice of humor.

Unlike Hazlitt, Thackeray postulated that humor has an ameliorative purpose, as it emanates from the sensibility of the writer and connects him with the reader. Written as lectures for large audiences, "The English Humourists of the Eighteenth Century" were first delivered by Thackeray in 1851. The lectures were more on the lives of the humorists than their humor, for Thackeray held that the author's personality and character, formed by their lives, would be evident in his works. There is little attempt at classification or definition. For Thackeray, humor has an ennobling, sympathetic aspect: "The humorous writer professes to awaken and direct your love, your pity, your kindness—your scorn for untruth, pretension, imposture—your tenderness for the weak, the poor, the oppressed, the unhappy" (4). Thackeray's sentimentality comes through in these lectures without the wit, irony, or intellect evident in his best fiction.

George Eliot, like Coleridge and Carlyle, was influenced by her reading of German authors. She discussed humor in a review entitled "German Wit: Heinrich Heine," published in the *Westminister Review* in January 1856. Like many other authors Eliot distinguishes humor from wit: "Humour is of earlier growth than wit" (68). While humor is allied with poetic tendencies and associates with sympathy, wit is allied with the reasoning intellect. Humor draws its material from situations and characters; wit seizes on unexpected and complex relations with a brief and sudden energy. Eliot finds that what is laughable varies with class, culture, and nationality. The writers who define humor as "the sympathetic presentation of incongruous elements in human nature and life" are describing only the later development of humor (70). In earlier ages, humor arose not from incongruity but from superiority. Yet the divisions, she finds, are less than clear cut, and often overlap, and indeed the result is often more successful when they are mixed.

Meredith developed a series of essays in 1877 that came to be published as *An Essay on Comedy*. Like many other writers on comedy at this time, Meredith attempts to distinguish the various types of comedy; he concurs with Eliot in seeing these types less as labels than as forces with a life of their own. Meredith considered the comic a pervading spirit affecting author, audience, and society, demanding both the subtlety of the author and the acuteness of the audience. He distinguishes among the different types of comedy by reference to the author's hold on his audience:

> If you detect the ridicule, and your kindliness is chilled by it, you are slipping into the grasp of Satire.
>
> If, instead of falling foul of the ridiculous person with a satiric rod, to make him writhe and shriek aloud, you prefer to sting him under a semi-caress, by which he shall in his anguish be rendered dubious whether indeed anything has hurt him, you are an engine of Irony.
>
> If you laugh all round him, tumble him, roll him about, deal him a smack and drop a tear on him, own his likeness to you, and yours to your neighbor, spare him a little as you shun, pity him as much as you expose, it is a spirit of Humour that is moving you. (*Essay*, 42)

Meredith notes the sympathy inherent in humor and humor's ability to indicate the infinite within the finite world. He does not try to distinguish wit and humor. However, he believes wit superior to humor as wit is founded in common sense and sees through folly. His essay argues for an intellectual approach to comedy, one that would do away with sentimental humor. The Comic Spirit breathes common sense and intelligence. Meredith also understood the central tenet of Carlyle's humor; he wrote to a friend: "In reading Carlyle, bear in mind that he is a humourist. The insolence offensive to you, is part of his humour. He means what he says, but only so far as a humourist can mean what he says" (*Letters* 1: 327).

III

"Thus has not the Editor himself, working over Teufelsdröckh's German, lost much of his own English purity?" (*SR*, 293)

From his close studies of the German writers Goethe and Jean Paul Friedrich Richter, in addition to those English theorists described above, Carlyle began to foster his own ideas about writing. Carlyle was aware of his debt to his German predecessors for his early development of philosophy and writing style. He wrote to his wife in 1826, "It is singular what a mockbird I am: I am writing here unconsciously in the very note of Jean Paul Friedrich Richter, on whose works I have been labouring for the last four weeks" (*Collected Letters* 4: 117). Richter gave Carlyle an early model for his style of writing and especially his brand of humor. J. W. Smeed points out that in 1858 an anonymous writer had noticed the shift in Carlyle's style between the *Life of Schiller* and *Sartor Resartus*, and suggested that the change began in Carlyle's 1827 essay on Richter (239–40). This shift occurred because of Carlyle's study and emulation of Richter. Carlyle's well-known description of Richter's style depicts many aspects of Carlyle's style as well, and perhaps shows us how competent a "mockbird" he was:

> There are few writers with whom deliberation and careful distrust of first impressions are more necessary than with Richter. He is a phenomenon from the very surface; he presents himself with a professed and determined singularity; his language itself is a stone of stumbling to the critic; to critics of the grammarian species, an unpardonable, often an insuperable rock of offence. Not that he is ignorant of grammar, or disdains the sciences of spelling and parsing; but he exercises both in a certain latitudinarian spirit; deals with astonishing liberality in parentheses, dashes, and subsidiary clauses; invents hundreds of new words, alters old ones, or by hyphen chains and pairs and packs them together into most jarring combination; in short, produces sentences of the most heterogeneous, lumbering, interminable kind. Figures without limit; indeed the whole is one tissue of metaphors, and similes, and allusions to all the provinces of Earth, Sea and Air; interlaced with epigrammatic breaks, vehement bursts, or sardonic turns, interjections, quips, puns, and even oaths! A perfect Indian jungle it seems; a boundless, unparalleled imbroglio; nothing on all sides but darkness, dissonance, confusion worse confounded! Then the style of the whole corresponds, in perplexity and extravagance, with that of the parts. (*Works* 26: 11–12)

Carlyle's rush of words and phrases imitates his subject. More remarkably, it becomes an accurate description of Carlylese, describing the use of metaphors, images, allusions, the creation and alteration of words, and the compounding of words, thoughts, and sentences that he was to employ so successfully in *Sartor Resartus*.

Richter wrote an influential theory of humor in which he equates the vantage point of the humorist with that of the religious person. Both are ever conscious of the dual aspect of the world and of man's place in it: "When man looks down, as ancient theology did, from the supernal world to the earthly world, it seems small and vain in the distance; when he measures out the small world and sees them together, a kind of laughter results in which there is pain and greatness" (Hale, 140). Richter describes the position of the humorist as looking down on the world, and placing this world on a level with the supernal world.

The humorist writes in earnest, for his use of humor is conscious and voluntary. The dual aspect of the world, the mutually exclusive propositions of humor, cannot exist simultaneously in the finite world and thus humor resolves the incongruities via leveling:

> Humour as the inverted sublime annihilates, not the individual, but the finite through its contrast with the idea. It recognizes no individual foolishness, no fools, but only folly and a mad world— unlike the common joker with his innuendoes. Humour lowers the great—unlike parody—in order to get the small beside the great. Humour raises the small—unlike irony—in order to set the great beside it. Humour thus annihilates both great and small, because before infinity everything is equal and nothing. (Hale, 135–36)

Richter's term for humor, the "inverted sublime," indicates the religious light in which he saw humor. For Richter, the sublime reconciles all divisions in the temporal world, including the split between man's sensual and spiritual natures. All aspects of the finite world mirror the infinite, leading to a process of mediation. The sublime does this by reaching towards the highest; humor and other forms of art mediate by lowering the great or raising the small and then comparing the result with the ideal. The humorist sees these relationships instinctively and conveys them to others through the force of his imagination. This theory was popularized in England by Carlyle in three separate reviews of Richter's work: an introduction to the translation of two works by Richter in Carlyle's volume *German Romance* (1827), "Jean Paul Friedrich Richter" (1827), and "Jean Paul Friedrich Richter Again" (1830).

In the first essay, Carlyle discusses the German writers, "here languishing in the transports of Sentimentality, there dancing the St. Vitus dance of hard-studied Wit and Humour" (*Works* 21: 2). How much easier the former sounds than the latter, and it was the latter that Carlyle aspired to create. In the second essay, Carlyle praises Richter's humor and looks to its essence "The essence of humour is sensibility; warm, tender fellow-feeling with all forms of existence" (*Works* 26: 16). Although Carlyle was capable of writing with sensibility, not all of his humor has this playful quality that is the outstanding attribute of Richter's. Carlyle also describes in this essay Richter's term for the highest humor, the "inverse sublime":

> True humour springs not more from the head than from the heart; it is not contempt, its essence is love; it issues not in laughter, but in still smiles, which lie far deeper. It is a sort of

> inverse sublimity; exalting, as it were, into our affections what is below us, while sublimity draws down into our affections what is above us. The former is scarcely less precious or heart-affecting than the latter; perhaps it is still rarer, and, as a test of genius, still more decisive. It is, in fact, the bloom and perfume, the purest effluence of a deep, fine and loving nature; a nature in harmony with itself, reconciled to the world and its stintedness and contradiction, nay, finding in this very contradiction new elements of beauty as well as goodness. (*Works* 26: 17)

While the humorist must be conscious of the infinite, his feet must be planted in reality. The humorist exalts, loves, and raises the ordinary towards a higher level. Like Thackeray, Carlyle believes that humor produces compassion. Although he follows Richter's definition in the main, Carlyle does not explicate humor's ability to lower the great or to compare the finite with the infinite. Raising the lowly sounds kindlier than lowering the great. Carlyle admired Richter's ability to raise the lowly, but in his use of humor, Carlyle frequently lowers the great. Both are keenly aware of the dualistic nature of the world and of man's place in it. Both accept the ameliorative ability of humor, although Carlyle finds the world more in need of improvement than approval. Humor performs a mediative process like that of art in changing our perception of things. Carlyle may have been reconciled to some aspects of the world and able to treat them with the "inverse sublime,"[4] but he saw much of the world as in need of radical transformation. In Carlyle's view, the "inverse sublime" is contrasted with irony: "That faculty of irony, of caricature, which often passes by the name of humour, but consists chiefly in a certain superficial distortion or reversal of objects, and ends at best in laughter, bears no resemblance to the humour of Richter" (*Works* 26: 16). Carlyle delineates irony as distinct from the transitory nature of wit and irony.

In his third essay on Richter, Carlyle found that humor was inimical to Richter. He had said so before, but here Carlyle's argument is filled out:

> [I]t is impossible for him to write in other than a humorous manner, be his subject what it may. His Philosophical Treatises, nay, as we have seen, his Autobiography itself, everything that comes from him is encased in some quaint fantastic framing; and roguish eyes (yet with a strange sympathy in the matter, for his Humour, as we said, is heartfelt and true) look out on us through many a grave delineation. (*Works* 27: 143)

This description sounds the depths of Carlyle's own mature style, a style built out of the individual words, the structure of the sentences, and the composition of a symbol system. What he only hints at here is the tone of the whole, but he does indicate the layers and complexity with which he endowed it. Carlyle himself recognized the similarity to his own patterns of style, but commented that there were several more important influences on his style than Richter, such as that of his parents.

As much as Carlyle admired the style of Richter, it would not work for him. His subject matter differed greatly from Richter's. He appreciated the "inverse sublime" and incorporated it into his own style, along with a wide range of other comic weapons. Carlyle's humor is more than mere denunciation or frippery; it is a method of vision. Carlyle's humor is a pervasive attitude composed in part of aggression, but he used his humor as an aesthetic device to recreate the world in his works. Frequently Carlyle rails in bitterness at the actual. He does this because of his belief in the ability of the individual to better himself and his world. Carlyle's humor develops from a dual perception of the world—of its potential and its present ludicrous reality—and his perception of mankind as one with both the angels and the apes. The gulf between the two propositions provides the substance of his humor. Incongruity arises from Carlyle's belief that the universe is at once finite and infinite, ludicrous and sublime, and humorous and tragic. He yearns for the sublime reconciliation of the incongruities of the world, a result achieved only through humor and art. Carlyle had acquired from Richter a means of incorporating humor into his text, but Carlyle differs radically from Richter in his explicit and implicit subject matter. He had been influenced by Richter, he had matured, and he had found a suitable subject.

IV

> "Sarcasm I now see to be, in general, the language of the Devil; for which reason I have long since as good as renounced it."
> (*SR*, 129)

Carlyle developed a manner of writing for *Sartor Resartus* that grew out of his natural temperament and his thinking and reading on the subject of humor. In counterpoint to his desire to convey the "genial sympathy with the under side" or the "inverse sublime," another factor appears in Carlyle's humor. He frequently resorts to sarcasm, satire, and irony because of his inability to be reconciled with the follies of the world. Carlyle felt repelled by mockery and satire where he identified these traits both in himself and in others. Voltaire, "the most impudent, blaspheming, libidinous blackguard that ever lived," personified this aspect of the comic in Carlyle's mind. Yet Carlyle's attraction to, and admiration for, Voltaire's writing shines through his avowal of distaste: "yet were we not continually shocked with some indecent, vicious or profane allusion—[Voltaire's work] would not be unentertaining" (*Collected Letters* 1:

43–44). Entertainment via moral sterility, through the destruction of the world without offering a replacement, called forth Carlyle's intellectual rejection.

During the 1820s and early 1830s, Carlyle wrote for the popular magazines of the day—*Blackwood's, Fraser's,* and the *Edinburgh Review.* Carlyle later rejected the ironic type of humor favored by these magazines. He wrote to his wife in 1836, "O that 'Edinburgh style of mockery'! Me too, with its hand withering influences, its momentary solacement fataller than any pain, it had well-nigh conducted to Hades and Tophet; but I flung it off, and am alive" (*Collected Letters* 9: 33). Carlyle desired that his work contain sportful, sympathetic humor rather than satire and irony; thus he fought his own tendency towards wit, sarcasm, irony, and satire. Masson recounts a conversation he had with Carlyle while walking together on a beautiful night, speaking of human behavior:

> "There was too much jesting in it, he said, too much of mere irony and of laughter at the absurd, too little of calm religiousness and serious walk with God." In speaking of the over-prevalence of the habit of irony, sarcasm, and jesting he used this phrase of "self-humiliation" "Ah! and I have gone far too much in to that myself—*sniggering at things.*" (*Edinburgh Sketches*, 83)

Carlyle looked beyond the immediate cleverness of mind that creates wit. This intellectual tendency, Carlyle revealed, lead to the "self-humiliation" of irony, sarcasm, and jesting. He wanted a humor composed of earnestness and wisdom, a humor with an ability to raise the lowly—to show the world as better than it is. Carlyle does not "snigger at things" for the sole purpose of pointing out their worthlessness. Rather, he undercuts man's basic assumptions about the world in order to prompt him to reexamine his premises—especially those about himself. Carlyle needed the presence in his work of the religious feeling that was to be the basis for the "inverse sublime." Carlyle constantly criticized superficial comedy, writing in his *Two Note Books* in 1832: "Nothing in this world is to me more mournful, distressing and in the end intolerable, than mirth not based on Earnestness (for it is false mirth); than wit, pretending to be wit, and yet not based on wisdom" (246). Carlyle always advanced a humor based on intellect and sympathy, used towards an ameliorative goal. At one point in *Sartor Resartus*, the Editor discusses Teufelsdröckh's work: "A wild tone pervades the whole utterance of the man, like its keynote and regulator; now screwing itself aloft as into the Song of Spirits, or else the shrill mockery of Fiends" (31). The Editor finds that Teufelsdröckh's humor verges too much towards satire and irony. Teufelsdröckh himself, much like his creator, claims to be rid of sarcasm: "Sarcasm I now see to be, in general, the language of the Devil; for which reason I have long since as good as renounced it" (129). Teufelsdröckh, like Carlyle, could denounce satire, irony, and sarcasm and yet continue to use it to enforce his points. Carlyle's style incorporates every form of humor he could create in his attempt to prod and awaken his readers. As he wrote to John Sterling in defense of his style, "But finally do you reckon this really a time for Purism of Style?" (*Collected Letters* 8: 135). The time demanded every weapon at Carlyle's disposal.

V

> "Up to this hour we have never fully satisfied ourselves whether it is a tone and hum of real Humour, which we reckon among the very highest qualities of genius, or some echo of mere Insanity and Inanity, which doubtless ranks below the very lowest." (*SR*, 32)

Away from the world with his wife at Craigenputtock, Carlyle wrote to his brother John in 1830, "What I am writing at is the strangest of all things.... A very singular piece, I assure you! It glances from Heaven to Earth & back again in a strange satirical frenzy, whether *fine* or not remains to be seen" (*Collected Letters* 5: 175). This "strange satirical frenzy" begins to describe Carlyle's tone in *Sartor Resartus*. The advance from Carlyle's earlier prose to that used in this work can be understood by examining two passages next to each other, the first from "Wotton Reinfred," the other from *Sartor Resartus*. In "Wotton Reinfred," Carlyle attempted to alternate a romantic tale involving a great deal of rushing about with Wotton's rests from traveling, at which time different philosophic positions were stated and considered by their adherents. Below Wotton pauses in his travels to see his beloved, Jane:

> One morning he found his fair Jane constrained and sad; she was silent, absent; she seemed to have been weeping. The aunt left the room. He pressed for explanation, first in kind solicitude, then with increasing apprehension; but none was to be had, save only broken hints that she was grieved for herself, for him, that she had much to suffer, that he must cease to visit her. It was vain that the thunderstruck Wotton demanded, "Why? Why?" "One whom she entirely depended on had so ordered it, and for herself she had nothing to do but to obey." She resisted all entreaty; she denied all explanation: her words were firm and cold; only by a thrill of anguish that once or twice quivered over her face could a calmer man have divined that she was suffering within. Wotton's pride was stung; he rose and held out his hand: "Farewell, then, madam!" said he, in a low steady voice; "I will not—" She put her hand in his; she looked in his face, tears started to her eyes; but she turned

away her head, hastily pressed his hand, and sobbing, whispered, scarcely audibly, "Farewell!" He approached in frenzy; his arms were half raised to encircle her; but starting back she turned on him a weeping face—a face of anger, love, and agony. She sternly motioned to him to withdraw, and Wotton scarce knew where he was till with mad galloping he had reached his own solitudes, and the town, and the fair Jane, and all his blessed dreams were far away. (36–37)

The story, as the would-be lovers touch and Jane sobs, is almost touching in the lack of communication between the two characters. There is no intentional humor here. It is intended to be a mysterious scene, the lady hiding her secret, her lover being hurt by the rejection without realizing that the lady is being forced to reject him because of a secret. The intended sentimentality and emotion does not come through successfully. Wotton feels resignation, the end of dreams and emotions. Carlyle recounts the events here in a stilted manner, overloaded with emotion, indicative of his inability to compose within the confines of traditional fiction. The scene becomes quite different, however, in book 2 of *Sartor Resartus*:

"One morning he found his Morning-star all dimmed and dusky-red; the fair creature was silent, absent, she seemed to have been weeping. Alas, no longer a Morning-star, but a troublous skyey Portent, announcing that the Doomsday had dawned! She said, in a tremulous voice, 'They were to meet no more.' The thunderstruck Air-sailor is not wanting to himself in this dread hour: but what avails it? We omit the passionate expostulations, entreaties, indignations, since all was vain, and not even an explanation was conceded him; and hasten to the catastrophe. 'Farewell, then, Madam!' said he, not without sternness, for his stung pride helped him. She put her hand in his, she looked in his face, tears started to her eyes; in wild audacity he clasped her to his bosom; their lips were joined, their two souls, like to dew-drops, rushed into one,—for the first time, and for the last! Thus was Teufelsdröckh made immortal by a kiss. And Then? Why, then—thick curtains of Night rushed over his soul, as rose the immeasurable Crash of Doom; and through the ruins as of a shivered Universe was he falling, falling, towards the Abyss." (145–46)

Looking at the two passages side by side, many words and phrases remain the same, but the feeling of the whole has changed. In "Wotton Reinfred" the heroine is named Jane and she is described as "constrained and sad" in the first sentence. The portrait of the woman is more real; she has her own story which we never are told, but she remains flesh and blood and tears. In *Sartor Resartus* the heroine has been given the name Blumine, already a symbolic name that the Editor ponders, but cannot successfully decipher. In this passage, she is his "Morning-star," a term already associated with her (143), and thus conjuring up with it what we already know of Blumine. This "Morning-star" is a further remove from reality, and she is "dimmed and dusky-red," words that describe a star in the sky, and a woman only metaphorically. Women, in *Sartor Resartus*, have previously been connected with angels and heaven showing the reverence with which Teufelsdröckh holds women. There is no longer any emphasis on the woman, she is there only to show the development of the hero.

In "Wotton Reinfred," Wotton presses on to ask Jane the story, and the narrator hints that the cause does not emanate from her. In *Sartor Resartus*, the result is announced symbolically in that the Morning-star has become a Portent of Doomsday before Blumine speaks. Teufelsdröckh now becomes the "thunderstruck Air-sailor," rather than the "thunderstruck Wotton" to give the scene an encompassing metaphoric reality in comparison to the original. The term "Air-sailor" may have several different references. Teufelsdröckh may be a soldier going into battle—the battle of the sexes; he is also a man traveling to the stars. And it may also be a tribute to Richter as the Germans are in control of the air as Carlyle mentions in his essays on the Germans. Blumine has previously been referred to as an "Air-maiden" (133). The construction "wanting to himself" is an archaic formulation, meaning "to fail to do justice to oneself, to fall below the exaggerative standard imposed by one's character and abilities" (*Oxford English Dictionary*). In this way Teufelsdröckh is a traditional hero. The editor announces, "We omit the passionate expostulations, entreaties, indignations," a euphonious listing of Teufelsdröckh's responses to Blumine. In these images of the Morning-star and the Portent and Air-sailor we have the "inverse sublime," the author playing with the heavens and the earth. The images first cause us to see the distance between earth and heaven, but then progress to a transcendent level.

The story in its later version becomes a parody of a romance, rather than a romance. We are presented with a new view of the romance, and must look at love anew. In this exaggeration and overstatement, in the wild rush of words and ideas, there is humor. The situation is universal, we have all been rejected, and here he is rejected after being united with his love and having a taste of immortality. The humor may be described as transcendence through incongruities, or as the "inverse sublime." There is a sense of worlds colliding, of the small being compared with the great, of a "strange satirical frenzy." The result is beyond the tawdry, and makes the ordinary extraordinary. The didactic purpose points out the seriousness of love, of all human emotion. In the same section from *Sartor Resartus*, the touch becomes a kiss, and for once they are joined. The kiss is a transcending experience, told in an overly dramatic manner, "for the first time, and for the last!" The fateful kiss has led Teufelsdröckh not to his damnation, but his salvation through his discovery of the Clothes Philosophy. Sartor has been made immortal by the kiss, in the tradition of Marlowe's Doctor Faustus being kissed by Helen of Troy and subject to the sin of demonality. The finite, a kiss, has led to the infinite, the uniting of the lover's souls. Through his use of imagery and allusions Carlyle succeeds in uniting the finite (failed love) with the infinite (the state of the soul). But the eternal is contrasted with the real as the mention of immortality is followed by the very earthly question, "What then?" Carlyle has previously defined love as "a discerning of the Infinite in the Finite" (141). The result is not the hero rushing off, but the close of the "curtains of Night" (no longer any "Morning-star"). The sense of finality is at a cosmic level; the curtains of night closing over his soul, the crash of doom, the ruins of the universe, the falling towards the abyss. Here the end of the possibility of earthly love becomes the end of the universe. Many of the phrases and the phrasing of the sentences refer to other works of literature. The words also refer to other usages occurring both before and after this passage in *Sartor Resartus*. With each use of these words, the meaning is enhanced and built up, adding to the dense texture of the work as a whole. The result is an exaggeration, true only on an imaginative and metaphoric level, and a transcendence through incongruity.

The passage from *Sartor Resartus* is beautiful, fascinating to read in its unique and startling use of words. Although shorter than the passage from "Wotton Reinfred," the passage from *Sartor Resartus* contains references to nature and the cosmos, allusions to other works of art, and a certain playful tone. The syncretic nature of Carlyle's style leads to humor. This is the mature style of humor that Carlyle developed for *Sartor Resartus*. It owes much to the romantic aspects of Richter's "inverse sublime," as indicated by the constant movement from the earth into the cosmos and by the connection of humor with pathos. Happenings on earth pale by comparison with the infinite, but are raised to the level of the sublime. Carlyle's style transcends the specific experiences of Teufelsdröckh and Blumine.

VI

"God must needs laugh outright, could such a thing be, to see his wondrous Manikins here below." (*SR*, 181)

In *Sartor Resartus,* humor occurs not in incidental flashes, but as an important element in understanding the work in its entirety. The constant use of humor in Carlyle's language, allusions, and in the tension between Teufelsdröckh and the Editor causes the reader to attend closely to the texture of the work, to enter into the universe evoked by Carlyle and to reexamine his usual means of thinking about the world. Humor establishes the prevailing tone of the work. The use of incongruity, the "inverse sublime," the juxtaposition of opposites, produces a result that incorporates the incongruous elements, thereby creating a transcendent reality. Carlyle's humor does not work as a sugar-coating to make the serious aspects of the work easier to swallow; rather, the humor forwards his didactic goal by shocking his readers and by providing a transcendent vision of the ludicrous and the sublime. Carlyle hoped to produce humor based on his characterization of the "inverse sublime," but he does not always succeed, for his tendency towards bitterness and mockery, stemming from disappointment, ill-health, and temperament, vies with his ideal of humor.

For all of Carlyle's early concern with distinguishing irony from humor, from working out his own theory, it is a subject which did not come up again in his letters or works. Once Carlyle had written *Sartor Resartus* and found his audience and his style, he did not seek to change his formula, but to apply it to other subjects through other works. He continued to use both kinds of humor throughout his work, as well as any other inventions of humor that helped him work towards his larger goal of educating his reading public to rethink everything in the world.

If Carlyle did not emphasize humor, it was always there, part of a larger picture. He describes his ideal audience in his essay, "The Opera" (1852), as "Populations of stern faces, stern as any Hebrew, but capable withal of bursting into inextinguishable laughter on occasion—do you understand the new and better form of character?" (*Works* 29: 403). This is how he wished to populate the universe, with people who can start to see through to the truth of things, who are able to explode the untrue with laughter. This is the audience that Carlyle tried to create for his own works. Such a population could only be created by exposing them to humor, both through the "inverse sublime" and through sarcasm, irony, and satire.

All that he had read and thought conspired with what was innate to him to develop a style now known to the world as Carlylese. His ideas were serious, and he presented them in a manner both personally and in his writing that included exaggeration, irony, and humor. Carlyle's seriousness of purpose, his desire to change the world, forced him to go beyond the sportive, to make use of the weapons of irony he had attempted to divest himself of. The variety of moods created by Carlyle indicate the vast, multifaced nature of the world. This style, consciously developed for *Sartor Resartus*, stayed with him with minor variations throughout his life. It was developed to produce a means of examining the world anew, to force his readers and listeners to confront their assumptions about their world and mankind, and to find a means of transcending the incongruities of life.

Notes

1 See Shine.
2 I am indebted throughout this discussion of Victorian humor to Tave and Martin.
3 I am indebted to Kinnaird's discussion of Hazlitt's essays.
4 Dale, Dunn, and Sutton discuss Carlyle's use of the "inverse sublime."
5 Charles Frederick Harrold points out the similarities between various passages in "Wotton Reinfred" and *Sartor Resartus* (318).

Works Cited

Aristotle. "Poetics." Trans. S. H. Butcher. *The Great Critics*. 1939. Ed. James Harry Smith and Edd Winfield Parks. 3rd ed. New York: Norton, 1967.

Carlyle, Thomas. *The Collected Letters of Thomas and Jane Welsh Carlyle*. Ed. Charles R. Sanders, Clyde de L. Ryals, et al. Duke-Edinburgh Edition. 25 vols. to date. Durham: Duke University Press, 1970.

———. *Reminiscences*. Ed. C. E. Norton. New York: Dutton, 1932.

———. *Sartor Resartus: The Life and Opinions of Herr Teufelsdröckh*. Ed. Charles Frederick Harrold. New York: Odyssey Press, 1937.

———. *Two Note Books of Thomas Carlyle*. Ed. Charles Eliot Norton. 1898. Mamaroneck: Paul Appel, 1972.

———. *The Works of Thomas Carlyle*. Ed. Henry Duff Traill. Centenary Edition. 30 vols. New York: Scribner, 1896–1901. New York: AMS, 1980.

———. "Wotton Reinfred: A Romance." *The Last Words of Thomas Carlyle*. Illustrated Cabinet ed. Boston: Dana Estes, 1892.

Clubbe, John, ed. *Two Reminiscences of Thomas Carlyle*. Durham: Duke University Press, 1974.

Dale, Peter Allan. "*Sartor Resartus* and the Inverse Sublime: The Art of Humorous Deconstruction." *Allegory, Myth, and Symbol: Harvard English Studies* 9 (1981): 293–312.

Dunn, Richard J. "'Inverse Sublimity': Carlyle's Theory of Humour." *University of Toronto Quarterly* 40 (1970): 41–57.

Eliot, George. "German Wit: Heinrich Heine." *The Writings of George Eliot*. 25 vols. Boston: Houghton, Mifflin, 1948. New York: AMS, 1970. 21: 68–124.

Froude, James Anthony. *Thomas Carlyle: A History of the First Forty Years of His Life, 1795–1835*. 2 vols. London: Longmans, Green, 1882.

Hale, Margaret R. "Jean Paul Friedrich Richter's *Vorschule der Aesthetik*: Fulcrum for its Period." Diss., Yale, 1970.

Haney, Janice L. "'Shadow-Hunting': Romantic Irony, *Sartor Resartus*, and Victorian Romanticism." *Studies in Romanticism* 17 (1978): 307–33.

Harrold, Charles Frederick, ed. *Sartor Resartus: The Life and Opinions of Herr Teufelsdröckh*. New York: Odyssey Press, 1937.

Hazlitt, William. *The Complete Works*. Ed. P. P. Howe. 21 vols. London: Frank Cass, 1967.

Heffer, Simon. *Moral Desperado: A Life of Thomas Carlyle*. London: Weidenfeld & Nicolson, 1995.

Higginson, Thomas W. *Carlyle's Laugh and Other Surprises*. New York: Houghton Mifflin, 1909.

Hobbes, Thomas. *Leviathan, The English Works of Thomas Hobbes*. Ed. William Molesworth. 9 vols. 1839–45. London: Bohn, 1939.

Hopkins, Gerard Manley. *The Correspondence of Gerard Manley Hopkins and Richard Watson Dixon*. Ed. Claude Colleer Abbott. London: Oxford University Press, 1935.

Kant, Immanuel. *Critique of Judgment*. Trans. J. H. Bernard. London: Macmillan, 1967.

Kinnaird, John. *William Hazlitt: Critic of Power*. New York: Columbia University Press, 1978.

LaValley, Albert J. *Carlyle and the Idea of the Modern: Studies in Carlyle's Prophetic Literature and its Relation to Blake, Nietzsche, Marx, and Others.* New Haven: Yale University Press, 1968.

Martin, Robert Bernard. *The Triumph of Wit: A Study of Victorian Comic Theory.* Oxford: Clarendon Press, 1974.

Masson, David. *Carlyle Personally and in his Writings.* 1885. Folcroft Library Ed., 1973.

———. *Edinburgh Sketches and Memories.* London: 1892.

Meredith, George. *An Essay on Comedy and the Uses of the Comic Spirit.* 1897. Port Washington, NY: Kennikat Press, 1972.

———. *The Letters of George Meredith.* Ed. C. L. Cline. 3 vols. Oxford: Clarendon Press, 1970.

Shine, Hill. *Carlyle's Early Reading, to 1834, with an Introductory Essay on his Intellectual Development.* Occasional Contribution No. 57. Margaret I. King Library. Lexington: University of Kentucky Libraries, 1953.

Smeed. J. W. "Thomas Carlyle and Jean Paul Richter." *Comparative Literature* 16 (1964): 226–53.

Sutton, Max Keith. "'Inverse Sublimity' in Victorian Humor." *Victorian Studies* 10 (1966): 177–92.

Tave, Stuart M. *The Amiable Humorist: A Study in the Comic Theory and Criticism of the Eighteenth and Early Nineteenth Centuries.* Chicago: University of Chicago Press, 1960.

Tennyson, G. B. *Sartor Called Resartus: The Genesis, Structure, and Style of Thomas Carlyle's First Major Work.* Princeton: Princeton University Press, 1965.

Thackeray, William Makepeace. *The English Humourists; The Four Georges.* New York: Dutton, 1929.

Vida, Elizabeth M. *Romantic Affinities: German Authors and Carlyle: A Study in the History of Ideas.* Toronto: University of Toronto Press, 1993.

Wilson, David Alic and David Wilson MacArthur. *Carlyle in Old Age (1865–1881).* London: Kegan Paul, 1934.

9

"Falling into Philistine Hands": Swinburne's Transgressive Correspondence

Nicholas Freeman

Cecil Lang's six-volume edition of the Swinburne letters (1959–62) has been a cornerstone of research into the poet since its appearance. Although selections from Swinburne's vast body of correspondence had appeared as long ago as 1917, when his cousin, Mrs. Disney Leith issued *The Boyhood of Algernon Charles Swinburne ... with Extracts from Some of His Private Letters,* Lang's meticulously annotated edition revealed the full extent of Swinburne's creative diversity. Here was the personality of the poet exposed as never before. An acute critic, an arch-pedant and quibbler (especially when harassing Andrew Chatto, his long-suffering publisher), Swinburne also possessed greater powers of vituperative invective than any writer since Swift. He was a solicitous son, a keen recorder of the beauties of nature, and a man equally at home with punctilious social niceties and disturbing Sadean fantasy. This almost heteropian diversity, with its attendant contradictions and inconsistencies, makes the letters endlessly fascinating. Lang's edition has informed all subsequent biographies, and while it has been supplemented by letters which have been discovered since its publication, it is unlikely ever to be surpassed as a resource for Swinburne scholars.

In view of the centrality of the letters in examining the poet's *oeuvre,* it is remarkable that such cursory attention has been paid to the comic writer who lurks within them. Lang himself calls Swinburne "the greatest parodist who ever lived" (introduction, *Letters* 1: xv) and praises his "satiric and epigrammatic gifts" (xvi), but differentiates between the formal production of the *Heptalogia* and the day-to-day humor of his correspondence, which he characterized in his preface to *New Writings by Swinburne* (1964) as "a robust comic gift" (preface, x): "Humor and logic were not Swinburne's strong points—he would have anathematized anyone who said this—and the heavy-handedness of the former is as amusing as the shiftiness of the latter" (introduction, *Letters* 1: xxxviii). This essay seeks to assess the truth of such estimation. Is Swinburne's humor the product of a thirty-three year old "adolescent" as Philip Henderson claimed in 1974 (161), or is the poet, as David G. Riede has argued more recently, a writer of "wonderful burlesques"

(38) whose refusal to incorporate such effects in the poetry of his mature years can only be regretted? Swinburne's most effective comic writing, outside the well-known items collected by Lang in *New Writings by Swinburne*, are to be found in volumes 1 and 2 of the letters which cover the years 1854 to 1875. Within these collections, the most rewarding letters begin with those to Balliol friends such as John Nichol in around 1857, and start to peter out with the dissolution of what might be called the Rossetti circle in the early 1870s. The key events here are D. G. Rossetti's mysterious estrangement from Swinburne in the summer of 1872 and the arrest of Simeon Solomon for homosexual offences in February 1873. The loss of these friends, coupled with the escalating chaos of Swinburne's own life, gave the poet less and less time and inclination for comedy, and while his gifts did not disappear with his retreat to Putney his opportunities for their use were much curtailed.

Any examination of the letters of this period is handicapped by the destruction, or continued unavailability, of many of these documents. Swinburne's letters to Solomon may still be in existence, but if so they are zealously guarded. Numerous letters to Nichol were burned by his daughter after his death, while those to Edward Burne-Jones were regretfully destroyed by the artist in the 1890s.[1] While wondering what other treasures have perished, it is more profitable to speculate as to why the letters were destroyed. Whose reputation was served by their destruction? Elderly gentlemen with aging eyes fixed on posterity would quite naturally remove any evidence which might expose unfavorable aspects of themselves to future generations, but what were the unfavorable aspects in question? Did the letters constitute an affront not just to the prevailing social standards of their composition but to more enduring values? Is the distinction they reveal between the idealized image of the artist and the human being an unpalatable one? Did Swinburne's recipients seek to protect him as well as themselves, having perhaps a greater awareness of the risks involved in writing so freely than a poet who never entirely lost a slight unworldliness? While Lang maintains that "yesterday's scandal has long since lost its power to shock" (introduction, *Letters* 1: xlix), it might be argued that the Swinburne letters continue to challenge English propriety, and thus refuse to be relegated to a convenient historical niche.

The letters essay a variety of comic modes. A favorite tactic is allusion. Swinburne enjoys combining his extraordinary knowledge of the Bible with his equally detailed knowledge of de Sade, producing a problematic amalgam of the religious with the aggressively atheistic; a volatile compound which can rarely be maintained for long because of its inherent instability. Then there is pastiche, especially the writing as schoolboy characters, where again the ferocity of Sadean imaginings combines uneasily with the slangy effusions of a supposed teenager. Here Swinburne appropriates a classic technique from pornographic fiction, where male authors frequently write as young women who are then made to display the paradoxical knowing innocence so typical of the genre.[2] However, by adapting the technique to male subjects, he draws once more upon an unlikely textual palette which has as its primary colors *Justine* and F. W. Farrar's *Eric or Little by Little* (1858). Swinburne also ventures frequently into parody of his contemporaries, revealing himself in the process to be a keen critic of Elizabeth Barrett and others. Margaret Rose has noted that the "ambivalent" nature of parody stems from the Greek "para-," which can be translated as "nearness" or "opposition" (33), and Swinburne's most accomplished rewritings foreground this ambiguity, straying at once as far as possible from their source and yet reinforcing its presence. The technique is displayed with particular clarity in his most sustained serial creation, the "Bogshire Banner," a Rabelaisian account of diocesan business which exploits the technique of mixing apparently incompatible linguistic registers to riotous effect.

Before considering these tactics in more detail, it is worth positing their intended audience. Evelyn Waugh once observed that "We cherish our friends not for their ability to amuse us but for our ability to amuse them," a remark which seems apposite in considering Swinburne's friendships (*Diary* [10 June 1963] 790). Certainly, throughout the early letters he seems consciously to be fulfilling the role cast for him in Pre-Raphaelite social gatherings. Edmund Gosse quotes a description of "the wild Walpurgis night of Swinburne's talk," before mentioning that Swinburne's "criticism in conversation was exceedingly stimulating, partly because it was independent and resolute, and partly because it was illuminated, far more than his written criticism, by whimsical flashes of humour and startling colloquial images" (294). As the fellowship broke up and relied more upon correspondence than spoken discourse, Swinburne seems to have attempted to remain the figure his friends had known during the painting of the Oxford Union murals in the late 1850s and the shared tenancy with Rossetti in Chelsea in the early 1860s, eras he recalled as the happiest periods of his life. It meant however that he was increasingly unable to adapt to the changes of the intervening years, especially to the growing public respectability of friends such as Burne-Jones and Nichol. Freed from domestic obligation, Swinburne was able to pursue his personal interests in a way in which many of his associates could not. This unappreciated but growing gulf between them implies that Swinburne's writing teetered on the edge of being an embarrassment, and that his correspondents destroyed his letters in order that he bequeathed to future generations the image of a great poet, not that of a psychological curiosity bedevilled by an arrested development.

While part of the "Rossetti circle," Swinburne seems to have enjoyed being at the center of conversation, and his letters reflect the same desire to

command the reader's attention using whatever materials come to hand. They
certainly suggest a high-spirited burning up of extraneous creative energies,
but in some cases at least they go beyond this into more collaborative
endeavors. Richard Monckton Milnes (Lord Houghton) and Swinburne were
able to write to each other "in character" to produce a series of letters
which blur the boundaries between personal utterance and epistolary
fiction, the medium of Swinburne's novel *A Year's Letters*, reprinted in
1905 as *Love's Cross-Currents*. To judge from Solomon's replies to
Swinburne's letters, their relationship may have been a similar one, for all
that Solomon played a lesser role. The use of recurrent running jokes—the
blasphemous squibs sent to D. G. Rossetti, the Sadean monikers and
situations of the letters to Monckton Milnes—further strengthens this idea
of combined comic energy rather than virtuoso exhibitionism.

The fixed points of Swinburne's satirical rewriting are the Bible and de
Sade. To see these poles as those of authority and rebellion which so
dominate his poetry is to oversimplify the issue, but the dialogue between
the two of them is certainly productive. Swinburne's study of Blake may
have encouraged him to believe that "Without contraries there is no
progression," and by combining antithetical ingredients, he was certainly
able to create a variety of comic opportunities. After these sources, his
favorite point of reference is Dickens, of whom he never tired, and from
whom he much enjoyed reading aloud favorite passages. Mrs. Gamp
appears in the letters in a variety of unlikely surroundings, and Swinburne
saw no reason why Dickens should not be used in legitimate criticism long
before George Gissing made similar claims in his 1898 analysis of the
novelist. Examining Swinburne's prose in his critical study of 1912,
Edward Thomas drew attention to Swinburne's attack on F. J. Furnivall,
whose writings he maintained combined "the double display of an
intelligence worthy of Mr. Toots and a dialect worthy of his friend the
Chicken" (117). While characters from *Dombey and Son* are here used for
the purposes of ridicule, Swinburne obviously admires Dickens's invention,
and by implication applauds in him the very qualities he finds lacking in his
adversary.

Swinburne's most accomplished verse parodies, excepting the self-parodic
"Poeta Loquitur," unpublished until 1918, appeared in his collection the
Heptalogia (1880). However, parody, pastiche, and paraphrase were such
intimate aspects of his creative technique that it is almost inevitable that his
letters should feature frequent comic examinations of other writers. His letter
to D. G. Rossetti of 1 March 1870 contains several examples of this rougher
parodic mode. Having offered detailed and intelligent comments on Rossetti's
work in a clutch of letters surrounding this one, he seems to have needed to
let off steam, and the result is a riot of Rabelaisian outrage. The *Memorials of
Edward Burne-Jones* suggest that Swinburne never made mock of "absent

friends," and that his comic method obeyed aristocratic codes of politeness.[3] In letters such as this, however, Swinburne's mockery of absent friends, authors who were unable to defend themselves, was particularly acute. It seems that propriety could only go so far, and that beyond social convention or the obligations of class there was a harsher aesthetic law which Swinburne enforced in the interests of literature, following the example of Juvenal, Swift and W. S. Landor, the influences he identified in a letter to W. M. Rossetti of 27 October 1871 (*Letters* 2: 163–65). His detailed critical comments on D. G. Rossetti's poetry, for instance, show both a keen awareness of the potentialities of language and a refusal to be overawed by the older man's reputation, while his harsh though accurate comments on William Morris show that friendship alone could not blunt his critical sword. In view of this, it is predictable that writers who were not close associates should receive unfettered mockery. The Brownings are treated with particular severity, Robert in a reworking of "James Lee" spoken by "Mrs. James Lee" and Elizabeth in Sadean rewritings of her "Cry of the Human" and other poems from her collection *Poems* (1844). Both these writers would feature in the *Heptalogia*, although Swinburne frequently praised their work in other contexts. In such instances, notes Philip Henderson, Swinburne's writings "reveal a curious complexity of temperament which combines admiration with parody of what it admires" (68).

Nobody would claim that the parodies of the Brownings are Swinburne's funniest or most subtle pieces, but they do provide some clue as to his motivation for satirizing the work of writers he professed to value. The parody of "James Lee" is, Swinburne suggests, "an improvement on the obscurity and equivocal tone of the original." Here he contrasts scholarly delicacy with the cruder lines preceding it:

(Mrs. James Lee *loquitur*, with self-satisfaction)—

That is a p——,
　　But *this* is a c——!
For a cripple, a stick;
　　For the hounds, the hunt;
　　　And for *you*, my duck,
(As you *are* such a brick
　　As care to f——,)
Here's a q—— to lick,
　　And an a—— to suck!

His parodies of Elizabeth Barrett Browning essay the same aggressively scatological mode, fascinated by dildoes, sodomy, and the sexual proclivities of royalty, the recurrent obsessions of his unfinished and perhaps unfinishable mock-French novels of the early 1860s, *La Soeur de la Reine*

and *La Fille du Policeman*. The second of the three parodies of E. B.
Browning, written in "rimes très libres," is probably the most effective:

> "There is no c——," the b—— saith,
>   But none, "There is no bottom";
> And Paphos oft, with bated breath,
>   Will use the terms of Sodom:
> And what, when seen by girls in front,
>   Was but a lank limp tassel,
> Becomes, though puny near a c——,
>   Gigantic near an a—hole.[4]

Here, the pragmatic Christianity (rather like that of A. H. Clough's
"Dipsychus") of Barrett's original offends Swinburne's atheistic pride in
suggesting that in times of "bitter need," he will revert to faith rather than the
resources of the intellect. His response is motivated, however subconsciously,
by an affront to his own belief system, and the parody becomes in a sense
an act of vengeance, deliberately twisting the religious language of the
original to a resolutely secular and "immoral" purpose. In these savage
rewritings of the esteemed, Swinburne never spells out the offending terms,
even though there is no doubt as to those which he intends the reader to
assume. The parodies seem to suggest a lingering reverence for the power
of transgressive language. Recognizing the totemic quality of forbidden
discourse, Swinburne contrives to draw it ever more to his reader's
attention—he at once avoids and yet magnifies its obscenity, inferring too
the inability of the original author to ever employ such idioms. There may
also be a criticism of the Brownings' marriage, a union so far removed
from his own background and creative practices that it is viewed almost
with contempt. The terms of "cunt" and "arse" are simultaneously implied
and erased, playing upon Rossetti's anticipated complicity in creating the
poem, the conventions associated with the representation of such language
and the inevitability of its rhyme scheme. There remains a schoolboyish
relish of outrageousness, but there is also an understanding that in the
1870s, even private letters risked becoming public once they were posted.
The Post Office Act of 1853 had placed tighter controls on the transmission
of subversive or indecent material than ever before, and the guidelines on
what was to be considered "indecent" or "obscene" had been sharpened by
the case of *R. v. Hicklin* in 1868. Swinburne must have been aware that his
notions of humor were not sanctioned by the state, and he resorted to
implying offensiveness rather than stating it in black and white. Such
caution, even though his intended meaning remained obvious, was sensible.
The sensational correspondence of Boulton and Park was to be a central
feature of the prosecution's case against them between April 1870 and May
1871.[5] Swinburne and Solomon followed developments with great interest

(the latter attending the trial on at least one occasion), and thus must have been aware of the activities of the Metropolitan Police in seizing private communications with or without legal permission. Swinburne's letter finishes with the disingenuous remark, "I am not responsible for the lady's rhymes," another example of the way a decorous observation intensifies the provocative lines which preceded it. This comment also suggests that Swinburne was playing not just with literary ideas, but with the escape clauses of criminal activity, although he surely did not intend any unwelcome reader to be assuaged by so half-hearted an alibi.[6]

Swinburne's satirical targets in his letters are attitudinal as much as textual. Despite the Browning parodies, he rarely attacks another author directly, preferring instead to mimic particular modes of language so as to get at the views behind them. Anthony Trollope's conservative politics and insipid Anglicanism seem to have been particularly provocative, but open ridicule of Trollope is rare, as once more Swinburne admired elements of his writing.[7] In a letter to Monckton Milnes of 11 July 1879, Swinburne made the mischievous suggestion that Trollope had prepared a version of de Sade's *Justine* for the stage, but his attacks on the novelist generally took the form of concern with propriety.[8] Swinburne was delighted by the way in which extreme linguistic precision could magnify obscenity and its offence, a tactic Joe Orton was to employ in his plays a hundred years later. The impeccably coy and euphemistic style of Trollope could also be noted in *The Times* press reports and in court and ecclesiastical circulars of the period, and it was here that Swinburne employed a favorite parodist's trick of employing a dual language, that is, mixing one mode of expression with the concerns of another. Hence the politeness and linguistic niceties of his "Bogshire Banner" reports make them far funnier, and more satirically effective, than they would have been if expressed in coarser terms. Swinburne also frequently parodied writers whom he admired, not least de Sade, and himself, using the same merciless critical acumen as had lambasted Trollope.

Bakhtin and other theorists have argued that parody is a metatextual form; that is, that it serves as an exploratory critical tool as well as a style of creative expression. Swinburne seems to have understood this very quickly. At Eton, he composed a tragedy called *The Unhappy Revenge*, inspired by Webster's *The Duchess of Malfi* and Massinger's *The Virgin Martyr*. In a letter to the critic Churton Collins of 11 December 1876, he claimed that he had "contrived to pack twice as many rapes and about three times as many murders as are contained in the model … It must have been a sweet work, and full of the tender and visionary innocence of childhood's fancy" (*Letters* 3: 229). Philip Henderson describes it as "an astonishing achievement for a boy of twelve" (15) and notes how Swinburne's imitative facility allowed him to ventriloquize the speech of long dead playwrights while yet adding a twist of his own evolving style. Evidently, the young poet already saw elements of absurdity in the final act of a play such as *Women Beware Women* which could easily be taken to a comic extreme, although it has to be admitted that Swinburne's own sensibilities derived more amusement from the martyrdom of female saints than those of most people. At Oxford, he wrote another play with the Ortonesque title, *Laugh and Lie Down*, a line derived from Cyril Tourneur. Here again he seems to revel in the tragic paraphernalia of Elizabethan drama while yet finding it vaguely silly. Swinburne's textual allegiances were frequently surprising. He defended the publication of Rabelais against the Society for the Suppression of Vice in 1875, and admired Aristophanes, yet he condemned Thomas Wycherley's "prurient and leprous" mind, and was appalled by *Troilus and Cressida* and the fourth act of *Pericles*. At the same time, he remained eternally grateful to Thomas Bowdler for first introducing him to Shakespeare. Here again, Swinburne shifts between the expected and the startling (see Edward Thomas, 107).

The "Bogshire Banner" shows Swinburne's interaction with further unlikely textual sources: On one hand, the daily business from the *Church Times*, and eminently respectable works such as George Eliot's *Scenes of Clerical Life* (1858) and Trollope's Barchester Chronicles (1855–67) (the name of which may have suggested Arseborough); on the other, Rabelais. In rewriting one author in the style of a very different other, Swinburne helps to create a literary echo chamber in which texts comment on each other and on the editor who sought to blend them together. In this example, he explores abstract notions of humor; is Rabelais only funny in terms of his own work, or is the "Rabelaisian" a transferable mode, able to thrive when replanted in the arid soil of the Victorian rather than medieval clergy? The question was certainly an interesting one for Swinburne, who in the early 1870s was adding Rabelais to his pantheon of esteemed French writers. In a letter to Rossetti dated 12 February 1870, he attacks the reviewers of "the Asinaeum" as "turdilousifartishittical buggeraminous ballockwaggers," adding "I have not the French of the passage under my eye, but the translation is no doubt—and very properly—softened down to the standard of English delicacy. The original probably verges on coarseness" (*Letters* 2: 89). The masterly understatement of the final line again suggests that Swinburne was not always as heavy-handed as Lang believes. Rabelais would resurface the following month in a key letter to D. G. Rossetti of 1 March (*Letters* 2: 107–108). Here Swinburne responds to a question from his friend in a passage which goes some way to suggesting the outrageousness of his conversation:

> As you were kindly interested in the literary fortunes of the
> "Bogshire Banner" I send you a sample of the excerpts I lately

forwarded to Etretat from that periodical. (The divorce case—
Codsham v. Codsham is not on yet.) "We are authorized to state
that there is no foundation for the report lately current that a
matrimonial alliance was on the *tapis* between the Hon. Monica
Friggins, of The Dildoze, Tongueham, and her cousin Mr.
Suckling Cunter, of St. Onan's. Since the death of old Bishop
Tollywegg, the diocese of Arseborough has been the scene of
continual disputes. Bishop Buggeridge (late Archdeacon—the
Ven. Athanasius Buggeridge) being most High, even Ritualist,
is on bad terms with the most influential clergy—even his own
relations, the Very Rev. Dean Buggeridge, who is Broad
Church, and their cousin the Hon. and Rev. Onan Buggeridge,
who is *very* low. Oil has been thrown on the waters by the
appointment of the Rev. Simplicius Pricksmall, of Little
Pissing, to the Perpetual Cure of St. Onan's. The tenantry of
Mount Scrotum (the country seat of the Dowager Duchess of
Arseborough) celebrated with old English games (pitching the
crowbar, shooting at the prick, running at the ring, filling up the
hole (also called the nine—or even more than nine—men's
Morris) bugger my neighbour, piss in the corner, back
throwing, cleaving the pin, and, to wind up with, a general
cockfight—her Grace for that day only permitting the free use
of her cock-pit) her Grace's recovery from a bad attack of
gonorrhoea. The prayers of the congregation were last Sunday
desired in Arseborough Cathedral for Viscount Fitzarse, who is
suffering from syphilis, contracted at Poxford." (2: 108)

Such humor is undoubtedly a matter of taste. However, if one does find
it amusing, to what elements does one respond? Its juxtaposition of wildly
contrasting linguistic registers? An anticlericalism keenly aware of
divisions within the Victorian church? The suggestion of rural England's
scabrous underbelly? The mid-Victorian nostalgia for the countryside is
here challenged and subverted by a catalogue of urban vices which
infiltrate not only the landed gentry but also place names and even rural
sports. There are certainly elements which seem to have a certain
adolescent joy in outrage for its own sake—Swinburne is evidently
delighted by the mere association of respectable figures with sexually-
transmitted disease—but beyond this is a more ambitious assault on
Victorian propriety. In suggesting that an apparently innocent country town
seethes with corrupt carnality, Swinburne forms a bridge between the high-
spirited relish of obscenity in Rochester—although Swinburne does not
refer to the Restoration satirist in the letters of this period, he must surely
have known such works as "Signior Dildo" and "Tunbridge Wells"—and
the post-World War I "Mortmere" stories of Christopher Isherwood and
Edward Upward. The targets are very similar in each; the clergy, social
pretension, and sexual hypocrisy have changed little since the classical

period as far as satirists are concerned. However, what marks Swinburne out as a particularly acute critic is his ability to mimic prevailing discourses. Perhaps at no time in English history has the country been so exact in its notions of linguistic nicety as in the second half of the nineteenth century, and Swinburne takes this very rigor as the basis for his comic technique. Without recourse to taboo utterance, he contrives to create an environment in which the conventional standards of morality which he so despised are triumphantly overturned. Innuendo is a key weapon in this assault, as is exactitude of nuance in asides such as "*very* Low," and the Dickensian inventiveness of names such as Suckling Cunter. As stated already, linguistic registers compete and collide. The Dowager Duchess seems to have strayed in from mid-Victorian pornography, while the doctrinal disputes draw upon Barchester and the *Essays and Reviews* controversy, which had involved Swinburne's friend Benjamin Jowett. At the same time, Swinburne picks away at the aggregation of euphemism and history which have robbed many English place names of their pagan associations and consequent vitality. The letter is thus not merely a caprice dashed off to amuse a friend, but a statement entirely consistent with Swinburne's wider artistic beliefs of the period, which similarly rejected Christianity, conventional sexual morality, and normative decorum.

Edward Thomas remarks that Swinburne "had in fact something like the standards of any other Englishman of his class in most matters excepting art and beauty" (104). In matters of humor, he was aggressively aristocratic, or rather, suggested that the artist himself was a being who could not be judged by bourgeois social norms, the classic aesthetic position of Baudelaire, Whistler and Oscar Wilde, among others. Although Monckton Milnes had been an outspoken opponent of the Obscene Publications Act of 1857, Swinburne himself had little interest in attempting to redefine the meaning of obscenity. In his article "Pornography and Obscenity" (1929), D. H. Lawrence suggested that the word "obscene" had lost its meaning—rather than having a precise definition, it was in fact a social construction decided upon by "the mob." "If the lower ten million doesn't know better than the upper ten men, then there's something wrong with mathematics" he argues, a wounded artist attempting to justify his art to an outraged audience. Lawrence maintains that words have different meanings for the mob and for the artist, and here his argument is much like that which can be deduced from Swinburne's letters. There is, however, an important difference. While Lawrence was urging society to reexamine its language and moral attitudes, Swinburne has no such reforming zeal. For him, the obscene is relished precisely because it is obscene. To have assimilated de Sade into everyday language would have robbed him of the sacred aura which Swinburne found in his writing, and would also have reduced social divisions rather than maintaining them. Here Swinburne seems to inhabit two worlds simultaneously. Although he rejected many elements of his background, he never abandoned his pride in his illustrious lineage; his aristocratic *hauteur* is well illustrated in letters to Chatto and in his replies to critics throughout his life. At the same time, he allied himself with another aristocracy—a loose assemblage of artists and writers who flouted bourgeois convention just as arrogantly. It is tempting to assume that Swinburne's final break with Solomon was occasioned not by the nature of Solomon's sexuality but by his being apprehended by the police; that Swinburne accepted the judgment of society in the case, and thus was caught between endorsing the opinion of a public to whom he felt superior, or facing up to the full implications of Solomon's nature, which may have illustrated the fatal divide between the world of literature and that of everyday life. While not excusing Swinburne's shabby treatment of his former friend, the recognition of such attitudes goes some way to explaining his behavior.

Swinburne's humor is much influenced by a belief that what is funny for gentlemen and artists would appall and disgust more timid social classes. His blasphemy is casual and light-hearted in letters to D. G. Rossetti, although even a couplet such as "So *this* is your bloody religion / To father your kid on a pigeon" (*Letters* 2: 98) comes complete with a bogus guarantee of authentication: "It is not part of a carol, but occurs in the Breviarium S. Mariae in Silvis, ed. R[everend] Pater Severinus," an allusion to Dom Severino of *La Nouvelle Justine*. This type of allusion to fictitious works, a technique Swinburne had taken to a high pitch of accomplishment in his *Spectator* hoaxes and the first series of *Poems and Ballads* (1866) means that the brief joke becomes contextualized in a wider world of Sadean extra-textuality; Swinburne is able, through his source, to jeer not only at Christianity but also at the mechanisms of exegesis through which it is propagated. His facility in inventing fake but convincing literary sources allows him to destabilize many of the scholarly traditions which he otherwise reveres, and once more creates a division between the creative literary consciousness and the more parasitic critical mechanisms springing from it. While Swinburne, like Matthew Arnold, seems to have had no difficulty in accepting his dual role as poet and critic, he remained fiercely skeptical of criticism which came from those not entitled to wear the purple of artistic accomplishment.

Throwaway blasphemies litter the letters of the 1860s and early 1870s, frequently accompanied by Sadean disquisitions. On other occasions, especially in writing to Monckton Milnes, Sadean themes predominate to the exclusion of almost everything else. As Lang observes, those who do not share Swinburne's propensities may well find such effusions tedious, but there are times when de Sade collides with the quotidian to considerable comic effect. In February 1863, Monckton Milnes sent Swinburne a clipping from the Liverpool *Daily Post* which had appeared in *Punch*. The inclusion of the advertisement itself raises interesting questions about Victorian notions of humor, but Monckton Milnes can scarcely have foreseen the ingenuity of his protégé's response. A Liverpool widower sought a young housekeeper to care for his three young sons. Prospective applicants were instructed to apply giving details of age, address, and willingness "to give corporal punishment" (*Letters* 1: 76, note 2). The advertisement inflamed Swinburne's imagination, and he suggested that he and Milnes "answer it privately, and desire him [the advertiser] to address Mme. de Clairwil, Poste Restante, Bournemouth, Care of M. le chevalier de Sade." On 12 February 1863, Swinburne sent Monckton Milnes a long letter in French (*Letters* 1: 79–83) supposedly replying to the advertisement in the style of de Sade's *Justine*—had this piece ever been sent in reply to the original advertiser, one can only wonder at the man's response! Swinburne claimed that his first exposure to de Sade left him helpless with laughter, but the Marquis's hold upon him became increasingly sinister as the poet's obsession with his work intensified. The reply to the advertisement reveals something of Swinburne's complex relationship with de Sade at this time, and an attitude which walks a thin line between revelling in the absurdity of *Justine* and endorsing its attitudes. Swinburne must have relished the idea of Sadean ideologies taking root in Bournemouth, even in 1863 the quintessential English holiday resort, but the sheer thoroughness of his reply robs the idea of some its comic vitality. Here perhaps is an early example of Swinburne not knowing when to stop; in the process he mars an originally amusing and subversive creation.

Set-pieces such as Sadean and schoolboy pastiche and the "Bogshire Banner" reveal Swinburne's ability to develop comic ideas at some length, yet he is often funnier when indulging in brief asides, the types of remark which enlivened his conversation at this time. Swinburne's comic eye was drawn to aptness and absurdity; he delights in discovering a creditor called Mr. Pincebourse (*Letters* 2: 168) and later in life collected newspaper clippings concerning namesakes of famous poets.[9] He was also rarely at a loss for an appropriate or amusing quotation. What the reader of the Swinburne letters regrets is that there are not more moments like these. When not over-elaborating his obsessions, Swinburne could issue delightful vignettes, such as a plan apparently involving the ultra-respectable Lady Pauline Trevelyan to dress Swinburne in women's clothing and introduce him to Georges Sand as "the typical *miss anglaise émancipée* and holding the most ultra views" (*Letters* 1: 76). Even here though, Swinburne combines a farcical social situation with a literary rationale, finding his feminine alter ego to be "the British Mademoiselle de Maupin." It is a pity that Edmund Gosse in particular did not seek to preserve more examples of Swinburne's verbal humor, and that Simeon Solomon, whose quick wit provoked his best inventions should have been similarly ill-served by biographers.[10]

R. B. Martin has noted how as the nineteenth century progressed, critics became increasingly fascinated by how humor worked. Before Freud opened up the psychological exploration of jokes in *Jokes and Their Relationship to the Unconscious* (1905), theorists as far removed as W. M. Thackeray, George Meredith, and Leslie Stephen were grappling with definitions and trying to make sense of the ways in which language manipulated its listeners. Victorian commentators, like their scientific contemporaries, seem to have been fascinated with the process of classification, the bringing of order to an apparently chaotic lexical universe. At the same time, there were many highly skilled parodists, C. S. Calverley, J. K. Stephen, Owen Seaman and so on, who, like Swinburne, were practical rather than theoretical critics of comedy. Swinburne's understanding of what was funny and what was not seems to have been an intuitive one, and, as in so many other areas of his career, he was often unable to recognize or observe the natural limits of particular inventions. Again, his study of Blake and Shelley may have counseled him against too analytical an approach to humor; he did not need to put the comic violet into the crucible, and knew that "If the sun and moon should doubt they would immediately go out." He regarded letters as individual performances tailored to the needs and tastes of the recipient, and, if he occasionally substituted his own preferences for those of his readers, this does not invalidate his strategy *per se*.

In spirit at least, parodists are often either young radicals who use humor to ridicule an establishment with which they are in dispute, or the older conservative voices of that very establishment who use similar weapons to defend their own values. Although this distinction is true only in a general sense, it encapsulates Swinburne's changing attitudes as his political affiliations began to ossify in the latter part of his life. His poetry challenged the complacency he saw in Tennyson's "Idylls of the Prince Consort," and the hypocrisy of a culture which was perfectly happy to study the depravities of classical civilization as long as these remained in Latin or Greek. In private correspondence, one might expect Swinburne to have made even bolder assaults on Victorian literary and social conventions, yet, for all their outrageous detail, the letters remain more conservative than Swinburne realized. In his essay "Swinburne and Romantic Authority," David G. Riede paraphrases Michel Foucault's argument that "the way for an artist to challenge the prevailing discourse of power is by transgressing the allowable limits of that discourse—and Swinburne's explicitly erotic and blasphemous language in *Poems and Ballads* ... was nothing if not transgressive" (25). By publishing poems such as "Dolores" or "Laus Veneris," Swinburne was bringing his ideas into the public sphere, exactly where they could do most damage to his readers' sensibilities, generating outraged debate and causing what amounts almost to panic in some areas.[11] The letters, though, are private utterances, and Swinburne only writes in his most transgressive modes to a few like-minded individuals. As one might expect, there is no hint of this side of his character in letters to his mother or mere acquaintances. The effect of this is a limiting quality of self-determined response. By sending the "Bogshire Banner" to Rossetti, or George Powell, or Simeon Solomon, Swinburne was creating an enclosed coterie in which such ideas could be bandied about with impunity. That the members of the fraternity were alarmed about the response of society to their behavior is evidenced by a number of letters to Swinburne and the destruction of others. Swinburne faced blackmailers on several occasions.[12] On others he sought to minimize the potentially explosive contents of his epistles. Writing to C. A. Howell in February 1873, Swinburne worries that Joseph Hotten, his erstwhile publisher, possesses "some papers relating to me in the mass of his collection, of which an unscrupulous man might possibly make annoying use ... I should of course not like any scrap *signed* with my name which in the dirty hands of a Grubstreet libeller might be turned to ridicule or to any calumnious or vexatious purpose to fall into such hands if such an accident could be avoided." He continues, "Neither Hotten nor for that matter any man alive has in his possession anything from my hand for which I need feel shame or serious regret or apprehension even should it be exposed to public view" before drawing a distinction between what he terms pieces written "in moments of chaff or Rabelaisian exchange of burlesque correspondence between friends who understand the fun" and "communications" on the subject of flagellation (*Letters* 2: 227). Clearly Swinburne was more alarmed by the possibility of the latter being exploited by blackmailers than the former, but he still recognized that his aristocratic good name stood a chance of disgrace if certain papers were ever to come to light.

This was not the first time he had worried about the matter. Rossetti wrote to Swinburne on 6 November 1871, telling him that

> every line you have ever written will one day be religiously raked up by greedy and often doubtless malevolent exploiteurs, and it is very hard for those who receive these wonderfully funny things of yours to resolve on taking the only safe course with them for your sake—that is, to destroy them after they have been abundantly laughed over by a circle of friends who know what mere fun they are. (*Letters* 2: 167, note 5)

Swinburne's reply to this is a revealing one. Four days later he told Rossetti that Powell had promised to take every care to prevent Swinburnian effusions from "falling into Philistine hands." "As to privacy," he wrote, "if we are to be shackled in our inmost intercourse with our closest friends by fear of future vermin, we may as well resign all liberty, and all thought of elbow-room for fun or confidence of any kind, at once" (*Letters* 2: 167). Here is a defense on two counts. Like Boulton and Park, Rossetti argued that the letters in question were "mere fun" and written solely to amuse. This separated the letters from the "literary" work, even though the two shared many similar concerns. Swinburne's argument is their private nature; that they were intended only for a social elite, not the vulgar "Philistines" who could never hope to properly understand them. The letters, for all their subversive wit, eventually lose their force through being addressed only to the converted. The risks of prosecution were too great for their author to venture into more public spheres, and the comic energy of the pieces remained another of Swinburne's secrets, revealed, like the full extent of his alcoholism and interest in flagellation, only after his death.

Swinburne never developed into a novelist, despite the promise of *Love's Cross-Currents* and *Lesbia Brandon*. It is tempting to see his withdrawal from society as having denied him the raw material of prose fiction, but there are other explanations. Changes in his social group, especially the absence of D. G. Rossetti and Solomon, robbed his ideas of vital sounding boards, while his attachment to the cause of Italian liberty led to increasingly serious studies of political issues, rather than the fantastic world of Bogshire. Of course, Swinburne's unmanageable alcoholism and attendant chaotic behavior also prevented him from involvement in prolonged prose works. The letters of the early 1870s show a man on the point of collapse, even though his intellect remains as sharp as ever. He is continually requesting books and making intelligent comments upon what he has read, while at the same time being unable to find essential household articles or look after himself. Frequent changes of address, and the losses and disorganization which followed in their wake meant that extended projects were difficult to pursue. It is telling that Swinburne's most complex historical dramas and most of his detailed critical works were accomplished at The Pines. Whether the products of these years represent worthy substitutes for the gradual disappearance of his comic work remains arguable. Watts-Dunton, for all his virtues, was unlikely to inflame the satirical imagination.

Swinburne's letters have chiefly been read by biographers, eager to expose their writer's psychological and sexual quirks to the public gaze. While the letters represent an essential resource for those interested in the poet's life, their significance for his work remains largely unexplored. To read Swinburne's poetry or prose without them is, in some sense, to do him a disservice, as well as to misrepresent the complex creative tensions of the 1860s and 1870s.

Notes

[1] By the time of his death in 1897, Edward Burne-Jones was a pillar of the artistic establishment he had once challenged (see Fitzgerald, 227). John Nichol had served as Professor of English at Glasgow University in the course of a long and respected academic career.

[2]   There are many examples of this technique in H. S. Ashbee's *Index of Forbidden Books* (1877–1885) and Steven Marcus's *The Other Victorians* (1964).

[3]   "The biting wit which filled his talk was at times to leave his hearers dumb with amazement always spared one thing, and that was an absent friend" (Georgiana Burne-Jones, *Memorials of Edward Burne-Jones* 1: 215).

[4]   The original, from Barrett's *Poems* (1844) begins:

> "There is no God," the foolish saith,
>   "But none There is no sorrow,"
> And nature oft the cry of faith
>   In bitter need will borrow:
> Eyes, which the preacher could not school,
>   By wayside graves are raisèd
> And lips say "God is pitiful,"
>   Who ne'er said "God be praisèd."
>   Be pitiful, O God!

[5]   For details of the case, and a politicized reading of its significance, see Bartlett; for further details see also Roughead.

[6]   For a summary of the Hicklin case and its implications, see Robertson.

[7]   See Hyder, 14, 210.

[8]   For the full text of this letter, see *Letters* 4: 72–73. All quotations of Swinburne's letters come from Lang's six-volume edition.

[9]   The best example is in a letter to William Bell Scott of 20 June 1881. Enclosing a cutting, Swinburne writes: "The enclosed is the most scandalous example of genius degraded by eccentricity that I have seen since Robert Browning was taken up for running stark naked down Hyde Park, through the Marble Arch, at noon—'his second offence' according to the *Times* reporter of some years ago." The cutting reads as follows: "Matthew Arnold, a printer [Swinburne altered this to 'a poet'] and two postmen named Evans were fined 10s. each at the Wandsworth police-court for playing 'tip-cat' in the street. The magistrate said that he thought men of their age should know better than play at a dangerous game of that kind in the street" (*Letters* 4: 222–23).

[10]   Many of Solomon's quips were recorded by his friend Henry Holiday. A selection of these, together with an estimation of Solomon's humor by Sir William Richmond, is reprinted by Croft-Cooke, 40–41.

[11]   Donald Thomas notes that "even in such poems as 'A Ballad of Life' and 'A Ballad of Death,' with their Pre-Raphaelite pictorialism and their almost Spenserian lushness, there were passages detailing a girl's breasts and nipples in a manner calculated to bring a family reading to an abrupt halt" (120).

[12]   For further bulletins from Bogshire, see *Letters* 2: 60 (#326) and 2: 140–41 (#384). There are accounts of several blackmail attempts; for example, the unsavory business of copyright negotiation with George Redway in the 1870s (see Donald Thomas, 116).

Works Cited

Ashbee, H. S. *Index of Forbidden Books*. London: privately printed, 1877–85. Republished as *Bibliography of Prohibited Books ...: Biobiblio-icono-graphical and Critical Notes on Curious, Uncommon and Erotic Books* (By Pisanus Fraxi [pseud.]. 3 vols. New York: Brussel, 1962.

Bartlett, Neil. *Who Was That Man? A Present for Mr. Oscar Wilde*. London: Serpent's Tail, 1984.

Burne-Jones, Georgiana. *Memorials of Edward Burne-Jones*. 2 vols. London: Macmillan & Co., 1904.

Croft-Cooke, Rupert. *Feasting with Panthers*. London: W. H. Allen, 1967.

Fitzgerald, Penelope. *Edward Burne-Jones: A Biography*. London: Michael Joseph, 1975.

Gosse, Edmund. *The Life of Algernon Charles Swinburne*. London: Macmillan, 1917.

Henderson, Philip. *Swinburne: Portrait of a Poet*. London: Routledge, 1974.

Hyder, Clyde K. *Swinburne: The Critical Heritage*. London: Routledge, 1970.

Lang, Cecil Y., ed. *The Swinburne Letters*. 6 vols. New Haven: Yale University Press, 1959–62.

———, ed. *New Writings by Swinburne; or Miscellanea nova et curiosa*. Syracuse: Syracuse University Press, 1964.

Lawrence, D. H. "Pornography and Obscenity." In *A Selection from Phoenix*. Ed. A. A. H. Inglis. Harmondsworth: Peregrine, 1971. 306–27.

Leith, Mrs. Disney. *The Boyhood of Algernon Charles Swinburne*. London: Chatto & Windus, 1917.

Marcus, Steven. *The Other Victorians*. New York: Basic Books, 1966.

Riede, David G. "Swinburne and Romantic Authority." In *The Whole Music of Passion: New Essays on Swinburne*. Ed. Rikky Rooksby. Aldershot: Scholar Press, 1993.

Robertson, Geoffrey. "The Victorian Legacy." In *Obscenity*. London: Weidenfeld & Nicolson, 1979. 26–33.

Rose, Margaret. *Parody/Meta-Fiction: An Analysis of Parody as a Critical Mirror to the Writing and Reception of Fiction*. London: Croom Helm, 1979.

Roughead, William. *Bed Companions*. Edinburgh: W. Green, 1933.

Thomas, Donald. *Swinburne: The Poet in his World*. London: Weidenfeld & Nicolson, 1979.

Thomas, Edward. *Algernon Charles Swinburne: A Critical Study*. London: Martin Secker, 1912.

Waugh, Evelyn. *The Diaries of Evelyn Waugh*. Ed. Michael Joseph. Harmondsworth: Penguin, 1979.

10

Arnold's Irony and the Deployment of Dandyism

James Najarian

"Modern critics tend to take Arnold seriously," R. H. Super has written (186). As Super notes, Arnold's contemporaries did not see him as grave; on the contrary, Arnold was decried for his foppishness and flamboyance. A famous caricature by Max Beerbohm shows a tiny Augusta Ward pleading with a vast Matthew Arnold "Why, Uncle Matthew, will you not be wholly serious?" Plenty of Arnold's work—"On the Translation of Homer," the preface to his *Essays in Criticism*—ridicules his opponents. At the same time, Arnold often ridicules himself, stationing a self-consciously aesthetic persona he labels as "weak," "feeble," or "defective." Arnold's self-irony, I believe, derives from a particular element in his psychic history: his early dandyism. Arnold's activities at Oxford were, as Trilling puts it, "jorrockesque" (19). Park Honan sums up the young Arnold in a short paragraph:

> Matthew's formal achievements were unimpressive, but his clothes, laughter, antics, and minor feats were remarkable. People recalled his leap over Wadham's railings. They even remembered him naked. Capering on a riverbank one day, he made such a show of himself that a clergyman "came up to remonstrate," according to G. H. Lewes's diary. "Is it possible," Matthew replied while waving a towel, "that you see anything indelicate in the human form divine?" (51)

Arnold's concentration on his antics, rather than his studies, was to result in the deserved humiliation of a second-class degree. He overcame that defeat by winning a fellowship a year later to Oriel. The dandyism continued unabated. Concurrent with the Oriel fellowship he took a post as private secretary to Lord Lansdowne. A sinecure in the fashionable world, it demanded little work from him. When he married, he dropped his Oriel fellowship and appointment under Lansdowne, took an exceptionally demanding post as a school inspector, and suppressed the outward signs of his foppery—the colognes, colored waistcoats, and expensive habits.

Biographers have largely interpreted the performance of the young Arnold as a stage of development that Arnold passed through and did not return to. In Trilling's view, Arnold chose this persona to counter the influence and the

memory of his father. Thomas Arnold single-mindedly reformed Rugby
and private education in England. The elder Arnold induced in the pupils
of his reformed Rugby a Christian seriousness which bordered on
"nervous priggishness." Matthew Arnold's dandy tried to deflate it. The
young man countered his father's earnestness and sincerity with an ironic
detachment. Instead of caring deeply about everything in the world,
Matthew was to care for nothing in particular. "He had been trained to
every sober virtue of England, taught everlastingly that life was serious,
yet every act that his friends recall of Matthew Arnold at this time is a
denial of his training, every word that he writes in his letters is an
assertion of his own pleasant difference from other men" (21–22). Trilling
sees Arnold's dandyism as a more or less calculated act. To Trilling, the
dandy worked as a shield or screen, behind which the real work of self-
cultivation went on: "Arnold indulged ... in a kind of muted Byronism of
conduct to preserve imagination and self from the corroding effects of his
society in order that he might still be a poet" (97). Park Honan also sees
Arnold's dandyism as a strategy that he used to conceal a volatile and
sentimental temperament (59). Arnold did keep the persona going in his
letters to Clough even after his real interests shifted from gamboling to
studying. We know this from the huge reading lists Arnold made up for
himself during the time he wrote some of the letters (Trilling, 94). E. K.
Brown writes that no one quite expected *The Strayed Reveller* from
Matthew Arnold; his first volume of poems surprised those who knew him
with its seriousness (34).

    Scholars disagree on the relationship that this youthful stance might
have to the rest of Arnold's work. Most scholars of Arnold have tried to
explain away this side of the man. A. Dwight Culler admires Arnold's
rejection of his youthful pose and christens it "self-mastery" (125). The
recent biography by Nicholas Murray hardly mentions it. This essay will
argue that dandyism was far more than a stage of Arnold's youth; rather,
it informs the complex stance and tone that Arnold constructs in his
criticism, a stance of mockery, theatricality, and ambivalence that together
we can label irony. In an earlier essay, I argued that Arnold's poetry
records the force with which Arnold repressed his dandyism when he
married and took up the respectable position as school inspector; I
connect the repression of his dandyism to both Arnold's sense of himself
vis-à-vis the Romantics and to Arnold's awareness of the androgynous
implications of the dandy's pose. But like all good repressions, Arnold's
dandyism returns. The suppressed dandyism returns in the style and the
content of his essays, particularly "The Function of Criticism at the
Present Time" and *Culture and Anarchy*. While Arnold's dandyism may
have begun as a mode of the body, it returns as a critical position.
Arnold's ironic stance derives in part from the stance of the dandy.

I

Dandyism as a phenomenon has come more fully into the critical radar in the last decade. As Rhonda Garelick and Ellen Moers have shown, dandyism was theorized already in the nineteenth century in works by Balzac, Barbey, and Mallarmé. Moers has delineated the pose from those famous dandies like Brummell and the Count D'Orsay to its literary representations in Bulwer-Lytton, Disraeli, and Beerbohm. Domna Stanton has traced its French sources to the early concept of the *honnête homme*. Beau Brummell, the famous gambler, man-about-town, and sometime friend of the Prince Regent, becomes, for all of these writers, the model dandy.

Critics have offered several explications of the dandy's activities. Many of these writers interpret the dandy's stance as a reaction to industrial capitalism. For Maryléne Delbourg-Delphis, the dandy lives a radical individualism born of the French Revolution. He fashions an aristocracy for himself, convinced of his power of superiority (199). James Eli Adams theorizes that the dandy, like the nineteenth-century ideal of the gentleman, is a redefinition of masculinity that responds "to pressures of modernity" (5). Both are male modes of being that are renegotiated while an industrial age was fast making traditional mode of masculinity obsolete. The dandy manufactures a mode of aristocracy when the genuine aristocracy has lost its power. The dandy is, in Adams's view, "a masculine figure defined in antagonism to the market" (25). For Delbourg-Delphis, originality is the dandy's supreme value (109). The dandy exhibits a radical detachment from the concerns of the normal human being into order to form a "radical alterity" or "singularity" that replaces aristocratic values. That singularity can be represented by distinct attitudes: the dandy's detachment is a primary example. One might note the infatuated Barbey on Brummell: "Sometimes there came into his clever eyes a look of glacial indifference, without contempt, as becomes a consummate Dandy ..." (54).

For Adams and other critics, the dandy represents his detachment with theatricality. This emphasis on display creates a male mode that is on as much display as traditional feminine modes (Adams, 11). The dandy's concern with the ephemera of daily life, then, is a stance that displays his autonomy. The dandy's attention to dress, many argue, is a conscious strategy. The dandy's oeuvre is passing, unstable, and futile, argues Françoise Coblence, and up-ends our ideas of permanence, artistic worth, and morality (11). For Coblence, the dandy's exhibitionism represents an anxiety about the failure of royal power; his life is lived as a public spectacle in part to replace the loss or vitiation of such spectacles after the fall of the *ancien régime*. "The dandy," Coblence writes, "does not exist if he does not appear to others" (12). In Adams's words, "the dandy is a fundamentally theatrical being, abjectly dependent on the recognition of the audience he professes to reject" (122). The dandy's fastidiousness is a strategy of display, and could reach absorbing heights. Asked if he ate any vegetables, Brummell replied, "I once ate a pea."

In the process of making himself a prose critic, Arnold adapts dandyism to the creation of a critical persona. Though many critics have wondered about Arnold's change from poet to critic, few have attended to the cultural sources of Arnold's prose persona. William Robbins sees Arnold's persona as performing in his criticism essentially the same role that Honan and Trilling see dandyism performing in his youth, concealing his selfhood: "The airs and graces of a 'kidglove' prophet of culture which the relentlessly earnest found so irritating were as much of a mask of the gay insouciance of the young man" (Robbins, 28). Arnold's only outwardly satirical work, the series of letters later collected as *Friendship's Garland*, manages jokes by manufacturing a series of voices deployed at the reader's expense. In it, the critic "Matthew Arnold" purports to introduce his friend Arminius, Baron von-Thunder-ten-Tronckh, who states with some violence the views that the real Matthew Arnold really took. Arnold represents "himself" here as foolish, ineffectual, and deeply concerned with appearances; Arminius says "it is impossible to enter into any serious discussion with him" (*Works* 5: 56). Recording a late "meeting" with "Matthew Arnold," Arminius writes, "poor Matthew Arnold, upon this, emerged suddenly from his corner, and asked hesitatingly, 'but will anyone still call him a man of delicacy?'" (*Works* 5: 326). Brian Nellist, in one of the very few critical works to mention *Friendship's Garland*, notes that the series of personae destabilizes the reader. Its "serious playfulness" "refuses to let the reader settle onto safe ground" (30). For Nellist, Arnold's play with critical personae has a definite object, a form of irony that makes the reader aware of his own discomfort, a discomfort with knowledge as its end. Arnold's irony "makes the reader anxious, but anxious for understanding, not for himself" (43).

Arnold's self-conscious display of his ability to play with personae, not to be himself, is evident early on. The foregrounding of the writing persona has a distinctive flamboyance; he draws attention to his own methods. Arnold foregrounds his own style as a method, and then foregrounds his foregrounding of his style. In his "Preface" to *Essays in Criticism*, even as he apologizes to Mr. Wright for almost saying there was no proper reason for Wright to exist (in his essay "On Celtic Literature"), he adds: "My vivacity is all but the last sparkle of flame before we are all in the dark, the last glimpse of color before we all go into drab—the drab of the earnest, prosaic, practical, austerely literal future" (*Works* 3: 287). Style becomes substance. Arnold's "vivacity" registers more than vivacity, but an attitude toward display.

It is interesting to note the literary manifestations of the young Arnold's self-conscious detachment from the religious and political concerns of his contemporaries. Again, following Trilling and Honan, the seriousness of Thomas Arnold (and of Arthur Hugh Clough) is theatrically rejected in Matthew's pose. When revolutionaries dethrone Louis-Philippe and precipitate revolutions all over the Continent in 1848, Arnold displays himself as hardly interested: "Even to such a man revolution and bodily illnesses are fine anodynes when he is an agent or patient therein; but when he is a spectator only, their kind effect is transitory" (*Letters* 1: 86). Arnold not only activates or advocates detachment, but turns it into a way of life. Arnold's constant advice to Clough is to cultivate detachment, but almost as interesting is the language that he uses in doing so:

> You ask me in what I think or have thought you going wrong: in this: that you would never take your assiette as something determined final and unchangeable for you and proceed to work away on the basis of that: but were always poking and patching and cobbling at the assiette itself—could never finally, as it seemed—"resolve to be thyself"—but were looking for this and that experience, and doubting whether you ought not to adopt this or that mode of being of persons *qui ne voulent pas* because it might possibly be nearer to truth than your own: you had no reason for thinking it *was*, but it *might* be—and so you would try to adapt yourself to it. You have I am convinced lost infinite time in this way: it is what I call your morbid conscientiousness—you are the most conscientious man I ever knew: but on some lines morbidly so, and it spoils your action. (*Letters* 1: 254)

For Arnold, Clough is too restless, too dissatisfied, and too involved. That "morbid conscientiousness" was instilled in Clough by Matthew's father, the ever-serious Thomas Arnold. (Clough and Arnold were friends at Rugby.) Arnold's letter is first of all a diatribe against earnestness—Clough's serious and repeated tries to search for and determine "the truth" as found or represented by other people. For Arnold, this truthful way of life is not constructed—Arnold's metaphor is taken from sculpture—but simply performed. The notion of the *assiette* ("pedestal") is important here; it assumes that its bearer is already on display.

Matthew's detachment is represented not only in the advocacy of indifference as performance, but also stylistically by self-quotation. Arnold quotes himself at Clough, precisely at the moment when one might expect Arnold to quote Goethe or Marcus Aurelius. "Resolve to be thyself" comes from his own poem "Self-Dependence." Arnold's quotation of his own work not only demonstrates "self-dependence," it enlarges his own authority. Arnold installs himself as an authority for himself—and even as an authority for his friend. Arnold does not chip away at his own *assiette*, but adds to it.

I would like to suggest that this 1853 letter to Clough exhibits the characteristics of literary dandyism that Arnold will work into a cultural and poetic program, as well as a style, in "The Function of Criticism at the Present Time." Arnold's work insists on its difference—not just his difference in opinion from other writers, but its essential alterity. This insistence on radical alterity bears the mark of the dandy. In the preface to *Essays in Criticism*, this emphasis on singularity is repeated several times: "I have always sought out to stand by myself," he writes (*Works* 3: 287); and on the next page, "I prefer to stand alone" (3: 288). This alterity is theorized in "The Function of Criticism," where Arnold takes dandyistic detachment to the sphere of literary criticism. Certainly Arnold's essay can be historically situated at a time when criticism and reviews bore a pronounced political bias and often a religious tinge. In the process of trying to remove criticism from these interests, he establishes a theatrical alterity as the basis for criticism:

> It is of the last importance that English criticism should clearly
> discern what rule for its course, in order to avail itself of the
> field now opening to it, and to produce fruit for its future, it
> ought to take. The rule may be summed up in one word,—
> disinterestedness. And how is criticism to show disinterestedness?
> By keeping aloof from what is called the "practical view of
> things"; by resolutely following the law of its own nature, which
> is to be a free play of the mind on all subjects which it touches,
> by steadily refusing to lend itself to any of those ulterior,
> political, practical considerations about ideas, which plenty of
> people will be sure to attach to them, which perhaps ought often
> to be attached to them, which in this country at any rate are
> certain to be attached to them quite sufficiently, but which
> criticism has really nothing to do with. Its business is, as I have
> said, simply to know the best that is known and thought in the
> world, and by in turn making this known, to create a current of
> life and fresh ideas. (*Works* 3: 269–70)

For Steven Marcus, "disinterestedness" manufactures a "transcendent value" to replace religion (438). While not disagreeing with Marcus's insistence on what disinterestedness does for Arnold, I would like to examine what it may be in the context of Arnold's self-making. Arnold emphasizes the true critic's otherness—his removal from unspecified "alien practical considerations." If criticism is to follow the "law of its own nature," clearly the critic is to follow the law of his own, too. As he wrote to Clough: "resolve to be thyself." "Disinterestedness," then, is a form of self-fashioning. The "ulterior, political, practical considerations" Arnold tries to avoid are exactly the considerations Arnold did without during his Oxford days—and exactly, it might be added, the alien and practical considerations that derailed Clough every time. The critic is the dandy; in order to preserve itself from the outside world, criticism proclaims itself essentially other. The critic and the dandy are really the only two people in

England who have the luxury of knowing "the best that is known and thought in the world."

"As an undergraduate," Honan writes, "Matthew defeated laws of purpose and consecutive time by doing the same thing over and over— throwing a line into a brook, repeating hilly walks or skiffing expeditions— or by turning logical discussions into circular ones by being solemn and absurd at once" (86). This portrait of Arnold as a young man sounds uncannily like a description of Arnold's prose. Even before we get to the level of interpretation, Arnold's distinctive word-choice establishes his alterity. The language Arnold uses to establish critical detachment displays itself in interesting ways. The earliest reviewers of Arnold noticed this tendency to repeat himself. This trick of repetition of phrases quickly individualizes his prose; the repetition of phrases not only substitutes for, but becomes a personal style. "Things as they are," "disinterestedness," "the best that is known and thought in the world"—Arnold's repetitions become a short cut to and shorthand for originality. In order to make his formulations memorable, Arnold makes sure that the reader will never forget them.

Most importantly, repeating oneself is a covert way of quoting oneself. I noted earlier that Arnold quotes his own poetry in his letter to Clough. The technique is one of autocanonization. Arnold not only relies on himself in an Emersonian way, he becomes his own authority, self-begotten, self-made. Garelick writes that the dandy's goal is to appear as if he begets himself: "All dandyism hints at a wish for male autochthony. The dandy, after all, longs to create himself as an emblem of complete originality, with no other progenitors save other dandies" (19). Arnold's autochthony is represented not only in the establishment of a persona with certain stylistic and argumentative tics, with the reliance on his own work to represent a tradition. "The Study of Poetry" begins with a whole paragraph of Arnold quoting Arnold. Very early on, Arnold sets himself up as canonical. If the dandy denies his sources, Arnold's critic becomes his own precursor. These moves solidify the character of Matthew Arnold—they begin to write him into the role of the critic which he describes. Kept away from practical considerations, the critic replicates himself as the only alternative. His own words become the sole doctrine that can oppose "alien practical considerations."

This necessary display of alterity and difference of the persona Arnold assumes in "The Function of Criticism" motivates the more famous and humorous turns of his argument. We can take the famous "Wragg is in custody" passage as an example:

> But let criticism leave church-rates and the franchise alone,
> and in the most candid spirit, without a single lurking thought
> of practical innovation, confront with our dithyramb this

paragraph on which I stumbled in a newspaper immediately
after reading Mr. Roebuck:—
"A shocking child murder has just been committed at
Nottingham. A girl named Wragg left the workhouse there on
Saturday morning with her young illegitimate child. The child
was soon afterwards found dead on Mapperly Hills, having
been strangled. Wragg is in custody."
Nothing but that; but, in juxtaposition with the absolute
eulogies of Sir Charles Adderly and Mr. Roebuck, how
eloquent, how suggestive are these few lines! "Our Anglo-
Saxon breed, the best in the whole world!"—how much that is
harsh and ill-favored there is in this best! *Wragg!* If we are to
talk of ideal perfection, of "the best in the whole world," has
any one reflected what a touch of grossness in our race, what an
original shortcoming in the more delicate spiritual perceptions,
is shown by the natural growth amongst us of such hideous
names,—Higginbottom, Stiggins, Bugg! (*Works* 3: 273)

The critic is so distant from "practice, politics, and everything of the
kind," that his objection to the jingoistic fooleries of Mr. Roebuck shrinks to
a mere syllable: "*Wragg!*" The critic, divorced as the dandy is from practical
considerations, can no longer object on the basis of morality, still less on the
basis of politics. Arnold's dandy attacks on the basis of aesthetics. Arnold's
mannered style certainly emphasizes his aestheticism, and aesthetics become
his point rather than simply support it. Like the dandy, Arnold self-
consciously occupies himself with ephemera—with precisely the least
important details of the story. Similarly, when Arnold sets himself on the
great projects of the middle classes, a "disinterestedness" that can only be
represented in terms of taste determines the direction of his attack:

> Everyone knows the British College of Health; it is that building
> with the lion and the statue of the goddess Hygeia before it; at
> least I am sure about the lion, though I am not absolutely certain
> about the goddess Hygeia. This building does credit, perhaps, to
> the resources of Dr. Morrison and his disciples; but it falls a
> good deal short of one's idea of what a British College of Health
> ought to be. In England, where we hate public interference and
> love individual enterprise, we have a whole crop of places like
> the British College of Health; the grand name without the grand
> thing. (*Works* 3: 279–80)

What is exactly wrong about the British College of Health remains a
mystery to the reader; we only know that the statue of Hygeia is perhaps
not well cast. The argument about the college serves mainly to introduce
another one of Arnold's self-begotten phrases, "the grand name without the
grand thing." In some way, these kinds of arguments are not just strategies

of his assumed disinterestedness, they are the inevitable products of it. Arnold's presents himself as an appearance who judges on appearances. Arnold puts forward "weak" or aesthetic arguments in the course of creating not only an essay, but a persona, who argues from style alone. This move helps create alterity or individuality by emphasizing the dandy's concentration on appearances and distancing his own concerns from the matter at hand. Arnold takes an ironic view of argument. His false arguments short-circuit argument; they cannot quite be taken seriously, which is their intention.

This emphasis on the aesthetic not only creates alterity, it creates alterity in a specific mode: the feminine. In his social criticism, Arnold continually puts himself forward as physically weak or lacking. As early as the preface of his *Essays in Criticism*, Arnold represents himself as "feeble": "the English middle class, of which I myself am a feeble unit" (*Works* 3: 289). Adams has written that the dandy's display creates a masculine mode of theatricality. But the mode of the dandy, with his concentration on traditionally feminine spheres of dress and deportment, does not necessarily, as Adams argues, create masculinity out of these materials. Rather, the dandy emphasizes his distance from traditional masculine ideals. Marie-Christine Natta remarks that the dandy's performance of alterity necessarily entails his removal from traditional notions of gender stability—particularly from sexuality and marriage, as marriage implied the acceptance of a whole series of social codes (139, 145). Marriage identifies one as masculine in a traditionally recognizable (and public) way. It includes one in the social system. But the performance of dress and deportment in a mode recognized particularly in England as feminine questions an unmitigated allegiance to gender.

II

Arnold was increasingly lampooned as a dandy in the course of the nineteenth century, both in England and America. Francis Attwood, in *Life*, was to draw him as a large-headed, supercilious man with his nose in the air, wearing a tight, dapper jacket, and even tighter trousers (Marks, 29–44). By the time *Culture and Anarchy* was published in book form, many critics had taken Arnold to task in reviews of his previous works or of the versions of the chapters of *Culture and Anarchy* published in the *Cornhill*. They seemed to object less to the specific points of his argument than to his foppery. His arguments seemed feminine, his style effete. Fitzjames Stephen called "The Function of Criticism" "very pretty reading," and continued:

> he really does work himself into an esoteric enthusiasm for the
> particular point which he enforces. It is also to be noticed that

his points are always of the same kind. His self-imposed
mission is to give good advice to the English people as to their
manifold faults, especially as to their one great fault of being
altogether, in an intellectual and artistic point of view, inferior
to the French. He is so warm about the subject that he has
taught himself to write a dialect as like French as true English
can be. (Dawson and Pfordresher, 683–84)

It is not stretching the matter much to see what is behind Stephen's idea
that Arnold's English sounds like French. For "French," read "Continental"
or "unmanly." Frederic Harrison wrote a supposed dialogue between an
enthusiast of Arnold and Arminius von Thunder-ten-Tronckh. When
exposed to Arnold's doctrines, Arminius compares the author to "some
petit-maitre preacher passing his white hands through his perfumed curls,
and simpering thus about the fringes of his stole" (Dawson and Pfordresher,
234–35). James Macdonnell all but called Arnold a eunuch:

Philistines as we are, we may be permitted to ask a sight of the
poet's credential. From what place does he hail? What has he
done that he should put on airs, and proclaim himself so
immensely holier than other men? The answer is simple; he is
the high priest of the kid-gloved persuasion ... A little arrogance
is no doubt pardonable in a Jeremiah denouncing the sins of a
people; but the assurance must first of all be given that the
Jeremiah is real. The time has not come for recognizing as a
Jeremiah the man who can write pretty verses, turn pretty
sentences, and express pretty sentiments. There is no analogy, we
would remind Mr. Arnold, between a poet and a fop. (Dawson
and Pfordresher, 165–66)

What precisely is Macdonnell is getting at when he calls Arnold a "fop?"
Macdonnell could not have known much about Arnold's youth; Macdonnell
was reviewing "On Celtic Literature," published in 1867, long after
Arnold's Oxford days. Foppishness not only registers that dandyistic
position of Arnold's persona, but at once encapsulates the political and
sexual dimensions of Arnold's persona. Macdonnell registers the aesthetic
turn of Arnold's argument—hence his own repetition of "pretty" as well as
the tone of Arnold's prose: "pretty sentences." This combination of
aesthetic argument and political detachment infuriates Macdonnell. Arnold
is able to poke fun at Liberals and Tories, high-churchmen and dissenters—
he refuses to align himself with any sect or party. Macdonnell thinks this
lack of commitment to any side uncommon and swank. It seems to him a
sort of political androgyny.

What is striking about *Culture and Anarchy* is Arnold's ability to exploit
his critics' marking him as a fop or dandy. Arnold does not really disagree
with his critics on this point. On the contrary, he purports to admit to their

criticism and then exploits them in the process of displaying his originality. Arnold not only quotes himself as he does in "The Study of Poetry" or "The Function of Criticism," he remakes his persona just along the lines of his critics' condemnation of him. In his spoof, Frederic Harrison pictured Arnold holding culture aloft with a pouncet-box: by book publication, Arnold pictures himself handing around that pouncet-box. Arnold not only quotes, but proudly displays, Macdonnell's handling of him in his introduction to *Culture and Anarchy* (*Works* 5: 88).

Arnold takes advantage of his enemies by becoming more foppish than they accuse him of being. "Culture" and "Anarchy" seem to be secondary considerations in the essay of that title. *Culture and Anarchy* is not just a study in culture, but a study of Arnold's place in that culture. It becomes an advertisement for his own theatricality:

> Still, I have often spoken in praise of culture, I have striven to make all my works and ways serve the interests of culture. I take culture to be something a great deal more than what Mr. Frederic Harrison and others call it: "a desirable quality in a critic of new books." Nay, even though to a certain extent I am disposed to agree with Mr. Frederic Harrison, that men of culture are just the class of responsible beings in this community of ours who cannot, properly, at present, be entrusted with power, I am not sure I do not think this the fault of our community rather than of the men of culture (*Works* 5: 88).

The reluctance to assume power cannot be represented more theatrically. "I—I—I"—certainly the real question is not what culture is, but who the I is. This I seems to displace the definition of culture, as culture's importance is in creating the writing persona. Culture's role is to foster detachment, much as criticism aimed for disinterestedness: "Culture indefatigably tries, not to make what each raw person may like the rule by which he fashions himself; but to draw ever nearer to a sense of what is indeed beautiful, graceful, and becoming, to get the raw person to like that" (*Works* 5: 96). Arnold expands the categories and definitions that infuriated Macdonnell. Any loyalty toward a definition of culture that breaks down traditional loyalties of class and sect makes its followers not only politically, but also artistically and socially, undefinable.

Arnold adapts one of the most powerful selections from dandy's *oeuvre*. For many critics, the dandy's accomplishment is his new solution to the problem of class. The dandy creates his own class—even in terms of economics, he seems not to spring not from the economic terms of the society but from himself. For Wilfred Ihrig, the dandy's rejection of industrial, political, and religious affiliations is itself an affront to the class most highly invested in affiliation: "the Dandy is the personified Antithesis to middle-class business" (28). At the same time, the dandy displays himself as separate from the aristocracy while using its techniques. For Delbourg-Delphis, Brummell created a new "stoicism of luxury, an aristocratism that mocked the aristocracy" (23). (Brummell famously literally mocked the aristocracy after the Prince Regent had dropped him; walking in Regent's Park he ran into an acquaintance in the company of George and inquired quite loudly, "Who's your fat friend?")

In his fabrication of the alien in *Culture and Anarchy*, Arnold adapts the dandiacal fantasy in order to claim a place for himself outside of the class system. Arnold self-deprecatingly disassociates himself from his own class in order to create and join this fourth estate of Aliens. In his discussion of the Barbarians, Philistines, and Populace, Arnold offers a concrete example of each class in its strength and in its defect. Arnold himself is once again the example of a "defect":

> I will venture to humbly offer myself as an illustration of defect in those forces and qualities which make our middle class what it is. The well-founded reproaches of my opponents declare how little I have lent a hand to the great works of the middle class; for it is evidently these works, and my slackness at them, which are meant, when I am said to "refuse to lend a hand to the humble operation of uprooting certain definite evil" ... the line, again, of a still-unsatisfied seeker which I have followed, the idea of self-transformation, of growing towards some measure of sweetness and light not yet reached, is evidently at clean variance with the perfect self-satisfaction current in my class, the middle class, and may serve to indicate in me, therefore, the extreme defect of this feeling. (*Works* 5: 138)

That display of himself as a "defect" of the middle class dates back at least to the preface to *Essays in Criticism*. Of course, Arnold is not really "slack" in all the works of the middle class. His work on education was as indefatigable as anyone else's. Nor does *Schools and Universities on the Continent* shy away from facts, numbers, and the "alien practical considerations" Arnold said (in "The Function of Criticism") were contrary to the spirit of criticism. Arnold merely manipulates a few words of his critics to make a ticket out of the middle class. After Arnold manages to escape that class he uses himself again as an example, this time of how one can be in sympathy with any class:

> I myself am properly a Philistine,—Mr. Swinburne would add, the son of a Philistine ... I have, for the most part, broken with the ideas and the tea-meetings of my own class, yet I have not, on that account, been brought much nearer to the ideas and works of the Barbarians or of the Populace. Nevertheless, I never take a gun or a fishing-rod in my hands without feeling that I have in the ground of my nature the self-same seed

> which, fostered by circumstances, do so much to make the
> Barbarian; and that, with the Barbarian's advantages, I might
> have rivalled him. (*Works* 5: 144)

When Arnold feels certain primitive emotions, he feels his connection with
the populace as well. The detached Arnold is able to have things two ways.
He is able to escape the censure reserved for members of any class, even the
class from which he springs, and at the same time have a sort of elemental
connection to all of the classes at once. It is a very easy step to copy himself
and project others who are also separated from their classes, and who must
also have the advantage of great sympathy. These are the aliens, or
intellectuals: "persons who are mainly led, not by their class spirit, but by a
general humane spirit, by the love of human perfection" (*Works* 5: 146).
There are problems with this designation—these aliens are probably all
economically middle class, getting and spending with the rest of us. Most of
them are identifiably Liberal in politics, even if they do not always toe the
party line; in short, these aliens may not exist. Even if they do exist, Arnold
has cleverly subsumed their class interests into "the general humane spirit."
By defining them only in opposition to the other three classes, the aliens'
interests are subsumed into "disinterestedness." Their own views become "the
love of human perfection." Matthew Arnold's alien replicates a whole class
of Matthew Arnolds. Arnold has created a whole class of critics, defined not
by their interests, but by their detachment from the whole idea of having
interests, whose interests are largely aesthetic, stylistic, and ephemeral.

Oscar Wilde wrote, "it is through Art, and through Art only, that we can
shield ourselves from the sordid perils of actual existence" (380). But Arnold
played this idea out even before Wilde. It was Walter Pater who noted in his
review of *The Picture of Dorian Gray* that Arnold was Wilde's precursor.
Though we tend to read Arnold in his high seriousness, usually in a line of
solemn critics that includes Eliot, Leavis, and Arnold's biographer Lionel
Trilling, it might be more productive to see him as Pater saw him, not only as
the progenitor of "serious" criticism, but of the kinds of irony that have lately
received attention and been labeled as "camp." Arnold, with his phrase-making,
persona-sculpting, and self-consciously aesthetic views, may not only have
shaped Wilde and his *aperçu*, but also engendered the ironic poses that made
Wilde possible. In short, Arnold may be the grandfather of what most critics
have attributed to Wilde himself. Arnold may be the grandfather of camp.

Works Cited

Adams, James Eli. *Dandies and Desert Saints: Styles of Victorian Masculinity*. Ithaca and
    London: Cornell University Press, 1995.
Arnold, Matthew. *The Complete Prose Works of Matthew Arnold*. Ed. R. H. Super. 11 vols.
    Ann Arbor: University of Michigan Press, 1960–77.

Arnold, Matthew. *The Letters of Matthew Arnold*. Ed. Cecil V. Lang. 2 vols. Charlottesville: University Press of Virginia, 1996.

Attwood, Francis. "Souvenir for Mr. Arnold." *Life*, 31 January 1884: 61. In Patricia Marks, "A Charivari to Matthew Arnold, American Style." *Arnoldian* 2 (1980): 29–44.

Barbey D'Aurevilly, Jules. *Dandyism*. Trans. Douglas Ainslie. New York: PAJ, 1988.

Brown, E. K. *Matthew Arnold: A Study in Conflict*. New York: Archon, 1966.

Coblence, Françoise. *Le Dandysme, obligation d'incertitude*. Paris: Presses Universitaires de Paris, 1988.

Dawson, Carl, and John Pfordresher. *Matthew Arnold Prose Writings: The Critical Heritage*. London: Routledge & Kegan Paul, 1979.

Delbourg-Delphis, Marylène. *Masculin Singulier: Le Dandysme et son Histoire*. Paris: Hachette, 1985.

Garelick, Rhonda K. *Rising Star: Dandyism, Gender and Performance in the Fin de Siècle*. Princeton: Princeton University Press, 1998.

Honan, Park. *Matthew Arnold: A Life*. New York: McGraw-Hill, 1981.

Ihrig, Wilfrid. *Literarische Avantgarde und Dandysmus*. Frankfurt am Main: AthenSum, 1988.

Marcus, Steven. "Conceptions of the Self in an Age of Progress." In *Progress and Its Discontents*. Ed. Gabriel Almond, Martin Chodorow, and Roy Harvey Pearce. Berkeley and Los Angeles: University of California Press, 1982. 431–48.

Marks, Patricia. "A Charivari for Matthew Arnold, American Style." *Arnoldian* 7 (1980): 29–44.

Moers, Ellen. *The Dandy: Brummell to Beerbohm*. New York: Viking Press, 1960.

Murray, Nicholas. *A Life of Matthew Arnold*. New York: St. Martin's Press, 1996.

Najarian, James. "'Curled Minion, dancer, coiner of sweet words': Keats, Dandyism, and Sexual Indeterminacy in *Sohrab and Rustum*." *Victorian Poetry* 35 (1997): 23–42.

Natta, Marie-Christine. *La Grandeur sans Convictions*. Paris: Editions du Félin, 1992.

Nellist, Brian. "Disconcerting the Reader: *Friendship's Garland* and the True Voices of 'Mr. Arnold.'" *Essays and Studies* 41 (1988): 30–44.

Robbins, William. *The Arnoldian Principle of Flexibility. English Literary Studies* 15. Victoria: University of Victoria, 1979.

Stanton, Domna. *The Aristocrat as Art*. New York: Columbia University Press, 1980.

Super, Robert H. "Sweetness and Light: Matthew Arnold's Comic Muse." In *Matthew Arnold in His Time and Ours*. Eds. Clinton Machann and Forrest D. Burt. Charlottesville: University Press of Virginia, 1988. 183–96.

Trilling, Lionel. *Matthew Arnold*. New York: Columbia University Press, 1947.

Wilde, Oscar. *The Artist as Critic: Critical Writings of Oscar Wilde*. Ed. Richard Ellmann. Oxford: Clarendon Press, 1968.

11

Salomé: Re/Dressing Wilde on the Rim

Rob K. Baum

A really well-made buttonhole is the only link between Art and Nature.
—Oscar Wilde, *The Chameleon*[1]

Studies of humor neglect *Salomé,* Oscar Wilde's dramatization of the biblical story of John the Baptist's decapitation. Although among the most tragic writing in Wilde's literary repertory, *Salomé* employs the linguistic twists and gender jokes common to Victorian humor. In Wilde's most successful comedy, *The Importance of Being Earnest,* Algernon sublimates his proclivities in cravings for cucumber sandwiches; in *Salomé,* the Judaen princess blatantly demands head. Where Ernest's name encodes a desire for men relieved by "Bunburying," Salomé destroys the only man towards whom she has felt attraction, then fetishizes his corpse. Betraying British obedience to royalty and pomp, Wilde portrays a spoiled princess, jealous queen and incestuous monarch; subverting Victorians' fetishism of virgins and dead children, Wilde beheads one virgin and flattens another. Comic dialogue undercuts the tragic fate of Salomé and her Beloved, and repetition oddly veils rather than reveals, burying same-sex signifiers in biblically-resonant poetic passages. Phrases and gestures, recontextualized by shared utterance, deny a queer presence while passionately inscribing its difference.

The Jews

Although necessarily identifying Jews as religious individuals whose speech resembles that of animals, Wilde's anti-Semitic depiction of Jews generally attacks Jewish philosophy rather than physiognomy. Reading the play, one can easily forget the unseen Jewish characters in the temple, who merely form a backdrop to Herod's entertainment. Production makes their presence more concrete, as when the First and Second Soldier remark on the ambient noise: "*First Soldier.* What an uproar! Who are those wild beasts howling? *Second Soldier.* The Jews. They are always like that. They are disputing

about their religion" (6).[2] The Jews' invisibility throughout the first part of
the drama ironically mirrors the subject of their intense conversation: "The
Pharisees, for instance, say that there are angels, and the Sadducees declare
that angels do not exist." As the soldiers summarize the in-fighting:

> *First Soldier.* The Jews worship a God that one cannot see.
> *The Cappadocian.* I cannot understand that.
> *First Soldier.* In fact, they only believe in things that one cannot
> see.
> *The Cappadocian.* That seems to me altogether ridiculous.[3] (9)

Jews' perversely passionate devotion to the unseen (in this dramatic sense,
the obscene) encrypts personal belief and public avowal as aspects of
identity, which can be questioned but not altered by outsiders: although in
disagreement, the philosophers are all nonetheless Jews. Wilde's public
behaviors continually marked him as belonging to another society, one whose
individuals disagreed as to appropriate decorum (while his own "angel," Lord
Alfred Douglas, would prove unstable and far from uplifting); like the Jews
in *Salomé,* gays were forever outside the dominant culture and—as the text
has proven for a century—equally unseen. The first mention of Jews,
moreover, contains a translator's pun, presumably Wilde's lover deploying
the playwright's own surname: the howling beasts are "wild." In the context
of Victorian society, Wilde's beliefs ally him with Jews, persecuted despite
their invisibility.

Besides mocking Jews, Wilde portrays the Tetrarch as weak, disgusting
and rather stupid.

> *Herod.* What does that mean? The Saviour of the world?
> *Tigellinus.* It is a title that Caesar adopts.
> *Herod.* But Caesar is not coming into Judaea ... (a)nd you ...
> heard nothing concerning this matter, did you?
> *Tigellinus.* Sire, I heard nothing concerning the matter. I was
> explaining the title. It is one of Caesar's titles.
> *Herod.* But Caesar cannot come. He is too gouty ... (38–39)

His commanding officer is not the only insubordinate person present. In
hilarious contrast to Wilde's well-received parlor comedies, especially *The
Ideal Husband* (1895) with its great male friendship and sentimental
marriage of unequals, marital bickering pervades *Salomé.* The following
dialogue between Herod and his queen reveals rich strains of boredom
relieved by needless argument:

> *Herodias.* You hear what he says about you. He says that you
> will be eaten of worms.

> *Herod.* It is not of me that he speaks. He speaks never against
> me. It is of the King of Cappadocia that he speaks ... mine
> enemy. It is he who shall be eaten of worms. It is not I.
> Never has he spoken word against me, this prophet, save
> that I sinned in taking to wife the wife of my brother. (49)

Herod surprisingly admits to the crime of incest, but a moment later shows his cunning by pinning blame on Herodias: "It may be he is right. For, of a truth, you are sterile." But Herodias is an excellent match for the fading monarch: "I am sterile, I? You say that, you that are ever looking at my daughter, you that would have her dance for your pleasure? You speak as a fool. I have borne a child. You have gotten no child, no, not on one of your slaves. It is you who are sterile, not I" (49).

Herod thinks to win the round by childishly out-shouting her, and again taunts his wife: "Peace, woman! I say that you are sterile. You have borne me no child, and the prophet says that our marriage is not a true marriage [but] ... a marriage of incest ... that will bring evils." He then changes tacks, using the play's trademark morose, self-conscious repetition—and sudden reversal: "I fear he is right; I am sure that he is right. I would be happy at this. Of a truth, I am happy. There is nothing I lack" (50). But Herodias sends the last volley: "I am glad that you are of so fair a humour to-night. It is not your custom" (49–50). Beneath the facade of royal ennui lies Wilde's true comic genius: the tongue is an instrument of desire and punishment; no one is innocent. The terrible pleasure at the *fin de siècle* is personified in this pubescent female who requests the unbelievable and does the unforgivable. Yet most of the artists who immortalized the princess as evil incarnate neglected the motif, present in the Gospel version, that in dancing Salomé yielded to an uncle's incestuous gaze.

Wilde recreates Salomé's dance as poetic justice for both Herod and Jokanaan, decapitation of crimes against women. By presenting Herod as despicable and risible, and Salomé as a virgin desperate to escape molestation, Wilde acquits Salomé of her historical "sin." Salomé becomes a sym/pathetic figure, a child who wins a game of bluff with an adult but wins an ugly prize. The true horror is that she cannot understand why the disembodied head does not respond, why her kisses leave no imprint. For answers, we follow a trail of blood.

Circles of Desire

A preoccupation with the making of a beautiful life replicating art necessitated concealment of an "underworld" of Victorian manhood, behind (or beneath) which lay the artfully corporeal queen. In the manifold joke of the Wilde coterie, evident in the title and events of Wilde's comedy *The Importance of Being Earnest* (1895), the fantasized male name[4] is less a comic pun on serious behavior than a terrible French pun for *Uraniste,* code for the anatomy of gay male culture.[5] The French term *uraniste* betrays the provenance of the sodomite, the planet Uranus (in British English rendered "your anus"); it also yields the Christian name "Ernest," homonymically "earnest." The "proper" name is thus of paramount importance, a sub/liminal joke for Wilde's invisible public.

Wilde's compulsion for buttonholes, cited in the epigraph, coyly alludes to the dandy in him and himself in the Other. Despite his flair for exquisite dress, evidenced in person and in his many articles on the subject, Wilde habited men of the lower classes, preferably those whose own buttonholes were empty, and butt(on)holes were dirty. London hoteliers were to complain that Wilde left a wake of bed sheets stained with blood and fecal matter. A predilection for vile and violable spaces accordingly surfaces in *Salomé,* the play's dialogue, symbols and stage settings reiterating circles, holes, fruits, flowers and white "moons." In the circles of Herod's eyes, Salomé voluptuously poises to dance; breasts, belly and buttocks reappear like the female moon, or references to silver light and mirrors. Drops of blood melt into "cheeks," moonlight, "rosy" petals, and the Herodian "wreath" which transforms into a signifying crown of thorns: masculine company could be openly enjoyed, but sodomy was a private, criminal act, and punishable by imprisonment. The jeweled crown Herod wears opposes the spiritual crown Jokanaan contemplates, paralleling the crown of the head (lofty principles) and rectal opening (base desire). Herod's crown simultaneously invokes a Freudian reading of jewels as fecal gifts—thus doubling the sign of anality while concealing it in florid language. Wilde dwells in both crowns as writer and lover of men, a Victorian queen living at the transgressive rim.

Herod's jewels spark round as rings, coins, hinter gems, gold, silver and shields, mirroring the silver charger which carries Jokanaan's head like a warrior into battle. Salomé will be destroyed by the weapons bent to defend her: shields defend but also crush the Other in us, like the secret which owns us. In their reflective surface we find ourselves immobilized or turned to stone, prey to the desiring gaze. Seen by all but Jokanaan, Salomé says of him, "It is his eyes above all that are terrible. They are like black holes burned by torches in a tapestry of the Tyre. They are like the black caverns of Egypt in which the dragons make their lairs. They are like black lakes troubled by fantastic moons" (21). Jokanaan's refusal to look at Salomé provokes in her a storm of poetic description calculated to externalize her desire, the linguistic equivalent of contumescence. But his "head" is spiritually bent. Salomé's amazement at the unresponsive head of the prophet is more comprehensible if examined as an element of (the) fore/

play, in which Salomé lavishes praise upon Jokanaan as a sexual object. His negations read as a kind of infantile rejection. Now that Salomé is actually possessing and fondling his head, Jokanaan's failure to respond is physiologically contraindicated. Salomé is right in expecting the head to stand, the mouth to open, and the virile *"red viper"* (65) to arouse her.

Wilde's play walks a dark edge of humor verdant with *double entendre*. The play's chief poetic source is *Shir Ha-Shirim* (the *Song of Songs*), the Hebrew Bible's most romantic writing, in which Shulamit appears as the Beloved; ostensibly discussing physical love between a man and woman, the *Song of Songs* metaphorizes spiritual love between the Hebrews and God.[6] The biblical text is thus already analogical, in notes of physical explicitness submerging an unspeakable love akin to what Lord Douglas called "the Love that dare not speak its Name." Calling *Salomé* a "religious" drama (Kuryluk, 217), Wilde's usage draws upon that subtext, locating masculine biblical verses in the mouth of an unnamed, untouched female (described in Mark 6: 20–28), speaking to an untouchable man. The narcissistic virgin has eyes only for the prophet whose eyes, unfortunately directed upwards, confirm this love as unrequited; the boldness of the princess's demands helps mask the impossibility of her desire.

Blackness is re-marked in connection with a gaze actively sought by Salomé, a look in which she thinks to find life, or a new life; "eyes like black holes ... like caverns" reflect the pit beneath the palace, a "strange prison ... an old cistern ... a poisonous place in which to dwell" (11). In this way the look without desire corresponds to Salomé's punishment, imprisoning her; to live without the look of men, of a particular man, estranges. The black hole/eye redirects us to the black eye of the body, site of corporeal poisons; the failure of the gaze fore/closes Salomé's own possibilities of liberating anality. Salomé cannot feel (gay) pleasure. The "cluster of black grapes" to which Salomé compares the prophet's hair are not the only "fruit" to feel the bite of Salomé's teeth; Herod desires to see her teeth's imprint in his own fruit. Biting of fruit hints at "original sin," a metaphor of prime/evil pain and never completely containable sexuality—either female sexuality or the appearance of a sexuality defined as female. This circle comes repetitively round to roses, reproductive but sterile fruits, and a distinctive darkness against the emphatic whiteness of Jokanaan's (and Salomé's) imagined body. Roses are therefore suggestively masculine, wrapped in forbidden scents, and as surpassingly hidden yet openable as the rectal ring. Through this code of secrecy we enter the cistern, open anus of wet earth, in which Jokanaan is, at the play's onset, "buried."

Language of Love

Melissa Knox comments on the conscious devices with which Wilde distances yet personalizes his drama:

> Cloaking his story in a foreign language, in exotic literary borrowings, and in a highly ornate, artificial style, Wilde gave the play the unreality of a dream, showing that he wanted it to be interpreted as a message, just as someone recounting a dream hopes that his listener, in decoding it, will accept it. (30–31)

Written in French, *Salomé* disguises even Wilde's native tongue, an idiosyncrasy with which Wilde's biographers continue to wrestle. The "queerness" of the French tongue further removes *Salomé*'s tragic characters from British normalcy, making their passions at once more foreign and more sophisticated.[7]

Wilde's choice of French is grotesquely clever, proving that, as he writes in "The Portrait of Mr. W. H.," "sincerity ... [is] often the unconscious result of style" (Ellman, 199). Just as German culture influenced Wilde's naming of sexual practices (apparent in other writings), French culture provided the young Wilde with a range of fashionable and subversive gestures, including the green carnation which became his trademark "buttonhole." It is this "little green flower" which Salomé offers to drop for the smitten Syrian soldier, a man who later kills himself in order to place his body before his rival's (Jokanaan's). Replacing the lily Wilde wore in his aesthetic period, the green carnation symbolized a life perfected by art, and became indelibly linked with the gay male underground whose members could restructure sexuality by eradicating female presence—or subsuming it in effeminate signs. In gay subculture to adopt such behaviors is to participate in a form of parody known as "drag," an acceptable mockery of women. French disguised Wilde's gender play even more effectively than *The Importance of Being Earnest* with its schizophrenic lover whose "name is Ernest in town and Jack in the country" (*Five Major Plays*, 233). Jack believes that married, c(o)untry life will quash his need to be—or have—Uraniste in town. At the end of his sham marriage to Constance Lloyd, Wilde already knows better. By writing Salomé's story in French—appearing to be "frank"—Wilde evaded censorship of the play but also within the play. By (dis)locating gay desire in an unsexed girl, he further disguised the quality of that love, permitting it to masquerade as a perverse heterosexuality rather than a tragic homosexuality.

"How black it is down there ... in so black a hole," says Salomé of the cistern (15). In order to broach its protective ring, Salomé strips off the adolescence unaccustomed to giving or taking mature pleasure,[8] dancing the Dance of the Seven Veils for Herod. Lowered veils tantalizingly reveal the female body in this distinctly Middle-Eastern and orientalized erotic dance whose final inferent veil is the hymen: while in prison, Wilde wrote to Salomé's illustrator Aubrey Beardsley of this implied, "invisible" veiling, sharing one of the play's underlying jokes.[9] As a male god, Hymen presides over marriage (but only the marriage of heterosexuals), thereby inadvertently assisting in the invisibility of gay male partnership. Salomé's hymen is certainly implied by the use of the veils, but "veil," a homonym of "vale" (valley), shrouds reference to the other breakable tissue of intercourse, while defining the way to it: through the crack of homosocial copulation.

From this crack in the earth its fruit, Jokanaan, eventually and briefly emerges, his misdirected gaze following his voice like branches upswelling, the vegetable god carrying his seed to the chosen one: maiden, moon, princess, Salomé, the one who has chosen him. Yet Jokanaan renounces Salomé as "Daughter of Sodom" (Wilde, 24), blatantly evoking the mythological incipience of sodomy. Wilde's re/emergence in Victorian England in the reconfiguration of the aesthete-as-dandy invoked a new fear of the effeminate, which eventually gave way to terror at "sodomitical posing" in Wilde's sex crimes trial; not surprisingly, the active sodomite was repugned. While it might seem that the prophet attributes responsibility for sodomitical practices to the "female" (receptive partner, or insertee), in fact Salomé functions as the active, "male" partner (insertor) in her deadly relationship with Jokanaan—the role Wilde himself enjoyed, usually by butt(on)holing young laborers for an evening's well-paid pleasure. Young men, such as those induced to testify against Wilde at the trial, were called "renters," yet another example of the Victorian mastery of euphemism.[10] The "renter" was both borrowed and burrowed. Hired for his body, orientalized by Wilde and Douglas (who called the men their "Arab boys"), the renter's deflowered butt(on)hole might well bleed—being rent as well as rented.

With its blood omens, *Salomé*'s biblical setting pre-s(t)ages the battle to come between England's tyrannical purity and the public perception, invoked through court testimony, of plagues of blood, sperm and the consequences of desire. As Leo Bersani writes,

> The normal fear of homosexuality has been promoted to a compelling terror as a secret fantasy becomes a public spectacle: the spectacle of men dying from what I called in "Is the Rectum a Grave?" "the suicidal ecstasy of taking their sex like a woman." (*Homos*, 19)

Disguising one's true passions is a recurrent theme in Wilde's *oeuvre*, elegantly hidden in fashions, predilections and polite servings at appropriate times. *Salomé* is rife with linguistic jokes hidden (as in his other plays) in characters' names, such as the place names of "Bracknell" and "Goring," two places where Wilde vacationed. There is every reason to believe that Wilde knew the Hebrew meanings of the names he ingeniously assigned: even while in Reading Gaol Wilde ordered in foreign language dictionaries, as well as tutorial programs, to help him with current writing projects. In the English translation the names have been somewhat altered, rendering them less meaningful; fortunately, the Hebrew translation restores the names' biblical spellings.[11] Names of slaves and soldiers carry their own linguistic humor: Tigellinus, Herod's officer, suggests a "small beam," or penis. The frightening Executioner's name, Naaman, means "pleasant." And when Herod calls at the play's end for Manasseh, Ish'shacar, and O'ziah to "veil the stage" (Wilde, 67), concealing the perversion, he actually calls out a kind of sentence: "I am trying/a male rent(er)/G-d's courage!"[12]

To discover a man for rent in the middle of Herod's cry for invisibility is clearly no accident of nature as these names are Wilde's invention; Herod and Salomé are the only two names linked with the original Gospel story. Herod contains two ciphers in English—"her/odd," which one might render as significantly "queer," and "he/rod," recalling Wilde's own sonnet "*Helas!*" in which he remembers that "lo! with a little rod / I did but touch the honey of romance" (Ellmann, xiv);[13] the connection between his rod and the other's honey is clear. Conversely, the Hebrew *herid* is related to the word "empty," which suggests the honeypot rather than (or after contact with) the Wilde rod. Salomé, or Shulamit, by queer coincidence, is related to the word *shula'im*, meaning "margin"—or "rim." In terms of a queer presence, and more significantly anal convergence, the play in her name buttonholes Salomé as—if not a male homosexual—at least one whose sexuality is predicated on (or in) that margin of difference.

Salomé's dialogue with Jokanaan—rather a monologue interspersed with his violent indictments—veils and unveils her sudden and mysterious interest in the prophet. Employing all her faculties in what Karl Toepfer calls "ecstatic speech," Salomé vacillates between adoration and excoriation, cyclically lavishing compliments, receiving another insult, and lashing back with curses. The manner of her praises is particularly interesting, involving as they do diatribes about Jokanaan's physical characteristics. Beginning with the body trunk and concluding with the mouth, Salomé dictates an image of the prophet as an unusually pale, thin man with black eyes and long black hair, but most of her insults oddly depict various stages of disease, from the emaciation of one dying to the serpent-like choke-hold of hair: even Jokanaan's hair becomes poisonous.[14] "Only sick people dream" (Wilde, 41), Herodias rebukes her gay Page, striking him. In the contemporary lexicon, Jokanaan resembles a victim of AIDS, but Wilde's own vision of disease was syphilis, another bloody end. The spectre of his coming death imprisoned Wilde, foretold by blood on the sheets and a dirty pen.

The Carnival Body

Perhaps the greatest intrigue of this play is its locus, the dreary dungeon of its hero. Jokanaan languishes beneath the surface of our vision in the building's belly, stopped-up, blind, a mole in the hole of the stage, the trap.

For much of the play he is unseen but heard, a fact which maintains his mysterious detachment; the prophet re/produces our most glorious visions, the second sight of God. Lying beneath Salomé's feet as she dances, eye at the keyhole of her body, he is the breath beneath her veil, intercessor and mediator for the gaze of the audience. Although the character Salomé's object (Jokanaan) is absent, the object Salomé herself is almost always present, her body as vulnerable to the hunt as a contemporary princess. Salomé remains an open wound in the flesh of the play, inviting the fouling matter of our interest. The play's binarisms produce maidens and prophets equally unsoiled, and soldiers and queens equally used; we witness extravagance and impoverishment, luxury and asceticism, loveliness and lovelessness, fantasy and evil, heads of state and stately headlessness, politics and poetry. The sense of bodies without voices, seen and obscene, infects the drama, redrawing the margins of social life. *Salomé* traffics in bodies and souls, invocations and provocations of a distant god, martyrdom and excess, excretion and execration. Such dichotomies exist in carnival's periodic cycles of violent difference, celebrations of habits typically reined in (like those involving eating, drinking, parturition, and sex), loci of pollution and therefore portals for license and formal riot.

> [N]ext to the bowels and the genital organs is the mouth through which enters the world to be swallowed up.... All these convexities and orifices have a common characteristic; it is with them that the borders between one's own and other bodies and between the body and the world are breached. (Bakhtin, 317)

In the extremism of carnival, inversions dominate; the body speaks for a sleeping brain in a topsy-turvy, betwixt and between, neitherworld. In *Salomé,* it is the netherworld which surfaces. A signifier for the ethic of waste, the cistern performs like the *vomitorium* of the Roman theater, as an arena for human disposal and Herodian appetites. Carnival, cockpit, and play-hole—or the *Uraniste* with a cistern at his center, primary as the hole in a music disc or human corpus. This prison is therefore also charnel house and gaming place, a stage for the playing, Wilde self-consciously insisting upon the theatricality of his own gay male body. A site for refreshing the living, the cistern becomes a dungeon for sexual difference: *c'est/urn.*

Prophet and political prisoner, Jokanaan speaks untold danger, violating the neat principles of authority. A symbol of Wilde's self-professed martyrdom, Jokanaan occupies the bottom of Herod's palace, last stop in a world without light or redemption, a cesspool of outrageous appetites. The bestiality of Herod's palace penetrates to the prisoner, animalizing him; in this arena the body's flaws are immediately discernible and any weakness leads irrevocably to death. The dank, empty socket would be an unsightly end for a man of vision—but there is no indication that he can see: Salomé repeatedly complains of his inability to gaze upon her, reproaching even the lifeless head. Jokanaan's sight is directed upwards and within as he cites previous visions of depravity and beauty; Earth's eyehole is blind. An ordinary prisoner might be reduced to his body, made female by personal powerlessness; Jokanaan overturns expectation by insisting upon his difference, denying his invisibility. He makes one living appearance, summarily severed when he rejects Salomé's advances: beheading propels Jokanaan into the limelight. Difference is not so terrible when it is already neutralized, neutered, destroyed, and only its icon remains—particularly when that difference is reminiscent of oneself. Jokanaan's death permits Salomé to mete her nascent sexuality upon the Other-become-Self without fear of reciprocation, and in a more public arena than the cistern's privacy offers. The death of the Other is liberating.

Mikhail Bakhtin's idea of actual liberation conflicts with Umberto Eco's notion of carnival as "authorized transgression." Confrontation between rank physicality and lofty spirituality is comic, carnivalesque. If the women suggest carnival, possibilities of unleashed desire, then the cistern (as central locus) is more than metaphoric resonator, metallic earth-hole. Cistern becomes prison becomes mouth becomes eyes becomes head, an algebra of punishments. Herod, not Salomé, is the man-eater. Because the mouth is the site where that which is alien is incorporated, the feast, according to Mikhail Bakhtin, is a time of "free interplay between the body and outside world," a time of victory over fear, for the feast celebrates the destruction of what the self encounters as threatening. Food "crowns" our relation to work: "the struggle of people against a hostile nature is crowned with food ... People 'swallow that which they have defeated'" (Yaeger, 4).

The cistern is the mouth of Herod, and therefore the king's true palace, inverted and subverted; the world is a cistern for sodomites and a satire on Victorian entrée. Herod's cistern exemplifies ancient worship, pantheon of gods, sublimation of the death wish, the Roman mission to consume; it is a house of the dead fed by horrible waters of forgetfulness akin to death. Hades is home to Charon the ferry-man (a pun Wilde would cheerfully have committed) and the mystery of women, in which men drown.[15] The death towards which *Salomé* inevitably drives cannot be avoided as long as desire for an Other like herself is read as perversion. Salomé must fall to the sword of a raging appetite bent upon heteronormative sexuality, towards primal but conceivable lusts.

Funny Looking

Offstage handling of death is not so much a trend of the tragic as an avoidance of the comic in the play and opera. Separation of a man's body from his head could not be anything but comic, evidenced by the ambivalence one experiences viewing images of decapitation. The French Revolution's *La guillotine* was a huge crowd pleaser; in an instant, she transformed subject into object, head into rolling ball. Fallen behind the death machine, the headless body may be tragic, but the severed head is (too) suddenly plastic and bizarre, a child's plaything; the jerking body becomes mechanical, involuntary, impulses gone awry, the essence of the comic. One sees the frozen face of one's own mortality, mimicry and mimesis.

By occurring offstage, Jokanaan's death becomes metaphorical, linked to the death of other prophets, a sum lost in the addition of bureaucracy and spirituality. This death is not the only instance of metaphor: the dance precipitating Jokanaan's execution is a better one, and as time-honored. The elaborate revealing of Salomé is pure sexual metaphor, for which the end flourish is *le petite mort* ("the little death" of Victorian orgasm), an end prefiguring Jokanaan's. He is never heard again; the pronouncements he makes prior to Salomé's dance are his last. The dance of desire thus becomes the dance of death, the stripping of psyche. At this juncture lies the point of realization, the coming-together or simultaneous proliferation of image and meaning, thought and reason, copulation and regeneration, collision and derailing. Or unveiling.

Salomé is the historical boundary marker between the ancient Roman and Hebraic cultures, virgin and sexpot—a cultural and sexual difference is dramatized in the ambiguous attention to her body and her treatment as a product of the period's waste. Not until the Dance of the Seven Veils is it apparent that Salomé is veiled. The absence of Salomé's cloth veil earlier in the play is not dramaturgically insupportable if one extrapolates from contemporary standards of Bedouin honor.[16] Salomé is chiefly in the company of family members, where to veil would be inappropriate for an unmarried female (although she may have been veiled at the party from which she has ventured). As an uncorrupted (that is, untouched) princess, Salomé commands high property value, a fact known to Salomé and all present; but the presence of her hidden "veil," assumed beneath her garments, is the only real guarantee of that value. Without this tissue, even her royal birth cannot elevate her above the commoners, the city's foundational cistern.

Salomé knows that she is currently the possession of the palace under the eye of her stepfather, who vigorously pro/tests her value by importuning her to dance for his private pleasure. Her eventual agreement raises the stakes in this primitive game of seduction, endangering both her virginity and its appearance—or unseen presence. Accord only further problematizes the sight and site of Salomé's body, one made obscene by repugnant/ different desires. She had only wanted to be seen, really seen. In the unfinished circle of erotic fantasy, Salomé is trapped *en centre* (or *en ceintre*)[17] and risks being crushed between diverse desires. Precisely this happens at the end of the play: at her sexual awakening, she calls for the (wrong) head. Woman and not-man give way to heteronormative sexuality, and in the crush of male bodies Salomé disappears. The last vestige of the Other is gone.

In this play the (visible) audience's wishes are finally granted, beginning with the release of Jokanaan from prison and the dung heap of Roman appetites. Salomé dances; Jokanaan is beheaded; intoning the formula of head and innocence, desire and decapitation, Salomé dances with a silenced partner. The body of Jokanaan drops away, a capsule of useless flesh, to rot unrecovered in the subterrain of cistern, memory, Wilde imagination. But the head must be handled gently lest its comic side be seen. To dribble the head like a basketball, comb its black locks, or press it dramatically to the bosom could easily move the audience to gales of laughter. There is little one can do with that head, not because it is a phony prop but because it represents something human now become awkward, metaphoric and perverse. Beside Salomé's near-nakedness it swiftly becomes a different sort of joke, hollow laughter from the prison. *Salomé* is underwritten with this coterie wit; at the base of *Salomé*'s baseness is metaphor, and metaphor is that which calls attention to itself by its absence. In her own murder, the danger of the wild, sexually conscious "female" is averted, the truly Wilde beast is put down.

The premoderns must be forgiven the orientalization of Salomé's naïvely erotic appeal. Salomé learns to live in the gaze of dark men, to turn towards its light like the auxins of a sun-seeking plant. Her best lesson is her last: she herself looks too hard; under the reflection of her own gaze she burns. Jokanaan's descent into the cistern begins Salomé's own downward journey, his death becoming her own. Salomé is no heroic or unambiguous creature: after her dance we accord her little sympathy; she goes down before us buried in her own dirt, prey to her passions like the other Victorian queen under her horses, as if she had invited her own disaster. Wilde's darker comic vision of Victoriana, *Salomé* is a play on psychic dysfunction and bodily functions, the transmission of language and the invisibility of difference. Inimically cryptic, Wilde bemoans the *fin de siècle*'s limitations on the exchange of tongues and giving of head. *Salomé* thus portrays Wilde's dirty y/earning for the proper buttonhole in which to place himself, flower of the Victorian age.

Notes

[1] "Phrases and Philosophies for the Use of the Young," *The Chameleon* (November 1884): 1.

[2] This is actually the second page of the play itself. All quotations from Wilde's play are taken from an apparent reprint of the English edition first published in 1894, and believed to have been translated by Lord Alfred Douglas but without his name on the title plate.

[3]   For an indication of the history of *Salomé*'s depiction, see Pressly.

[4]   See Sedgwick on "Ernest" as the "Name of the Father."

[5]   Patricia Flanagan Behrendt drew my attention to the code *"Uraniste"* in "Ferocious Idylls; Or, The Social Comedies of Oscar Wilde," a paper delivered at the Annual Conference for American Society of Theatre Research, November 1992, in Newport, Rhode Island. Wilde was to write from prison about the irony that a "poet in prison for loving boys loves boys. To have altered my life would have been to have admitted that Uranian love is ignoble. I hold it to be noble—more noble than other forms" (Hart-Davis, 705). For the origin of the term *Uranus* in connection with homosexuality, see 705, note 1.

[6]   Jews call the biblical text "The Song of Songs." Wilde draws heavily upon the Hebraic text while shaming Jews themselves. See Sander Gilman's treatment of Richard Strauss' opera *Salomé* and Jewish perversion in *Disease and Representation* (1988).

[7]   On the need to correct Wilde's colloquial French, see especially Stuart Merrill's reminiscences (Hart-Davis, 305); on the need to correct Lord Alfred Douglas's "schoolboy French" translation, to which Wilde refers by letter in 1893, see Hart-Davis, 344, note 3. Stuart Merrill was *Salomé*'s first stage manager.

[8]   The hymen is equally mysterious for *Salomé*.

[9]   Wilde inscribed the original edition of *Salomé* to Beardsley in March 1893, telling the artist that he was "the only artist who, besides myself, knows what the dance of the seven veils is, and can see that invisible dance" (Hart-Davis, 348, note 3).

[10]   On "renter" as British slang for homosexual, see Hart-Davis, 327, note 2.

[11]   For instance, the name Issadar ("to arrange") appears as *Ish-shacar* in Hebrew.

[12]   One could alternately translate the syllables as *Yesh shacar,* meaning "There is a rent(er)." In the English version Oziah is sufficiently close to *Tziaf,* meaning "veil or cover;" thus the complete "sentence" would read "I am trying to cover a renter!"

[13]   This poem was published at age 25, in 1861.

[14]   Jokanaan's body is depicted as alternatively virginal, frigid, soft, light-footed and ethereal—terms associated with effeminacy—and monstrous, leprous, rotten, infested and funereal. His mouth, a fragrant fruit, brazen, bloody, oceanic, and precious, is also seen as a weapon. In most of the play's characters, but especially Jokanaan and Salomé, the gender conventions of masculinity and feminity are radically violated.

[15]   It is no license to name the connection between the name of the waters—Lethe—and the word "lethal": surely the death of memory is the final death, by which we truly know the ethic of waste and ugliness that the Berlin *Salomé*'s later opera/tor Richard Strauss vacated—into which bodies tumbled, bones in a trench, with memory itself.

[16]   On veiling as codification among contemporary Muslims, see Abu-Lughod. An Arab population which roamed the Middle East, influencing and being influenced by indigenous populations, Bedouins may be found in Jordan, Israel, and Egypt, among other places; some tribes are no longer nomadic.

[17]   I owe this pun to Bert O. States on his reading of my original draft of this article.

Works Cited

Abu-Lughod, Lila. *Veiled Sentiments: Honor and Poetry in Bedouin Society*. Berkeley: University of California Press, 1986.

Bakhtin, Mikhail. *Rabelais and His World*. Trans. Helene Iswolsky. Cambridge: MIT Press, 1968.

Beardsley, Aubrey. *The Art of Aubrey Beardsley.* New York: Modern Library, 1925.

Bersani, Leo. "Is the Rectum a Grave?" *Aids: Cultural Analysis, Cultural Activism*. Ed. Douglas Crimp. 1st MIT Press Edition. Cambridge: MIT Press, 1988. 187–222.

Bersani, Leo. *Homos*. Cambridge: Harvard University Press, 1995.

Douglas, Lord Alfred. *My Friendship With Oscar Wilde, Being the Autobiography of Lord Alfred Douglas*. New York: Coventry House, 1932.

Eckardt, Wolf Von, Sander L. Gilman, and J. Edward Chamberlin. *Oscar Wilde's London: A Scrapbook of Vices and Virtues, 1880–1900*. 1st edition. Garden City, NY: Anchor Press, 1987.

Eco, Umberto. "The Frames of Comic 'Freedom'." In *Carnival!* Ed. Thomas A. Sebeok. New York and Amsterdam: Mouton Publishers, 1984. 1–9.

Ellmann, Richard, ed. "The Portrait of Mr. W. H." [1889]. *The Artist as Critic: Critical Writings of Oscar Wilde*. New York: Random House, 1970. 152–220.

Gilman, Sander. *Disease and Representation: Images of Illness from Madness to Aids*. Ithaca: Cornell University Press, 1988.

Harris, Frank. *Oscar Wilde: His Life and Confessions*. New York: Covici, Friede Publishers, 1930.

Hart-Davis, Rupert, ed. *The Letters of Oscar Wilde*. New York: Harcourt, Brace & World, 1962.

Kettle, Michael. *Salomé's Last Veil: The Libel Case of the Century*. London: Hart-Davis, 1977.

Knox, Melissa. *Oscar Wilde: A Long and Lovely Suicide*. New Haven: Yale University Press, 1994.

Kuryluk, Ewa. *Salomé and Judas in the Cave of Sex. The Grotesque: Origins, Iconography, Techniques*. Evanston: Northwestern University Press, 1987.

Pressly, Nancy L. *Salomé: La Belle Dame Sans Merci*. San Antonio: San Antonio Museum of Art, 1983.

Sedgwick, Eve Kogofsky. "Tales of the Avunculate: Queer Tutelage in *The Importance of Being Earnest.*" *Professions of Desire: Lesbian and Gay Studies in Literature*. Ed. George E. Haggerty and Bonnie Zimmerman. New York: The Modern Language Association of America, 1995. 191–209.

Showalter, Elaine. *Sexual Anarchy: Gender and Culture at the Fin de Siècle*. New York: Viking Press, 1990.

Toepfer, Karl. *The Voice of Rapture: A Symbolist System of Ecstatic Speech in Oscar Wilde's Salomé*. New York: Peter Lang, 1991.

Watney, Simon. "The Spectacle of AIDS." *Aids: Cultural Analysis, Cultural Activism*. Ed. Douglas Crimp. 1st MIT Press Edition. Cambridge, Mass.: MIT Press, 1988. 71–86.

Wilde, Oscar. *Five Major Plays*. New York: Airmont Publishing Co., Inc., 1970.

———. *Salomé*. Trans. Lord Alfred Douglas. Boston: John W. Luce & Co., 1912.

———. *Shlumah*. Trans. Beshmat Alon. Yerushalayim: Beit Ha-ozah Alishar, 1981.

Yaeger, Patricia. *Honey-Mad Women: Emancipatory Strategies in Women's Writing*. Carolyn G. Heilbrun and Nancy K. Miller, eds. New York: Columbia University Press, 1988.

12

The Laugh of the New Woman

Margaret D. Stetz

> You only have to look at the Medusa straight on to see her. And she's not deadly. She's beautiful and she's laughing.
>
> Hélène Cixous, "The Laugh of the Medusa" (289)

The laughing woman is the least remembered woman of the Victorian period. (Just say the words "Victorian period" and no smiling female faces will come to mind.) New Women writers are probably the least remembered authors of the Victorian period. And so—to follow out this formula—New Women writers who employed the comic mode are the most forgotten among the forgotten, their jests at the expense of patriarchal attitudes and social conventions lost to readers today, and even to most feminist scholars. You will not find their comedy discussed in studies of New Women's fiction, such as Ann Ardis's *New Women, New Novels* (1990), Rita Kranidis's *Subversive Discourse* (1995), or Sally Ledger's *The New Woman* (1997). Neither do they receive so much as a mention in recent works on feminist comedy, such as Frances Gray's *Women and Laughter* (1994) or the two volumes of essays edited by Regina Barreca, *Last Laughs: Perspectives on Women and Comedy* (1988) and *New Perspectives on Women and Comedy* (1992). Even Ada Leverson, a New Woman who was perhaps the best-known female satirist of the 1890s, has been shut out entirely from *The Penguin Book of Women's Humor* (Barreca, 1996), a volume billed on its back cover as "a landmark anthology ... [with] extravagantly wide-ranging selections ... [that] span three centuries." Yet, though the peculiar character of the New Woman's laughter remains unexplored, there is much to be learned from it, both about the strategies that women have used in times of intellectual assaults upon them and about their hesitations and reservations when taking up forms identified with the exercise of masculine prerogative.

Conservative male contemporaries may have feared the rebellious will of the New Woman and regarded her personally as so sinister and destructive a figure that she would have to be ridiculed into submission, if not physically clubbed. The evidence suggests, nevertheless, that when New Women writers actually took up a cultural weapon such as the cudgel of laughter, they wielded it with some ambivalence, conscious of its problematic and double-edged nature. Though they were portrayed by their detractors as man-slaying monsters, the New Women of the 1890s—like the transformed icons of

Hélène Cixous's 1975 essay, "The Laugh of the Medusa" ["Le Rire de la Méduse"]—appear, when looked at "straight on," not to have been so "deadly" at all in their intentions (Cixous, 289). In fact, the comedy authored by New Women was in general far less vituperative and fierce than the comedy directed at them.

Is this discrepancy a sign that the New Women writers, many of whom were members of the middle classes and thus burdened with the training appropriate to "ladies," were too timid, too repressed, or just too nice to fight fire with fire? Perhaps. My own research, however, suggests that the avoidance of no-holds-barred satire did not merely represent unconscious feminine discomfort with aggression, but also conscious rejection of such masculine posturing, on both moral and practical grounds. Though their antagonists may have believed that driving women back into their original place through intimidation by ridicule would put the world right again, New Women of the 1890s were too clear-sighted to imagine that merely laughing at men or at male-generated institutions would solve their difficulties. And, in the long run, they proved to be correct in their assessment of comedy's limitations. The lampoons of turn-of-the-century feminism that circulated regularly both in the popular press and in intellectual circles were insufficient to destroy the movement or to silence its demands; ridicule may have been an effective weapon for inflicting injury, but it could not deliver a fatal blow. New Women writers did laugh and did attempt to make their readers laugh, but their attitude toward laughter, unlike that of their adversaries, was complex and rooted in skepticism. Laughter was, for them, only one element of social or psychological liberation, and a somewhat uncertain one at that.

I

As Sandra Gilbert and Susan Gubar have rightly described them in *The War of the Words*, the first volume of *No Man's Land*, the closing decades of the nineteenth century were a time of "women's invasion of the public sphere," when female movement out of the realm of domesticity and silence was perceived by many male observers as "an act of aggression that inaugurated a battle of the sexes" (65). By the 1890s in England, a change too great to be ignored was occurring: "[N]ever before had women been so visible in British society and culture—and hardly since, either, until the 1970s and the new women's movement" (Bjørhovde, 4). Accompanying this growing prominence of women—particularly of middle-class women—was a masculine backlash that struck out first at the most obvious instigator of this change, the so-called New Woman, she who was most conscious of and vocal about the injustice of present-day social and sexual hierarchies. Not merely in England, but throughout the Continent and in the United States as well, Elaine Showalter reminds us, "the New Woman, university-educated and sexually independent, engendered intense hostility and fear as she seemed to challenge male supremacy in art, the professions, and the home" (38).

In the period between 1880 and 1900, the bolts drawn down by this cultural lightning-rod often took the form of derisive laughter, satire, and caricature. As Patricia Marks has documented in her study, *Bicycles, Bangs, and Bloomers*, the popular press on both sides of the Atlantic was especially virulent in its comic attacks, hoping to shame and to "tame the rambunctious feminist spirit and return it to its domestic sphere" (2). Cartoonists in particular often used the charge of female humorlessness as a weapon to make the New Woman unappealing in the public's eye, as they depicted hatchet-faced, scowling sourpusses going about the business of winning equal rights. But even a better-informed and sporadically sympathetic figure, such as the English novelist George Gissing would assert in his 1898 study of Charles Dickens, that women—the New and the more familiar ones alike—were deficient in the all-important comic spirit, and that a "humourist never strongly appeals to that audience" (Gissing, 131–32). Looking back, just a few years later, upon the heyday of the New Women of the 1890s, C. E. Lawrence would entitle an essay "Wanted—Humourists" and carry the same charge into a new century. Begging for an antidote to the recent female "nastiness," when "those mouthing animals misbehaved, and were proud of it," Lawrence would opine that "It was all as depressing as cold tea after a funeral. An ill year for literature and fun! The Woman Who Did frowned, and humor fled. That achievement was the one triumph of Mrs. Morbidly-Neurotic" (551). Women in general and feminists in particular at the close of the nineteenth century were allegedly too psychologically unbalanced to appreciate the sanity and healthfulness of jokes.

The British New Woman writer of the end of the century was forced into self-consciousness, therefore, about how she positioned herself on the issue of laughter. She faced on the one hand a variety of misogynistic comic attacks upon her goals and programs, whether those involved reform of the marriage laws, access to higher education and entry into the professions for women, the end of the class system, or the abolition of the double standard in sexual morality. In addition, she met with satirical portraits of herself designed to make her seem personally ridiculous—loathsome of face and deformed in body. And then, moreover, she found herself decried as incapable by nature of laughter of her own—humorless, without wit, unable to address a reader except through harangues or angry sputters. Thus when Arthur Rickett, the English literary satirist, published in 1895 "Miss Maud's Three Notes," his parody of a New Woman-ish volume entitled *Keynotes* by

"George Egerton" (Mary Chavelita Dunne), he depicted the feminist heroine as a grim and violent creature, hurling a flower-pot at a random man and ranting incoherently, "'I feel,' said Maud, 'I don't know—I can't express—I hate men; I loathe men. I don't know why, but I do'" (Rickett, 14–15).

According to the opposition, the greatest error of such a New Woman was her refusal to keep these sentiments to herself and her insistence instead upon making them public, even turning them to literary purposes. Her pretensions to authorship, however, were inevitably a mere nuisance or joke, as Rickett made clear in a further squib from 1895, "The New Cinderella. An Up-to-Date Fairy Tale." There is scarcely a more foolish character in literature of the 1890s than Rickett's female protagonist, who decides, on the advice of her fairy godmother, to write novels—"turgid prose full of asterisks and hysterics"—just as all the other New Women do, and who produces "a sickly exotic of first-class morbidness" (66).

But a woman did not have to consider herself "New" in order to experience the scourge of masculine wit; indeed, "George Egerton," who was the target of Rickett's laughter, as well as of a two-part anonymous parody in *Punch* (10 March and 17 March 1894) and a separate caricature (28 April 1894), denied repeatedly in published interviews that her work concealed any socio-political agenda or that she herself was associated in any way with those she called the "advanced" and the "unsexed." To merit lampoons or worse, nonetheless, it was enough for a female author merely to seem willful and incompliant to the male observer. So keen, in fact, was this comic scrutiny of female temperament and actions throughout the 1890s that it went beyond consideration of actual women. Even fictional characters from earlier Victorian literature were subject to retrospective judgment and punishment, as a warning to all contemporary transgressors of the rule of female subordination.

Perhaps the most extraordinary example of how this climate of ridicule extended itself in diffuse and unexpected directions for the purpose of intimidating both the New Woman—and her less political sisters who might have been tempted to air their own grievances—can be found in George Gissing's *Charles Dickens*. This 1898 volume on the works of Dickens, issued in Blackie & Son's "Victorian Era Series," was at once an encomium of past satires of women and itself an exercise in 1890s misogyny. For Gissing, whose ambivalence ran so deep in his fiction that it produced both the tremendously sympathetic portrayals of feminists in *The Odd Women* (1893) and the vicious displays of contempt for self-assertive women in *The Whirlpool* (1897), this study became the occasion for justifying his own fiercest prejudices by linking them with the attitudes of his esteemed literary predecessor.

Gissing noted with pleasure the mockery of a "gallery of foolish, ridiculous, or offensive women" (133) in Dickens's novels:

> For ... it is obvious that Dickens wrote of women in his
> liveliest spirit of satire. Wonderful as fact, and admirable as art,
> are the numberless pictures of more or less detestable widows,
> wives, and spinsters which appear throughout his books.
> Beyond dispute, they must be held among his finest work; this
> portraiture alone would establish his claim to greatness." (133)

It was Gissing's argument in *Charles Dickens* that what had always been
viewed as a deliberate comic distortion in the satirical portraits of women—a
heightening of the characters' ridiculous traits for the sake of laughter—was
nothing of the sort. On the contrary, Dickens was practicing in his comedy
the strictest truth-to-life, as rigorous as that of any latter-day French
Naturalist:

> Here—I cannot remind the reader too often of this fact in
> regard to Dickens's women—one discerns absolutely nothing of
> "exaggeration"; not a word, not a gesture, goes beyond the very
> truth. Here the master would have nothing to learn from later
> art; he is the realist's exemplar. (155)

Dickens was, for Gissing, "the social historian of his day" (154), who
recorded from experience, rather than created or enhanced, the defects
present in his female characters: "Through his early life, Dickens must have
been in constant observation of these social pests ... His women use
utterance such as no male genius could have invented" (135). And the test of
Dickens's artistry was the likeness between such portraits and what, according
to Gissing, a dispassionate scientific "inquirer" of the present, a figure such
as the author himself, would perceive about actual women around him:
"There needs no historical investigation to ascertain the truthfulness of these
presentments ... [for] such women may be observed to-day by an inquirer
sufficiently courageous; they are a multitude that no man can number" (134).

Having established then to his own satisfaction that there was no
distinction between misogynist satire and sober truth, Gissing felt free in
Charles Dickens to indulge his comic inclinations at the expense of noisy,
demanding women, conflating his descriptions of Dickens's female characters
with his own malicious flights of fancy:

> In the highways and by-ways of life, by the fireside, and in the
> bed-chamber, their voices shrill upon the terrified ear. It is
> difficult to believe that death can stifle them; one imagines them
> upon the threshold of some other world, sounding confusion
> among unhappy spirits who hoped to have found peace. (133–34)

In none of these satirical passages did Gissing ever fix upon the New
Women of his own time by name, as representing the latter-day equivalents

of Dickens's obstreperous shrews. Nevertheless, by singling out for
opprobrium those very characteristics in a woman—restlessness, loudness,
immodesty, neglect of housekeeping, defiance, and discontent—for which
his rebellious female contemporaries were being publicly vilified in the
press, he encouraged the reader to make that identification for him. As he
said of Dickens's women, employing criticisms unmistakably similar to
those used against New Women of the middle classes:

> In general their circumstances are comfortable; they suffer no
> hardship ... nothing is asked of them but a quiet and amiable
> discharge of household duties; they are treated by their male
> kindred with great, often with extraordinary, consideration. Yet
> their characteristic is acidity of temper and boundless license of
> querulous or insulting talk. (133)

The connection between the comic literature of the past and the sexual
politics of the present deepened, moreover, as Gissing moved the chapter
called "Women and Children" toward a serious discussion of both
Dickens's and his own "ideal" woman—a figure who contrasted in every
way with the so-called emancipated female of the 1890s:

> I have left her [Ruth Pinch] to the last, because she will serve
> us as the type of all that Dickens really admired in woman.
> Truth to tell, it was no bad ideal. Granted that the world must
> go on very much in the old way, that children must be born
> and looked after, that dinners must be cooked, that houses
> must be kept swept, it is hard to see how Ruth Pinch can ever
> be supplanted ... [A] little house, a little garden, the cooking
> her own peculiar care, a little maid for the little babies—this
> is her dream. But never, within those walls, a sound of
> complaining or of strife, never a wry face, acidly discontented
> with the husband's doings or sayings. Upon my word—is it a
> bad ideal? (161–62)

In contrast to the sugary tone of this brief tribute to the traditional
housewife—the "thoroughly kind-hearted and home-loving woman" (161)—
was the vitriol of Gissing's extended satirical attack, which filled the rest of
the "Women and Children" chapter, upon those Dickensian females guilty of
kicking against their domestic circumstances. Over the head of Mrs. Varden
from *Barnaby Rudge*, for instance, he poured a torrent of sarcasm for the
crime of poisoning her household with "persistent sourness and sulkiness"
(137):

> She has in perfection all the illogicality of thought, all the
> maddening tricks of senseless language, which, doubtless for
> many thousand of years, have served her like for weapons. It is

an odd thing that evolution has allowed the persistence of this
art, for we may be quite sure that many a primitive woman paid
for it with a broken skull. Here it is, however, flourishing and
like to flourish. (137)

In commentary such as this, George Gissing and those of his masculine
contemporaries who shared his dislike and distrust of unsubmissive
women seemed to be establishing a new precedent for turn-of-the-century
comedy. Earlier Victorian theorists had defended satirical portraiture as a
mode of inciting the "correction" of its victims' manners, the kind of
correction that one sees, for instance, in the male protagonist of George
Meredith's "The Case of General Ople and Lady Camper" (1877), who is
stung to self-improvement by the scathing caricatures of him produced by
the story's artistic heroine. It was for this reason that Meredith had
spoken of satire, in his 1877 essay called "On the Idea of Comedy and of
the Uses of the Comic Spirit," as a form of "hard-hitting, with a moral
purpose to sanction it" (Meredith, 42). Much of the misogynistic comedy
of the 1890s, however, was notable for its attacks not upon manners but
upon what it labeled "woman's nature," which it blamed for such
eruptions as the New Woman's insurgent spirit. Deeming this condition
quite incorrigible, end-of-the-century theorists advocated a kind of
comedy that practiced pure assault for assault's sake, meant to dispose of,
rather than to educate and amend, the nuisance at hand.

Thus in his study of Charles Dickens, Gissing praised the depiction of
Mrs. Gargery from *Great Expectations* as capturing precisely the "shrew
of the most highly developed order," whose obnoxious complaining is
entirely unprovoked, groundless, and unchangeable: "Cause there is none
... It is the peculiarity of these women that no one can conjecture why
they behave so ill. The nature of the animals—nothing more can be said"
(143). But while reveling in the laughter aimed at her type, Gissing could
not be content with ridicule alone to do what Meredith had referred to as
"hard-hitting," and a more blatant call to arms accompanied his jibes. In
his remarks upon the female character's fate, Gissing made plain the
violence and malignity that underlay many of the comic attacks upon
women in the nineties, as well as the readiness of some male authors to
move beyond the text into action:

Mrs. Gargery shall be brought to quietness; but how? By a half-
murderous blow on the back of her head, from which she will
never recover. Dickens understood by this time that there is no
other efficacious way with these ornaments of their sex. A
felling and stunning and all but killing blow, followed by
paralysis and slow death. A sharp remedy, but no whit sharper
than the evil it cures. (143)

II

Obviously, the animosity and antagonism that fueled misogynist satire in the 1890s did not go unremarked by its victims. But the comedy produced in turn by New Women of the period seldom went for the kill. More often, it kept intact the Meredithian tradition of using laughter merely to inspire change and improvement. The satire that it favored was usually limited and localized in its targets—not "the nature of the animal" for "many thousands of years," but the particular conduct of present-day men and male-dominated institutions. Its tone, moreover, was often quite temperate—a version of ridicule moderate enough to allow for continued relations between the jokester and the object of mockery. And indeed, in a world where men would continue to wield greater economic and cultural power long after the laughter had died away, no New Woman with an ounce of pragmatism could afford to alienate her masculine targets completely.

A good example of the tempered and more carefully focused comedy of the New Woman was "The Last Ditch," from *A Pomander of Verse*, E. [Edith] Nesbit's volume of poetry issued in 1895 by the Bodley Head, a firm strongly associated with New Women's texts in general, especially by authors such as "Victoria Crosse," Netta Syrett, and Evelyn Sharp. As a founding member in the 1880s of the Fabian Society, Nesbit had long been acquainted through debates involving the socialist movement with the rhetoric of anger and abuse; certainly, she could have drawn such weaponry from the arsenal of memory in order to write satire, had she so wished. What she published instead was a wry comedy with a feminist slant—an address to a coercive male lover who is an aesthete and who has fixed notions of how women ought to conform to the visions of men, especially those of popular painters and illustrators:

> Love, through your varied views on Art
>   Untiring have I followed you,
> Content to know I had your heart
>   And was your Art-ideal, too.
>
> As, dear, I was when first we met.
>   ('Twas at the time you worshipped Leighton,
> And were attempting to forget
>   Your Foster and your Noel Paton.)
>
> "Love rhymes with Art," said your dear voice,
>   And, at my crude, uncultured age,
> I could but blushingly rejoice
>   That you had passed the Rubens stage.
>
> When Madox Brown and Morris swayed
>   Your taste, did I not dress and look

Like any Middle Ages maid
In an illuminated book?

I wore strange garments, without shame,
  Of formless form and toneless tones,
I might have stepped out of the frame
  Of a Rossetti or Burne-Jones.
I stole soft frills from Marcus Stone,
  My waist wore Herkomer's disguise,
My slender purse was strained, I own,
  But—my silk lay as Sargent's lies.

And when you were abroad—in Prague—
  'Mid Cherets I had shone, a star;
Then for your sake I grew as vague
  As Mr. Whistler's ladies are.

But now at last you sue in vain,
  For here a life's submission ends:
Not even for you will I grow plain
  As Aubrey Beardsley's "lady friends."

Here I renounce your hand—unless
  You find your Art-ideal elsewhere;
I will not wear the kind of dress
  That Laurence Housman's people wear! (83–84)

The speaker of "The Last Ditch" does not rail against patriarchy or against heterosexual power arrangements in general. Neither does she complain about the burden—not even about the economic burden upon her "slender purse"—of having to fashion and refashion her appearance, while obliterating her individuality, to suit the lover's shifting artistic whims. Instead, her only objection is to his latest enthusiasm: a taste for a new mode that offends her own aesthetic sense and feminine pride by making women homely. Thus, the immediate comic target of the poem is the lover's one particular excess—a specific and corrigible fault; its long-range target, rather than being any general deficiency in the attitude of men, is the grotesque stylization practiced by British illustrators of the nineties. And even this seeming poke at contemporary masculinist British art turns out to be more of a sly, in-house dig among colleagues, delivered by someone who expects to maintain connections with the butts of her joke. In 1895, the year when "The Last Ditch" appeared, E. Nesbit, Laurence Housman, and Aubrey Beardsley were, in fact, all under contract with the Bodley Head press (though Beardsley, unbeknownst to Nesbit at this point, would soon be dropped by the firm in the wake of the Oscar Wilde scandal). Indeed, *A Pomander of Verse*, the volume containing this apparently anti-Decadent-art poem, was designed by Housman himself, complete with a title-page illustration of an attenuated female figure; moreover, when the poem was published, Nesbit had every reason to believe that her forthcoming collection of stories, *In Homespun*, for the Bodley Head's "Keynotes Series," would feature covers, spine, and title-page by Beardsley, who was in charge of the series's format.

As a group, New Women writers tended not to expend their energies on abusive and alienating forms of satire, favoring instead a version of humor that recognized the inevitability of an ongoing relationship with the masculine objects of their laughter, as well as the need to reform and improve the character of that relationship. This was not merely a reflection of some inherent female preference, of the kind that the sociolinguists such as Deborah Tannen have identified, for joke-telling that increases "affiliation" and "intimacy" with others. It was rather an acknowledgment of the fact that women's comedy in the 1890s had to remain palatable to a male audience in order to achieve publication at all. (In the case of Nesbit's poem, this meant gaining the approval first of a publisher's reader, Richard Le Gallienne, who was himself a social acquaintance of Beardsley and Housman, and then of a male publisher, John Lane, at the Bodley Head). It was further grounded in the recognition that social change on either a narrow or a broad scale still depended upon the cooperation of men who held the reins of power.

At the same time, however, that New Women were creating their own versions of comedies in the 1890s, they were consciously exploring, both in criticism and in fiction, the issue of laughter in general, sometimes approaching it from a theoretical standpoint and sometimes in terms of consequences for the individual woman who laughs. Their concerns were ethical and also practical, arising out of questions not only as to whether ridicule of the other sex and its culture were just, but whether it did a woman any good or perhaps even exposed her to greater misery. The jeers and sneers directed at the New Women themselves had done nothing to reconcile them to the point of view of their attackers, so there was little reason for them to believe unconditionally in such weapons as effective political strategies for bringing about institutional change. Instead, since comedy had first presented itself in a problematic form to them, used in targeting and humiliating women, they continued to see laughter in all its guises, from scathing mockery to mere wry smiles, as a problem requiring careful scrutiny.

We can begin to get a sense of the range of turn-of-the-century women's philosophical positions on the issues surrounding laughter by contrasting the responses of two prominent female commentators, Alice Meynell and Laura Marholm Hansson, each of whom moved into and out of the category of "New Womanhood" at various points. The purpose of their arguments differed: in Meynell's case, to object to the injustice of what had passed as masculine wit and humor and to reclaim comedy as women's province, too; in Marholm Hansson's, to uncover the well-hidden tradition of women's laughter at men that did not express itself chiefly in literary texts, but also to raise troubling questions about how much this female laughter could accomplish in any case. What these critics shared was an acute sensitivity to the role of masculine comedy in supporting and maintaining unequal power relations between men and women and a moral revulsion against the infliction of pain through laughter, as well as a deep skepticism about the possibility of changing the power balance merely by reversing the gender of the joke's practitioner and the joke's victim.

Alice Meynell, the British Roman Catholic poet, may be better known now for her lyrical verse, but she was also a literary and social critic who used the platform of her essays to "be sarcastic on the subject of those men who were themselves sarcastic on the subject of women" (Sackville-West, 22). In both her private and public life, she voluntarily played out traditional feminine roles. She was, as Vita Sackville-West described her in a 1947 essay, "womanly ... [in] her clothes, her manner, her quiet assumption of her right as a woman towards whom homage was due" (21), as well as in the way that she took on the identities of "mother" and "hostess" (21). Nevertheless, her own New Woman-ish sympathies came through in an essay such as "A Woman in Grey" from *The Colour of Life* (1896), her paean to the female bicyclist as the embodiment of "watchful confidence," female "courage," readiness to assume "equal risk," and ability to overcome having been as a "woman ... long educated to sit still" (*Colour*, 68–71). But most of all, her feminist spirit of dissatisfaction with the social order of the day exercised itself in protests against the disrespectful treatment of women by male writers.

In an essay titled "Laughter" that was collected in her 1909 volume, *Ceres' Runaway and Other Essays*, Meynell would note with displeasure the efforts of her turn-of-the-century male contemporaries to arrogate to themselves the right to decide what was funny:

> There is, in a word, a determination, an increasing tendency ...
> [for] laughter [to be] everywhere and at every moment proclaimed
> to be the honourable occupation of men, and in some degree
> distinctive of men, and no mean part of their prerogative and
> privilege. The sense of humour is chiefly theirs, and those who are
> not men are to be admitted to the jest upon their explanation. (30)

Such a situation, as Meynell had stated in an earlier meditation on the subject of laughter titled "Penultimate Caricature," left the female spectator in a difficult position—not only excluded from the process of defining the comic, but, in some cases, subject to scorn for even daring to point out the implications of a so-called jest. As she wrote in that essay in 1893,

"Obviously to make a serious comment on anything which others consider or have considered humorous is to put one's-self at a disadvantage. He who sees the joke holds himself somewhat the superior" (*Rhythm*, 101).

Meynell risked placing herself at a disadvantage, nonetheless, in order to protest against what she identified as a continuing trend of "derision of the woman" in nineteenth-century culture (*Rhythm*, 105). She began "Penultimate Caricature," the essay to which she gave the honor of closing her 1893 volume called *The Rhythm of Life*, with an acknowledgment that hers was a minority position, for she was taking exception to a characteristic of earlier Victorian art by which few evidently had been troubled: "There has been no denunciation, and perhaps even no recognition, of a certain social immorality in the caricature of the mid-century and earlier. Literary and pictorial alike, it had for its notice the vulgarising of the married woman" (101). Preceding George Gissing's book on Charles Dickens by just five years, Meynell's essay singled out Dickens and some of his contemporaries (including Jerrold, Leech, and Keene)—not, this time, for praise, but rather for tough critical scrutiny. In Gissing's eyes, Dickens could do no wrong as a satirist. But were these mid-Victorians, Meynell asked, really models worthy of emulation by artists of the nineties? In their works, she found what seemed to her both unfair and unwarranted expressions of disgust at women's conduct and physical being, especially in their role as wives:

> There is in some old *Punch* volume a drawing by Leech ... where the work of the artist has vied with the spirit of the letter-press. Douglas Jerrold treats of the woman's jealousy, Leech of her stays. They lie on a chair by the bed, beyond description gross. And page by page the woman is derided, with an unfailing enjoyment of her foolish ugliness of person, of manners, and of language. (102)

The word that she chose to describe such proceedings was an interesting one. In 1893, at a time when male critics reserved the use of "immorality" almost exclusively for their descriptions of contemporary European and British Naturalism and for novels by New Women writers, Meynell applied it not to literary offenses against the prevailing code of sexual propriety but, more daringly, to offenses against the good name of Woman.

As might be expected, Meynell's portrait of Dickens in "Penultimate Caricature" differed radically from the one Gissing would draw soon afterward in his own critical sketch. For Meynell, Dickens was not at all the so-called social historian, whose satires of women approached in technique the scientific accuracy of the later French realism and whose example, therefore, could be used to validate all subsequent attacks upon women's existence; instead, he was an artist with a dreadful blind spot that made him treat his female subjects unjustly:

> In that time there was, moreover, one great humourist; he bore
> his part willingly in vulgarising the woman; and the part that fell
> to him was the vulgarising of the act of maternity. Woman
> spiteful ... woman incoherent, woman abandoned without
> restraint to violence and temper ... in none of these ignominies is
> woman so common, foul, and foolish for Dickens as she is in
> child-bearing. (102–103)

It would have been clear to Meynell's audience that her intention in this
essay was not to malign Dickens's reputation or to suggest that his novels
made unsuitable reading, even for women. Indeed, there is no sign either here
or in her later essay entitled "Dickens," from the 1917 collection *Hearts of
Controversy*, of the antipathy toward his work that George Gissing would
attribute to female readers in general because of their alleged lack of a sense
of humor (Gissing, 131–32). On the contrary, Dickens was, for Meynell, a
writer whose inspiration often seemed to have been "celestial" and whose
creations were sometimes "ultimately to be traced, through Dickens, to God"
("Dickens," 110). And while announcing her admiration for his skill at
"dramatic tragedy" (110), she insisted even more strongly that "it be granted
that Dickens the humourist is foremost and most precious" (117). Her
unhappiness was solely with his choice of targets, and her criticism of
Dickens's comedy remained a precise and local one, focused only upon his
denial of fair treatment to women.

But the aim of Meynell's criticism in "Penultimate Caricature" was not
merely to blast the tastes in satire of fifty years earlier; rather, as was
evident from the conclusion toward which this essay built, its purpose lay
in addressing the present day and in shaping the literary and social practices
of the future. Referring boldly again to misogyny as an ethical crime,
Meynell finished by noting that "This great immorality, centring in the
irreproachable days of the Exhibition of 1851, or thereabouts—the pleasure
in this particular form of human disgrace" was still clearly traceable in her
contemporaries, especially in the "habit by which some men reproach a
silly woman through her sex, whereas a silly man is not reproached through
his sex" (*Rhythm*, 106). Her method of dealing with this present-day
injustice was a subtle one: to create in her readers a revulsion against the
misogynistic excesses of the past that could make them wish to change
their own behavior. And by allowing the audience first to recognize the
evils of sexism in comic art from which it felt some detachment or
distance—such as that produced by the passage of forty or fifty years—she
could lessen the sense of personal threat that a male reader, in particular,
might experience with an example closer to home.

Meynell's tactics were those of a moderate, but that does not mean that
they were determined purely by considerations of what might reach or might

placate a male audience. Her arguments also made their appeal to those women readers of the 1890s who, frightened off by the hostile caricatures in *Punch* and other journals of middle-class opinion, had become reluctant to identify themselves with the more direct protests of the New Women against contemporary manifestations of woman-hating, but who could safely second a criticism of the mid-Victorians. Such women also suffered from a feeling of physical and spiritual humiliation, which they had no outlet for expressing, whenever they encountered representations of female "grossness"; for these middle-class female readers of the *Pall Mall Gazette*, the *Scots Observer*, and other periodicals in which her essays first appeared, Meynell served as a welcome and unthreatening defender of women's rights.

Female critics of the 1890s produced a wide spectrum of response, both to the pressing issue of male ridicule of women and to the problems attaching themselves to the concept of laughter as a whole. Clearly, Meynell's reactions came down on the side of optimism and potential for reform; her complaints about masculine satires of women were meant to inaugurate a process of change, first in artistic representations and then in life. But not all feminist theorists seemed to believe in such a hopeful outcome. Very different in tone and in underlying assumptions were the writings, for instance, of Marholm Hansson. Her book-length study called *Modern Women*—issued in 1896 by the John Lane, the Bodley Head, publisher of much New Women Literature, in a translation from German by Hermione Ramsden—appeared in England at a moment when public events had revealed the vicious and sadistic undercurrent running through laughter in general at the end of the century. Only months before, on the afternoon of 21 November 1895, Oscar Wilde had stood on a railway platform at Clapham Junction, waiting to be transferred by his jailers to Reading gaol. "Handcuffed and in prison clothing," the most celebrated comic playwright of the decade, having been convicted on charges of indecency for homosexual activity, met his audience: "A crowd formed, first laughing and then jeering at him. One man recognized that this was Oscar Wilde, and spat at him" (Ellmann, 465).

The outbursts of extreme malevolence that seemed to arise especially around the issues of gender roles and sexuality and that expressed itself through ridicule were hardly confined to England in this period. In a second volume of literary criticism published by the Bodley Head in 1899, *We Women and Our Authors*, Marholm Hansson would title one of her chapters "The Women-Haters, Tolstoy and Strindberg" and would devote much of her discussion of the latter figure to recording how, in his representations of women, he could "never depict them ludicrously and repulsively enough" to satisfy himself (160). Marholm Hansson, an author who was "a German-speaking Dano-Russian from Latvia with Norwegian relatives" (Brantly, 5), spent much time in Denmark and in Sweden with her husband, the Swedish writer Ola Hansson. Thus she became well aware of the relationship, at least in Northern European and Scandinavian culture at the turn of the century, between masculine anger and ridicule directed against women and the upsurge of feminist political agitation. As she noted in placing Strindberg's plays of the 1880s and 1890s in their social context:

> In the course of a few years there appeared a collection of dramas evincing a hatred of woman quite unparalleled in the literature of the world. It was just at the time when the Scandinavian movement for the emancipation of women was in full swing, with its natural accompaniment of women authors. (*We Women*, 169–70)

Yet though Marholm Hansson fervently condemned misogyny, whether masked as comedy or not, her own support of the "movement for the emancipation of women" proved ambivalent and wavering. Her intellectual stance throughout the nineties was a deliberately provocative one, yoking together elements of the New Woman and the so-called Womanly Woman arguments in an irresolvable tension. A believer in essentialism and in biology as destiny, she claimed that "[o]wing to her physiological structure woman is a creature of instinct," born with an "unfathomable ... incomprehensible nature" that produces an "utter disregard for law and justice and all the rest of the intricate building of common sense upon which human society is founded" (56); thus, any demand that women be given a university education, the vote, or training for intellectual careers was, to her, fundamentally misguided. But while extolling the glories of female "instinct" and condemning those who would educate women for the professions, Marholm Hansson herself displayed more than her share of "common sense," as well as a learned acquaintance with contemporary literature and philosophy from across Europe and an unquenchable ambition to see her own writings published and taken seriously. This divided temperament made her a fitting mediator, however, between more traditional women readers and the New Women writers, the role that she created for herself in the 1896 volume called *Modern Women*. It was, indeed, in the capacity of a kind of feminist go-between that she appeared in the chapter from *Modern Women* entitled "Neurotic Keynotes," reflections inspired by her reading of two volumes of short stories (*Keynotes* from 1893 and *Discords* from 1894, both published by the Bodley Head) by the Anglo-Irish writer "George Egerton" (Mary Chavelita Dunne).

Throughout that chapter, Marholm Hansson's discussion of the comedy of heterosexual relations became an occasion for expressing her ambivalent view of women's position. She was, on the one hand, strongly attracted to the concept of femininity as a form of power to be exercised and enjoyed—something that gave women the ability to tease, manipulate, control, and, especially, to mock men. But she was also aware of the restrictions on that power imposed by the economic and political disparities of gender. And, most of all, she felt enormous sympathy for those women who began by using the advantage of feminine laughter in their dealings with men, only to find themselves yoked eventually in marriage to men whom they could not respect and who would not respect them, locked forever in a socially sanctioned arrangement where their powers could do them no good.

The conflicts between these notions of female power and powerlessness begin to emerge as Marholm Hansson describes the secret comic perspective of women, which rarely finds representation in literary form:

> It is almost universal amongst women, especially Germans, that they do not take men as seriously as he likes to imagine. They think him comical ... Men have no idea what a comical appearance they present, not only as individuals, but as a race. The comic part about a man is that he is so different from women, and that is just what he is proudest of. The more refined and fragile a woman is, the more ridiculous she is likely to find the clumsy, great creature, who takes such a roundabout way to gain his comical ends. To young girls especially, man offers a perpetual excuse for a laugh, and a secret shudder. When men find a group of women laughing among themselves, they never suspect that it is they who are the cause of it. And that again is so comic. The better a man is, the more he is in earnest when he makes his pathetic appeal for a great love, and woman, who takes a special delight in playing a little false, even when there is no necessity, becomes as earnest and solemn as he, when all the time she is only making fun of him. (*Modern Women*, 64–65)

Marholm Hansson outlines a scenario in which women can counter masculine supremacy and dominate men through their laughter—a triumph all the greater, because it occurs without the victim's knowledge. Only recently, she asserts, has the literary evidence of this mocking attitude toward men finally appeared, in the short stories published as *Keynotes* by a writer such as "George Egerton," whom she classes as a new or "modern" female type (although, in the private correspondence between Marholm Hansson and "George Egerton" that ensued, the latter would once again disavow the New Woman label).

But even as Marholm Hansson argues for her vision of women's power over men, she also presents a more sinister picture of heterosexual relations in action in the social world. Using "George Egerton's" work as her illustration, she describes how the supposed comedy of "difference" inevitably degenerates, under the institutionalized inequality of marriage, into something violent and sordid, culminating in physical danger to the "little" woman from the "big" man, as well as psychological alienation and frustration on both sides:

The ... shudder is the deepest vibration in Mrs. Egerton's book. What is the subject? ... in every story it is the same little woman with a difference, the same little woman who is always loved by a big, clumsy, comic man, who is now good and well-behaved, now wild, drunk, and brutal, who sometimes ill-treats her, sometimes fondles her, but never understands what it is that he ill-treats and fondles. (*Modern Women*, 65)

What had started with female laughter ends on a very different note—the despairing sound of the narrative voice that Marholm Hansson hears throughout "George Egerton's" second volume of stories, *Discords*:

The tone of bitter disappointment which pervades "Discords" is the expression of woman's disappointment in man. Man and man's love are not a joy to her, they are a torment. He is inconsiderate in his demands, brutal in his caresses, and unsympathetic with those sides of her nature which are not there for his satisfaction. He is no longer the great, comic animal of "Keynotes," whom the woman teases and plays with—he is a nightmare which smothers her during horrible nights, a hangman who tortures her body and soul during days and years for his pleasure; a despot who demands admiration, caresses, and devotion, while her every nerve quivers with an opposite emotion; a man born blind, whose clumsy fingers press the spot where the pain is, and when she moans, replies with coarse, unfeeling laughter, "Absurd nonsense!" (*Modern Women*, 86–87)

By the end of Marholm Hansson's discourse, the issue of laughter has come full circle. Once again, the laugh is reinstated as a characteristic of male privilege, a symptom of masculine hatred of women, and an instrument of female humiliation and entrapment, rather than of female liberation. Given the context of the social and legal realities of late nineteenth-century marriage, the "comedy" of sexual relations remains, for Marholm Hansson, a questionable concept and the laughing woman herself a problematic figure. And indeed, the version of the New Woman that she admires—the one whose voice she finds in *Discords* and interprets for more conservative women readers—is not prone to comic flights. On the contrary, this New Woman has an "intense and morbid consciousness of ... [her own] ego" (*Modern Women*, 79), "delicate nerves" on which "the sand of time falls drop by drop" (83), and a "tired, worn ... restless ... bitter, [and] hopeless" mien (83). She is a character who has given up on satire as a strategy, and her former attempts to "tease ... and play ... with" men and to treat them as humorous subjects are revealed as dangerously naïve errors.

For Marholm Hansson, then, the ultimate usefulness of female laughter was greatly in doubt. The impulse, in which the author herself indulges, to view men as comical and to look down at them coexists uneasily here with the recognition of male power within patriarchy as absolute and of male hostility toward women as irremediable. Contemporary readers would have been at a loss to decide what course of action Marholm was recommending: whether to go on countering the ferocity of the "Women-Haters" by "making fun" of man for being "so different from women" (*Modern Women*, 64–65), as she claimed women had been doing all along in secret, or whether to acknowledge the futility of such efforts and abandon them. Certainly, the fact that Marholm Hansson did not believe in or support any organized feminist movement for social change meant that she could not proffer any way out of this deadlock—this vision of women first laughing at suitors and then finding themselves helpless, laughed at, and abused by their captors after marriage. She could only present the issue of laughter as a complex socio-sexual problem, bound up with the unequal status of women, to be solved by someone else.

III

Long before Freud published his findings about the links between comedy and aggression, women intellectuals of the late nineteenth century were pressed by circumstances into discerning this connection. There was no doubt that women in general—and any discontented, self-assertive, and vocal ones who could be labeled New Women, in particular—were being subjected on a wide scale to what Meynell called the "great immorality" of sexist ridicule and that an angry, belligerent misogyny was behind this. Agreement broke down, though, over the proper response in a such a climate. Did it help or hurt women, as a group or individually, to laugh back? If this question ran as a continuing preoccupation through the works of female literary and social critics, such as Meynell and Marholm Hansson, it proved an even greater issue for women writers of fiction. Through fiction, whether itself comic or serious in tone, New Women could explore the ramifications of being a woman who laughs, by figuring the personal consequences of making jokes at the expense of patriarchy and weighing the ultimate effects of such gestures in terms of other women's lives.

The fate of the middle-class woman who applies a comic perspective to her dealings with men became the special province of Ella Hepworth Dixon, especially in her works of the early nineties, such as "A Literary Lover" and *My Flirtations* (1892). Like her contemporary Ada Leverson, who also moved socially among the Oscar Wilde set (Dixon contributed several pieces, as well, to the *Woman's World*, the magazine that Wilde edited), Dixon valued the exercise of wit in others and excelled in it herself. But wit, for her, could not be a virtue in itself, detached from other moral and political considerations. She was also a New Woman, as would be clear with the publication of her novel of social protest, *The Story of a Modern Woman* (1894), in which her characters dared to hope for a time when women would be "united ... [and] could lead the world" (Dixon, *Story*, 259). And as a feminist, therefore, she refused to view any comedy that touched upon relations between the sexes as separable from the serious business of women's unequal status under patriarchy.

The potential of laughter, within this context of inequality, to do women more harm than good became the subject of one of her early short stories for the magazine *Woman's World*. In "A Literary Lover" (1890), the female protagonist finds herself alone in the sitting-room occupied by her houseguest, with whom she is in love and from whom she anticipates receiving a proposal. He is a novelist who has gone away overnight to consult with his publisher. As she pauses "reverently ... wrapt in a happy dream" before the stray sheets of a manuscript that he has left lying on a writing desk, her eyes alight first upon a "page ... full of clever paradoxes written in a slightly precieux style, and then [upon] ... a brilliant phrase, the phrase of a master-mind, which rent the veil of convention and laid bare a palpitating human soul." Riveted, she moves on to a sheet of notes ready to be incorporated into his witty, satirical novel of contemporary life: "She read on and on, until a hard smile gathered at the corners of her mouth and her fingers clenched the fragile scrap of paper ... The notes, elaborate, searching, brutal in their frankness, were about a woman—and that woman was herself" ("Literary Lover," 641).

Her reaction is an interesting one. Stung though she is by her recognition of "the cruelty, the cynicism" involved in his leading her on for the sake of "using her as a painter uses a model, to copy and thrust aside," she still pays him the compliment of attributing his behavior to the "egotism of the artist," rather than to mere caddishness. What is more, she allows herself to register that "hard smile" which signals bitterness and rue, but which also serves as a kind of tribute to the power of his words to amuse, even when the amusement comes at her own expense. So strong is her own artistic sensibility—so much is she, too, the "literary lover" of the story's title—that she can acknowledge almost admiringly the "brutal fidelity" with which he has rendered "her foolish, half-tender speeches, her appealing looks, her innocent little subterfuges for seeing him alone," while also feeling betrayed and exposed (641).

The course of action on which she settles in response is a further indication of her literary temperament. Knowing that he "had only done a third of his book, and he would want to study her for a long time to come," she decides to punish him by writing him out of her own history, long before he has finished with her for his story. As she says to herself, employing the language of a novelist ridding herself of an unsuccessful fictional creation: "It was he who should be blotted out of her life as if he had never existed" (641).

Her method of accomplishing this end, moreover, shows that her sensibility is not only that of an artist, but of a comic artist in particular. She salves her damaged ego and restores herself to a position of superiority through the use of the smile. When her novelist-lover returns the next day, she greets him both with the news that she must unexpectedly leave him and with "her prettiest smile," an action that defies his analytic abilities: "He looked at her curiously, but her imperturbable smile baffled him." Expecting her to announce that she has given up this summer-house in the country to settle in London, where he can have ready access to her, he is stunned to hear instead that she has made very different plans: "'I signed the lease last night for fourteen years. I am going to live here,'" she tells him "lightly," capturing perfectly a comic tone in her delivery. She counters the sentimental melodrama of his final attempt to "press ... her hand" with a parting gesture of her own: "And then as the pony started off at a brisk trot, she turned and smiled back at him for the last time" (641). Her smile is a weapon that disarms him in many senses, depriving him at once of an explanation of the situation, of a model for his work, and of his control over women.

Published at a historical moment when Woman served as the object of unprecedented satirical dissection and demolition by male authors, Dixon's story appears to present the kind of resistance to such abuse that late twentieth-century feminist theorists might applaud. The protagonist's method of re-erecting the boundaries that have been violated by her lover's literary caricature—her way of ensuring that he "at least, should never know the truth" (641) about her pain—would seem to be one endorsed by Regina Barreca, for instance, who asserts that "The strategic use of humor by a woman backed into a literal or figurative corner can have enormously positive results" (*Snow White*, 95). In her 1991 work of feminist comic theory, *They Used to Call Me Snow White... But I Drifted*, which takes its title from a line penned by Mae West, Barreca argues throughout for the necessity of developing female "punch lines"—audacious comebacks to masculine hostility that disguises itself as humor. As Barreca delineates them, these "punch lines" depend, to paraphrase Oscar Wilde, far more on style than on sincerity. Speaking directly to her female audience, Barreca advises, "If and when you decide to use aggressive humor, you have to be sure to do it with finesse. It has to appear not to matter to you at all, otherwise it won't work. Like any joke, it depends on concealing the true feelings underneath" (97). Managed correctly, such behavior becomes a category of performance art. Indeed, the narrator of "A Literary Lover" points to just such a theatrical component, commenting upon the protagonist's success at carrying off the impenetrable smiles that function as her punch lines: "Most women are consummate actresses when their pride is at stake" (641).

In late twentieth-century terms, the protagonist of "A Literary Lover" proves triumphant; Dixon's story records the victory of a character who first refashions herself through humor into an unreadable text, no longer available to exploitation by male authors, and then into a writer-performer who gets both the last word and the last laugh. Vengeance is hers, for as Barreca says, "Making a joke at the joker's expense is like making a cheat pay the tab when he thought he was going to be the one who got the free meal" (98). And the protagonist's actions would be exemplary in a world such as Barreca envisions in *They Used to Call Me Snow White*, where only positive consequences follow from a good exit line: "When a construction worker shouts at you as you walk down the street, 'Hey, honey, I want to get into your pants,' by all means shout back, 'Nah, I got one asshole in there already.' His pals will give him a hard time all day, and they might even applaud you" (98).

For an end-of-the-nineteenth century feminist author such as Ella Hepworth Dixon, comedy represented neither so complete nor so simple a solution to women's dilemmas. In "A Literary Lover," to be able to deliver the lines that frustrate her lover's purposes and buffet his vanity—"I signed the lease last night for fourteen years. I am going to live here" ("Literary Lover," 641)—the protagonist herself must pay a fearful price. Victory over her opponent comes at the cost of a self-imposed banishment to South Devonshire, far from the "artistic and intellectual set" (638) in London with which she feels most at home. The satisfaction produced by one minute of smiling revenge weighs against the sacrifice to be endured through fourteen solitary years ahead. Thirty-six years old at the end of the narrative, she dooms herself to spend the prime of her creative and sexual life "stitching her ... thoughts into the tea-cloth she was embroidering" (639). The choice that she had framed so drolly only days before, in hopes of gently prodding her lover on to a proposal—"I must settle what is to become of me—if I am to be a civilised being again, and live in London, or if it would be better for me to stay in the country, and end my days in a sober and sensible manner—'planting cabbages'" (640)—has in fact become the augury of her grim fate.

Women's comedy here is indistinguishable from women's tragedy, for the laughter leads to no transformation of the oppressive circumstances. Though the exercise of her wit may have provided temporary relief from pain, it has done nothing either to increase the protagonist's own options by helping her to imagine and to realize better ways of living or, on the other hand, to create new options for the female audience that exists beyond the text. To be the comic victor in this situation, Dixon's narrative appears to suggest, does not mean that one has escaped victimization; if anything, the attempted one-upping has further limited the protagonist's prospects and opportunities. Reacting to the male author who manipulates women and takes them "lightly" by giving him a taste of his own medicine still leaves the woman of 1890 with only a bitter pill to swallow herself. Indeed, if her "literary lover" were to observe the boredom and isolation of the retirement into which his actions have driven her, it is he who might have the last laugh.

What did the laugh of the New Woman leave as its legacy? Perhaps the chief contribution of late-Victorian feminist humorists was in the area of attitudes, rather than of form. Paradoxically, they did most for comedy by alerting their readers to its limitations and by reminding audiences not to ask the impossible of it. New Women writers showed themselves quite capable of being funny. When, therefore, they chose to mute or temper their ridicule, or to write about the problems surrounding laughter, instead of merely reveling in laughter itself, they did so for a reason. Partly, this had to do with the moral complexities that they saw attached to the act of targeting an enemy for ridicule; but doubts about the effectiveness of laughter as a concrete political strategy proved an even more important factor. Focused as they were on the world beyond literature—on the specific social and economic conditions of actual women around them—they hesitated to put all their faith and energies into an activity that offered only limited potential for creating reforms. The New Women had no illusions about the power of comic literature alone to bring down the old order or to inaugurate a new one. The warning that Audre Lorde would issue to feminists in a different context almost one hundred years later—"For the master's tools will never dismantle the master's house. They may allow us temporarily to beat him at his own game, but they will never enable us to bring about genuine change" (Lorde, 99)—was one that they already knew to be true and tried to live by.

Today, at a time when American feminist academic culture seems inclined to overvalue the role of laughter as a "subversive" force in art and politics, turning to it reverently, whether as a corrective or as a guide, and holding up women comics from Mae West to Roseanne to Ellen DeGeneres as heroes, it might be wise to remember the skepticism of the New Women one hundred years ago. Even as they laughed, they recognized that satire is no substitute for political solidarity and that poking fun at patriarchy cannot do the work of organized action.

Works Cited

Ardis, Ann L. *New Women, New Novels: Feminism and Early Modernism.* New Brunswick, NJ: Rutgers University Press, 1990.

Barreca, Regina, ed. *Last Laughs: Perspectives on Women and Comedy.* New York: Gordon & Breach, 1988.

———, ed. *New Perspectives on Women and Comedy.* Philadelphia: Gordon & Breach, 1992.

———, ed. *The Penguin Book of Women's Humor.* New York: Penguin, 1996.

Barreca, Regina. *They Used to Call Me Snow White ... But I Drifted.* New York: Viking, 1991.

Bjørhovde, Gerd. *Rebellious Structures: Women Writers and the Crisis of the Novel, 1880–1900.* Oslo: Norwegian University Press, 1987.

Brantly, Susan. *The Life and Writings of Laura Marholm.* Beiträge zur nordischen Philologie, Bd. 21. Basel and Frankfurt am Main: Helbing & Lichtenhahn Verlag AG, 1991.

Cixous, Hélène. "The Laugh of the Medusa." Trans. Keith Cohen and Paula Cohen. In *The Signs Reader: Women, Gender, and Scholarship.* Eds. Elizabeth Abel and Emily K. Abel. Chicago: University of Chicago Press, 1983. 279–97.

Dixon, Ella Hepworth. "A Literary Lover." *The Woman's World.* Vol. 3. London: Cassell & Co., 1890. 638–41.

———. *My Flirtations.* By Margaret Wynman [pseud.]. London: Chatto & Windus, 1892.

———. *The Story of a Modern Woman.* New York: Cassell, 1894.

Ellmann, Richard. *Oscar Wilde.* London: Hamish Hamilton, 1987.

Gilbert, Sandra M., and Susan Gubar. *The War of the Words.* Vol. 1 of *No Man's Land: The Place of the Woman Writer in the Twentieth Century.* 3 vols. New Haven: Yale University Press, 1987.

Gissing, George. *Charles Dickens: A Critical Study.* London: Blackie & Son, 1898.

Gray, Frances. *Women and Laughter.* Charlottesville: University Press of Virginia, 1994.

Kranidis, Rita S. *Subversive Discourse: The Cultural Production of Late Victorian Feminist Novels.* New York: St. Martin's Press, 1995.

Lawrence, C. E. "Wanted—Humourists." *The Book Monthly* (London). May 1906: 549–552.

Ledger, Sally. *The New Woman: Fiction and Feminism at the Fin de Siècle.* Manchester: Manchester University Press, 1997.

Lorde, Audre. "The Master's Tools Will Never Dismantle the Master's House." In *This Bridge Called My Back: Writings of Radical Women of Color.* Eds. Cherrie Moraga and Gloria Anzaldua. New York: Kitchen Table, 1983. 98–101.

Marholm Hansson, Laura. *Modern Women: An English Rendering of Laura Marholm Hansson's 'Das Buch der Frauen' by Hermione Ramsden.* London: John Lane, The Bodley Head, 1896.

———. *We Women and Our Authors.* Trans. Hermione Ramsden. London: John Lane, The Bodley Head, 1899.

Marks, Patricia. *Bicycles, Bangs, and Bloomers: The New Woman in the Popular Press.* Lexington, KY: University Press of Kentucky, 1990.

Meredith, George. "On the Idea of Comedy and the Uses of the Comic Spirit." In *Comedy: "An Essay on Comedy" by George Meredith and "Laughter" by Henri Bergson.* Ed. Wylie Sypher. Baltimore: The Johns Hopkins University Press, 1980.

Meynell, Alice. *Ceres' Runaway and Other Essays.* London: Constable, 1909.

———. *The Colour of Life and Other Essays on Things Seen and Heard.* London: John Lane, 1896.

———. "Dickens." In *Alice Meynell, Prose and Poetry: Centenary Volume.* Eds. F. P. [Frederick Page], V. M. [Viola Meynell], O. S. [Olivia Meynell] and F. M. [Francis Meynell]. London: Jonathan Cape, 1947. 108–22.

———. *The Rhythm of Life and Other Essays.* London: Elkin Mathews and John Lane, 1893.

Nesbit, E. [Edith]. *A Pomander of Verse.* London: John Lane, The Bodley Head, 1895.

Rickett, Arthur. *Lost Chords.* London: A. D. Innes, 1895.

Sackville-West, Vita. "Introduction." In *Alice Meynell, Prose and Poetry: Centenary Volume.* Eds. F. P. [Frederick Page], V. M. [Viola Meynell], O. S. [Olivia Meynell] and F. M. [Francis Meynell]. London: Jonathan Cape, 1947. 7–26.

Showalter, Elaine. *Sexual Anarchy: Gender and Culture at the Fin de Siècle.* New York: Viking Press, 1990.

Notes on Contributors

John S. Batts has taught at the University of Ottawa in Canada for thirty years. He has particular interests in the literature of the Victorian and Transition periods, in the diary as a literary genre, and in literary humor. An original member of the International Society for Humor Studies, he also has spoken at WHIM (Wit, Humor, and Irony Membership) and ALA (American Literature Association) conferences. Some of his work has appeared in *Satire*, in *Humor: International Journal of Humor Research*, and in *The Encyclopedia of British Humor.*

Rob K. Baum teaches performance movement and theory at the University of Haifa, Israel. She has written numerous essays on gender and absence in Victorian literature, on identity politics, and on Judaic performativity and contemporary ethnic theater in Israel. She has also published original poetry and feminist plays. She is preparing a manuscript on female absence in dramas and novels, and continues to work on Victorian topics—including J. M. Barrie and the "Wilde body."

Abigail Burnham Bloom is Managing Editor of the journal *Victorian Literature and Culture.* She is co-editor, with John Maynard, of *Anne Thackeray Richie: Journals and Letters* (1994) and is currently editing a reference work on nineteenth-century British women writers. She also teaches courses at The New School and at New York University (Gallatin Division).

Nicholas Freeman teaches at the University of Bristol, and is currently working on a book about London and the Edwardian literary imagination. His publication and research areas include nineteenth- and twentieth-century poetry, the novel, and the relationship of literature to other art forms and to film. He has also contributed several entries on British writers to the *Dictionary of Literary Biography.*

Joseph H. Gardner is Professor of English and Director of Graduate Studies at the University of Kentucky. In addition to *Dickens in America: Twain, Howells, James and Norris* (1988), he is the author of numerous articles on Beardsley, D. G. Rossetti, T. H. Huxley, and other Victorian worthies.

Eileen Gillooly is the author of *Smile of Discontent: Humor, Gender, and Nineteenth-Century British Fiction* (1999), and of articles and reviews in such publications as *Victorian Studies, ELH (English Literary History)*, and *The New York Times Book Review*. She teaches English and comparative literature at Columbia University.

Patricia Marks, Professor of English and the 1997–98 Regents' Distinguished Professor at Valdosta State University, has published numerous articles on Victorian periodicals, on caricature and satire, and on the novel. She is co-author of *The Smiling Muse: Victoriana in the Comic Press* (1985), and author of both *American Literary and Drama Reviews: An Index to Late Nineteenth Century Periodicals* (1984) and *Bicycles, Bangs, and Bloomers: The New Woman in the Popular Press* (1990).

Patricia Murphy teaches at Missouri Southern State College. She has completed a book manuscript entitled *Time is of the Essence: Temporality, Gender, and the New Woman*, and has also completed an anthology, *Psyching Out the Sex: Victorian Writings on the Female Mind*. Her essays on the New Woman and on various Victorian texts have appeared in such journals as *Victorian Literature and Culture, SEL (Studies in English Literature)*, and the *Victorian Newsletter*.

James Najarian is Assistant Professor of English at Boston College, where he teaches Romantic and Victorian literature. He has completed a book entitled *The "Unmanly Poet": Keats, Keatsianism, and Victorian Desire*, and has published articles that have appeared in *Victorian Poetry* and *Midwest Quarterly*. He has also contributed to *The Gay and Lesbian Literary Heritage* (1992), and to *The Encyclopedia of Romanticism* (1992).

David Nash is Senior Lecturer at Oxford Brookes University. He has published widely on aspects of the secular movement and community as well as the history of blasphemy in British society. His publications include *Secularism, Art and Freedom* (1992) and *Blasphemy in Britain 1789–Present* (Ashgate, 1999). He has also published articles in *History Today, The Journal of Religious History*, and *Victorian Periodicals Review*.

Margaret D. Stetz is Associate Professor of English and Women's Studies at Georgetown University. She is co-author, with Mark Samuel Lasner, of *England in the 1880s: Old Guard and Avant-Garde* (1989), *England in the 1890s: Literary Publishing at the Bodley Head* (1990), and *The Yellow Book: A Centenary Exhibition* (1994), the catalogues of their library exhibitions on late Victorian cultural and publishing history. She is also author of numerous essays on nineteenth- and twentieth-century literature, and is currently writing a work on "George Egerton" for the Eighteen-

Nineties Society's monograph series. Finally, she is co-editing a volume of essays on Asian "comfort women" of World War II.

Jennifer A. Wagner-Lawlor is Associate Professor in the Department of English at The University of Memphis, where she also serves as the director of the Marcus W. Orr Center for the Humanities. She is author of *A Moment's Monument: Revisionary Poetics in the Nineteenth-Century Sonnet* (1996); she has also published articles on Keats, Shelley, Hopkins, Rossetti, Swinburne, and Browning, as well as on contemporary British drama. She is currently working on Victorian drama, and also on nineteenth-century literary parody.

Carolyn Williams is Associate Professor in the Department of English at Rutgers University in New Brunswick, New Jersey, where she also serves as Associate Director of the Center for the Critical Analysis of Contemporary Culture (CCACC). She has published articles and book chapters on various Victorian topics; she is also author of *Transfigured World: Walter Pater's Aesthetic Historicism* (1989). Recently she guest-edited a special-topics section on "Victorian Studies and Cultural Studies" for an issue of *Victorian Literature and Culture*. She is currently working on several related topics in Victorian theater: melodrama, comic opera, minstrelsy, and the music hall.

Index

á Beckett, Arthur, 68
Aborigines' Protection Society, 73
Academy, 91
Adams, James Eli, 193
Adcock, Arthur, 92, 93
aestheticism, xvii, xix, 4, 5, 7, 8, 9, 76 ff,
    182, 191, 211
Albert (Prince), 70, 74
Alington, C. A., 4
All the Year Round, 68
Altick Richard D., xiv, 77
Anstey, F., 68, 78
anticlericalism, 45, 49, 55, 56, 181
anti-Semitism, 61, 62–63
Anti-Slavery Society, 73
Arata, Stephen D., 38
Ardis, Ann, 219
Aristophanes, 4, 180
Aristotle, 158
Arnold, Matthew, xiii, xix, 76, 77, 80, 183,
    191–204
    Works:
    Culture and Anarchy, 192, 199, 200,
        201, 202
    Essays in Criticism, 191, 194, 196,
        199, 202
    "Function of Criticism at the Present
        Time, The," 192, 196, 197, 200,
        202
    Friendship's Garland, 194
    "Self-Dependence," 195
    Strayed Reveller, 192
    "Study of Poetry, The," 201
Arnold, Thomas, 192, 195
Ashley, Leonard, 10
Athenaeum, 99
Attwood, Francis, 199
Auerbach, Nina, 135

Bakhtin, Mikhail, xx, 24, 48, 61, 179, 211,
    214
Balzac, Honoré de, 193

Barbey D'Aurevilly, Jules, 193
Barr, Robert, 92
Barreca, Regina, 219, 238, 239
Barsley, Michael, 92
Baudelaire, Charles, 182
Beardsley, Aubrey, 210, 227, 228
Beerbohm, Max, 93, 94, 104, 191, 193
Benchley, Robert, 104
Bentham, Jeremy, 141, 142, 143, 144
Bernhardt, Sarah, 80
Bersani, Leo, 211
Biron, Sir Chartres, 25; *see* "Hyder
    Ragged," pseud.
    Works:
    King Solomon's Wives, xvii, 23–42
Bivona, Daniel, 24
Blackwood's, 165
Blake, William, 176, 185
blasphemy, xvii, 45, 46, 55, 61, 62, 64, 65,
    185
bluestocking women, 84, 85
Bodley Head, 226, 227, 228, 232
Bolt, Christine, 73
Bowdler, Thomas, 180
Boz, 118, 131, 135, 136; *also see* Dickens,
    Charles
Brantlinger, Patrick, 23, 33
Bright, John, 70
Brown, E. K., 192
Browning, Robert, 177–78, 179
Browning, Elizabeth Barrett, 175, 177–78,
    179
Brummell, Beau, 193, 194, 202
Buchanan, Robert, 75, 83, 84
Bulwer-Lytton, Edward, 193
burlesque, 1, 10, 76, 150, 173, 186
Burnand, F. C., 73, 102
Burne-Jones, Edward, 79, 174, 175
Butler, Samuel, 141, 157

Calverley, C. S., 185
caricature, 222, 238

Carlile, Richard, 45
Carlyle, Jane Welsh, 154, 166
Carlyle, John, 166
Carlyle, Thomas, xviii, 141, 144, 153–72
　Works:
　"Cruthers and Jonson,"157
　German Romance, 162
　"Illudo Chartis," 157
　"Jean Paul Friedrich Richter," 161, 162
　"Jean Paul Friedrich Richter Again," 162
　Life of Schiller, 161
　"Opera, The," 170
　Reminiscences, 154, 157
　Sartor Resartus, xviii, xix, 153–72
　Two Note Books, 165
　"Wotton Reinfred," 157, 166–69
Carte, Richard D'Oyly, 17
carnivalesque, xvi, 61, 64, 213, 214
cartoon, xvii, 49, 51ff, 64, 70, 221
Chatto and Windus, 99, 173, 183
Chrisman, Laura, 36
Christianity, critiques/satires of, 6, 43–66
　passim, 180–83
Church Times, 180
Cixous, Hélène, 219, 220
class issues, xvii, xviii, 4, 5, 11, 15 ff, 55,
　67 ff, 91, 92–93, 94, 98, 101, 104,
　108, 182, 183, 201–3 *passim*, 224, 232
Clough, Arthur Hugh, 178, 192, 195, 197
Cockney, 7, 67, 70, 85, 102, 103, 108
Coblence, Françoise, 193
Coleridge, Samuel Taylor, 159
Collins, Churton, 179
comic opera, 17
"Comic Spirit," xvi, 160, 225; *see also*
　Meredith, George
Cons, Emma, 80
Cornhill, 199
cross-dressing, 128, 129, 132; *see also*
　transvestism
Crosse, Victoria (pseud.), 226
Culler, A. Dwight, 192

D'Orsay, Count, 193
Daily Post (Liverpool), 184
Daily Telegraph, 75, 83
dandy/dandyism, xix, 191–204
Darnton, Robert, 43
Darwin, Charles, 23, 75, 86, 143
De Generes, Ellen, 240

de Sade, Marquis, 174–75, 176, 179, 182,
　183, 184
Delbourg-Delphis, Maryléne, 193, 202
Dickens, Charles, xviii, 68, 102, 126, 130,
　131, 133, 134, 135, 136, 141–52,
　176, 221, 222–24, 225, 230–31
　Works:
　Barnaby Rudge, 224
　Christmas Carol, 126
　Dombey and Son, 135, 176
　Great Expectations, 225
　Hard Times, xviii, 141–52
　Pickwick Papers, 133, 135
Disdéri, André, 76
Disraeli, Benjamin, 70, 72, 74, 193
Dixon, Ella Hepworth, 235–39
　Works:
　"A Literary Lover," 235–39
　My Flirtations, 236
　Story of a Modern Woman, The, 237
Dodero, Louis, 76
Douglas, Alfred (Lord), 206, 209, 211
Doyle, Richard, 79
Du Maurier, George, 68

Eco, Umberto, xiv, xvi
Edinburgh Review, 165
Egerton, George (pseud., Mary Chavelita
　Dunne), 221, 222, 233, 234, 235
　Works:
　Discords, 233, 235
　Keynotes, 221, 233, 234
Eliot, George, 159, 180
Eliot, T. S., 203
exaggeration, 93, 95, 96, 97, 103, 106,
　107, 129, 154, 168, 169, 170, 223
extravaganza, 11, 12, 13, 14, 16, 17, 18

Farrar, F. W., 175
Foote, George William, 47, 48, 49, 51, 55,
　56, 57, 60, 61, 62, 63, 65
Forster, E. M., 144
Foucault, Michel, 185
Fraser's, 165
Freethinker, xvii, 47, 48, 49, 51, 55, 56,
　57, 58, 61, 63, 64
freethinking movement, 46–66 *passim*
Freud, Sigmund, xix, 126, 185, 236
Froude, J. Anthony, 155–56, 157
Fun, 9

Furnivall, F. J., 176

Gainesborough, Thomas, 79
Garelick, Rhonda, 193, 197
Gaskell, Elizabeth, xviii, 115–40
    Works:
    Cranford, xviii, 115–40
    Mary Barton, 135
    "The Poor Clare," 119–21
Geertz, Clifford, 43
gender/sexual ideology, xix, 4, 5, 12–13,
        15–16, 70, 81–85, 86, 118, 191–204
        passim, 205–18 *passim,* 219–41 *passim*
Gentleman's Magazine, 68
Gilbert, Sandra and Gubar, Susan, 220
Gilbert, Sir William Schwenck, 9, 10, 11,
        13, 14, 18, 91; *also see* Gilbert and
        Sullivan
Gilbert and Sullivan, xvii, 1–21 *passim*
    Savoy Operas, xvii, 1–21 *passim; see
        individual titles below*
    Works:
    HMS Pinafore, 2, 4, 10, 11
    Happy Land, 10
    Harlequin Cock Robin and Jenny Wren ...,
        11
    Iolanthe, 1, 9, 13, 14–17
    Mikado, The, 2
    Patience, 1, 2–9, 15
    Pirates of Penzance, The, 10
    Princess, The, 10
    Princess Ida, 10
    Rosencrantz and Guildenstern, 18
    Ruddigore, 11
    Wicked World, The, 10, 12, 15
Gissing, George, 176, 221, 222–24, 230–31
Gladstone, William Ewart, 72, 76, 81, 83, 91
Goethe, Johann Wolfgang von, 160, 195
Gosse, Edmund, 91, 175, 184
Gray, Frances, 219
Grosvenor Gallery, 79

Haggard, H. Rider, xvii, 23–42 *passim*
    Works:
    King Solomon's Mines, vxii, 23–42
        passim
    She, 38
Hansson, Laura Marholm; *see* Marholm
        Hansson, Laura
Harcourt, Sir William, 55

Hardy, Thomas, 91
Harrison, Frederic, 200
Harte, Bret, 92
Hazlitt, William, 158–59
Henckle, Roger B., 104
Henderson, Philip, 173, 177, 179
"high" vs. "low" culture, 4–6, 8, 9, 18, 76
Hindle, E. B., 18
Hobbes, Thomas, 150, 157–58
Holcroft, Thomas, 11
Holyoake, George Jacob, 46
Home Chimes, 105
homoeroticism, 205–18 *passim*
Honan, Park, 191, 192, 194, 195, 197
Hood, Edwin, xv, xx
Hood, Thomas, 70, 135
Hotten, Joseph, 186
Household Words, 115, 135
Housman, Laurence, 227
Howell, C. A., 186
humor and literary form (*see* blasphemy;
        burlesque; caricature; cartoon;
        comic opera; exaggeration; extrava
        ganza; irony; lampoon; mock-
        heroic; nonsense; pantomime;
        parody; pastiche; satire)
    "New" (American), xviii, 91–113 *passim*
    theories of, xiii–xvi, xviii, xx, 104,
        158 ff, 185
    as anger/aggression, xviii, xix, 116–17,
        119, 121–22, 128–29, 132–33, 136,
        164, 236, 238
    as ideological "unmasking," xv, xvi, xx
    as incongruity, xiii–xiv, xviii, 158–60,
        164, 170
    as "inverse sublime," xviii–xix, 153–72
        passim
    as social/political criticism, xiv, xv, xvi,
        xix, 9, 23–24, 43, 67–89 *passim,*
        185, 240
    as superiority, 158, 160, 238
    as sympathy, 159–60, 165
    as trangression, xvi, xx, 64, 128, 173–
        89 *passim,* 213–14
    wit vs. humor, xiv, 104, 158–9, 162
    and the "new woman," 81–5, 219–41
Hunt, G. W., 72
Huxley, Thomas Henry, 75, 143
"Hyder Ragged," pseud., xvii, 23–42
        passim; see Biron, Sir Charles

Works:
   King Solomon's Wives, 23–42

Idler, 91, 92
Ihrig, Wilfred, 201–2
imperialism, xvii, 23–42 *passim*, 48–49,
   70 ff, 86
intertextuality, xiv, xvii, xx, 1, 9, 12, 17
"inverse sublime," *see* humor, theories of
irony, xviii, xix, 1, 73, 145, 146,
   151, 155, 159, 164, 165, 166, 170,
   191–204 *passim*
Isherwood, Christopher, 181

Jameson, Fredric, 1
Jerome, Jerome K., xviii, 91–113
   Works:
   Idle Thoughts of an Idle Fellow, 105
   My Life, 94, 99, 100
   On the Stage-and Off, 93–94, 99, 100
   Stage-land, 93, 94–100
   Tales Told After Supper, 99
   Three Men in a Boat, 91, 95, 102, 103,
   105–8
Jerrold, Douglas, 230
Jerusalem Star, 64
Jewish World, 63
Jews, 61, 62–64, 205–18 *passim*; *see* anti-
   Semitism
Johnson, Samuel, 118, 122, 131, 135, 136
Jowett, Benjamin, 182
Juvenal, 177

Kant, Immanuel, 157
Katz, Wendy R., 38
Keats, John, 102
Keene, Charles, 68, 230
Kingsley, Charles, 68
Kipling, Rudyard, 91
Knox, Melissa, 209–10
Kranidis, Rita, 219

lampoon, xvii, 43, 45, 49, 222
Landor, W. S., 177
Lane, John, 228, 232
Lang, Andrew, 91, 92, 98
Lang, Cecil Y., 173, 174, 180, 183
Landsdown, Lord, 191
LaTouche, Rose, 77
Lawrence, D. H., 182

Lawrence, C. E., 221
Leacock, Stephen, xiii, xiv
Leavis, F. R., 146, 203
Ledger, Sally, 219
Leech, John, 68, 230
Le Gallienne, Richard, 228
Lehmann, R. C., 102
Leith, Mrs. Disney, 173
Leverson, Ada, 219
Levy, Leonard, 63
Lippincott's, 79
Linton, Eliza Lynn, 83, 84
Livingstone, David, 23
Lorde, Audrey, 240

Macaulay, Thomas Babington, 80
Macdermott, G. H., 72
Macdonnell, James, 200–201
Mallarmé, Stéphane, 193
Marcus, Steven, 189, 196
Marholm Hansson, Laura, xix, 228, 232–
   36
   Works:
   Modern Woman, 232–36
   We Women and Our Authors, 232–33
Marlowe, Christopher, 169
Marks, Patricia, 221
Marsh, Joss, 48
Martin, Robert Bernard, xiv, 104, 184
Masson, David S., 156, 165
May, Phil, 68
Mayhew, Henry, 70
McCalman, Ian, 45, 46
melodrama, 4, 5, 7, 10, 11, 95
Meredith, George, xv, 91, 104, 159, 160,
   185, 225, 226
   Works:
   An Essay on Comedy, 160
metacomedy, xviii, 141, 148, 150
metatheater, 1, 2, 4
Meynell, Alice, xix, 228–32, 236
   Works:
   Ceres' Runaway and Other Essays, 229
   Colour of Life, The, 229
   Hearts of Controversy, The, 231
   Rhythm of Life, The, 229–30
Mill, John Stuart, 143, 154
Miller, J. Hillis, 134
Milliken, E. J., xvii, xviii, 67, 68, 70, 73,
   75, 76, 78, 83, 85, 86

Milnes, Richard Monckton (Lord Houghton), 176, 179, 182, 183, 184
mock-heroic, 7, 10
Moers, Ellen, 193
More, Hannah, 45, 46, 55
Morning Leader, 49
Morning Post, 74
Murray, Nicholas, 192

National Reformer, 47, 61
National Review, xv
Natta, Marie-Christine, 199
Nellist, Brian, 194
Nesbit, Edith, xix, 226–28
"New Woman," xvii, xix, 81–85, 219–41
New York Times, 100
Nichol, John, 174, 175
Nilsen, Don, 92
nonsense, 5
Norton, Charles Eliot, 156

Obscene Publications Act, 182
Orel, Harold, xiii

Paine, Thomas, 45
Pall Mall Gazette, 47, 232
Palmer, Jerry, 91, 105, 112
pantomime, 11, 12, 13, 14, 16
parody, xvii, xix, 1–2, 5, 6, 8, 9, 10, 11, 12, 13, 17, 18, 23, 24, 25, 29, 30, 32, 34, 35, 37, 38, 39, 40, 102, 103, 168, 173–89 *passim*, 221
Partridge, Bernard, 99
pastiche, xvii, 1–2, 3, 7, 8, 9, 11, 17, 18, 174, 176, 184
Pater, Walter, 203
Piggott, E. F., 80
Pixérécourt, 11
Planché, James Robinson, 13, 18
Playgoer, 94
Pope, Alexander, 86
Powell, George, 186
Pratt, Mary Louise, 33
Pre-Raphaelites, 76, 77, 79, 175
Price, R. G. G., 75, 113
Priestley, J. B., 91, 92
Punch, or The London Charivari, xvii, xviii, 67, 68, 70, 74, 75, 76, 79, 82, 84, 85, 86, 92, 93, 94, 100–105, 184, 222, 230, 232

Rabelais, François, 157, 175, 176, 180–81, 186
race, 23–42 *passim*, 73, 86, 98; *see also* anti-Semitism
Racine, Jean Baptiste, 80
Rambler, 126
Rickett, Arthur, 221–22
Riede, David G., 173, 185
Richter, John Paul Friedrich, xviii, 156, 160–64, 169
Robbins, William, 194
Robertson, John, 49
Rose, Margaret, 1, 175
Roseanne (Barr), 240
Rossetti, Dante Gabriel, 173–89 *passim*
Rossetti, William Michael, 176, 177
Rousseau, Jean Jacques, 75
Roy, Donald, 18
Royal Academy, 79
Ruskin, John, 77–78, 91, 115
Russell, Leonard, 94

Sackville-West, Vita, 229
Salvation Army, 51, 58, 64
Sand, Georges, 184
sarcasm, 164–65, 166, 170, 229
satire, xvii, xviii, xix, 1, 4, 5, 9, 17, 49, 64, 67, 70, 73, 86, 159, 164, 165, 166, 170, 177, 178, 181, 182, 194, 219, 220, 223, 224, 225, 226, 228, 230, 231, 237
Saturday Review, 83
Scots Observer, 232
Scotson-Clark, George, 72
Seaman, Owen, 185
Secular Review, 47
Secular Chronicle, 47
secularism, 44, 45, 46, 48, 49, 51, 55, 56, 63, 64
Shakespeare, William, 11, 12, 158, 180
Sharp, Evelyn, 226
Shaw, George Bernard, 141, 142
Shelley, Percy Bysshe, 185
Showalter, Elaine, 221
Simon, Oswald J., 63
Smeed, J. W., 161
Smithers, Leonard, 91
Society for the Suppression of Vice, 180
Somerset County Gazette, 68
Solomon, Simeon, 174, 176, 178, 183, 184, 186, 187

Southwell, Charles, 61
Spencer, Herbert, 91
Spielmann, Marion B., 68, 70, 101, 102
Stallybrass, Peter and White, Allon, 48, 64, 65
Stanton, Domna, 193
Stead, W. T., 47
Stedman, Jane, 14
Stephen, Leslie, xv, 185
Stephen, Fitzjames, 199
Stephen, J. K., 185
Sterne, Lawrence, 157
Strindberg, August, 233
Sullivan, Sir Arthur Seymour, *see* Gilbert
    and Sullivan
Super, R. H., 191
Swift, Jonathan, 157, 177
Swinburne, Algernon Charles, xix, 91,
    173–89
  Works:
    "Bogshire Banner," 175, 179, 180, 184
    Essays and Reviews, 182
    Heptalogia, The, 173, 176, 177
    Laugh and Lie Down, 180
    Lesbia Brandon, 187
    Love's Cross-Currents, 176, 187
    Poems and Ballads, 183, 185
    Unhappy Revenge, The, 179
Syrett, Netta, 226

Tannen, Deborah, 228
Tave, Stuart M., 159
Taylor, Tom, 67, 68, 70
Tennyson, Alfred, 10, 70, 185
The Times, 70, 179
Thackeray, William Makepeace, 79, 101,
    102, 159, 185
theatricality, xvii, xix, 7–8, 192, 199, 201
Thomas, Edward, 176, 182
Thurber, James, 104
Titbits, 47
Toepfer, Karl, 212, 218
Tolstoy, Leo, 144
Traill, H. D., xv
transvestism, 13, 14; *see also* cross-
    dressing

Trevelyan, (Lady) Pauline, 184
Trilling, Lionel, 191, 192, 194, 195, 203
Trollope, Anthony, 179, 180
Turner, Joseph Mallord William, 77
Twain, Mark, xviii, 91–113 *passim*
  Works:
    "American Claimant, The," 92
    Innocents Abroad, The, 93, 95, 97, 98,
      103, 105, 106, 107
    Roughing It, 95, 98, 107, 108

Universal Review, 83
Upward, Edward, 181

Victoria (Queen), 74
Voltaire, 164

War Cry, 51
Ward, Artemus, 92, 98, 100
Watts-Dunton, Theodore, 187
Waugh, Evelyn, 175
West, Mae, 238, 240
Westminster Review, 159
Wheeler, Mazzini, 63
Whistler, James Abbott MacNeill, 78–9,
    182
Wilde, Oscar, xix, 76, 78–79, 91, 94, 98,
    104, 108, 182, 203, 205–18, 227,
    232, 236, 238
  Works:
    Ideal Husband, The, 206
    Importance of Being Ernest, The, xix,
      205, 208, 210
    Picture of Dorian Gray, The, 79, 203
    "Portrait of W. H., The," 210
    Salomé, xix, 205–18
Winnicott, D. W., 122, 133, 134
wit vs. humor, *see* humor, theories of
Woman's World, 236, 237
Wycherley, Thomas, 180

Yeats, William Butler, 91

Zangwill, Israel, 92

For Product Safety Concerns and Information please contact our EU
representative GPSR@taylorandfrancis.com Taylor & Francis Verlag GmbH,
Kaufingerstraße 24, 80331 München, Germany

Printed and bound by CPI Group (UK) Ltd, Croydon, CR0 4YY
01/05/2025
01858342-0012